FIRE CANOE

FIRE CANOE

Prairie Steamboat Days
Revisited

Theodore Barris

McClelland and Stewart

Reprinted 1978

The Canadian Publishers
McClelland and Stewart Limited
25 Hollinger Road, Toronto

Printed and bound in Canada

CANADIAN CATALOGUING IN PUBLICATION DATA

Barris, Theodore.
    Fire canoe

Bibliography
Includes index.
ISBN 0-7710-1025-7

1. River steamers — Prairie Provinces — History.
2. Lake steamers — Prairie Provinces — History.
I. Title.
VM461.B37   386′.22′409712   C77-001295-7

ACKNOWLEDGEMENTS

First, for allowing the author the luxury of expressing a published acknowledgement at all, thanks must go to the Canada Council, whose Explorations grant launched *Fire Canoe* in the spring of 1974.

Subsequently, nearly a thousand prairie residents will recall two summer travellers on their doorsteps with a tape recorder, on the opposite end of a telephone line, or with pen and paper in hand, listening. At the end of a 12,000-mile May-through-August research expedition that year, my wife Jayne MacAulay and I had accumulated more than a hundred hours of audio-taped interviews, boxes of unpublished background data, over a thousand photographs from private and public collections, 150,000 words of daily journals, and a host of new friendships. These friends, mostly the elderly, who had pioneered the prairies, and who opened their living rooms and their memories to us, compose the basis of this book. They allowed the author to revisit moments of the prairie steamboat era first hand.

With the people whose decades of filing have created places like the Public Archives of Canada, the Provincial Archives of Manitoba, the Saskatchewan Archives Board, the University of Saskatchewan Archives, the Provincial Archives of Alberta, the Glenbow-Alberta Institute, and a fleet of other local museums, libraries, historical-site centres, historical society offices, and archives across the prairies, the author shares any success of this manuscript.

All descriptions of steamboats and steamboatmen, as well as the mood and colour of the times, have been kept as accurate and authentic as possible. Every effort was made to base all descriptions except the most general on the written and verbal sources that comprise the background research of the book. All dialogue attributed to the various participants has been taken from existing written sources or transcribed first hand from persons describing their own experiences in this era of receding history. The sources of all quotations cited are listed at the end of the text.

The task of reaching the primary sources which make up the body of this work was facilitated by cohorts in the media. Among those outlets instrumental in encouraging prairie pioneers to come forward with their early steamboat reminiscences and recollections were: CFQC Radio-Television, Saskatoon; CKBI Radio-Television, Prince Albert; CKCK Television, Regina; CBK Radio, Regina; CJNB Radio, North Battleford; CJCA Radio, Edmonton; the *Star-Phoenix,* Saskatoon; the Prince Albert *Times*; the *Advertiser Post,* North Battleford; and the Lloydminster *Times.*

The landlord and landlady of a central Ontario farmhouse where the author found the peace and time to write for a year deserve special acknowledgement. So do a boatload of individuals who encouraged the writing of this book: the Sorrenti family who helped buy the time; Robert Weaver, who believed in an unknown author; Katy Lonsdale, who read evenings away with the raw chapters in her lap; Myrna Schneider, who found the unfindable; the Henderson, Medd, Rowan, and Nairn families, of which we felt a part; the Dulls, who saved us many dimes; Jim Rieger, a friend of the subject; Alan Bradley, who planted the idea; David Scollard, another transplanted Torontonian who also fell in love with the prairies, believed in this subject, and edited it with that love and belief; and finally the Doig family, who continued to wonder when there would be a book in hand. Here, at last!

For the two ladies who flow between the lines
– Lake Agassiz and Lady Jayne

CONTENTS

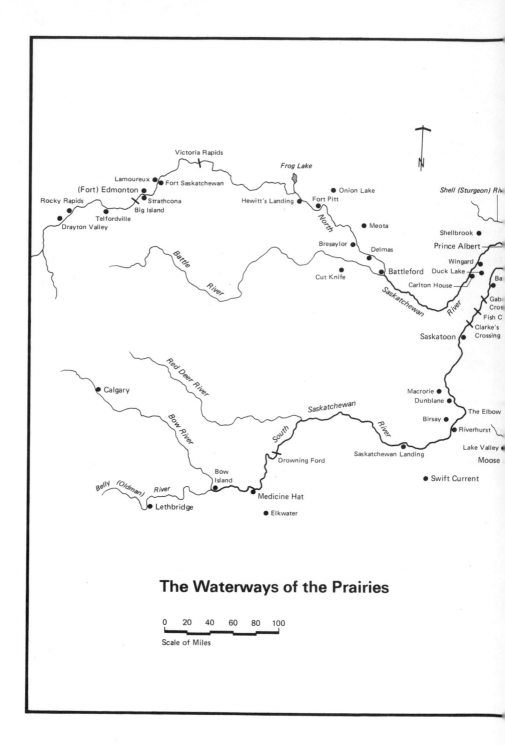

The Waterways of the Prairies

Victoria Rapids
Frog Lake
Lamoureux Fort Saskatchewan
Onion Lake
Shell (Sturgeon) Riv
(Fort) Edmonton
Rocky Rapids Strathcona Hewitt's Landing Fort Pitt
Big Island
Telfordville Meota
Shellbrook
Drayton Valley
Bresaylor Prince Albert
Battle Delmas Wingard
River Battleford Duck Lake Ba
Cut Knife Carlton House
Gab
Cros
North Saskatchewan River Fish C
Clarke's
Saskatoon Crossing
Red Deer River
Calgary Macrorie
Dunblane
Saskatchewan The Elbow
Bow River Birsay
River Riverhurst
South Lake Valley
Saskatchewan Landing Moose
Bow Drowning Ford
Belly (Oldman) River Island
Lethbridge Medicine Hat Swift Current
Elkwater

0   20   40   60   80   100
Scale of Miles

PROLOGUE

It was Wesukechak, the great spirit and creator, who bestowed upon the Swampy Cree the intricate, almost endless watercourses at the heart of North America – but to do this he first had to overcome a formidable test. Flood waters had overwhelmed the earth, leaving him and his animal brothers adrift on a raft. For days on end they searched for dry land. Finally, in desperation, Nehkik, the otter, retrieved a small piece of mud from beneath the flood waters. Wesukechak rolled the mud between his hands and blew on it, until the mud became an enormous ball. Putting ashore on the great land mass, Wesukechak set about reshaping the world. He ordered trees and grass to appear. He told Maheekun, the grey wolf, to jump about with his large feet in the soft earth to form hollows for lakes, and to push up piles of mud with his nose for mountains. And then he had Misekenapik, the great snake, cut rivers into the earth. And this is how the Cree world was made.

The Cree story of the great flood is augmented by the more mundane geological explanations for the formation of the great plains. For a million years before the Cree, the glacial masses of the Quaternay period gripped and gouged the high latitudes of the North American continent. When the warm climate finally returned, approximately 14,000 years ago, and the ice was driven northwards by the melting sun, a vast inland sea was created, that submerged more than two hundred thousand square miles of territory in present-day Minnesota, North Dakota, Ontario, Manitoba, and Saskatchewan. The watershed and basin of Glacial Lake Agassiz encompassed nearly the entire north central plains. In its few thousand years of life, Agassiz wore away at the flesh of the plains, shaping a system of waterways and flatlands which for millennia would determine the migration of animal and man, the way of agriculture, the means of survival, the pattern of settlement, the growth of nations, and the method of transportation.

Locked within the core of the continent by the sprawling Arctic Ocean watershed to the north, by the Hudson Bay and Great Lakes networks to the east, by the Mississippi and Missouri arteries across the south, and by the quick ascent of the Rocky Mountain range on the west, lay the modern descendant of Lake Agassiz – the Lake Winnipeg basin.

Lake Winnipeg, dominating the topography of Cree hunting grounds, drew no less than five major watercourses to its centre. Rising in the American territories, the Red River meandered northward through boulder-strewn rapids, overgrown riverbanks, and crooked channels five hundred water miles to the south shore of the lake. Two prairie-born rivers approached Lake Winnipeg from the west: fed by the streams and chain lakes of the open grassland, the Qu'Appelle (or Calling) River joined the Assiniboine River below her parkland source, and, as the main Assiniboine channel, wound 350 miles to meet the Red River en route to the lake. Also from the west, Lake Manitoba and Lake Winnipegosis, totalling in area nearly four thousand square miles, flowed through the Dauphin River into Lake Winnipeg. The most generous fresh water source, the Saskatchewan River, poured into the lake at its northwestern extremity. Weaving together a dozen principal tributaries, the combined forces of the north and south branches of the Saskatchewan, converging halfway across the plains, deposited silt and glacial run-off from the Rocky Mountain interior into Lake Winnipeg. And in dramatic fashion – falling on an average six feet per mile over its one thousand miles of flow across the prairies, the Saskatchewan thundered through the Grand Rapids cataract, descending nearly a hundred feet inside three miles.

Awesome though they were, the prairie waterways were brotherly spirits to the Cree natives, personalities upon which the Indians depended for fish, game, and travel. And as theirs was a friendship with rivers and lakes, the Cree lived in harmony with the Lake Winnipeg basin. But the fair-skinned newcomers and their gods, their habits, and their experiences were foreign to the basin and to the natives. The newcomers' attitude toward prairie watercourses was one of exploration and exploitation – an attempt to own the western interior of the continent. The Europeans never considered prairie rivers and lakes as spiritual brothers. For them, entering the western plains was a discovery of profitable resources and a conquest over bothersome adversities.

Prairie waterways brought Cree and European together. In their creeks, sloughs, and swamps, the waters of the western interior harboured the beaver. Amisk, as the Cree knew him, clothed the Indians. But for the traders of New France and the Hudson's Bay Company men, beaver pelts meant premium prices in seventeenth-century Europe. Consequently, all along the Hudson Bay watershed whites rivalled whites to trade simple foreign articles for the Indians' surplus furs. Each year the water highways of the interior carried the Cree birch-covered canoes, laden with beaver skins, from the distant basins of the Athabasca, the Peace, and the North Saskatchewan rivers to this lucrative trade with the white man. The fresh waters of the interior offered their natives bountiful fur to trade and easy transport to eastern trading posts at Hudson Bay, while they frustrated and puzzled the British and French novices who were pushing their fur monopoly contention further inland.

The Saskatchewan River buffeted its first European visitor in the summer of 1691, when the young adventurer Henry Kelsey canoed west on a mission of reconnaissance for his Hudson's Bay Company. The first white to see the Canadian prairies via the Saskatchewan, Kelsey noted the violent nature of the riverway, running "strong with falls," and barricaded by "thirty-three Carriages." Fifty years later, the southern Lake Winnipeg basin resisted an invasion from New France. Vanguard explorer Sieur de la Verendrye, rivalling the British, built fortifications along the lower Red River, and then canoed upstream to claim the Assiniboine River, uncooperative with its "water very low . . . winding, strong currents and many shallows." Rivalry on the plains and abroad ultimately pushed the French and British to global blows in the Seven Years War, diverting all attention from the North American interior. Thus the prairie lakes and rivers flowed undisturbed for several years following 1756, while Britain defeated France, won sovereignty over North America, and granted its Hudson's Bay Company exclusive monopoly of the interior territory of Prince Rupert's Land, which comprised all territory drained by Hudson Bay.

Inland waters again bore the rivalry of heavy freighting canoes by 1780, when the Montreal-based North West Company challenged the Hudson's Bay Company along the frontier. Nor'Westers thrust their fur trade deep into the Lake Winnipeg basin, and upset the Hudson's Bay Company monopoly. But despite their lightning probes into the West, they lacked the skill and, in particular, the knowledge of the waterways, of the Cree natives. Each summer the Saskatchewan River rose suddenly with the melting of the snow in the Rocky Mountain headwaters; in 1786, this phenomenon dumbfounded North West Company journalist Edward Umfreville, just as the expansive sprawl of the Lake Winnipeg basin had confused and amazed fellow North West Company explorer Alexander Mackenzie. In contrast to this European puzzlement with prairie waters, the subsequent travels of cartographer David Thompson reflected a greater understanding and rather remarkable foresight: "Although the heads of this River give several passages to the Mountains, from the labor being so great, and also [being] exposed to attacks from hostile Indians, [it seems] that Steam Vessels are the only proper craft for this River; and even to these, its many shoals and sands offer serious impediments, for its waters are very turbid. . . ."

Was it conceivable in those days of the early nineteenth century that steam-driven vessels might ever navigate the tortuous waterways of the northwest river system? The idea must have seemed incredible. Nevertheless, the first tentative experiments with steam navigation had already been successfully completed in Great Britain, and new innovations and improvements were following one another in rapid succession. William

Symington had successfully launched the steamboat *Charlotte Dundas* in 1801 on the Forth and Clyde canals. By 1809 the St. Lawrence between Montreal and Quebec carried the first Canadian steamer, *Accomodation*. Still, London directors of the Hudson's Bay Company knew that steamboats were some years from their Rupert's Land territory. So, while the river routes of the North West Company lived with the occasional passing of low-capacity voyageur canoes, the British-controlled waterways awoke to the nineteenth-century buzz of Hudson's Bay Company men ceaselessly building and launching their future in long, broad, wooden vessels – the famous York boats.

Uniformly built with standardized ribs and hull planks, sharp at both ends, forty feet long and nine feet across, and propelled by as many as a dozen oarsmen, the York boats formed the spearhead of the Bay Company retaliation. The murmur of the Saskatchewan, the Red, and the Assiniboine was increasingly overpowered by the commotion of York boat fleets – the clatter of the portage, the whine of the oar locks, and the whoop of their singing. Cathedral bells for St. Boniface, wheeled carriages for Company officials, pianos for factors' wives, six and nine-pounder guns for Upper Fort Garry, even young buffalo – all travelled the water trails in prairie York boats. By 1821, their superior economy and efficiency had forced the North West Company into amalgamation with the Hudson's Bay Company, whose factors then moved their entire York-boat/fur-trade operation inland to bolster their monopoly. But again the very nature of the Lake Winnipeg basin defied total domination by any single organization. Of necessity, all York boats were constructed of prairie soft woods from the river banks and lake shores of the plains; consequently, the repeated transportation of three-ton cargoes down rapids, across portages, and through waterlogging rivers deteriorated the Company's York boats before their time.

Despite the short life expectancy of the York boats, each year the rivers carried more Company freight. And each year the lakes delivered more newcomers to the brink of the prairies – hunters, scientists, naturalists, and military men, all on expedition – arriving to change the pace of the prairie basin. In 1819, a British Navy captain, John Franklin, led a collection of scientists upstream into the West. Somewhat later, two American missions – one despatched by the federal government in 1823, and another by the Washington Territory governor in 1853 – slipped above the forty-ninth parallel to search out potential transportation routes. The greatest impact on the Lake Winnipeg basin resulted from two expeditions launched in 1857 – one British, led by John Palliser, and the other Canadian, led by Henry Y. Hind. Travelling by paddlewheeler up the Missouri, Palliser, the "solitary rambler", came northwest to study the feasability of prairie agriculture; his reports invited western settlement, and spelled the end of fur-trade control. Simultaneously, the sensitive naturalist Hind boarded a Great Lakes steamer en route to the prairies' edge; surveying prospective passages into the Canadian plains, he foreshadowed a transportation revolution on the prairies, and wrote the York boat off to far northern frontiers: "There are large quantities of goods imported by [various] lines of communication – chiefly through the United States territory at present; and as the York Factory route is to be partially abandoned, a large portion of the importations of Rupert's Land will have henceforth to enter the Winnipeg Basin from the south, so that there will doubtless be sufficient commerce in view of the great water facilities afforded by the country, to encourage the initiation of steam navigation."

Within a year, Hind's prediction was reality. Steam-powered, propelled by paddle or screw, wide, low, shallow-drafted, flat-bottomed or keeled, and crowned by one or more deck levels, with smokestacks and a pilothouse, the water vessel of a new era arrived – the prairie steamboat. Prairie watercourses and Cree natives faced a mechanical encroacher. For Lake Agassiz's descendant– the Lake Winnipeg basin – prairie storms, unpredictable water levels, shifting sandbars, deceptive shallows, and shoals and snags were sufficient defence. But for the Cree, this thrashing river beast, screeching evil shrieks and belching sparks, was an overwhelming monster.

"An Indian was standing on the bank, when the boat came 'round the bend of the river, with navigation lights on and smoke pouring from her funnels. Never having seen a steamboat before, the apparition made him run so fast that his hair swept out behind him . . . ."

Kuska pahtew oosi! Fire canoe!

CHAPTER ONE

First Down the Red

The westerly winds seldom relented as they struck with a force built up across half a continent of prairie grasslands. When, rarely, the wind subsided and the wild prairie grasses stood motionless and silent, the only sound heard by the five thousand inhabitants of the Red River Settlement was the ceaseless rumble and wash of the Assiniboine and the Red River that met below the fort to flow north to Hudson Bay. Otherwise, for its fifty-year existence the Settlement had lived in the silence of isolation. At a precise moment in time – on Friday, the 10th of June, 1859 – this pastoral harmony came abruptly to an end. On that spring day a young Indian girl playing on the walkway of the fortress walls heard a different sound, like the low echo of someone blowing across the lip of a bottle. It was a sound unlike anything ever heard before in the Settlement.

Within moments there was pandemonium. Panic-stricken Indians fleeing to the river forks cried out that a fiery monster was pounding down the river towards them. Then the "monster" appeared, as suddenly as an apparition. Little more than a tub ninety feet long and twenty-two feet across, and surmounted by a great house-like superstructure, the *Anson Northup,* shrouded by swirling steam and woodsmoke, rounded the final bend and bore down on the Red River Settlement. The Red River was in its annual flood, but even the tumult of the rushing water was drowned by the violent thrashing of the *Northup's* stern paddlewheel. The Hudson's Bay Company colours rose above the fort walls to greet the Stars and Stripes flying from the prow of the ungainly vessel.

The inhabitants of the Settlement were taken completely by surprise by this American invasion of their territory.

"The boat arrived unexpectedly in the centre of the colony ... no one anticipating its coming," wrote Bishop Alexandre Taché, a spectator on the riverbank. "Its arrival was treated as quite an event, and, to the surprise of the public, cannon thundered and bells pealed forth chimes to signal rejoicing. The puffing of steam moving about on our river told the echoes of the desert that a new era for our country was being inaugurated. Each turn of the engine appeared to bring us nearer by so much to the civilized world."

Horses with buckskin riders, oxdrawn two-wheeled carts from the fields, and cautious Indians clad in feathers, leggings, and moccasins streamed to the fort landing. Children thronged at the riverside to see "an enormous barge, with a watermill on its stern" emerging from the wilderness like a demon churning up water and spitting sparks. The few carriages available rushed to the scene with flounced and furbelowed ladies attended by bearded gentlemen in tall hats – the Governor's entourage.

The steamer nosed into the Assiniboine to glory in the fort's impromptu welcome. Owner and builder Captain Anson Northup allowed a smile to cross his granite face as the proud mate Edwin Bell tugged a line releasing high-pressure steam through the whistle. The screech clattered off the clay riverbank to the fort wall and reverberated across the distant prairie space, initiating two decades of steamboat supremacy over the territory of the Red River settlers. With the whistle blast, the Scottish descendants of the original Lord Selkirk settlers cheered; the children danced to the new music; the French and Scottish half-breeds looked on undecided; the Indians with hair on end "ran and jumped into the bulrushes close by to hide"; the Governor offered reserved congratulations; and Northup grinned confidently.

Each reaction indicated the tremendous importance that this first day of the steamboat signified for the prairies of the British Northwest. For the Anglo-Saxon Red River settlers, the political fence around their District of Assiniboia now had significance; now their world could grow from isolation to a coming nationhood. The French half-breeds could see their casual agricultural interests and their freedom to rove the riverside plains curtailed by the arrival of a new order spoken exclusively in English. Whites described the surprise and consternation of the natives as "a perfect circus," and to be sure, the Plains Indians never stopped running. When Indians complained that the boats and their whistle screams drove game away and disturbed the spirits of their dead, the boat owners appeased them with gold, and agreed to sound whistles at arrivals and departures only. Demand after demand would anger the Indians and send their game and spirits retreating with the frontier.

Well might the appointed Governor reserve his enthusiasm over this pioneer steamboat which now linked the Settlement with Fort Abercrombie, Minnesota, only three hundred miles away. The American free traders had competed in Company-dominated territory before, but the *Anson Northup* marked the first time the Americans had enjoyed the advantage of a more efficient transportation system. The superior capacity, speed, and economy of the steamboats made the York Factory route of the Hudson's Bay Company obsolete. The remoteness that the Company had exploited for centuries ended; suddenly Hudson's Bay men had to grapple with a rival more ominous than competitive independent fur traders – American Manifest Destiny.

Captain Northup's smile was not only that of an agent of Manifest Destiny; he had just won himself a small fortune. The aggressive Americanism stemmed from a St. Paul Chamber of Commerce that had eight months before offered money to the first man or company to put a steamer on the Red, the challenge being to overcome the land divide between a now fully navigable Mississippi River system and an untouched Red River system. Bull-headed and greedy, Northup persuaded the St. Paul businessmen to double the prize money to two thousand dollars. He immediately purchased an abandoned light-draft steamboat, the *North Star* (previously constructed on the lower Mississippi as the *Governor Ramsey* with machinery from Maine). His suggestion to build a fifty-mile canal joining the Mississippi and Red rivers in Minnesota was laughed down, so Northup decided to walk his boat overland from Crow Wing on the Mississippi to Lafayette on the Red.

Through the winter of 1858-59 Northup appeared to be the only contender for the St. Paul money. Guiding seventeen span of horses, thirteen yoke of oxen, and thirty teamsters, he carted the *North Star's* extracted 11,000-pound boiler, engine works, and rough timbers for a new hull over 150 miles of Minnesota forest, drift-snow, and a series of makeshift bridges – no minor miracle. However, by spring breakup on the Mississippi River, another captain, John B. Davis, had quietly slipped a small, flat-bottomed, square-bowed steamer, the *Freighter,* into the upper Minnesota, a tributary of the Mississippi. Confident his light craft and his own ability would bring him success, Davis made a lightning dash for the Red at the peak of the spring thaw, when flooding submerged the land between the Minnesota and Red rivers. Davis was set on the two thousand dollars and a claim on gold struck on the Saskatchewan River in the Northwest. He lost his *Freighter* to the shallows of the flooded divide and his crew to a barrel of whisky, and left Northup alone in the bid for the money.

Meanwhile on the banks of the Red, Northup fashioned his "pine basket" steamboat around the innards of the dismantled *North Star,* and christened it, not surprisingly, the *Anson Northup.* And by May 17, 1859, assisted by two Mississippi skippers, Russell Blakely and Edwin Bell, and a crew of three, Captain Northup had launched his steamer bound for Fort Garry, the prize money, all the glory, and a winner's smile.

The magnitude of his achievement fresh in his mind, Northup returned to Fort Abercrombie proclaiming to all, including the Hudson's Bay Company, that the Red River trade was his. The Company challenged him, however, by refusing to pay his monopoly rates. Boycotted by the Company, Northup settled for the $8,000 sale of his steamer to J. C. Burbank & Company (whose silent partner was the Hudson's Bay Company), and disappeared forever. But Hudson's Bay Company Governor Sir George Simpson had miscalculated. His company had thrived on the isolation of the Northwest and hoped the threat of development would go away. In allowing brothers J. C. and H. C. Burbank ownership of the Northup steamer, the Hudson's Bay Company opened wide the door to its domain, and unleashed a competition for river commerce that set the pace and pattern of northwest steamboating for the quarter century to follow.

The struggle for power, territory and trade on the Red was only half the battle. The Red River itself still remained an unconquered third party. Any steamboatman venturing into the little-known lower reaches of the Red was faced with a vexing dilemma. Because of the tremendously difficult river conditions, he had to sacrifice the glamour and luxury of his boat merely to ensure the vessel's survival. The further he sailed from St. Paul and the lazy waters of the Mississippi, the less important became the frills and the comforts, and the more vital grew the raw efficiency of the steamboat. Attractive gingerbread trim became secondary to a reinforced gunwale. The personality of the Red rendered steamers "clumsy and uncouth in their huge white-washed bulk," wrote passenger Joseph J. Hargrave. In Hargrave's opinion, the *Pioneer* (the *Anson Northup* refurbished and re-named) was, for all its prestige as a symbol of the Burbank partnership with the "Honourable Company", a vessel outclassed by the river.

"In consequence of the shortness of the *Pioneer,*" Hargrave wrote, "it was found very difficult to manage her in turning the numerous and sharp points which we passed on our way. . . . For more than an entire day the crew was engaged pulling the vessel over [rapids] by main force, by means of a rope attached to the capstan, and fixed to a spot ashore at some distance ahead. At intervals during this tedious series of operations the *Pioneer* would partially ground, while the greater part of her keel would be floating in water flowing like the sluice of a mill. On such occasions she would whirl cork-like around, setting at defiance the utmost efforts of the rude stern wheel to regulate her motions."

Probing the river like this the full length of the journey made each day exciting without relief. Because the comfort of paying passengers was secondary, even the nights offered little peace. The steamboat was a floating closet, over-crowded, over-heated, and constantly in an uproar. The walls of Hargrave's stateroom might as well have been curtains like those in the temporary berths of the saloon; Hargrave overheard each swallow of whisky, shuffle of cards, and drunken ballad of the night revellers. And if quiet did settle on the *Pioneer,* moored at night to the riverbank, clumsily boarded walls and loose-fitting window frames gave easy passage to hordes of mosquitoes. A straight distance of 250 miles, by river the trip from Burbank's Minnesota Stage Company station on the Red to Fort Garry was 500 miles. Hargrave spoke of his days aboard the *Pioneer* as his "detention."

From the ragged pine deck of the *Pioneer,* passage down the Red held very little glamour; often it brought hardship. But from behind his polished oak desk in the St. Paul metropolis, J. C. Burbank envisioned quite a different story. His private lane to the Northwest would soon replace labouring cart brigades en route to the District of Assiniboia. He had made agricultural history by shipping the first four sacks of seed wheat out of the British prairies, and he forecast more to come. He promised a regular ten-day or fortnightly service to Fort Garry and back, and maintained that "from Red Lake River to Fort Garry there is at all times a depth of water sufficient to float the largest craft of the Mississippi. . . . The journey from Fort Garry to St. Paul by steamboat and stage will ere long be regarded as one of the most agreeable of trips." Conveniently for Burbank, J. J. Hargrave's eight-day ordeal on the *Pioneer* wasn't published until many years later.

Despite the truth about steamboat travel on the Red, the idea continued to attract numerous travellers. Trappers, daring immigrants, and naturalists trickled into the Burbank steamboat offices for tickets. The Hudson's Bay Company joined the trend, shipping its sugar, guns, hardware, soap, tea, dry goods, tobacco, nails, shot, and seeds to Fort Garry with Burbank. One season found an astronomer, a mathematician, a naturalist, and a humourist aboard the Red River steamer en route to the Saskatchewan River to view a total eclipse of the sun. Burbank's romantic vision of his steamer was bluntly contradicted by the humourist, who wrote, "Nothing could have been more awkward than that tub of a boat, plunging every now and again headlong into the banks despite the frantic exertions of the pilot."

An 1857 gold strike in the Crown Colony of British Columbia had brought a steady flow of Canadians, Californians, and eastern Americans clambering to Burbank & Company's doorstep. In the spring of 1862, a mass of pick-carrying workers left Toronto for Georgetown, Burbank's new head of navigation, on the promise that Burbank would transport them to Fort Garry aboard a new Red River steamer. The task of fulfilling the promise to the Canadian Overlanders (as the gold-seekers were

23

called) and building Burbank's dream, fell to the ambitious Cornelius P.V. Lull. A one-time Minnesota sheriff who married into the Burbank family and became manager of Burbank's Minnesota Stage Company and its stations and hotels, Lull was "an august individual, who is squire, justice of the peace and head cook and bottle washer of this town [Georgetown], while he is also pilot of the steamer betwixt here and Fort Garry."

To everyone's surprise, Burbank resurrected the *Freighter* (John Davis's poor second in the St. Paul Chamber of Commerce race to Fort Garry), and refurbished it in grander form as the *International*. One hundred and thirty-seven feet long, triple-decked, with a twenty-six-foot beam and a draft of forty-two inches, the *International* was launched on May 20, 1862 – only ten days later than promised. That afternoon, Cornelius Lull piloted the dazzling Burbank showpiece out of the Georgetown timber yards with 160 Cariboo-bound Canadian prospectors and forty well-wishers all headed for Fort Garry. The *International's* grandiose motto *Germinaverunt speciosa deserti* ("The deserts have bloomed") told only part of the story. The Burbank blossom had cost his silent partner the Hudson's Bay Company $20,200. And with the news that spring that the *Pioneer* had been crushed by ice below Fort Garry, Burbank & Company could use all the business they could get their hands on.

Fort Garry's *Nor'Wester* newspaper praised the *International* enthusiastically, claiming that "its size and finish would make it respectable even amid the finest floating palaces of the Mississippi," and trumpeted its May 26 arrival as nothing less than spectacular, describing its docking as "a grand affair."

But the shouts of welcome had scarcely faded when Burbank & Company encountered further problems. As the Red River's June flooding peaked and fell, so did business for the *International*. Water levels in the Red River channel severely limited her movement. Smallpox brought immigration to a halt, so the passenger trade died. The Civil War dragged on further than either Union or Confederate experts had predicted, and with the war went the manpower available to move Red River trade. By 1862 the fundamental incompatability of the Hudson's Bay Company and the Burbank organization had undermined the partnership. Burbank sought immigration and free trade; the Hudson's Bay Company desperately wished to delay the opening up of Rupert's Land for the sake of preserving the fur trade. But more critically, buying off the Indians along the Red River with "kegs of yellow money" – gold – wasn't enough. Some bands had resorted to confiscating steamboat goods as a form of toll for crossing Indian territory. And gradually the Sioux, Crees, and Chippewas of the riverbanks refused to allow the woodhawks (the woodcutters who

24

supplied chopped cordwood fuel for the steamboats) the right to live and work along the river. This growing hostility scared away even the most faithful of Burbank's customers.

In August of 1862, enraged Sioux cut all communication lines between Fort Garry and the United States; they killed drivers of the Minnesota Stage Company, burned way stations, chased frontier settlers into forts and town sites, and forced garrisons to guard a most vulnerable Red River resident – the *International*. Marooned on the riverbank, unemployed, and under the guns at Fort Abercrombie, the second Red River steamer sat idle, symbolizing the mood of the entire Northwest – afraid to move, desolate, and resigned to a renewed isolation that would prevail until the end of the decade. For eight years the Red carried no steamship trade.

On a July evening in 1870, the *International* steamed unsuspectingly into the centre of the greatest storm that western Canada had to that point experienced. The political forces at work in the Northwest were complex and dangerously volatile. American free traders, fresh from conquest over the Southern Confederacy and hostile Indians, hungrily eyed the unprotected territory. Among the traders, violence-bent Irish Fenians brought with them their hatred of Britain and all things British. The three-year-old Dominion of Canada was seeking British help to purchase the Northwest Territories from the Hudson's Bay Company. A horrified Hudson's Bay Company was fighting a rearguard action to protect its empire from crumbling under the onslaught of new settlers who would drive out the fur-bearing animals – the Company might endure the loss of its deed to the Red River Valley, but to survive, it had to out-trade all its competitors. Caught in the middle, a restless District of Assiniboia population, primarily half-breeds of both Anglo-Saxon and French descent, had the feeling their land and lives were being bartered like cattle. Canadian officials had already arrived with surveyors who disregarded existing river-lot farms and Indian game lands. The Red River neared explosion when the oratory and the vigorous personality of Louis Riel defied all the forces competing for the region. In the autumn of 1869 Riel had led a bloodless coup against the Hudson's Bay Company stronghold at Fort Garry. By Christmas he had established a provisional government. And in the summer of 1870, having just tried and executed his antagonist Thomas Scott partly as an example to discourage resistance, Riel learned of the *International's* first approach of the season and of its valuable cargo.

As the *International* steamed north towards Fort Garry, one of the passengers, a young Canadian military intelligence officer named Captain

William F. Butler, was planning a meeting with Riel. Butler had booked passage as a civilian at Frog Point, Minnesota; sent on a mission to ascertain the mood of the whites and Métis at Assiniboia and the likelihood of attack by Fenians from Dakota or Minnesota, he had decided to visit Fort Garry and meet the Métis leader. Butler's plan was to introduce himself as a representative of the Dominion government and then try to dissuade Riel from rebellion. At the border Butler learned that his real identity as an intelligence officer had been found out, and that his life was in genuine danger. Calmly, he planned his escape as the *International* moved through the dusk toward Fort Garry. At midnight Butler and an accomplice took a six-shooter and a rifle into the bow of the ship. The steamer chugged through the forks from the Red into the Assiniboine. Light from lanterns at the fort landing revealed figures gathered for the boat's arrival. As the steamboat answered the Assiniboine's current, now pounding her broadside, her bow touched the north bank. Two figures leapt ashore and scrambled up the bank two hundred yards from the chains that Riel had brought for Butler, the captain, and the *International* herself.

Having foiled Riel's attempt to imprison him, Butler gained a better bargaining position with the Métis leader. From a sanctuary in Lower Fort Garry, a predominantly Protestant community twenty miles up the Red River, the young army officer engineered a summit meeting with Riel over a billiard table. Butler made clear the strength of Colonel Garnet Wolseley's approaching 1,200-man force, and consequently discovered Riel's preference for a Canadian Fort Garry rather than an American one. Tension eased at the fort, Butler canoed off to meet Wolseley's expedition, Riel fled, the Métis won rights to custom, property, and language in the 1870 Act that made Assiniboia Canada's province of Manitoba, and the freed *International* returned to Georgetown on the eve of the golden era of prairie steamboats.

With the *International* unchained and the political question mark of the Northwest resolved (at least for the moment), steamboating was reborn. Telegraph lines had come to the Red River Valley. The steel rails of the American Northern Pacific Railroad reached the east bank of the Red at Moorhead, thereby terminating forever the ox-cart trains, and gave the river a more accessible steamboat terminus. But the Hudson's Bay Company was lagging behind the pace of events. Finally realizing that their attempt to freeze the development of Manitoba was futile, the Company had to scramble to share in the profits. The unkempt *International* was pressed into 'round-the-clock service. Norwegian Sven Heskin, who had hired on in the fury of an industry breaking wide open, gladly took the meager pay of thirty-five dollars a month and board.

Russian Mennonite immigrants debarking at Fort Garry, 10 August 1874. Paying passengers like these made the *International* the pride of J. C. Burbank & Co. *(Provincial Archives of Manitoba)*

Not even the eclectic *Anson Northup* – composed of machinery from Maine, timbers from lower Mississippi, and planking from Minnesota – could eclipse the grace of a hand-hewn canoe in 1859. *(Provincial Archives of Manitoba)*

"Our work consisted of loading and unloading freight, besides carrying aboard a cord of wood apiece a day. The *International's* two boilers needed twenty-two cords burned each day. [The steamer] had, in addition to itself, two barges about thirty feet long, on which additional freight was loaded. At Moorhead the barges were loaded first and set adrift downstream, oars serving as steering devices. All hands turned to when loading began. . . . Had a crew of twenty-two deckhands besides the captain, pilot and other officers. We travelled day and lanterns were used to light our way at night." The Company hurried machinery, seed, and food stuffs into Fort Garry, and returned with furs and healthy profits. Soon deck space for cargo was shared by a steady rush of immigrants to the Northwest. Though she had lost her exclusive dominance of the land, the Hudson's Bay Company held great pride in her control of river traffic.

Proud and blind. In the spring of 1870 a young St. Paul merchant offered the Company an unprecedented contract: to carry all Company freight from New York City to Fort Garry for the lowest rates. Unruffled by come-lately competitors, the Company rejected the offer. The decision was unwise. Recognizing a superb opportunity to take business from the Hudson's Bay Company, whose rates were uncompetitively high, especially on merchandise of American origin, a previously inconspicuous St. Paul firm launched a steamboat at McCauleyville, Minnesota, in 1871. Freight piled to the hurricane deck, the *Selkirk* docked at Pembina customs house on the international border with a devastating announcement – her owners proclaimed that she was the only bonded boat on the Red River. A dead-letter law suddenly grounded the *International* – all goods passing through American territory destined for Canada were now required to be bonded at United States customs. The Hudson's Bay Company found herself snagged in a governmental loophole and at the mercy of her new competitor, Hill, Griggs & Company. The same James Jerome Hill, turned away the year before, had joined with one Chauncey Griggs to form the rival enterprise. Jovial but with a razor-sharp mind, Hill "was always gathering facts and thinking, silently thinking, of the opportunities scattered here so lavishly for the foresighted and the energetic." Determined to capture the steamboat and mercantile business on the Red, Hill now held the power to set freight rates. Indeed, returns from her first cargo into Fort Garry almost paid for the construction of the *Selkirk*.

Hill, Griggs & Company monopolized most of that season. But a resourceful Hudson's Bay Company Chief Commissioner, Donald A. Smith, evaded the bond issue by transferring the *International* to an American citizen, who just happened to be the Hudson's Bay Company's St. Paul agent, and who knew James Hill from a previous rivalry during the Mississippi steamboat packet days of the 1860's. Norman W. Kittson had studied the trading game for twenty-five years, had sat as mayor of St. Paul, had calmed hostile Indians in 1864, and had become a millionaire overnight. Securing bonding rights for "his" *International*, "Commodore" Kittson revitalized the western operations of the Hudson's Bay Company and, like Burbank before him, became the Company's front man. Kittson capitalized on the disgust Fort Garry merchants felt over Hill's monopoly rates and put the *International* back on the Red chasing new business.

"It wasn't a race exactly," recounted a Manitoba *Free Press* correspondent, "but they – the *Selkirk* and *International* – both wanted to get a lee-tle ahead of the other. They left here a week ago Monday evening, the *International* having three hours start, which she kept till arrival at Pembina, where a delay caused by the breaking of one of her cam yokes allowed the *Selkirk* to catch up. Both boats left that place, nose and nose together; the *Selkirk* took the lead ... till she broke a wheel arm which occasioned a stoppage for repairs, during which the *International* passed her. At Grand Forks [in Dakota Territory] the *International* stopped, but the rival boat hadn't time. Mitchell had just placed a rooster [crewman] on the safety valve and was standing over him with a monkey wrench to see that he kept in his place. Both boats tore up the River, stole wood from each other – the *International* reaching Fisher's Landing [in Minnesota] an hour and a half ahead, one says, and fifteen minutes ahead, according to the *Selkirk* version."

For the full season of 1871 the Red was churned by competition, but when ice thawed the following spring it left behind only one enterprise, a new one – the Red River Transportation Company – which was managed by Norman Kittson and which boasted ownership of both the *International* and the *Selkirk*. By appearances, it looked as if Hill, Griggs, & Company had sold out to Kittson. Actually, the Red River Transportation Company represented the combined interests of Kittson, Chief Commissioner Donald Smith, and James Hill; it was an expanded monopoly of the Fort Garry/Moorhead route and produced enough profit for Hill, Kittson, and the perpetual benefactor, the Hudson's Bay Company. Dubbed the "Kittson Line", the Red River Transportation Company absorbed every potential competitor – the *Dakota*, a sternwheeler launched at Breckenridge, Minnesota in 1872; the compact and polished sidewheel steamer *Cheyenne,* built in 1873 at Grand Forks; and the small *Alpha,* owned by J. W. "Flatboat" McLean, who was forced to sell out because his British citizenship disallowed his navigating in American waters. Kittson paddlewheelers ruled a complete monopoly.

Powerful as the capitalists were who seemed to command the very flow of water in the Red River from their arm-chaired offices, the prairie river, its inhabitants – man and machine – and the adventurous nature of a young America and a younger Canada bred a homegrown steamboat culture in the Northwest with a quality that was uniquely its own. "Ever since I arrived here in midwinter," a slightly puzzled newcomer to Manitoba wrote, "I've been bored with that confounded vessel. Everybody has friends coming by that First Boat. It was to be the medium for a tremendous flood of immigration and no matter of trade could be contracted without its valuable assistance." He computed that the First Boat would have to have been twenty miles wide, fifty miles long, and able to carry thirteen thousand passengers – "a veritable Noah's Ark." Aboard were farmers moonlighting as firemen or storekeepers on as pursers, and their daughters hired as maids. Extravagant foods in the saloons provided a comfortable diversion from the outside wilderness. Poets found Wordsworthian pastorals to put to rhyme. Mosquitoes swarmed in clouds for the new blood of naive immigrants. And half-breed roustabouts struggled to keep the steamboat from snagging on bends of the Red, so winding that the prow "points as often towards the Antarctic as the Arctic pole."

Shallow and twisting, the Red seasoned skippers aboard the Kittson steamers in practices unique to navigation. Building wing dams on the spot to raise river water, or winching steamers over boulders and ordering crew and passengers overboard to execute a simple brute-strength push, were commonplace. Some steamboat masters, surviving on their ingenuity, constructed a battering ram to run through ice jams; others, relying on teamwork, commanded a crew on "butter-knives" (paddle-rudders mounted on the gunwales) to navigate horseshoe river bends. All the captains operated on nerve.

All the captains operated on nerve, but some, like Captain Alexander Griggs, carried it to almost unbelievable limits. The *International* steamed through the evening of May 10, 1873, to meet a provincial customs house deadline. En route to Fort Garry, Griggs was piloting a large consignment of liquor for the Hudson's Bay Company. At midnight on the 10th a new tariff would come into effect, which would cost the liquor importers thousands of extra tax dollars. The Red River, in flood, had spilled its banks and submerged the prairie for miles on either side of the river. The captain's resulting action, witnessed by a *Manitoban* reporter, was perhaps the most spirited feat ever performed on the Red. "Capt. Griggs on taking command, resolved to make a bold stroke to reach the goal in season, and very coolly turned the boat out of the bed of the river and made a short cut over the prairie ... thereby reducing the distance very materially and gaining the Customs House" before the midnight tax hike on his liquid cargo.

Never again would the Red River sleep. The rattle of the machinery was unceasing as the steamboats doggedly pursued their schedules up and down the valley. There was no such thing as a "routine trip", but a typical voyage would not have been dissimilar to the one taken in May, 1874, by the *Dakota* from the Fargo levee to the newly incorporated city of Winnipeg. Steamed up, with her complement of crew and 175 passengers, Captain Sam Painter as usual had freighted Kittson's lanky steamer to the limit. Quarters were so cramped that the clerk's berth was under his office desk.

Tenant farmers from England ached to see their 160-acre plots of land, Scottish crofters and evicted farmers from Ireland exchanged visits and danced hours away, and Métis deckhands bucked wood and fed the *Dakota's* leaky boilers to the rhythm of their songs and laughter. Above on the cabin deck, Englishmen and their wives of "Lord and Lady" class gossiped with young sons of English and Scottish nobility and remittance men. Hudson's Bay Company chief factors laid plans for the new "Little Sticks" land of the Mackenzie River which they would soon supervise. Three sisters cloaked in the habit of their Order of the Gray Nuns studied maps of their new mission home – the Saskatchewan and Great Slave country. In one stateroom a third district court judge for the Territory of Dakota, a United States marshal, and the district attorney played whist and waited for their stop at Pembina, where they would hold a term of court. An Indian agent, a member of the boundary commission for the Northwest, a sergeant and his squad of Mounted Police recruits, and a party of Canadian Pacific Railway engineers en route to survey the territory east of Winnipeg all slept along the stuffy cabin deck. And the middle-aged wife of British army officer Captain George U. White from Port Perry, Ontario, surveyed the antics of her six children; the family was off to join Captain White on a new farm at Teulon, Manitoba, just outside Winnipeg.

A buffalo-robed historian-pioneer, Gordon Keeney, had climbed to the texas deck atop the steamer early this May morning. For amusement, he inspected the United States marshal's fifteen shackled and hand-cuffed prisoners, now headed for trial at Pembina. But he inspected from a distance. A guard with orders to shoot should a prisoner attempt to escape, barred anyone passage across the texas near the prisoners. Among this collection of accused murderers and grand larceny cases, George Billhymer, a plain man, sprawled on the deck just out of range of the sternwheel spray. Thrown out of work when the Northern Pacific Railroad ceased to operate west of Fargo, and needing food for his young wife and son, Billhymer had broken into a commissary building at Fort Seward, Dakota Territory, and was quickly arrested. Without bail money and only just able to bring his family aboard the Dakota for the trip, he too was off to trial at Pembina.

"The call to breakfast had just sounded," Keeney recalled, "when a woman's cry of 'My child' and a man's voice calling 'Child overboard' came up to us from the cabins below." Emma, the lively, pretty, red-haired daughter of the Whites from Ontario, had clutched at an over-hanging tree branch and hadn't let go soon enough; just three and a half years old, she was whisked overboard and was instantly struggling in the swirling Red. "As we started to get up on our feet, we heard Billhymer shout, 'Don't shoot, Ollie.' And he threw himself over the low railing at his side. As he dropped out of sight twenty-five feet toward the river, a revolver cracked and a bullet splintered the wood of the railing just above him." The *Dakota* was under full steam heading downstream, so by the time word reached the pilothouse for the cumbersome paddlewheel to reverse, the drama in the river had begun.

"The child struggled in the water, buoyed up by the air caught in the folds of her garments. Billhymer was striking out sideways with his hands, held close together by the handcuffs. . . . The child drifted towards him and just as she sank out of sight, Billhymer let himself under. When he came up he had the child in his hands. . . . With a backward fling he threw her across his shoulder, holding on by taking grip of her dress band in his teeth. In her struggles, the child threw Billhymer off balance. Both went under. He had lost the child, but still clutched a piece of coloured cloth torn from the child's dress. . . . Raising his shackled hands above his head, he twisted and wrenched at them until the blood ran down his arms. He could not break the iron. As he sank he saw the instant appear-ance of the child's arm. With all his strength he pulled himself farther out into the centre of the river. We could plainly see his shackled limbs stick-ing out of the water. The irons glistened in the sunshine before they disappeared, as we all thought, for the last time. Billhymer again came up and once more he had the child, again by the waist of her dress."

A boat lowered from the *Dakota* reached a shivering Emma and the ironclad rescuer. Passengers immediately collected a purse of sixty dollars and presented Billhymer with a testimonial signed by eighty witnesses, including Captain Painter. A sentence against Billhymer was reduced at Pembina and he took his family north to find work with an appreciative Captain White in Winnipeg.

"Man overboard" was a frequent cry on the Red, but not always did it mean tragedy. A commotion aboard a steamer during one trip brought crew and passengers running to the promenade, where "a stranger was trying a waltz across the deck with an umbrella under his arm for a part-ner, and who took a round too much, and without trying, waltzed off most beautifully into the river. Assistance was rendered and after a struggle, the unfortunate votary of the mazy was lugged out by one of the roustabouts belonging to the craft. Damages sustained – ruined clothes, one plug hat, umbrella and one shoe." One Kittson steamer was involved in no fewer than three collisions; it sank once; it had a minor fire in its hold; and it lost one passenger overboard, all within three seasons. The *Keewatin,* a local Manitoba boat, had all its minor disasters in one trip – a man fell overboard, another stumbled into the hold and dislocated his shoulder, and a third accidentally discharged a gun, nearly killing another man on deck. With a little luck, passage on a steamboat might provide some excitement – a grounding, a shooting match, a race, or a song-and-dance fest. Incidents aboard the steamboats kept crews on their toes, and kept the customers coming.

Thousands paid fees to the Kittson Line – and to Kittson, that's all they were, numbers, or statistics in the Red River Transportation ledgers, each passenger one more fee to be collected. In 1874 in two weeks nearly nine hundred Mennonites from Russia arrived on the decks and tow barges of the *Cheyenne* and the *International.* That same season, 1,100 Icelanders shuffled down Winnipeg gangplanks to new Manitoba homes. The 1870's, the Red, and Kittson steamboats dumped hordes of nameless travellers into Manitoba.

With so many near-anonymous souls travelling aboard the Kittson steamers, it is not surprising that crimes should occasionally be commited, including one which occurred aboard the *International* which remains unsolved today. A purser discovered, after disembarking all his passengers at Winnipeg, that one cabin remained occupied and locked. Knocking yielded no response. The captain authorized a break-in, and the smallest steward crawled through the porthole's broken glass. "A man's lying in the bunk," quivered the boy removing the chair wedged under the door lock inside the cabin. "And there's blood on the pillow. . . . Looks like he's dead."

But for his name, which could have been assumed to avoid creditors or law officers, this passenger carried not one paper of identification, nor were there manufacturers' trademarks on his clothes. He had no distinguishing body marks and apparently had spoken with no-one. The *International's* records showed no debarkations between Grand Forks and the Winnipeg landing. Tracing travellers was impossible; stages met the boats and departed as quickly as people disembarked, scattering their patrons for miles in every direction, and not returning for weeks. G. Orton, as the stranger identified himself to the Purser, had boarded the *International* from a stage that connected the Northern Pacific with the steamer's departure port, Grand Forks. He carried two handsome leather bags (the steward recalled they were heavy) to his cabin. About forty-five, dressed inconspicuously, he had a short brown beard, and his hands looked well cared for and unaccustomed to hard work. The night before the Winnipeg docking, Orton was struck from behind. A knife blade severed a neck artery. Blood spattered the cabin walls. There was no struggle. Death followed in minutes on undisturbed bed linen. The victim was robbed. One clue, a gold Masonic pin with square, compass, and letter "G" on the man's vest lapel, produced nothing. Fingerprint files did not exist, there was only limited wire communication, and the absence of photographic aids left the authorities empty-handed. If the murderer had calculated the attack, he chose the perfect victim and the perfect time, aboard the perfect vehicle. And with little effort the killer left the *International* and was swallowed up by a veil of frontier anonymity.

Lawlessness and the vacuum of identity did not impede the boom of the Kittson empire. For six months of every year the screech of steamboat whistles coming and going brought citizens of Winnipeg scurrying to the docks at the foot of Post Office Street. Special police were hired to restrain the surging boat-watchers who jammed the landing to meet relatives and claim their belongings. A multitude of immigrant languages hummed in the street as deckhands unloaded a huge variety of cargo, from printing presses to church pipe organs. The hurricane decks of the Kittson steamboats carried the flesh and blood of a growing province. In came new citizens, food, and work staples for pioneer settlement, and delicacies for the nouveau riche of Winnipeg; out flowed exports of a budding frontier economy – furs, buffalo robes, and increasingly prevalent sacks of Manitoba wheat. And for half the decade the Red River Transportation Company had called every shot. Even when the Dominion government moved at one point to legislate the American monopoly out of Canada, Kittson mustered more support for his steamboat line than the nationalists could for Canada.

But the Kittson bubble was growing dangerously thin. By 1873 the rates charged by the autocratic line had climbed to astronomical figures. Increasingly frequent newspaper editorials criticized the Kittson enterprise. The Winnipeg Board of Trade threw darts at an apathetic government unwilling to place Manitoban trade on Canadian transportation facilities. Talk of a rival venture to force rates down culminated with the incorporation of the Merchants International Steamboat Line. At first planned as an exclusively Winnipeg concern, the Merchants Line was thwarted by the denial of navigation rights in American waters. The Merchants plan of reaction broadened to include a handful of St. Paul businessmen, who, they hoped, would enable them to overcome the problem. On May 21, 1875, the curtain rose on yet another steamboat rivalry on the Red.

"The gem of the Red" plashed into the Post Office Street wharf that day. Built at Moorhead over the winter, the *Manitoba,* a colossal one hundred and ninety feet long and nearly three hundred tons displacement, had just set a speed record – Moorhead to Winnipeg in forty-five hours. The first of the Merchants' two new paddlewheelers, she received all the pomp accorded a queen.

"Just before dark a large number of ladies and gentlemen congregated in the spacious saloon of the sidewheeler," reported a gloating *Free Press.* "Mrs. P. Sutherland, on behalf of the ladies, presented Captain Webber with two magnificent red ensigns. The captain acknowledged the degree of pride that he felt and wrapped a flag around himself, remarking that he never had felt so happy in his life. The colours were hoisted and saluted by several rounds from a piece of artillery on board."

But Norman Kittson wasn't one to sit idly by and let a competitor move in unopposed. The first indication of his response to the interloper appeared in slashing *Free Press* editorials that accused Kittson of plotting the customs snags which delayed the *Manitoba* on numerous trips. Meanwhile, the Merchants Line christened the *Manitoba's* sister ship, the *Minnesota,* and launched her into the competition. Rates crashed to new lows. Races between Kittson and Merchants steamers highlighted the struggle for business. The fever pace on the river brought its first serious incident just three weeks after the *Manitoba's* triumphant maiden arrival at Winnipeg.

After another record-breaking run of forty-five hours from the upper river port at Moorhead into Winnipeg on June 4, 1875, the *Manitoba* had quickly reloaded for the return upstream trip. By eleven o'clock that night she had put nine miles behind her; she was rounding a sharp point where a small tributary met the Red when Kittson's *International,* steaming downstream for Winnipeg, suddenly loomed up from the twilight. Telegraph dispatches at Moorhead and Winnipeg flashed the encounter over the wires:

"Stinking River, Manitoba. Captain [John] Segers of the *International*, says he was on watch at the time. He saw a steamboat approaching. He blew the whistle for port side, as the descending boat always has the choice in passing."

"The *Manitoba* answered for the starboard side."

"The steamers were then within one hundred and fifty feet of each other."

"Segers reversed his engine and blew again for port side as it was impossible for him, owing to the position of the boats and surrounding, to go to starboard."

"The *Manitoba* was then right across the bow of the *International.* The *International* struck the *Manitoba* just abreast the stacks at her lower stairs and cut into her ten feet. The deck of the *Manitoba* was under water in a minute."

One man was pinned between an icebox and the ceiling of the *Manitoba's* galley and suffered broken ribs. Others were injured, but most aboard the *Manitoba* jumped to safety on the *International* or dove overboard and swam ashore. The disaster was not human but political. Both captains – Webber and Segers – claimed to be in the right. Excitement over the event brought more editorials blasting Kittson for deliberate sabotage. The curious flocked to the "tent colony" started on shore. "A sign on a shingle adorning a tree at the colony reads 'Collision Villa'," explained the Red River *Star* editor who had dashed aboard the *Minnesota* en route to the wreck site. By the end of July, however, the *Manitoba* returned, her name blazed in gold paint with her badger and green leaf emblem glowing beside the English and American ensigns.

But regenerated enthusiasm in the Merchants' cause couldn't overcome hard financial reality. By September of the same year, the *Manitoba* had been seized for a $1,700 debt, and the *Minnesota* had sustained heavy fire damage at the Moorhead levee. Again speculation of a Kittson plot, but again the inevitable Kittson takeover. The Red River Transportation Company snuffed out another rival by purchasing the two Merchants' steamers for a tidy $15,000. Even with ten steamboats plying the Red by late 1875, Kittson with his fleet of seven* blanketed the river trade with an expanded, tighter monopoly.

A creeping civilization was also gaining ground. The Dominion government had initiated surveys at Winnipeg for their planned trans-Canada railway. American railroaders meanwhile had reached Fisher's Landing, Minnesota, drastically cutting the steamboat trade along the Red. Immigration was filling the gaps between St. Paul and Winnipeg. The North West Mounted Police force had brought effective law and order to Manitoba. A new king was emerging on the Canadian prairies – wheat. And a Northwest revelling in its new-found sophistication imported traditions of an elegant East.

The river and her parade of chugging steamboats took on a dashing air. Suddenly they were colourful and romantic, and it was fashionable to be aboard. Mingling with immigrant passengers and crew were inquiring industrialists, gentleman adventurers, journalists, and curious well-to-do eastern farmers. The Kittson steamers also had a new clientele – tourists. Accordingly, the *Minnesota* dressed up to show off her hospitality, her glamour, and a lighthearted crew. The pilothouse buzzed with anecdotes, the captain told of steamboat life on the Mississippi and the Red River, while passengers stood spellbound with fascination. A traveller aboard

*The Kittson line included the *International, Selkirk, Dakota, Cheyenne, Alpha, Manitoba,* and *Minnesota.* The other steamers were the *Maggie, Prince Rupert,* and *Swallow.*

the *Minnesota* described being awoken one night to the shriek of blowing steam whistles. "A night race was on between the *Minnesota* and the *Manitoba*," he wrote in a letter. "The great lights of the two steamers gave a weird appearance to the scene. What a racket: the pilots leaned over their wheelhouses and cracked jokes with each other; and the roosters on deck crowed over each other, and the great chimneys puffed and threw out great clouds of sparks in unison, but we didn't spill any coal oil into the furnace nor break up the cabin furniture to make steam, but we forged quietly ahead and soon left the *Manitoba* far in our wake."

Charles B. Thimens, a genial pilot-captain who had once owned steamboat packets on the Mississippi and Missouri and had survived the Civil War with a sense of humour, commanded the colourful *Minnesota* in her record-setting escapades. First to venture down the Red River through spring ice to Winnipeg in 1876, Thimens and the *Minnesota* also risked being caught in the freeze-up by delaying departure until October 28 that same season, so as to load aboard 856 bushels of Canadian prairie-grown wheat, the first major grain shipment from Winnipeg to Fisher's Landing.

The hussy steamer was only two years old when she and her publicity-prone crew carried Lord Dufferin, the first Governor General of Canada to visit the West, from Fisher's Landing to Winnipeg, in August of 1877. The Governor General's party enjoyed the primitively regal ceremony, and endured the hazards of a muddy, narrow, sinuous Red. "We go from one bank to the other," Lady Dufferin lamented, "crushing and crashing against the trees, which grow down to the waterside; I had just written this when I gave a shriek as I saw my ink-bottle on the point of being swept overboard by an intrusive tree. The consequence of this curious navigation is that we never really go on for more than three minutes at a time. . . . Our stern wheel is very often ashore, and our captain and pilot must require the patience of saints. . . .

"Slowly we turned a point and saw another boat approaching us. It looked beautiful in the dark, with two great bull's-eyes, green and red lamps and other lights on deck, creeping towards us; we stopped and backed into the shore, that it might pass us. It came close and fired off a cannon and we saw on the deck [of the *Manitoba*] a large transparency with 'Welcome Lord Dufferin' on it, and two girls dressed in white with flags in their hands; then a voice sang 'Canada, Sweet Canada', and many more voices joined the chorus, and they sang 'God Save the Queen' and 'Rule, Britannia', and cheered for the Governor General as they began to move slowly away disappearing into the darkness."

Within a month, Lord Dufferin completed his historic tour across Manitoba, including a cruise around Lake Winnipeg on the Hudson's

Bay Company screw steamer *Colvile*. Back in Winnipeg, the Governor General reboarded the *Minnesota*. Firing guns, shouting, and waving capped the send-off, at which a Member of Parliament "quite overcome by the grief of parting with us, almost fell into the water because he continued his parting speeches until the gangway was removed." The *Minnesota* wheeled the Dufferin expedition back up the Red to rendezvous with the Northern Pacific at Fisher's Landing. More merriment and presentations accompanied this final leg of the steamboat trip, including autographed photographs of Lord and Lady Dufferin for the skipper, "as mementoes of his lordship's very pleasant trips on Captain Thimens' boat." But bonfires and fanfares for the vice-regal party dissolved in the October rains. A week passed and prairie winds left little evidence that any festival had brightened the banks of the Red.

An uneasy captain paced the texas outside his pilothouse and tossed down directives to hands on the main deck. The steamer *Selkirk* and her skipper, Captain John Griggs, had seen six years service on the Red in two major enterprises. A heavy load and low water at season's end had given the captain a trying night of navigation. Cleared of customs at Pembina and wooded up in the early hours of October 8, 1877, the *Selkirk* had only a hundred miles of river before her; she would reach Winnipeg that afternoon.

Pausing between checks with his pilot over channel conditions, Griggs overheard a gentleman on the hurricane deck talking with a lady; he was describing the collision between Kittson's veteran *International* and the Merchant's flagship *Manitoba* two years earlier. Recognizing the voice, the captain forced a smile and tipped his cap to the gentleman, Joseph Whitehead, a self-made CPR contractor who was making the journey aboard the *Selkirk* to superintend the ship's special cargo. Once the pride of Hill, Griggs & Company, the *Selkirk* this trip was pushing yet another cluster of barges laden with railway supplies. The year before she had freighted a record 725 tons of rail iron. This day she carried the cargo which would soon be the centrepiece for a major celebration in Winnipeg, but which at the same stroke would also be her own and her sisters' tombstone.

Shored between six braced flat cars and a caboose on the centre barge rested a monster glistening in the midday sun: the Countess of Dufferin, Manitoba's first steam locomotive. Her cone-shaped funnel already shimmered with the heat from a blazing furnace below, and steam pressure was building up for a screeching blast from her whistle on the approach to Winnipeg. Ensigns topped the flat cars and leafy branches dressed the

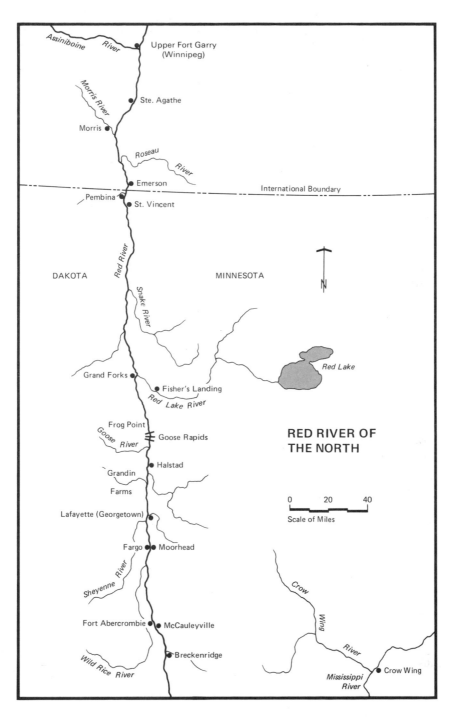

Assiniboine River

Upper Fort Garry
(Winnipeg)

Ste. Agathe

Morris River

Morris

Roseau River

Emerson

International Boundary

Pembina

St. Vincent

Red River

DAKOTA

Snake River

MINNESOTA

N

Red Lake

Grand Forks

Fisher's Landing

Red Lake River

Frog Point

Goose River

Goose Rapids

RED RIVER OF
THE NORTH

Halstad

Grandin
Farms

Lafayette (Georgetown)

0   20   40
Scale of Miles

Fargo   Moorhead

Sheyenne River

Fort Abercrombie   McCauleyville

Crow Wing River

Breckenridge

Wild Rice River

Crow Wing

Mississippi River

39

caboose. "Canadian Pacific" was inscribed on the yellow painted cars, and a banner with the initials "C.P." fluttered from the *Selkirk's* twin stacks.

Nearly twenty years of steamboats had struggled up and down the Red since the *Anson Northup* splashed into tiny Fort Garry for the first time. This autumn afternoon, sunlight danced on the roof-tops of an established city, across church spires and over oceans of ripened grain. Most attractive in the sun to Captain Griggs were the silent steamboats, moored at the riverside in a natural white glow and trimmed with bunting. Instinctively, he reached for the whistle cord and held it long and hard as the *Selkirk's* voice roared an almost defiant blast at a city preparing to crown a new queen of the Red River region – the Canadian Pacific Railway.

CHAPTER TWO

The Scot, the Wolf, and the Honourable Company

The pandemonium that the first Northup paddlewheeler had unleashed on the lower Red River two decades before broke forth again. The City of Winnipeg declared this early October day a public holiday. The Manitoba *Free Press* printed a special edition directing citizens to the warehouse and docks in St. Boniface for four o'clock. Bunting, ribbons, and banners clattered in the air above the Post Office Street landing, while mill whistles hooted and cathedral bells chimed a constant din through the city. Seated aboard the new locomotive, a young Negro stewardess from the *Selkirk* clanged the bell steadily, while vigorous cheers answered her from the enthusiastic spectators on shore. Ironically, she was ringing the death knell of steamboating on the Red River.

The applause continued well into the next year, as the last spike was driven on the St. Paul and Manitoba Railroad line linking Pembina, at the international border, with the southern hinterland of the United States. And the Canadian Pacific Railway wasted no time in connecting the border to St. Boniface; this line was complete by December of 1878. So excited about the iron horse were Winnipeggers that they unanimously voted three hundred thousand dollars for a railway bridge to span the Red and bring the first train from St. Paul in a running time of thirty hours and forty minutes. Scarcely anyone now noticed the thrashing sternwheels of the steamboats fleeing down the Red and up the Assiniboine.

It had not taken much foresight to estimate the future of steamboating along the Red River. By the time the polished Countess of Dufferin had debarked at St. Boniface, the Red River Transportation Company had already lost its celebrated manager, Norman W. Kittson, who had jumped ship and moved quickly to more lucrative interests as co-owner of the St. Paul and Manitoba Railroad. The days of the Kittson steamship

41

monopoly ended. Yet, unlike the crushing defeat that westward-tracking American railroads handed the Mississippi rivermen overnight in the 1850's, the northwest captains, pilots, and crews were not left looking for their next meal.

Built into the fiber of the companies, the crews, the management, and the mechanisms of the steamboats themselves, was an ability to move with the frontier. By their very nature, these men and machines were nomads. In contrast to their Mississippi predecessors, who woke one morning to find trestles and bridge piers choking their river lane, the northwest steamboatmen had all the space and untouched territory they needed to re-establish themselves. Winnipeg was just the fringe of the prairies, or more importantly, just the beginning of a water highway that stretched for thousands of miles. And while the Northern Pacific Railroad choked off the livelihood of Minnesota rivermen, the Northwest Territories grew because its transportation network of locomotive, steamboat, York boat, canoe, stage, and ox-cart lived symbiotically – each mode of transportation was a partner feeding the next in line with business beneficial to all. Leading this harmony of transport was a constantly moving vanguard of scouts – adventurers who mapped for themselves and their enterprises new routes to prosperity.

The need for steamboats had not died – it had been transplanted. The Red River led naturally to three unvisited horizons – to the sixth Great Lake, Lake Winnipeg; through the Manitoba lakes to the Saskatchewan River and the Rockies; and west to the fertile Palliser Plain via the Assiniboine and Qu'Appelle rivers.

Through the 1860's the Hudson's Bay Company had attempted in vain to discourage exploitation of the Red River as the primary trade route to the Canadian Northwest. Sir George Simpson, the governor, coveted the Hudson Bay/York Factory/Lake Winnipeg/Fort Garry passage. However, others in the Company hierarchy examined a wider horizon. To an extremely hard-nosed Company man like Donald Smith, the future of waterways leading out of Fort Garry and Winnipeg meant prosperity within reach. During the 1870's, proponents of a Company transportation system extending across the Manitoba lakes to the Saskatchewan prepared a survey of the Saskatchewan River and its navigability. Smith confidently envisioned steamboat lines bringing twice the goods out of the West to Fort Garry; he saw settlement on the Saskatchewan as new business; and he saw York boat veterans manning the new river and lake steamboats.

In May, 1872, in Lower Fort Garry, the first Hudson's Bay Company steamer destined for the Saskatchewan River was launched, the *Chief Commissioner,* named in Smith's honour. Almost immediately, a major problem became apparent: the one-funnel screw steamer designed by Captain D.W. Hewitt had too deep a draft to reach the Saskatchewan. Unsuited for lake or river, she was eventually dismantled, her vital parts transplanted in other less ill-starred vessels.

The Company was not prepared to give up. Captain Frank Aymond, skipper of the *International*, came to Grand Rapids (at the mouth of the Saskatchewan) in 1873 to command the launching of the Company's second attempt at a Saskatchewan River steamer line. Nine thousand English pounds and three months later, a somber governor, Lord Stafford Northcote, reported to Company shareholders in England that the unnamed 142-foot sternwheeler "in working her way up the rapids, between the place of her construction and the waters on which she was to ply, was unfortunately stranded and so much injured as to be rendered useless." Two hundred kegs of sugar, hardware, and numerous bolts of cloth were lost in the sinking. Some of the cloth was later salvaged by local Indian women, who spread it to dry on the trees and bushes of one of the islands in the river; the Company's humiliation was commemorated when the spot was named Calico Island.

Thus the first two ventures to navigate the Saskatchewan failed dismally. To complicate matters, Chief Commissioner Donald Smith had abandoned steamboating to join the ex-manager of the Red River Transportation Company, Norman Kittson, and two other entrepreneurs, J.J. Hill and George Stephen, in the operation of the arch-enemy Canadian Pacific Railway. Despite these setbacks, however, the establishment of a steamboat line on the untapped Saskatchewan remained a top Company priority.

Of the forty-five prisoners taken by Louis Riel in his coup of 1869, three escaped, one was shot, and a number of others were released on swearing allegiance to Riel's cause. The remainder were set at liberty through the efforts of an Imperial government and the Hudson's Bay Company commissioner, the same Donald A. Smith. Among those released through Smith's diplomacy was a 29-year-old Scot, whose clan swore "There is nothing older, unless the hills, McArthur, and the Devil." Peter McArthur was given twenty-four hours to flee the district or be shot by Riel and his followers. The fragile-looking McArthur immediately embarked on a 450-mile trek overland in mid-winter to St. Cloud, Minnesota, to escape the death threat, and to begin a singular career that would eventually establish him as one of the dominant figures of the prairie steamboat era.

The black sheep of seven children, McArthur had sailed to Toronto from Nairnshire, Scotland, in 1862, worked as a cabinet-maker in

Ontario until the American Civil War ended, opened a woodworking plant in Iowa, homesteaded at Portage la Prairie, and worked as a carpenter on the Dawson Road project until Riel captured him at Christmas, 1869. Perhaps as a result of his diverse experiences, he believed that "hardship and struggle are beneficial discipline, especially for the young, that they toughen character." Having withstood imprisonment and the winter trek to freedom, young McArthur was called to Ottawa and received an unexpected hero's welcome. As a prize and compensation for helping defend British interests at Fort Garry, McArthur won rights to land and resources in the West. "The future that beckons," McArthur insisted, "is in timber and transportation."

"In the fall of 1870," he wrote, "I made preparations to cut logs in the forest nearest Fort Garry ... on the Brokenhead River, about 50 miles northeast. First it was necessary to get a permit to cut the timber from the local band of natives. I introduced myself to Chief Prince of the Brokenhead band with a present of a box of raisins. The Chief informed me that this novel and weighty problem of state could be decided only at a full and formal council.... A council was assembled; gifts ... a plow and grindstone, and for each family a sturgeon net, a dress length and a quantity of beads ... were displayed; long speeches made and the desired boon was finally granted.

"At breakup, the logs were driven down to where the mill was being built and they filled the river for half a mile, which was a point of grievance with the natives, and a council of protest was called. After hours of argument I was worried. My foreman, Tom Stewart, motioned me outside and said, 'Leave this to me,' so I retired and presently one by one the Chief and councillors were summoned to the mill office and one by one they reappeared smiling and happy." Aware that his employer was an abstainer, but that the Indians were not, Stewart solved the difference with whisky, a practice that McArthur abhorred.

Bound to his puritanical principles, but fully aware of the opportunities for capitalizing on a booming Manitoba, Peter McArthur watched the coming of steamboat transport; he was not unprepared. On May 6, 1873, the *Dakota*, of the Red River Transportation Company, paddled her 92-foot keel and 118 tons against the previously unchallenged Assiniboine River. Captain Sam Painter received laurels for his ten-mile penetration of the Assiniboine, while the *Free Press* prophesized: "It is likely from present indications that our continuous line of settlements will extend a distance of 200 miles or more, west of Winnipeg. In view of this fact it is hoped that some enterprising citizen will test the navigation of the Assiniboine to Fort Ellice through that region with a steamer built for the purpose." Few read the prediction and plea more soberly than Peter

The steamer *Selkirk* and her cargo, the *Countess of Dufferin,* the first Winnipeg steam locomotive epitomized the coming struggle between steamboats and railway on the prairies on 9 October 1877. *(Provincial Archives of Manitoba)*

The first prefabricated steamboat, the steel-hulled *Lily* was shipped in pieces from the Scottish shipyards of Yarrow & Co. British machinists Bodden and Tobbin assembled her at the mouth of the Saskatchewan River in 1877. *(Saskatchewan Archives Board)*

McArthur, who the previous season had already launched a thirty-ton two-engine double-decked sidewheeler, the *Prince Rupert,* on the Broken-head River. The first steamer built exclusively in Manitoba, the *Prince Rupert* was small, experimental, and designed primarily for McArthur's lumber interests. Extreme exertion and worry over the paddlewheeler played havoc with his plans and left his health in an ulcerous condition, but his determination to be the "enterprising citizen to test navigation of the Assiniboine" remained undiminished.

Like the caulking between hull planks, lines of immigrants, sand-wiched between piles of freshly cut Minnesota oak wood ordered for the Hudson's Bay Company, arrived at Winnipeg on barges of the Kittson steamer *International* in May, 1874. The precious 15,000 feet of lumber would face many more miles of travel beyond the St. Boniface landing on its way to Captain J. Reeves and the boatbuilding crews of the Hudson's Bay Company at Grand Rapids. There, a sternwheeler nearly twice the length of the Red River's pioneer *Anson Northup*, with twin smokestacks and the engine works from the unnamed steamer that had been wrecked the previous season, was taking shape at a cost of fifty thousand dollars. The Saskatchewan River and the Company's migrant steamboatmen were about to collide in a decade of struggle.

"August 26, 1874 – The long expected steamer North-Cote [*sic*] came puffing up in sight," wrote Reverend Henry Budd, the Church of England missionary at The Pas, Manitoba. A handful of native teepees, the church, the schoolhouse, and the peace of isolation were all that greeted the newly christened steamer, named in honour of the Hudson's Bay Company Governor Stafford Henry Northcote. "They blew the whistle so loud they made the very cattle rear up their heels, and took to full gallop with their tails up in the air in full speed to the woods. But, not only the cattle but the people of all ages and sexes were no less excited at the sight of the boat, the first boat of the kind to be seen by them all their life; in fact, the first steam boat going in this river since the Creation."

For nearly five hundred miles up the Saskatchewan, the *Northcote* created a similar spectacle wherever she landed; the shrieks of her whistle attracted anyone within ear-shot of the river, as press forecasts from the outside world claimed she was "the forerunner of a great fleet of steam craft which is hereafter to navigate this long line of waterways ... through Lake Winnipeg and the North Saskatchewan to Fort Edmonton at the foot of the Rocky Mountains."

The success of the *Northcote's* maiden voyage as far west as Carlton House, Northwest Territories, bolstered the career of her designer and builder, John Reeves; the Hudson's Bay Company rapidly re-hired his talents for the construction of a new screw-propelled steamer for Lake Winnipeg, the *Colvile*. The hull was laid at Grand Forks under Reeves's supervision and then moved to Lower Fort Garry, where Company engineer Edmund R. Abell, a self-taught mechanic, supervised the transplant of machinery from the ill-fated *Chief Commissioner*. The launching was September, 1875, two months after the *International* had rammed the *Manitoba* at Stinking River. Almost overpowered by the gingerbread elegance that the Kittson and Merchants lines both liked to flaunt, the squat ark-like 108-foot *Colvile* laboured her way northward down the flood waters of the Red. John Reeves, the proud skipper, hadn't worried about the frills that the other Red River lines depended on to attract passengers and merchant business. Undeniably ugly on the Red River, the *Colvile* would have no rival in grace on Lake Winnipeg.

The river air above the Post Office Street wharfs droned with the shouts and frenzy of deckhands bucking freight aboard the *International* and the *Minnesota;* the race for business didn't stop to notice the Hudson's Bay Company newcomer as it unobtrusively made its way towards open water. And no-one seemed to note the presence of a square-faced youth who stared at the shore activity from the *Colvile's* maindeck. The young man's name was William Robinson.

Out from Guelph, Ontario, Robinson had freighted to Fort Pitt, Northwest Territories, for the Dominion government, and had helped lay track over muskeg in northwestern Ontario for the CPR. To the young adventurer, Lake Winnipeg was vast, unexploited, and waiting for him. So he booked passage on the *Colvile's* maiden voyage north around the lake to appraise its potential; aboard he mingled with Hudson's Bay Company traders and trappers and met with dignitaries of Lieutenant-Governor Alexander Morris's expedition to sign Treaty Number Five with the Swampy Cree Indians. Robinson discovered that local residents of the lake had cut lumber and fished and freighted for years at Gimli, Hecla, Warren Landing, Norway House, and Grand Rapids, but none, not even the Company, had operated on a grand scale. This short history was gathered as the *Colvile* chuffed through its itinerary of treaty appointments and across seven hundred miles of inland sea. Robinson absorbed everything, ironically planning his future move into Hudson's Bay Company domain from the deck of the Company's touring lake steamer.

With William Robinson's arrival at Lake Winnipeg, the stage was set for a partnership – which would before long turn into bitter rivalry – that held exceptional significance for the history of western steamboating. Along with Peter McArthur – the McArthur who had already founded a prosperous lumber business, and launched his first paddlewheeler, the *Prince Rupert* – Robinson would become one of the dominating titans of the western waterways. Before him lay the not-inconsiderable task of securing financial backing, but already he was preparing to build his empire and a reputation as "the lone wolf" and the "Commodore" of Lake Winnipeg.

A dry season in 1876 limited steamboat traffic to small boats on rainy days, but the following year brought with it the promise of better conditions. News from up the Assiniboine River smashed the lull early in the spring of 1877. Pushing one hundred and twenty tons on three flat barges laden with general merchandise and telegraph wire, the sidewheeling *Prince Rupert* had struggled for three weeks to reach Pratt's Landing, south of Portage la Prairie. With its crooked, winding course, the Assiniboine had left the *Rupert's* crew dizzy and exhausted; but their effort was rewarded by the enthusiastic reception that greeted them. "Excitement [reigned] amongst the merchants, the butchers, grocers and bakers, as the whistle of the steamboat was heard turning the bend of the river, a short distance from the landing," a riverbank observer wrote. "Buckboards, buggies, and waggons of all kinds went rattling down the River Road, the desideratum being who could get there first. Very cheering, and yet strange, that whistle sounded from the wooded banks of the river, like a voice from the great outer world breaking in on the silence and loneliness of our prairie homes." Peter McArthur had broken into the Assiniboine trade; several days later his steamer returned to Winnipeg towing 2,000 bushels of wheat, 1,250 sacks of flour, and 2,000 bushels of oats. It was only the beginning.

The same banner season, excursions around Winnipeg branched out to the new water routes. A garrison from Pembina partied aboard the *International* en route to pay the lower Red River a good-will visit. The gesture was reciprocated by the Masons of Winnipeg who visited Pembina. Another Manitoba boat, the *Keewatin,* initiated moonlight cruises with dancing aboard. The "gem of the Red" dressed in her finest for a pleasure trip to Lake Winnipeg that year; with 170 excursionists and her rails lined with poplar trees, the *Manitoba* eased down the Red like a floating garden with roses blooming in every fire bucket. Not to be outdone, the independent American steamboat *J. L. Grandin,* from the famous Grandin Farms of Minnesota, chugged down the Red with a full circus troop aboard, the first to visit Winnipeg.

Closer to the delta of the Red, near the town he would soon put on the map, the bearded young opportunist from Guelph, Ontario, launched his first experimental steamboat, named, immodestly, after himself; the *William Robinson* would initiate freighting out of the port of Selkirk, Manitoba. All this in the same summer that the steamer *Selkirk* had barged a hooting iron horse, the Countess of Dufferin, into Winnipeg for the CPR.

The *Colvile* handled heavy Grand Rapids-bound traffic that season of 1877. In April, the newly appointed inspector of steamboats for the Manitoba, Keewatin, and North West Division of the Department of Marine, Edmund Abell, disembarked to give rubber-stamp approval to the Hudson's Bay Company's three-year-old *Northcote*. On another trip, a hundred tons of rail and tramcars came ashore under the supervision of the capable CPR civil engineer Walter Moberly; his job was to assemble a narrow-gauge rail by-pass at Grand Rapids. A travel-worn Lady Dufferin, en route with the Governor General's viceregal tour, arrived at Grand Rapids on the *Colvile* in September; she was unimpressed with the new steamboat hub of the Saskatchewan River. "There is not very much to see at this particular spot," her journal narrated. "Trees on each side of the river, two large wooden houses at the wharf, and some groups of Indians sitting about. They had put up decorations and fired off their guns as usual."

Another paying passenger aboard the *Colvile* to Grand Rapids in the summer of 1877 was the latest addition to the Saskatchewan fleet, the *Lily*. In knocked-down form, her prefabricated sections had travelled eight thousand miles from the Scottish shipyards of Alfred Yarrow & Company. From the same mold as steamers the Glasgow firm had sent to South America and Africa, the *Lily's* steel hull, unique to the Saskatchewan, measured one hundred feet in length, twenty-four feet across, and four feet deep. Captain John Griggs, a recent refugee from the wilting Red River steamboat trade, guided the *Lily* west up the Saskatchewan River two hundred miles to Cumberland House.

On Queen Victoria's birthday in the spring of 1879, Captain John H. Smith completed his wagon travels overland from Winnipeg to Carlton House, Northwest Territories, to assume command of the *Lily*. A veteran of the Red River paddlewheelers *Dakota* and *Selkirk* (on which he had served as mate) and the Lake Winnipeg steamers *Chief Commissioner* and *Colvile*, Smith piloted the *Lily* into a season of ceremony and bruises. Up the Battle River (a Saskatchewan tributary) to her first entry to the town of Battleford, six hundred miles above Grand Rapids, the *Lily* had the distinction of catching a Northwest telegraph line on her forward jack-staff, and wrenched out wire and poles up and down both sides of the riverbank. At the end of July, David Laird, Lieutenant-Governor of the Northwest Territories, his secretary, A. E. Forget, and magistrate Colonel Richardson joined the *Lily* at Battleford. For Laird the trip was part of an official visit, by now a popular habit of V.I.P.'s, to Fort Edmonton, while Richardson travelled to the Fort Saskatchewan barracks to deliberate a cannibalism trial – an Indian had been accused of eating his family during the bitter winter of '79.

"On the morning of Tuesday, the 5th inst.," recorded Battleford's *Saskatchewan Herald,* "when the steamer, which was gaily decked with bunting came in view of the Hudson's Bay Company fort at Edmonton, situated on a steep bank upwards of a hundred feet above the river, numerous flags were displayed. ... A salute of thirteen guns from two pieces of ordnance planted on the bank outside the stockade announced the arrival of the Lieutenant-Governor."

After a day of touring, speech-making, and gift-exchanges, the Lieutenant-Governor's excursion returned to the flats below the fort to rendezvous with the *Lily.* A night's rest aboard was abruptly ended as the *Lily* whistled her departure back down the North Saskatchewan, expecting to reach Battleford from Edmonton in no more than two days. By nine o'clock the sunshine had dissolved the river mists and the day was clear with only a light breeze tripping over the river. The *Lily* wheeled ten miles below Fort Saskatchewan. Captain Smith was on duty in the pilothouse when the steel hull rushed hard against a boulder just below the river surface. Smith dashed below to find the rock had punched a hole near the centre of the hull, twenty feet from her stern, and the rear compartment was taking water rapidly. He shouted out orders to beach the boat, but with steep banks hindering the crew's efforts, the sparring to keep the *Lily* afloat with steam-driven poles was in vain. The Saskatchewan's queen of speed sank in eight feet of water. His Excellency and company spent an uneasy night waiting to be picked up, then rowed down the river the next day in an open skiff (sent from Fort Saskatchewan) under a blazing summer sun; however, the party reached the Hudson's Bay post at Victoria by four o'clock, in time for tea. Thus the ostentatious tour and the impregnable sternwheeler came to a ragged season's end in the shallows of a treacherous North Saskatchewan. Captain Smith never forgave the Saskatchewan. On a later occasion, while on an overland trip from Winnipeg to Edmonton, he complained that he had to "navigate a buckboard across the plains in deep water," whereas on the Saskatchewan River the level was often so low that he had to "carry the steamer through shoal waters."

Wherever the source of the steamboat lanes – the spring run-off, the annual rise with the melted snows from the Rockies, or flooding in heavy rains – the timing for navigation had to be perfect. Sufficient water to keep a steamer's hull afloat was as precious as gold. And steamboat skippers hoarded their water lifeline. An Assiniboine riverbank resident dipped his pail into the current one day and had to answer to the wrath of a passing riverboat skipper who screamed, "Hey you! Put that water back!"

50

Peter McArthur's *Marquette* could whistle-stop from the foot of Post Office Street in Winnipeg through a dozen ports of call and a thousand miles of shallow Assiniboine channel to Fort Pelly and back inside a week. *(Saskatchewan Archives Board)*

Named for the Marquis of Lorne, Canada's governor general in 1882, the steamer *Marquis* lived up to her name in power and elegance. At open throttle her eighty-five-horsepower steam engines caused every piece of silver and china to shudder. *(Saskatchewan Archives Board)*

Winnipeg navigation authorities even formulated maritime law, and imported one Judge McKeagney from a Nova Scotia seaport to act as marine judge for Manitoba waterways. "In the riverboat boom days," recalled a riverside Manitoban, "there was much navigational litigation, and from my recollection, the natives, owners and boat officers were surprised at the breadth and adequacy of the law as it applied to their pioneer conditions. The judge explained that these laws were based on the Roman laws of the Justinian Code, modified by British usage. They dealt not only with the rights and obligations of boat owners, but also with riparian rights of the riverbank owners, with insurance and collision, with jetsam and piracy and defined Acts of God. . . . If a spark from a passing steamer set fire to a thatched cow-byre or haystack, the owner was careful not to put it out because the expected compensation for damage was sure to be far beyond the replacement value."

The Assiniboine by 1879 had a bumper crop of governing laws and authorities – the traditional maritime law, a nine-year-old provincial legislature, land speculators of the CPR, factors of an omnipresent Hudson's Bay Company, homesteaders, and a new Winnipeg and Western Transportation Company. The w. & w.t.c. represented a half-dozen merchants, lawyers, and bankers who had pooled fifty thousand dollars ready cash. The company had no small objective – it would control freighting by steamboat not only on the Assiniboine, but throughout the waterways of Manitoba, the District of Keewatin, and the Northwest Territories. Very quickly the new enterprise became a leading force in the northwest steamship industry. By the spring of 1879 the w. & w.t.c. had left the Red River Transportation Company to the history books. The cream of the Kittson Line – the *Cheyenne, Alpha, Manitoba,* and *Minnesota* – were purchased, and the remnant of the once-proud Kittson fleet disintegrated under the onslaught of irresistible competition. With daily service between Winnipeg and Selkirk, a semi-weekly boat to Portage la Prairie, and a tri-weekly boat from Winnipeg to Emerson, the w. & w.t.c. far surpassed any of her rivals.

The *Cheyenne* had her fourteen staterooms, her ladies' cabins between the paddles, and her saloon refurnished with white, green, and gold-striped panelling and oak and walnut inlaid flooring. Muralists painted a complete buffalo hunt scene above her paddles with the proud inscription "Selkirk and Emerson Packet". She catered for the excursion trade, carrying loads of holiday picnickers and cricket teams to St. Andrews Park on the Red River. The flagships *Minnesota* and *Manitoba,* moored in the Grand Forks, Dakota, shipyards, were embellished with an additional fifty feet of elegance (but not, unfortunately, with an equal proportion of stability). Meanwhile, the country bumpkin steamer *Alpha,* built for dry days on the Assiniboine, broke speed records on the Winnipeg to Portage la Prairie run – with a full cargo and passenger list, she took less than five days.

Impressive new vessels were also added to the line. Drawing an extremely light fifteen inches and, according to her owner, Peter McArthur, "able to navigate on a light dew," the 130-foot *Marquette* whistled her way into Winnipeg from her April, 1879, launching at Moorhead, Minnesota. On board was her designer, John S. Irish. Irish, born in Maine and a veteran of boatbuilding yards on the Atlantic seaboard and on the Mississippi and the St. Croix River, had been Norman Kittson's Fort Garry and Breckenridge foreman. Credited with the original designs for the *Manitoba,* the *Minnesota* and two American Red River paddlewheelers (the *Pluck* and the *Henry W. Alsop*), Irish had built a reliable reputation into his "plain modern" steamers.

Close by McArthur on the *Marquette* the day the steamer first met the current of the Assiniboine was another graybeard of American steamboating: Captain Jerry Webber, sporting his traditional black frock coat, a semi-dress white shirt, a string tie, and a broad-brimmed hat. Captain Webber embodied over forty years of steamboat experience. He epitomized the Huck Finn character, having run away from his East Liverpool, Ohio, home at eleven to become a pilot's apprentice on an Ohio River packet. A pioneer skipper on the Minnesota River in the 1850's, Webber won great respect among rivermen when he piloted the *Fanny Harris* and her valuable artillery cargo down the crooked and violently flooding Minnesota and Mississippi rivers for Union forces when the Civil War broke out in 1861. In the seventies Webber saw Red River service aboard James Hill's *Selkirk,* Kittson's *Dakota* and the Merchants' *Manitoba.* McArthur felt Captain Webber was the perfect match for his challenge – to pilot the *Marquette* on a 1,000-mile round trip up the unpredictable Assiniboine from Winnipeg to Fort Ellice, Northwest Territories, where the untouched Qu'Appelle River bubbled into the Assiniboine.

With his showpiece *Marquette* broken in, a daring folk-hero captain hired, Hudson's Bay Company freight loaded, and a sizeable complement of passengers and crew aboard, Peter McArthur steamed out to capture the Assiniboine on the afternoon of May 10, 1879. For five days a party atmosphere carried the venture west along dazzling clay bluffs, sand-hill chasms, and lush spruce woods. After Crawford's Landing, however, the sightseeing ended. The *Marquette,* having travelled further up river than any steamer before her, faced a twenty-mile-per-hour current and a two-mile climb through the churning Assiniboine rapids.

A steam-driven nigger engine on the forward boiler deck depended on riverbank trees for anchoring a towline. But the Assiniboine had foiled Captain Webber; there wasn't a tree for miles. The only alternative was a "deadman", a heavy log buried horizontally in a deep riverbank ditch with a sloping T-shaped outlet, through which a strong hawser line ran, joining the secured log and the boat winch.

"After getting the yawl into the water [and] with ropes, spades and axes to put in the deadman," recorded purser A.D. Robinson's journal, "Messrs. Griggs, Read, Williams and Gibson . . . stemmed the swiftly flowing water. They reached the opposite shore amid applause from passengers and crew. . . . They went about putting the deadman in, then made preparations for returning to the steamer. They came down (the rapids) with lightning-like velocity, which made the onlookers turn pale with fright. Were they to be dashed to pieces? A dexterous throw of rope by one of the crew and a skillful catch by Bill Griggs, and the downward course of the yawl was checked. . . . We then put the hawser rope around the nigger and commenced hauling away. We had gone a distance of about twenty feet when the rope broke . . . after three hours of hard work. 'Try again,' came from the Captain's lips, and at it they went again. But with not as much success as before. Coming down stream and nearing the steamboat, another line was cast for them to make fast to . . . but the suddenness with which the boat stopped, threw Griggs and Gibson overboard. Gibson held fast to the yawl, but Griggs was thrown farther out. As he came dashing down with the current past the steamboat, one of the men reached out and grabbed him by the hair, and yanked him on board, doubtless saving him from a watery grave."

Griggs lost a little hair, the yawl a few tools, Webber fourteen valuable hours, and two ladies fainted with the excitement. However, by the morning of the eighth day, success was theirs. "The *Marquette* arrived at Fort Ellice, amid loud cheering from the officers stationed at the place, and the blood-curdling yells of the Indians. We returned their salutations by blowing the whistle several minutes." The remainder of the day Webber, McArthur, and the boat's company celebrated the occasion; the following morning the *Marquette* headed back downstream. Webber docked the steamer at Winnipeg in five days (crossing those same Assiniboine rapids in only three minutes), and thereby set the pace for future Assiniboine steam navigation – one thousand miles in fourteen days.

Peter McArthur's grand step inland with the *Marquette* was made possible almost totally by the plucky Captain Webber. From boat owner, crewman, and passenger alike, the indefatigable skipper commanded enormous respect. McArthur had nothing but praise for Webber's ability in tight spots. "The *Marquette* was descending the Assiniboine light, Jerry Webber at the wheel, and the *Manitoba* hove in sight facing upstream with her loaded barge fast aground on a sandbar. Moreover, she had a line ashore fast to a deadman, taut and spanning the channel just above the water. This would normally call for some neighbourly assistance or at the least, respect for the property of a rival. It was not so in this case. . . . [Webber] bore down, at the same time ordering a deckhand forward with an axe. At the touch of the axe, the *Manitoba's* hawser parted, causing loud curses and violent gestures from her officers and amusement to the [*Marquette*] crew. . . . To the surprise of myself and everyone, the wash of our wheel floated the barge free and there was no after trouble."

Tales of Webber's impulsive and superstitious nature followed him about. On the Red in '75 he had wrapped himself in the ensign presented by the City of Winnipeg in honour of the *Manitoba's* arrival. A cackling raven, distinguished by the crimson ribbon Webber had strung around its wings, was the captain's constant companion on his trips up the Assiniboine in '79. In the early 1880's Webber was captain of the *Northcote;* a story of mutiny, related by a Hudson's Bay Company clerk known as O-ge-mas-es, or Little Clerk, suggests that Captain Webber brought his idiosyncrasies with him to the Saskatchewan.

"The captain of the *Northcote*," O-ge-mas-es reported, "was an artist in many and strange oaths, and when these failed him in moments of emergency, down went his hat on the deck and on it he jumped with both feet. His desperate language had made trouble on several occasions and he was warned to guard his speech." The day after the Company steamer departed Grand Rapids with 160 tons of freight, word came from the skipper of the *Northcote* that he was tied up with a strike at Chemahawin and all his crew were ashore. O-ge-mas-es rushed to Cedar Lake to find that the captain "could hardly articulate for rage and every second word was an oath (the poor beggar did not seem able to help it). I noted the men all sitting down and smoking on the bank and grinning at the boss's discomfiture. I at last coaxed him into his cabin and told him the situation was a serious one with the river falling daily, and he was liable to lose his job if he did not cool down."

Having waylaid the captain, the clerk gossiped his way into the midst of the disgruntled Indian stevedores, and then hustled the *Northcote's* steward to prepare a feast. Over the meal, O-ge-mas-es challenged the leader of the strikers to a competition; each took half the shore hands in a race to unload the freight. Company wares flew one way and cordwood the other through the night under flares, all in record time. The clerk ordered a dumbfounded steamboat crew to build steam up for an early morning departure. O-ge-mas-es warned the skipper to stay clear of the native deckhands until their tempers cooled, and sent the *Northcote* on her way, concluding that "poor Captain W———— was an able steamboat man, but when trouble of any kind arose, he became wild with excitement and his language was unwritable."

The *Northcote* made history every summer. In the season of 1880 she steamed up and down the Saskatchewan five times. For about ten cents a mile, cabin passengers rented a berth in a stateroom, while deck passengers brought their own bedding for a portion of the open deck; meals were fifty cents apiece. But if the steamer grounded or became stranded, every passenger was on his own. Generally, the Hudson's Bay Company and its steamboat crews had little concern – outside of fares – for their passengers.

There were exceptions to this attitude. Early one Saturday in late July of that 1880 season, the *Northcote* paddled downriver out of Prince Albert, Northwest Territories. On the passenger list was Joseph Reader, a Church Missionary Society minister reassigned from Touchwood Hills to The Pas in Manitoba. A day out of The Pas, near Cumberland House, Mrs. Reader gave birth to a boy in the cabin of the captain, who insisted that the child be named Northcote Reader. The first of two infants born aboard this steamer (the second was Mary Northcote Belcher, born to a young Mounted Policeman and his wife the following July), Northcote Reader not only began his days touched by steamboating, he would grow up with steamboats an integral part of his life.

The Indian community at The Pas was shockingly poor and racked by scarlet fever and whooping cough. Rev. Reader pleaded with his bishop to send food and clothing for distribution among these Swampy Cree. Bishop Bompas told Reader his mission was to be self-sufficient; Reader resigned, determined he would administer his own brand of Christianity without the Church of England.

"By the wildest coincidence," Reader's equally unorthodox grandson explained, "bang came a ten-horsepower big-shot from Ottawa, with the express purpose of setting up Indian agencies where none existed. And none existed here [at The Pas] . . . the Indians weren't even under treaty; it was a loose end and Ottawa wanted to button it up. When he arrived, people told him about that crazy Englishman who had jumped his job. It was fall and grandad had no resources when this big-shot came down; they hit it off real well. He made grandad the new Indian agent with carte blanche authority . . . for the princely salary of $1,200 a year plus so many pieces of hardtack and lard." Reader's territory comprised a 500-mile agency that included Birch River, Shoal Lake, Cumberland House, Moose Lake, Red Earth, Cedar Lake, and Grand Rapids.

Reader hiked off into the woods north of The Pas with his growing family and built his agency headquarters – a modest log cabin and chapel on the shores of his Reader Lake – from which he could paddle to the foot-hills of the Rockies, or portage three miles and paddle to Hudson Bay or the Gulf of Mexico. From Oonikup, his "meeting place" and cross-roads, Reader could travel anywhere. But annually at treaty time an agent had to pay each treaty Indian five dollars; he had to transport clerks, inspect reserves, hire and fire school teachers, conduct agency justice, and even haul cattle. A birch bark canoe would not suffice, so Reader pressed the Dominion government and received a six-horsepower wood-burning twin-screw steam launch, which he christened the *Glad Tidings*. "There was no reason why his steamboat should be named the *Royal Albert* or the *Jolly Sturgeon*," Reader's grandson continued. "As a missionary he believed his message was glad tidings, and someone bringing a fistful of five dollar bills, isn't that glad tidings?"

When the *Glad Tidings* arrived from Toronto, Joseph's two teenage sons, Herbert and Northcote, poured over the steam engineering instructions for operating the double-expansion, steeple, compound Bertram engine and the Roberts flash boiler. From a cold start, in fifteen minutes, with dry willow wood burning in her firebox, the *Glad Tidings* could be on her way, but "you'd lose about two of the four knots you had if you blew the whistle a prolonged blast," Reverend Reader would say. Three self-taught Reader steamboatmen distributed treaty money, enumerated newborn Indians, performed marriages, and presented booklets, alma-nacs, hymn books, excerpts from the Bible, and school lessons in Cree syllabics to eager hands. From Grand Rapids to Cumberland House, The Pas Agency was administered from the deck of the *Glad Tidings* for fif-teen years.

Three years had passed since the *Marquette* took possession of the Assi-niboine rapids away from the Assiniboine herself. The Winnipeg and Western Transportation Company steamer *Alpha* and her rival – McAr-thur's *Marquette* – joined the spring flood waters of the 1881 Assiniboine season. But prospects for a lucrative year suffered a setback when the Canadian Pacific Railway announced it would soon complete its line to Brandon, 145 miles west of Winnipeg and six miles above the Assiniboine rapids. Again, Canadian steamboats took up the trek westward with the march of settlement, just ahead of the steel rails.

Nonetheless, the *Alpha* rushed to begin routine runs between Brandon and Fort Ellice; the *Manitoba* augmented service to Fort Ellice; and in an extremely dry August, the *Marquette* contested the same river territory "practically walking on stones from Ellice to Portage," as her skipper claimed. Yet railway construction west hadn't put boat-builders out of work. In May 1881 Peter McArthur launched another John Irish creation at Moorhead. Seasoned Wisconsin oak planked the 200-foot hull of the largest sternwheeler the Northwest had known. The most modern boiler system, engines with unmatched stroke and leverage, a 120-foot cabin deck housing 80 berths, the highest-set hurricane deck, and a commodious pilothouse outfitted the $27,000 *North West.* With carpenters putting final touches to her two bridal chambers, the *North West* arrived at Winnipeg with a lumber consignment that netted $22,500 in fees. But her first coup wasn't on a navigational venture up the Assiniboine to join her sister ship *Marquette;* rather, the *North West* was the first steamboat in her territory to display a piano on board, and a $5,000 grand piano at that.

The same summer, McArthur put the oldest member of his fleet to rest – the steamer *Prince Rupert* was condemned and dismantled at Winnipeg. Also that summer, McArthur dispatched his latest American import, Captain John Scribner Segers, a seaman with global experience, in command of the *Marquette* up nearly 150 untried miles of the Assiniboine beyond Ellice to Fort Pelly, Northwest Territories. Segers ran his crew to the exhaustion point, but succeeded in his objective; the *Marquette* made the round trip from Ellice to Pelly inside one week.

The boom and gloom season of 1881 climaxed on the west bank of the Red River. For five months, Winnipeg residents at the foot of Bannatyne Avenue – young boys fishing, stevedores for the Assiniboine packets, and ships' carpenters – had seen it coming. A 154-foot skeleton of a steamboat was taking shape steadily, if slowly. An axle on a drawn truck crumpled while transporting crated marine engines and even three teams of Clydes couldn't rescue the rig from Main Street mud. An 11,000-pound boiler was tediously inched on rollers from the railway depot to the construction site. But word of the Governor General's pending visit to Winnipeg in August to christen the city's Louise Bridge gave the project new impetus. The steamer's owner, once a roustabout aboard the *Marquette,* had invited the Queen's chief Canadian representative to christen his creation as well. Carpenters and engineers worked frantically to meet an August deadline, so that the Marquis of Lorne could launch the *Princess,* the pride of Lake Winnipeg's new commodore, Captain William Robinson.

August 2, 1881. Winnipeg hummed like it had on similar occasions so many times before. Band music swelled sporadically along the city side of the Red; crowds swirled toward the riverside with the Governor General's entourage. McArthur steamers and Winnipeg and Western boats dotted the banks adjacent to Bannatyne Avenue. The *Cheyenne,* still a proud survivor of the Red River trade, and the two Missouri-type "mountain" boats – the *Marquette* and *North West* – all listed with the excess weight of spectators. Warehouse roofs, carriages, and even the trees anchoring the safety lines were loaded with onlookers. At the centre, flying English, French, and American flags, the *Princess* awaited her escape from land. Her bow was open to the main deck, like a river steamer, but with solid bulwarks for her lake work; her steampipes and ventilators, her serrated pilothouse roof, and the beaver emblems painted over the sidewheel housing, were all sparkling. Six o'clock drew near.

Greetings, bows, and hat-raising went round the launch platform, so littered with decorations that it was difficult to distinguish the officials from the bunting. Mayor Conklin began to speak. He described the rise of a native eastern Canadian from his days of freighting, railroading, roustabouting and barging on Lake Winnipeg, to his incorporation of the new North West Navigation Company. With his partners – C. J. Brydges, the Land Commissioner for the Hudson's Bay Company, and Winnipeg lumberman-boatbuilder Peter McArthur – the 31-year-old William Robinson was initiating a new era of luxury steamboats. The speech finally ended as the last of the wooden struts supporting the *Princess* splintered. Grinding timber and rushing furrowed water answered the cheering crowds, ropes whipped taut, anchor lines strained against the trees, and spectators tumbled from the top limbs. For a moment the *Princess* drifted unchecked in mid-stream, until workmen drew her back to shore. The *Princess*, capable of ferrying the largest passenger load in Manitoba – six hundred people – encountered Lake Winnipeg a month later and began a colourful career that no-one thought would ever end.

The parade of newborn and reborn steamboats passing through Winnipeg was as constant as the Red and Assiniboine themselves. Excitement accompanied another paddlewheeler down the river from Grand Forks to Winnipeg in 1881. "The *City of Winnipeg* is a finely appointed, three-decked steamboat, gaily painted and upholstered and kept in the most spotless and shining order throughout," reported one Manitoba newspaper on Victoria Day. "The boat is capable of carrying several hundreds of passengers and a crew and large quantity of freight."

"The *Minnesota,*" the Winnipeg *Daily Times* announced, using the *City of Winnipeg's* former name, "presents an imposing appearance, as the result of her enlarged dimensions and numerous improvements. Seventy feet of her hull, cabin and deck have been constructed entirely new.... The increased comfort of the passengers has been provided for by placing spring mattresses in all the staterooms. A large and convenient wash room and barber shop has been added, the water for which is supplied from a reservoir on the hurricane deck.... The new smoke stacks are lofty and handsome. Derricks and spars, with guys and pulleys ... will greatly facilitate the process of landing."

The "Grand Saloon", so called by the skipper, occupied the entire centre of the refitted Winnipeg and Western Transportation steamboat. "The saloon at meal times became the dining room," disclosed one traveller, "with a long table down the centre, the Captain presiding at the head. Most excellent meals were served from a small kitchen at the end of the boat by a real Chef, and the steward summoned the passengers to meals by beating with a spoon upon a tin pan."

Astonished by the wall-to-wall carpets, huge pier glasses and the $1,000 grand piano, another passenger wrote, "I had dinner on the *City* and was fascinated. I noted the flatware was monogrammed; the side dishes completely encircled the dinner plate and the butter was smothered in lumps of ice. The waiters were fast, young and colored. The piano was of course against the far wall, the chandeliers had pendant crystals and the skylight windows were all patterned, frosted glass."

As impressive as the *City's* ornamental interior was her imposing master, James Sheets. An 1840's veteran riverman from the American West, Sheets had joined the Red River trade first as mate in the news-prone *Manitoba* in 1876, and then as a skipper on the Assiniboine packets. Captain Jimmy Sheets enjoyed great popularity "and was indeed an autocrat as he walked his deck," pictured one excursionist. "Certainly no mutiny by either passengers or crew dare raise its head while he commanded the ship. The Captain was a past master in the art of using 'language', his speech being terse, epigrammatic and picturesque to a degree. In fact, the passengers often remarked that that 'language' ran the boat." Like Webber and others, Sheets took full advantage of jocular moments aboard his steamer. One minute he showered orders down over a crew that "absolutely flew about in and out of the water, pushed, pulled, poled or dragged with ropes [while] the engines started and snorted, trying to 'back water' and shaking the boat from stem to stern ... while passengers all held their breath." The next minute he plotted with his crew to overgrease the bow of a novice violinist aboard who "insisted on torturing the passengers of the *City* with his screeds." The highlight of one evening's social in August, 1881, arranged by ladies aboard the two steamers moored at Brandon, was the crooning harmonics of Captain Segers from the *Marquette* and Captain Sheets from the *City of Winnipeg*.

The *City* was wrecked one month later. Flaws – mechanical shoddiness, and weaknesses in the hull created when the ship was lengthened – first appeared in August when the heads of her cylinders blew out. She limped in tow back to the Red River and then to Selkirk, where her machinery was partly removed and her hull loaded with 42,000 board feet of lumber. The *City*, her owners decided, would become the first Red-Assiniboine steamboat transferred to the Saskatchewan River. An experienced Lake Winnipeg steamboatman was required for the transfer operation, and the obvious choice for the task was Commodore Robinson. And so the *Princess*, with Robinson at the helm, steamed north on Lake Winnipeg in early September, towing the *City of Winnipeg* with Captain Sheets aboard. It was a disastrous trip. Three storms battered the northbound vessels and even hugging the west shoreline didn't help.

"The sea ran mountain high," remarked Captain Sheets, "and the *City*, although of fragile build, stood the storm bravely for a while. She then tossed and pitched and rolled, her chains snapped, her timbers creaked and strained, and it was not until the cabin was taken off and danger was apprehended for her consort, the *Princess*, that she was cut loose and left to drift ashore." She struck shore at Long Point, where one side was torn away and her decks ripped loose. The beach rocks soon destroyed her, and in so doing, shook the confidence of the Winnipeg and Western Transportation Company.

The disaster on Lake Winnipeg had a catalytic effect on the major steamboat concerns on the Canadian prairies. Three years earlier, the Winnipeg and Western Transportation Company had wrested the charter to run steamboats on the Red, Assiniboine, and Saskatchewan rivers and on Lakes Winnipeg, Manitoba, and Winnipegosis from the Hudson's Bay Company. When the North West Navigation Company was formed by McArthur, Robinson, and Hudson's Bay Company Commissioner Brydges to compete in the same territory, it looked like the Honourable Company was up to its old tricks again – wiggling its way back into the centre of the northwest steamboating business. Rumours of a third contender in the same trade zone – the Saskatchewan Transportation and Trading Company (a private-enterprise threat that fizzled) – was likely one reason for the Hudson's Bay Company's regenerated interest. However, the loss of the *City of Winnipeg,* coming simultaneously with the rumour of a rival company being formed, forced decisive Company action. The North West Navigation Company (with Hudson's Bay Company investment) and the Winnipeg and Western Transportation Company (whose major freight customer was the Hudson's Bay Company) by summer's end in 1881 had joined forces; the overlapping directorship appointed Peter McArthur as Inland Navigator, with a mandate to transfer some of the Red and Assiniboine steamers belonging to both companies to the Saskatchewan. Robinson, who was blamed for the City of Winnipeg disaster, resumed operation of his Lake Winnipeg enterprise. The arrangement also assured the Hudson's Bay Company a berth in profiteering up the Saskatchewan. From 1881 to 1884 the Hudson's Bay Company held controlling interest in the w. & w.t.c. which, in the same three years, secured ownership of all Saskatchewan River sternwheelers.

A further contra deal with Robinson, who controlled the Lake Winnipeg and Assiniboine shipping lanes with the N.W.N.C. steamers *Princess* and *Marquette* respectively, put a firm Hudson's Bay Company hand on the helm of steamboating across the Canadian Northwest.

At forty, Peter McArthur presented the refined appearance of a Scottish gentleman, but his worn complexion and his continuing struggles with an ulcer gave a truer description of the real man. Always a strict Presbyterian, McArthur had risen from prairie labourer to an important principal in the developing economy of the West. By the spring of 1882 the card-like shuffling of controlling interests in the two remaining steamboat companies – the North West Navigation Company and the Winnipeg & Western Transportation Company – had dealt him significant power; he was now sole head of inland steamboat navigation for their mutual interests. The 1882 season was a busy one for McArthur. By Dominion Day he had captured public attention at the foot of Bannatyne Avenue when he launched his latest steamboat, named in honour of the Governor General, the Marquis of Lorne. A shipbuilder from Wisconsin named Gregory and a purchasing agent named Swinford had assembled 201 feet of the largest sternwheeler the Canadian prairies would ever know. With the finest hull and cabin wood from the oaks of Wisconsin, and precision enginery from the ironworks of Dubuque, Iowa, the $55,-000 *Marquis* steamed north with her riverboat sisters, the *Manitoba* and the *North West,* en route to join the *Northcote* and the *Lily* of the Saskatchewan steamboat fleet. In the three years that followed, the five boats would all be registered as W. & W.T.C., property, thus enhancing the monopoly of the Hudson's Bay Company on the Saskatchewan River trade.

Uniting the five steamers above the Grand Rapids cataract at the mouth of the Saskatchewan River was no pleasure cruise. Under McArthur, each steamer had to be warped up the rapids with nigger winches, four-inch-thick manilla rope hawsers, steam power, and as many oaths as a steamboatman could muster. In ten days of struggling the *Marquis* grazed a limestone bluff which showered her decks with rock, but she made it. The *Manitoba,* even with her jinx from the Red and Assiniboine days, mounted the rapids without incident. On the fifth day of thrashing her way up white water, the *North West* jammed on a boulder at the final rapid; a supporting hog chain snapped and her hull nearly cracked in two, but a towline from the *Northcote,* above the rapids, hauled her to safety. "And that's how Peter McArthur, Captain William Robinson's former employer, took over the job of warping the three boats up the rapids. He claimed he owed his success to Robinson mistakes," McArthur's son stated. "He got everything up the Grand Rapids without a hitch; studied the layout, had special equipment made, and performed the finest feat of inland navigation ever in North America. The conditions were worse than Five Fingers, Stikine, or Whitehorse [rivers], or Hell's Canyon ... an 85-foot drop in four and a half miles of the Grand Rapids, with one three-foot fall in the centre."

McArthur's prestige was short-lived. Though his own abstinence was entirely compatible with a strict prohibition against liquor in the Northwest Territories, it tangled with the Winnipeg and Western Transportation Company scheme of freighting whisky to Edmonton. McArthur lost the argument and was discharged; again his business affairs and health fell into a slump. But on a new frontier – at Westbourne, a small town on the Whitemud River at the south end of Lake Manitoba – McArthur soon launched another lumber enterprise with his new *Saskatchewan*. Operating most of her career in the red, this "heartbreak" sidewheeler would one day burn and be swallowed up by the lake, from whose shores her hull timbers had been cut.

Nor did the future seem hopeful for Commodore Robinson. A recession settled into the West in 1882, and immediately affected the fringes of frontier industry. During 1881, Robinson's steamers, laden with settlers for the districts of Grand Valley, Souris, Turtle Mountain, Little Saskatchewan, Birdtail Creek, and Shell River, climbed the Assiniboine. The boats bristled with agricultural implements bound for Fort Pelly, Prince Albert, and Edmonton. But by September, steel reached west of Brandon. The CPR had given priority to the southern prairie route west; this boosted Saskatchewan River steamshipping prospects, but also chased the paddlewheelers off the Assiniboine. The loss of revenue on the Assiniboine, added to the humiliation of losing the *City of Winnipeg* on Lake Winnipeg, nearly destroyed Robinson. "It was a sudden end to the wildest real estate boom the West ever saw," one Manitoban wrote, "and the beginning of the darkest recession. . . . Robinson soon found that the lumber [from his Black River sawmill] was unsaleable, and the danger of losing the investment was serious. There was only one liquid asset, the insurance with Lloyds of London on his tugboat [the *William Robinson*.] Robinson hired a couple of local Treaty Indians as crew and in the dark of the night ran his boat on the rock off the mouth of Winnipeg River. Twice the stout boat slid safely off the polished granite rock, but the third time it ran fast aground and was wrecked by the next storm. William Robinson collected $2,000. . . . The place is called Robinson's Rock to this day."

Recession failed to scuttle either Robinson or McArthur. As before, a dream and perseverance outlived the economic climate. With renewed financial backing, recovery would be quick; both the Commodore and the lanky Scot would return before long. The greater problem facing steamboat trade, now poised for full steam on the Saskatchewan River system, was not man-made.

Upriver two-hundred miles from Grand Rapids, an unexpected factor emerged to thwart the flat-bottomed paddlewheelers. For a hundred years, the Cumberland House settlement had relied on the spring rebirth of the Saskatchewan's normal east-west flow several miles to the south of their Cumberland Lake. But the years that saw the introduction of steamboats had also witnessed a startling change in the temperament of the river near Cumberland. At a sharp bend in the river known to pilots as Mosquito Point, water was leaving the main channel and flowing northward in the swamps and streams leading to Cumberland Lake. This "cutoff" directed the current into smaller, less navigable waterways than the old Saskatchewan. To be marooned up the Saskatchewan River became a genuine fear among rivermen in 1882, the very season the Saskatchewan fleet appeared ready to steam into high gear. But the season was terminated early. Schedules could not be met. Freight could not be shipped with safety. The credibility of steamboats was undermined, not by a railway, not by competition, not by warfare, but by a "conquered" river. Overnight, master became slave.

CHAPTER THREE

Paddles of Peace and War

The youngest of a large family emigrating from Bruce County, Ontario, to the prairies, three-year-old Jessie Thompson delighted in the timeless days and weeks of travel en route to a new home in Prince Albert, Northwest Territories. It was the spring of 1883. Frontier travel to a carefree child was a marvel of fantasies and new experiences; even the remnants of a bleak prairie winter were fascinating. The overland journey behind rattling locomotives had ended when the St. Paul and Manitoba Railroad train pulled into Winnipeg. Ice at the north end of Lake Winnipeg had delayed the first spring departure of the *Princess,* the North West Navigation Company steamer that carried the Thompson family to a rendezvous at Grand Rapids with the majestic Saskatchewan riverboat *North West.*

The *North West* left a lasting impression with the young girl. "An old Scotsman, that captain [Jimmy Sheets] was very impressive up there steering the boat. We children made our own pastime; we played on the deck. My sister took a shoe of mine; she ran around the deck, holding the shoe by the lace outside the railing and accidentally dropped it into the river. We played everywhere; we had lots of room to scamper around . . . . It was all quite new to us. . . . Mr. [Dan] Milligan was the cook on the *North West.* He had one of those doors in his kitchen divided in two; he swung the top part back and he handed out cookies to us children. We were all tickled to death to receive them, even though they were tough."

Towering nearly sixty feet above the water line, two steel-grey funnels belched a second river of woodsmoke well above the prestigious pilot-house that crowned the open hurricane deck of the ships. The steamer's 120-foot cabin deck had berths for the Thompson family and accommodation for 70 more travellers; the second level still sported a carousel-like strolling deck, the two bridal suites, and the $5,000 piano. All this elegance lay ten feet above a sturdy boiler deck where a steady throb of steel machinery powered the lightest-draught Saskatchewan steamboat upriver. Her proud crew of ten officers and a dozen deckhands had nicknamed the *North West* the "Greyhound of the Saskatchewan". Among the 196 tons of freight the *North West* had loaded this trip were the Thompson's heirlooms and their means of livelihood. "Father came out with full equipment for shoeing horses; it was a complete forge. He was a turner, or lathe-worker, and brought everything. Mother had packed trunks and tool chests with clothes and linen."

The Thompson family disembarked at Prince Albert on July 1. "It was a Sunday and the church bells were ringing. The people all knew the boat was coming in with passengers. The town was like one big colony," waiting with open arms for news, relatives, the season's goods, and proof that the Saskatchewan River had not defeated the sternwheeler. Jessie Thompson and her optimistic family had travelled in the shelter of an outwardly confident crew. But the *North West* hadn't steamed from Grand Rapids to Prince Albert with the ease of a Sunday excursion to St. Andrews Park on the Red. Shifting sandbars, cropping up under the "Greyhound", had slowed her trip, but at least the greater fear of skipper and deckhands never materialized – the disappearance of the Saskatchewan's fickle channel. The problem unquestionably was serious. The course of the Saskatchewan shifted at the "cut-off" in 1882; coupled with the abnormally low rise from the spring runoff in 1883, navigation was becoming almost impossible.

Four years of constant letter-writing to the Minister of Public Works in Ottawa had produced for Hudson's Bay Company Land Commissioner C. J. Brydges only vague promises from federal politicians. The CPR won greater attention and more money. Meanwhile, Brydges's superiors screamed for movement of precious furs. Most freight, if there was any, sat under lock and key, waiting for improved river conditions. During the off-season Brydges discovered an experienced river-improvements expert from the Mississippi-Missouri region. E. A. Burbank, a relative of the famous Burbank & Company steamship monopolists from the Red River of the 1860's, was appointed Superintendent of Saskatchewan River Improvements. But Burbank's 1883 surveys moved more paper than boulders, and won only a trickle of allotments where a torrent was required. One scow worked her way downriver from Edmonton toward the rock-stewn Victoria Rapids, clearing boulders at a snail's pace, while another dredge nosed downstream from Prince Albert to the Cole's Falls rapids at the forks of the North and South Saskatchewan rivers. Improvements were minimal. Consequently, whenever a captain reassured his crew and passengers of his confidence in the river, unspoken lay the more honest fear that round the next bend the river channel might disappear.

The August 1 issue of the Prince Albert *Times* attacked the Winnipeg and Western Transportation Company with accusations of irresponsibility and failure to fulfill commitments. The problem was not irresponsibility so much as adverse river conditions which made it impossible for the ships to fulfill their commitments. For instance, on her second upriver voyage of the 1883 season, the *Marquis,* the flagship of the Saskatchewan fleet, had approached the foot of Cole's Falls only to discover that she could not climb the rapids and complete her sortie to Prince Albert with her cargo of binders essential to the town's grain harvest. Captain Aaron Raymond Russell, once master on a snag boat on the upper Mississippi above St. Paul, and now commanding the *Marquis,* had charted the unnatural "cut-off" phenomenon above Cumberland the year before by following the Saskatchewan's new channel through the swamps along the treacherous Sturgeon River. He depended on his boldness and competence to overcome a defiant channel wherever it flowed. But Cole's Falls foiled his every attempt to steam the final fifty miles to Prince Albert to deliver the farm machinery. In the midst of a passage with more rocks than water, Russell dumped the freight ashore and turned the *Marquis* downstream into a nightmare-come-true.

Steaming light, the *Marquis* joined the new Sturgeon River channel above Cumberland Lake; the channel disintegrated into a rash of shallow, unnavigable streams. Russell reversed engines and backtracked to the "cut-off" to attempt the old Saskatchewan channel. Again the channel deteriorated in a labyrinth of waterways, none able to support the Saskatchewan's deepest-draught steamer. A calm Captain Russell ordered his crew over the side with shovels to dam every creek and diversion off the main channel to keep the *Marquis* afloat. After nine days of ceaseless impromptu canal-building, the *Marquis* found deep water and dashed to the safety of Grand Rapids to lay up for the winter. The Saskatchewan had shaken even Russell's Gibraltar-like confidence.

The North West Navigation Company and the Winnipeg and Western Transportation Company reacted in print with invented confidence. They proclaimed their intent "to handle all freight that offers, and of making the route a popular one with tourists. ... The trip presents to the pleasure seeker many points of grandeur and interest – fresh, and free from the hackneyed sameness that characterizes so many of the old so-called pleasure resorts of the East." Such a claim was less likely to have come from the pen of a Saskatchewan *Herald* reporter than from a Winnipeg and Western public relations officer. Accompanying advertisements referred to the "weekly line" and promised "comfort for passengers" as well as "prompt delivery of freight" with the w. & w.t.c.

The promotion was authoritatively signed by a new commodore of the Winnipeg and Western Transportation Company. The commodore also announced a panacea to navigation on the Saskatchewan. His advertised scheme was a kind of shuttle service up and down the river – the *Princess* and the *Colvile* would shunt cargo and passengers from the south across Lake Winnipeg to Grand Rapids; Captain Russell on the *Marquis,* Captain Webber on the *Northcote* and Captain Sheets on the *North West* would run weekly between the Rapids and Prince Albert; while the *Manitoba,* under one-time skipper of the steamer *Chief Commissioner,* Captain James W. Lauderdale of Iowa, would operate semi-monthly between Prince Albert and Edmonton. Prince Albert would emerge as focal point for all Territories steamboat trade. The commodore planned an overhaul for the *Lily,* which would then explore the South Saskatchewan River southwest five hundred miles as far as Medicine Hat, which would soon be reached by the rails of the Canadian Pacific Railway. The idea was sound. Unfortunately the choice of commodore was not.

Originally from Rock Island, Illinois, the new commodore had served his trade for thirty-five years on the Ohio, Mississippi, Missouri, Minnesota, and Red rivers. Seven years before his surprise appointment on the Saskatchewan, he had blindly bid low on a contract to supply the American military thrust to subdue hostile Indians in untame territory along the Yellowstone. The blueprints for a steamboat line he brought to the upper Missouri and Yellowstone rivers were those of a prairie steamship operation, incompatible with the rugged rivers of the Rockies. His Yellowstone Transportation Company was a stillborn effort. Fifteen years before Yellowstone, he had launched an abortive mission on the plains of Minnesota; his mad dash for fame and the same St. Paul Chamber of Commerce prize money that Anson Northup had won, had grounded the steamboat *Freighter* high and dry. It was singularly odd, therefore, that the Winnipeg and Western Transportation Company directors should have appointed this same American riverman, Captain John B. Davis, commodore of the Saskatchewan fleet. If his record had appeared attractive, the directors had been sadly misinformed. More likely, it was the Mississippi-gambler impulse that a desperate group of Winnipeg and Western executives found attractive in Davis's style.

Relaying cargo and customers from steamer to steamer on the North Saskatchewan brought mediocre success. It mattered little how the company ran the boats – if the Saskatchewan didn't co-operate and provide sufficient water, no plan could operate smoothly. However, Davis insisted that if the *Lily's* experimental probing of the South Saskatchewan reached Medicine Hat, the company would have a new supply depot and a navigable Saskatchewan route.

Davis put the fate of the *Lily* mission into the skilled hands of John S. Segers, the American skipper whom McArthur had sent on his *Marquette* to explore the Assiniboine as far inland as Fort Pelly. Born in 1834 at

Saskatchewan river captains (left to right) Aaron Russell, John Segers, William Robinson, and Jerry Webber pose in Ottawa on 15 October 1884 before embarking on a British expedition up the Nile River to relieve General Gordon's garrison at Khartoum. *(Public Archives of Canada)*

Bangor, Maine, Segers was another classic river rat, who joined the Minnesota packets at age nineteen. His experience included service aboard the *Anson Northup, International, Manitoba,* and *Minnesota,* and he had also been master on the *Marquette* of the Assiniboine trade; when he died in 1909, his obituaries described him as a global pilot, Indian fighter, mercenary steamboatman, and Klondike pioneer of "indomitable spirit," and above all, "a brave and kind-hearted man." With Segers at the helm of the *Lily* venture, Davis beamed with utmost assurance.

Prince Albert gave the steel-hulled *Lily* and her eminent crew – Captain Segers, Commodore Davis, and company – a rousing sendoff to the south branch of the Saskatchewan in mid-July. The Saskatchewan *Herald* subtitled the progress report up the South Saskatchewan "Navigation and Hunting Geese", for while the *Lily* laboured upstream for some seventeen days, towing a freight barge at top speed of four miles per hour, the commodore engaged in daily bird shoots from the deck. Plains Cree unfamiliar with the sight of a fire canoe on their river stood in awe as the *Lily* passed. "On the 21st the boat ran aground on a bar, so that two and a half hours were lost," noted Captain Davis, but the delay didn't seem to bother him. "Two wild geese were shot. A beautiful prairie land lay on both sides. . . . The farming country was excellent and the crops were superior. . . . Telegraph Crossing was reached at noon, and Saskatoon at 5:30 P.M. The whole population of 75 inhabitants came out to welcome the arrival of the first boat." And, Davis gloated, "the price of town lots advanced immediately." Above Swift Current Creek, Davis honoured an Indian chief by sharing afternoon tea; further upstream he honoured two vacant Métis shanties with a one-way trip to the *Lily's* firebox. "On the 28th the wind prevented much headway being made, and the steamer getting aground lost three hours . . . . Eight wild geese were captured . . . . A buffalo was seen and three men sent after him . . . . the crew were having lots of fun." And, by the way, "Medicine Hat was reached on the 3rd of August."

Davis felt certain he had initiated the Hat's prominence as feeder point for the South Saskatchewan, while securing Prince Albert as the northern rail terminus to supply the North Saskatchewan. *Marquis* Captain Aaron R. Russell joined the celebration at Medicine Hat and embarked with Segers and the commodore for the return trip. To reinforce his success Davis loaded fifty tons of Hudson's Bay Company bacon and a lumber consignment on two flat barges for Prince Albert. On the 29th of August the *Lily* and her proud company steamed northeast down the south branch, on her last sailing.

Appropriately, at Drowning Ford, forty miles downstream from Medicine Hat, in a river that had fallen six inches since the upriver climb, the

Lily's hull scraped long and hard over a boulder just beneath the surface. The added momentum of the downward current increased the damage; an eight-foot-long strip of her steel planking was peeled off by the rock on the starboard side. The *Lily* sank immediately in the three feet of South Saskatchewan water remaining in the current. In a few seconds Drowning Ford had scuttled Davis's master plans, and had added a third, and what proved to be fatal, black mark to the commodore's record. All recovered except Davis. The Hudson's Bay Company retrieved its bacon, the Winnipeg and Western Transportation Company recovered twenty thousand dollars in insurance, and Commissioner Brydges launched salvage plans to convert the wreck into a dredging steamboat for badly needed river improvements.

"All aboard the *Lily* reached shore safely," raconteur-actor Clarence Geldert later detailed. An Atlantic seaboard version of a British remittance man known as "the Boston Kid", young Geldert had boarded the *Lily* under duress; his misadventures at Medicine Hat had crossed the path of magistrate Sergeant Sam Steele, Mounted Police administrator of law and order over the vast prairie territory through which the CPR laid its tracks. Steele had deported "the Kid" to his father's custody at Fort Saskatchewan, below Edmonton. Marooned on a South Saskatchewan riverbank, the shipwrecked group held a conference. "Old Hoover," continued Geldert, describing Commodore Davis, "his son and daughter decided to continue on down the river. [I] with thoughts of the grim-visaged Sergeant Steele in mind, threw in with them. Anchoring the lumber raft, now salvage, [we] built a rough boat . . . and started off for Saskatoon, 330 miles down river." Provisions gave out after ten days; river berries and the discovery of a potato patch kept the group alive beyond that. At the end of a two-week ordeal, rounding the last bend they "spied the dozen-odd tents and shacks of the Temperance Colony, Saskatoon." Geldert claimed that he financed a recovery in a subsequent Saskatoon poker game, and Davis sold the raft lumber for passage up the North Saskatchewan. At any rate, the commodore arrived back at Prince Albert broken and "recovering from an attack of rheumatism, induced by exposure and exertion on his recent trip on the South Saskatchewan."

The river and steamboat trade drained to rock bottom. Commodore Davis and the Winnipeg and Western directors expected that things simply couldn't get any worse, but a poor thaw on the prairies in the spring of 1884 proved them wrong. The Saskatchewan's insult chased remaining freight back to the land; any remaining confidence in steamboating upriver vanished; channel waters below the forks retreated still further into the swamps; and Company Commissioner Brydges couldn't sell his *Lily* salvage project – in fact his river improvements were attacked. "Instead of actual boat channels being cleared," the *North West* crew complained, "a great deal of money was expended in making new channels, which owing to adverse currents, cannot be used, and in some cases rocks or pieces of rocks taken from the proposed impracticable channel have been dropped in the actual channel, thereby impeding instead of assisting navigation." Half the Saskatchewan fleet sat idle and the shuttle scheme broke down completely. The writing was on the wall for the commodore and the inevitable came at season's end – in November the w.& w.t.c. abolished the office of superintendent of the Saskatchewan fleet in order to save four thousand dollars per year. Captain John B. Davis slipped back into obscurity.

In 1883 William Ashmead Bartlett-Burdett-Coutts joined publisher William Lethbridge, his partner Honourable William H. Smith, Sir Alexander T. Galt, the Canadian High Commissioner in London, and his son Elliott T. Galt, in organizing the North Western Coal and Navigation Company. Recently discovered coal outcroppings along the bluffs of the Belly River, a tributary of the South Saskatchewan, were the target of their collaboration. Predicting the Canadian Pacific Railway's need for locomotive fuel on its projected prairie line through Medicine Hat, the Galts capitalized fifty thousand pounds sterling with their partners and commenced plans for construction of a fleet of coal barges and steamboats to transport the "black diamonds" down the Belly to the Medicine Hat market. The flagship would honour Baroness Burdett-Coutts, the aristocratic wife of one of the partners of the corporation.*

Upholding the prairie tradition, the North Western Coal and Navigation Company decided that its *Baroness* would be built by a member of the American riverman dynasty. Captain Josephus Todd, a man "not remiss in using strong language if crew members proved slow," was a product of the early Ohio packets. His post-Civil War career had sent him into the rugged upper Missouri trade where he mastered the *Rosebud* for the Coulson Line. Todd had earned a through-thick-and-thin reputation, piloting crews, passengers and cargo past the stickiest hazards to navigation, "often made more difficult," noted a *Rosebud* traveler, "by islands made in the river by the carcasses of hundreds and hundreds of buffalo

*Angela Burdett-Coutts was one of the fascinating figures of Victorian England. Born in 1814, the granddaughter of an affluent banker, at age twenty-three she inherited a fortune which made her the wealthiest woman in the country. A celebrated philanthropist and patron, she offered hospitality to renowned clergymen, soldiers, authors, actors, poets, and political figures. In 1871 Queen Victoria granted her the title Baroness Burdett-Coutts. In 1881, at age sixty-one, she married her American secretary, William Ashmead Bartlett, who was forty years her junior.

Refurbished and sunk in the same 1881 season, the *City of Winnipeg's* lavish decor and elite passengers supplied Manitoba society columnists with great feature material. *(Provincial Archives of Manitoba)*

[which] often drowned in their attempts to swim the river. This mass of dead buffalo would collect silt and branches and gravel, so forming huge mounds that were most difficult to avoid. In time this would form a permanent island that stood quite a height in the river waterway."

Mine shafts had already penetrated the plains east of the Belly under the North Western Coal and Navigation Company banners in 1883, when a Lethbridge pioneer wrote, "Shortly after New Years, Captain Todd and the Captain's two sons, William and John, Abe Whistler and Bill Hughes, all shipbuilders, came to work from Yankton, Dakota. In a shack 12 by 16 feet, they had to cook and sleep as it was 35 below zero. . . . One half lay in bed while the other half ate, as there was not room for them all on the floor at once." Nels, the skipper's brother, also joined the contract, which involved hauling pine by bull team 60 miles from the company's Porcupine Hills sawmill (whose machinery had been transported in the same manner, 250 miles overland from Fort Benton on the Missouri). Early summer found the 173-foot hull of the *Baroness* dominating the bank of the Belly. By July 2, 1883, she was in the water. Downriver 110 miles at Medicine Hat, steam machinery crated at Pittsburgh, Pennsylvania, arrived from the end of CPR steel at Swift Current. Miners recently hired from Nova Scotia and other citizens among the growing settlement at the Hat watched the steam engine implanted in the paddlewheeler.

"When the machinery was taken aboard and placed in position," North West Mounted Policeman Tom Clarke observed, "it was found that the copper pipe conducting steam to the engine was six inches too long. . . . How to get rid of that troublesome six inches of pipe was not the problem. . . . No cutting tool of a sufficient size was on hand and . . . a botch job was made of the babbiting of the joint, with the result that when a pressure of 200 pounds to the square inch was applied, the escape of steam was so serious that the supply had to be shut off immediately. It fell to the lot of an ingenious member of the ship's company to handle the situation, and he made a splendid job of it, being warmly congratulated and rewarded by Alexander Galt." Galt, relieved and delighted that the launching ceremony would proceed unmarred, had other, more substantial, reasons for satisfaction. The CPR had just signed contracts accepting twenty thousand tons of N.W.C. & N.C. coal over five years for five dollars per ton. Present to give the deal his personal approval was none other than ex-steamboat mastermind, now CPR magnate, Donald Smith.

The maiden jaunt of the *Baroness* took signatories Galt and Smith and a 125-ton cargo of farm implements eighty miles up the Belly above Medicine Hat to the mouth of the Bow River, where the freight was debarked; the coal-fleet flagship acquitted herself superbly. As she began her coal-barge towing duties, the expansion-minded N.W.C. & N.C. directors negotiated the importation of Minnesota oak to build a second steamboat at Medicine Hat for the fleet. The new vessel, a 100-foot sternwheeler, would honour another eminent lady, Her Royal Highness Princess Louise Caroline Alberta, the Governor General's wife. The *Alberta* would be the perfect towing steamer. Despite their careful plans, however, the overzealous Elliott T. Galt and company were a prime quarry for a perverse Saskatchewan River system that had already sabotaged the *Lily* and Commodore Davis that season at Drowning Ford.

"I made the return trip from Lethbridge to Medicine Hat as a hand on one of the river barges hauling coal ... a terrible trip it was and took us nearly two weeks," narrated crewman D. J. Whitney. "The river was dropping awful fast and we were continually getting stuck on sand and gravel bars. We finally got down to Medicine Hat. ... The return trip was even worse as we had to buck the current. The boat hands were out in the water most of the time with poles prying the boat off bars. It was hard, gruelling work and we often lay down to sleep for a very few hours in our wet clothes. We were continually running out of fuel for our boilers, and as there were seams of coal along the river banks, we dug out coal and packed it in sacks down to the boat." On a similar occasion, a grounded barge weighing one hundred tons forced six deckhands into the river with levers and block and tackle. Up to their waists for hours in the autumn-chilled Belly, the six struggled arduously against the numbing cold. Each was rewarded with a quart bottle of whisky for his efforts by Alexander Galt. Five accepted the warming liquor; one temperate crewman refused, subsequently fell with fever, contracted pneumonia, and died. His death necessitated the opening of a cemetery at Medicine Hat; his was the first tombstone, an unflattering monument to an already failing N.W.C. & N.C. coal fleet on the South Saskatchewan. The 1883 navigation season had yielded only two hundred tons of "black diamonds" for sale to the CPR.

Still, the N.W.C. & N.C. put the Todd family of boat-builders and steamboatmen back to winter work; a third brother, Wesley Todd, arrived at Medicine Hat. When the snows of 1883-84 retreated, they unveiled Wesley's new command, the 150-ton *Alberta,* and an additional 16 coal barges. Blood Indians, specially permitted to leave the nearby reserve, lined the banks of the Belly to witness the launching of a third sternwheeler for the coal fleet, a 73-foot tug appropriately christened the *Minnow,* which had arrived at the Hat buttoned to the back of a CPR flat car. Designed and created at Rat Portage (Kenora), Ontario, the *Minnow* looked more like a pleasure lake-yacht than a coal-hauling tug boat for the South Saskatchewan.

Despite their initial optimism, company confidence in the coal fleet fizzled completely when spring flooding on the Belly never materialized. "Our miserable river has played out after barely four weeks of good water [May 24 to June 28], and we are awfully disgusted," reported Alexander Galt. Indeed, Galt was already planning a narrow-gauge railway to transport his coal from Lethbridge to Medicine Hat for the summer of 1885. His boats, just breaking in, were obsolete.

Even while the feckless steamboats of the North West Coal and Navigation Company were struggling with the maddening inconstancy of the South Saskatchewan and her tributaries, the slow reverberations of a far-distant political tumult were already being felt in the Canadian West.

In 1880, Moslems in the Sudan and Egypt had rebelled against the rule of the British Empire. Mohammed Ahmed, claiming to be the prophet Mahdi, the almighty and invincible "divine guide", had embarked on his holy mission to perform his own brand of miracles and to bring about chastity and simplicity among his people. The fanatical dervishes flocking to his standard had struck down unsuspecting British and Egyptian garrisons. An initial British expedition to relieve Egyptian officials and soldiers, led by the equally mystical and occult General Charles "Chinese" Gordon, had bogged down and was isolated at the inland stronghold of Khartoum, 1,500 miles up the Nile from Alexandria.

In England, preparations were begun for a second mission to relieve the first, to be commanded by General Garnet Wolseley (who in 1870 had forced Louis Riel's hand for the Dominion government). For the relief mission, an expeditionary fleet would be needed, comprised of boats especially designed for the treacherous waters of the Nile, to be manned by sailors with the highly specialized skills required for shallow-water navigation. It was very quickly obvious that nowhere would more suitable such specialists be found than among the steamboatmen of the western Canadian river system.

"In 1884 the rivers here in Manitoba got low quite early, and released me to some extent from my duties," understated the goateed 35-year-old commodore of Lake Winnipeg. Even Captain William Robinson had felt the hardship of poor water levels that summer, the disaster of the *City of Winnipeg* still rankled, and with the bleak outlook of the lumber trade, he was not ill-disposed towards a spell of adventure in far-distant waters. "In England, preparations for the Egyptian campaign had been going on, and Yarrow, the boatbuilders, were turning out sternwheelers [like the Saskatchewan's wrecked *Lily*] in sections to be put together at Alexandria at the mouth of the Nile. Britain needed men who understood this type of craft, for British experience had been mainly in boats of deep water navigation . . . and they wanted to know if I would go to Egypt and take with me three competent men who understood sternwheel boats." Apprehensive about potential employment in the coming season of 1885, rivermen John S. Segers, Jerry Webber, and Aaron R. Russell accepted the fifty dollars per month that the British Imperial Government offered. The foursome assembled in Ottawa, underwent a master mariner's examination, travelled to New York City, and boarded the steamship *Republic* to Liverpool for instructions and the further connection to Egypt.

Wolseley and the relief expedition reached Alexandria in November, 1884. In addition to the two Yarrow steamers and the four Canadian rivermen, Wolseley had imported four hundred Canadian voyageurs to man eight hundred smaller boats for the voyage up the Nile.

Commodore Robinson assumed command of the first assembled Yarrow steamer, the *Water Lily,* with Webber and Segers as pilots and Russell as mate. Robinson's journal narrated that the 1,000-mile "run between Cairo and Wadi Halfa was very interesting because it was all new. In the early morning we would often see crocodiles stretched full length on the sand. . . . For at least the first 1,000 miles, rapids are not as bad as ours in Manitoba, but the capstans were not strong enough to pull the boat up. [The Egyptians] have been in the habit of having about 250 native men and women take a line on their shoulders to pull the boat. . . . My boat, the 130-foot *Water Lily,* carried ammunition, freight and mail all that winter. We took anything that called for quick transport . . . [but] it was impossible to get any higher than Wadi Halfa, because the river becomes too narrow and crooked."

As for Captain Russell, "impossible" didn't exist in his code. If he could pilot the old Saskatchewan channel, all but carrying the *Marquis* every inch of the way, Russell expected he and Segers could get a second Yarrow steamer, the *Lotus,* another 240 miles up the Nile to Dongola Island (coincidentally the birthplace of the Mahdi). On New Year's day 1885 the *Lotus* set out to cross the second and third great cataracts of the Nile; the second cataract punched a hole in the boat's steel hull and challenged each of her capstan hawsers; and the third forced Wolseley's troops into the water to perform Russell's Saskatchewan stunt – damming secondary channels to raise water levels in the deepest channel through. Inside four weeks the *Lotus* had reached her objective. But high spirits collapsed quickly; just two days earlier, on January 28th, the Mahdi's forces had razed Khartoum and put all British troops there, including General Gordon, to the sword.

The mission was cancelled; Captains Russell, Robinson, and Segers returned to Canada to public acclaim and handsome financial rewards, while Captain Webber stayed on in Egypt to see General H. H. Kitchener avenge the slaughter of Gordon's garrison by defeating the Mahdi at Khartoum and Omdurman.

Terse orders and an unsettled A. P. Caron, Minister of Militia, greeted the three Nile rivermen in Ottawa in March of 1885. Russell, Segers, and Robinson immediately placed themselves at the disposal of veteran Empire campaigner Major-General F. D. Middleton, the newly appointed commander of a mobilized Canadian militia. The Northwest was electric with tension. Chief Big Bear and his reservation Cree had grown violent with starvation; white prairie farmers had tired of the CPR monopoly and protective tariff; and English and Scottish half-breeds and French-speaking Catholic Métis no longer asked but demanded the same aboriginal land titles that Manitobans had won in 1870. In a show of strength, a group of Métis, commanded by military strategist Gabriel Dumont and their reborn Messiah, Louis David Riel, had clashed with the Mounted Police from Fort Carlton. In thirty minutes at Duck Lake, between the forks of the North and South Saskatchewan, four Métis, one Indian, twelve officers, and eleven volunteers were dead. A week later twelve civilians were massacred near a Cree reserve at Frog Lake, northwest of Battleford. The East was dumbfounded; a nervous Parliament dispatched Middleton's armed expedition to the West; the future of a young country was threatened; and prairie steamboats awoke with gunfire to the liveliest season in five years. To them the outbreak of violence in the Northwest meant work and paydirt.

The situation was ideal for Alexander Galt. As he had turned surface coal deposits into "black diamonds", so he would capitalize on warfare. Suddenly, the idle Galt steamboats became valuable assets. His "Turkey Trail", the narrow-gauge railway that carried coal from the Lethbridge mines to the Hat, would soon eliminate the need for the boats completely, leaving them beached non-paying tenants. But a desperate Dominion government two thousand miles away wouldn't have to know that.

"As the steamboats and barges of the North Western Coal and Navigation Company are now entering into the active service of the Government," wrote Galt, as if at that very moment he were shovelling coal into the fires of the *Baroness*, "I am instructed . . . to have a definite rate of compensation settled with guarantee of indemnity from damage by the rebels. . . . I suggest that the Government should pay all expenses and guarantee the boats against damage or loss, and should pay the sum of Six Hundred dollars per diem for the use of the entire flotilla." From a collection of wasting hulks the coal fleet was elevated to a Nelsonian armada. "And as you will want large supplies of canned goods, groceries &c," continued Galt, making all the mileage he could on his patriotic interests, "bear in mind that my son Jack is in business [in Winnipeg] and has the largest assortment, wholesale, of articles of this kind." The repeated assurance by Caron's ministry that the government would assume full risk for any damage to the boats was insufficient assuagement. Galt claimed he had lost "$25,000 . . . and it is absolutely cruel to throw this burden upon me . . . pray put an end to the embarrassment this business is causing me personally." Despite these entreaties, Galt boats were conspicuously absent at critical moments during the confrontation. Although the success of Middleton's advance on Métis forces at Batoche depended on the *Minnow's* arrival with munitions and medical supplies, her skipper sidetracked her to barge oats for a private customer; ultimately, the coal fleet would arrive at Batoche days after the decisive battle. And as government troops counted their dead, Galt wired Ottawa demanding Caron "deposit $20,000 with the Bank of Montreal on account of steamer service . . . [I] have to pay off crews at great expense."

If Galt and the North West Coal and Navigation Company were in a position to take advantage of the situation, the Winnipeg and Western Transportation Company found itself with an entirely different outlook. The four w. & w.t.c. steamboats still in existence had been scattered like tumbleweed by the sleepy 1884 season. Repairs were interminably stalled on the *North West,* which lay beached on a Prince Albert riverbank. Wintered in the ice-choked mouth of the Shell River above Prince Albert were the *Marquis,* which was undergoing renovations to her cabins and her steering mechanism, and the *Manitoba.* Moreover, the Duck Lake skirmish had solidified the Métis stronghold at the forks of the Saskatchewan, thereby effectively isolating these three potential troop carriers from Middleton's advancing militia and from the river captains returning from Egypt. With the fourth boat, however, the situation was more promising. Captain Sheets, that spring the only active steamboatman on the prairies, was busy preparing the *Northcote* for launch from the Medicine Hat shoreline that she shared with the three abandoned steamers of Alexander Galt's North West Coal and Navigation Company.

"All the Hudson Bay boats and the Galt boats will be at the disposal of troops," ordered Militia Minister Caron. Middleton's forces sped across the Palliser plain on new CPR steel, delivered by cantankerous William Cornelius Van Horne (who had marshalled American troops by train during Civil War crises). Middleton detrained at Qu'Appelle with eight hundred troops; Lieutenant-Colonel W. D. Otter detrained at Swift Current with seven hundred men for the march to Battleford; Major-General T. B. Strange moved northwest to reconnoiter the Blackfoot near Edmonton; and North West Mounted Police Superintendent W. M. Herchmer travelled to the end of steel at Medicine Hat to protect the only means of transport north and west – the steamboats.

By the first official days of spring, the North West Mounted Police and the Nile skippers had joined James Sheets aboard the *Northcote* at Medicine Hat. The Cree across the South Saskatchewan broke camp and disappeared. On April 9 the capacious steamer hit the water with three reliable helmsmen (Segers, Sheets, and Russell), who piloted her and two scows into what appeared to be an ordinary trip, battling only low water and sandbars.

Even before Captain Sheets and the *Northcote* had weighed anchor at Medicine Hat, most of western Canada was galvanized by news of the hostilities. Able-bodied men took arms against Riel's forces. In the Prince Albert area – behind the Métis lines – the Prince Albert Volunteers were formed for the defence of the community. One man who joined the volunteers, steamboat worker Archie Ballantine, recorded his impressions of the scene. "In the winter of 1884-5 I was working in a lumber camp. . . . We broke camp about the middle of March and came to Prince Albert. The town was in a state of excitement." Ice was clearing, hundreds of miles upriver. Word arrived that the *Northcote* and the Galt boats had been launched; that Colonel Otter had detrained at Swift Current with a relief column for Battleford; and that Deputy Surgeon-General T. G. Roddick's medical corps awaited river transport to support Middleton's move northward from Qu'Appelle to break the Métis occupation of the forks. "A stockade had been built around a block taking in the Presbyterian Manse and the little Church," Ballantine continued. "All the cordwood in the town was used in the stockade and all provisions had been put inside. . . . I was kept for the guard for a few nights, when the officers decided they wanted me to go to work at the steamboats."

"The steamboats" referred to by Ballantine were the *Marquis* and the *Manitoba*, both frozen tight in the jaws of twisted ice at the mouth of the Shell River, five miles west of Prince Albert. At any moment the current could rip the deep-freeze loose, so Ballantine bedded down in a riverbank shanty with Captain Julius Dougall. The night of April 9 closed in. "In the morning . . . we could hear water running . . . and found that the Saskatchewan had risen four feet during the night, the water nearing the tops of the hulls. . . . We got the bark canoe and paddled out to the ice. When we were about in the middle of the river, the *Marquis* moved and raised up, but as her rudders were frozen in the sand and ice, she did not let go . . . we could do nothing. . . . The old *Manitoba* was full of water and would not rise. . . . The water ran high and covered the old *Manitoba* out of sight. . . . The *Marquis* was at an angle of forty-five degrees, her rudders still frozen and all her hog chains broken." Ballantine and Dougall patched her chains, severed her rudders from the river bed, stoked her fireboxes, built steam, and miraculously nursed her to the mainstream. Without steering gear Captain Dougall ran a line from the steamer's stern to the shore and, pointing the prow of the *Marquis* downstream, dashed for the ice-free safety of the Prince Albert wharfs. The *Manitoba* was a total wreck.

April was racing by. While Ballantine and the others worked frantically to complete even rudimentary repairs to the *Marquis*, the *Northcote* was proceeding downstream at all possible speed. Poundmaker's Crees were freely besieging Fort Battleford. Riel and Dumont amassed their Métis and Indian allies at Batoche. Five days out of Medicine Hat, a wary crew coaxed the *Northcote* around the last shallow bend above Saskatchewan Landing on the South Saskatchewan, twenty-five miles north of Swift Current. At the sight of the 150-foot paddlewheeler, a throng of equally weary Canadian militiamen at the landing cheered frantically. Their voices broke the river silence and aroused the exhausted rivermen to a new urgency.

Colonel Otter, with his five hundred regulars and two hundred teamsters, was itching to cross the South Saskatchewan in pursuit of Big Bear and Poundmaker. For three days the *Northcote* butted both banks of the river ferrying troops and vehicles to the north bank trail that led to Battleford. However, General Middleton, two hundred miles northeast down the Saskatchewan, was growing impatient for reinforcement before challenging Riel at the forks. The *Northcote's* normal run in a moment had become a military manoeuvre. On April 23, the *Northcote* splashed downstream, Saskatchewan Landing behind her. Her paddles pushed a fully loaded hold, and towed two barges laden with ammunition, food and medical supplies, livestock feed, a 200-man company of the Midland Battalion, and members of the Number One Field Hospital Corps, all in support of Middleton. Vital among the *Northcote's* passengers was American Lieutenant Arthur L. Howard, a famed Indian fighter released from the Connecticut National Guard and informally attached to the Canadian Northwest Field Force. Equally precious was his knowledge and the rapid-fire Gatling gun from which he earned his nickname "Gat" Howard.

Northcote master Sheets had estimated a four-day trip to meet Middleton at Clarke's Crossing near Batoche, but six days later there was still no word of her whereabouts. On the 29th, Surgeon-Major C. M. Douglas volunteered to paddle downstream in his folding canoe from Saskatchewan Landing to search; he was certain he would find the steamer wrecked, scuttled by Métis forces, and no survivors. On the fourth day "I was somewhat startled by the unexpected boom of a steam whistle lower down the river," Douglas said. "I soon came in sight of the smoke stacks of a steamer, without doubt the *Northcote*. . . . I saw the red-coated line of militia soldiers, and rounding-to under the lee of the steamer, which was wedged on a sand bar, was greeted by a cheer from them. I spent a few hours on board the steamer, but soon tired of the monotony of seeing the ship, heavily loaded, with two barges alongside, warped or lifted from one sandbar on to another by means of her 'grasshopper legs'.

"While running, a man kept on each barge taking soundings and calling them off for the directions of the man at the wheel," logged Doctor H. A. Wright, aboard with the Field Hospital Corps; his diary detailed the reason for the *Northcote's* delay. "If a barge was stranded and the boat in a fair depth of water, the barge's cargo was transferred to the boat; if both boat and barges were stranded, all the cargo was taken ashore in small boats." Again and again the boat was crutched downriver. "Long poles geared with block and tackle were placed perpendicularly one on either side of the boat capstans; men called into play winding up the cables and thus raising the bow of the boat. When it was raised, the engine was started and all possible force exerted to send the boat forward." Lieutenant John A. V. Preston, out from Bethany, Ontario, with the Midland Battalion, recorded that there was little relief from the boredom "while we wrestled with sand bars or tied up for repairs," except when "Gat Howard occasionally did a little target practice with his gun for our edification. . . . a typical Yankee who believed that the only good Indian was a dead Indian." Morale plummetted further when the *Northcote* arrived at the Elbow; Dumont's marksmen had felled fifty of Middleton's untried militia of school teachers, farm hands, bookkeepers, artists, mechanics, and lawyers at Fish Creek on April 24. When the *Northcote* landed near Saskatoon to debark a hospital unit for Middleton's wounded, the fatigued boat travellers also heard about Otter's humiliating retreat from Cut Knife Hill near Battleford on May 2.

The *Northcote's* sternwheel scarcely stopped chopping up the river at Saskatoon, pausing only to accept a welcome cargo – some freshly caught jackfish, which a farmer named Eby delivered personally by wading out to the steamer. Middleton paced about his Clarke's Crossing camp waiting for Gat Howard's prized weapon and the Midland Battalion with the Field Hospital Corps. By May 5 the steamer caught up to Middleton. A robust New Brunswicker with heavy overcoat and full beard joined the *Northcote* crew at Clarke's Crossing. Just thirty-five, Captain E. Shelton Andrews was a fully papered master of the high seas; in 1884 the Temperance Colony of Saskatoon had hired him to skipper the launch *May Queen* down from Medicine Hat with a scow of lumber for their growing South Saskatchewan town. The captain had homesteaded and married

A series of "best on record" passages on the Saskatchewan River between Grand Rapids and Edmonton in 1884 moved one *North West* crew to rechristen their sternwheeler "Greyhound of the Saskatchewan." *(Ernest Brown Collection)*

The *Northcote* rots on the beaches of Cumberland Lake nine years after her "assault" on Batoche. Ten years later she was torched as an unsafe children's playground. *(Saskatchewan Archives Board)*

just before the Duck Lake incident, but "as they had no-one else to splice their wire ropes [the militia] took me on as a combatant, and I took part in the expedition of the *Northcote* against Batoche."

Perhaps the Métis sniper's bullet that shattered part of General Middleton's shaving mirror (to which the General responded, "Lucky shot. Never happen again," without missing a stroke around his walrus moustache) wrongly convinced the commander that his enemy were poor shots. After seizing Gabriel's Crossing (Gabriel Dumont's abandoned farm site) on May 8, Middleton ordered Dumont's stable dismantled for its planking, and Dumont's billiard table and washing machine removed to the *Northcote*. It was then that he announced his idea to convert the steamer into a gunboat! Under S. L. Bedson, Chief of Transport for the Field Forces, and Captain Smith of the Infantry School Corps, the *Northcote* dressed for the mission. The stable planks were tacked outside the maindeck walls, and oat sacks, boxed materials, and pressed hay were packed around the upper deck. Armed with thirty-five riflemen, one cannon, and her top speed of five miles per hour, the *Northcote* would perform a diversionary manoeuvre as "Middleton's Navy" in the assault on Batoche.

According to Middleton's precautionary strategy, the *Northcote* stirred the river mists at Gabriel's Crossing shortly after six on the morning of May 9th, 1885, and steamed down to the last bend above the Batoche settlement, where she was to await Middleton's bombardment of Riel's camp from the east, and then split the Métis defence by opening fire from the river. With two clumsy barges lashed to her bulwarks, the *Northcote* paddled gently into the current toward her delay point. The two skippers and the chief clerk eyed uneasily the flimsy shielding around their wheelhouse. Below on the cabin deck and boiler deck, sea-captain Andrews, Captain Smith and his thirty-five troops, and an ailing Lieutenant Hugh John Macdonald, son of the Prime Minister, casually positioned themselves. Raconteur-reporter George H. Ham enjoyed the early morning with a cigar; he had come aboard to get the story, handle a rifle, and (because his father, John V. Ham, ran a legal firm with partner John A. Macdonald in Ontario), keep a guardian eye on the Prime Minister's son.

The first gunshot ripped into the *Northcote* "at ten minutes past eight," a startled George Ham reported, "passing through the pilot house. The rebel spies had watched the steamer the previous night on the opposite bank from Gabriel's. . . . This first shot was evidently a signal to the rebels of the boat's approach, and as she rounded the bend a moment later, she was raked fore and aft with a storm of bullets coming from either bank." Dashing below to join his ward, Ham jabbed Macdonald's rifle through the protective sacks and returned the fire with Smith's infantrymen. Faithful scouts had given Dumont an explicit description of the *Northcote's* features; mounted, Dumont raced up and down the riverbank directing Métis gunfire. "Captains Segers and Sheets, who piloted the steamer, remained at the post of duty," Ham commended, "and with them was Talbot, the purser, who kept a steady fire from the pilot-house, which was made a special target of by the rebel marksmen, they being fully aware of the disaster which must overtake us if we were wounded in this vulnerable point. Dozens of bullets pierced the wheel-house. Segers received one in the coat sleeve; and in the cabin in which I write, a scene of wild disorder prevails." The skylights were smashed, and the additional two-inch stable planking stopped few of the bullets; troops in the staterooms scrambled for mattresses and bolsters to throw against the inside walls for protection. Middleton's Field Force was still four miles from his Batoche appointment, leaving the *Northcote* alone to face the entire Métis force. The general's surprise gunboat for Louis Riel at Batoche Crossing was herself surprised.

"O my God," Riel had written in his diary on April 20th. "I pray you, in the name of Jesus, Mary, Joseph and St. John the Baptist, grant that you use the cable of our ferry to upset the steamboat; that we may have the provisions, the useful things the boat contains, the arms and the munitions."

"In passing the Crossing," a decked correspondent Ham continued, "the ferry cable, which is strung from the upper banks, was lowered just as we approached it, the intention of the rebels being to corral the steamer, and in the confusion to capture the boat, and massacre its human freight. . . ." The cable caught the smoke-stack, spars, masts, and the whistle (the only way to signal the boat's location to Middleton), but fortunately for the *Northcote*, missed the pilothouse. Debris and hot metal came crashing to the hurricane deck, nearly igniting the steamer's Minnesota oak.

It was Middleton's expectation to break through Riel's forces at the Batoche ferry to find the *Northcote* tearing up the Métis rearguard just off the riverbank. The skipper, dodging wood splinters and shattered glass, had little time to think of throwing the anchor to hold his position. "The steamer, to avoid two large boulders directly in her course," narrated Ham, "was allowed to turn around, and floated down stream stern foremost. One barge barely grazed the bank, and the boat could have been boarded by the rebels were it not for the steady volley that our men poured at them.

"A withering fire was still maintained from the enemy rifle-pits . . . until nine o'clock. . . . As some of the red coats were seen coming up in skirmishing order in the distance, our small force gave three lusty cheers. . . . Dropping below the [Métis] batteries nearly three miles, anchor was cast in midstream, but the steamer, almost unnoticeably, drifted for another mile before the anchor firmly caught. . . . We had run the gauntlet of fire for five miles." Keeping the boat, her crew, and civilian Ham in check, straggling Métis cracked sporadic shots into the *Northcote*, "where, ensconced behind a pile of mail-bags, I kept up a steady fire at something unknown. . . . I don't know whether I hit any clouds or not, but I am assured of one thing: if any lead mines are ever discovered on the banks of the Saskatchewan, I should have a prior claim over anybody in their ownership." The combatants continued to pelt the shore as an argument raged aboard – army versus "navy". Bedson and Smith pressed for a return upstream to fulfill Middleton's rear attack order, but Segers refused to pilot the steamer in its (or his) present state back to Batoche. To the skipper at least, the *Northcote* had proven herself no gunboat, no matter how much the militiamen believed in Middleton's naval illusion.

The turkey-shoot on the river encouraged Métis forces momentarily, but the graver threat, Middleton's Field of one thousand, presented them with a more significant danger. By May 15, Batoche was occupied by Middleton's army; the Indians supporting Riel scattered to the north; Dumont, like his Messianic leader had done fifteen years before, fled to Montana; and a relieved General Middleton held victory in his palm. Skirmishes continued throughout May, but the militia victory had been decided at Batoche. Commander Middleton regrouped at an exuberant Prince Albert and then launched his pursuit of Poundmaker and Big Bear, this time using the steamers *North West*, *Marquis*, *Baroness*, and *Alberta* – realistically – as troop transports only. By mid-July Middleton's army was homeward bound, the fighting was over, and the aftermath left to businesses like Alexander Galt's North West Coal and Navigation Company and the Hudson's Bay Company's Winnipeg and Western Transportation Company, who charged an indebted Dominion government thousands of dollars for their services; to historians and raconteur George Ham to write about; and to stationed officers like Captain George H. Young to clean up after.

"Young's instructions," related a friend, "were to take the steamboat [*Northcote*] down to the Elbow with Louis Riel," taken prisoner four days after the fall of Batoche and brought to Saskatoon along with the wounded. "Then he was to commandeer some farmers' wagons and from the Elbow come on to Moose Jaw and put him on the train [to Regina]. And according to the official account then, that's what happened. But of course, we all know that's not how it happened. George Young wasn't born yesterday; he knew that on the boat they'd be sitting ducks with rebels in the brush taking all the time in the world to draw a bead on them.

Instead, Young commandeered the wagons right in Saskatoon and went all the way overland to Regina."

The Temperance Colony at Saskatoon hardly noticed prisoner Louis Riel pass through in late May; Middleton's Field Force kept Deputy Surgeon-General Roddick, pioneer Saskatoon Doctor J. E. C. Willoughby, Doctor James Bell, and the village women far too busy caring for its wounded. The summer ordeal ended for Saskatoon, however, with a peculiar sendoff at the river wharf on July 1. Galt's steamer *Alberta* chuffed out into the same South Saskatchewan channel that the *Northcote* had taken as gunboat two months before. The impression the *Alberta* created was vastly different. Strung around her bow like flower petals floated a cluster of four barges. To her port side the sixteen-by-fifty-foot barge dubbed "John A. Macdonald" with its rough pine hull and canvas canopy was the floating hospital for the twenty-seven wounded; starboard was a huge double barge to house two hundred troops of the Midland Battalion waiting at the forks; and directly off the *Alberta's* bow was the fourth barge holding meat supplies, vegetables, barrels of water, forage, and two nervous cows to provide milk for the invalids. With medical staff lodged in the steamer's staterooms, the *Alberta's* entourage steamed northeast on her smooth 500-mile ambulance run to Grand Rapids and a rendezvous with Commodore Robinson's *Princess* for the Lake Winnipeg crossing.

Returning to his Winnipeg *Tribune* desk, publisher George Ham wrote finally, "On arriving at Winnipeg the troops were received with unbounded enthusiasm. Business was at a stand-still, and the whole city gave itself over to rejoicing. . . . the manifestations of joy expressed in waving flags, variegated bunting and noble arches, but more especially in the thundering cheers from the throats of thousands of fellow-countrymen. . . ." In one hundred and twenty days of campaign, fifty so-called rebels, a dozen civilians, and thirty-nine troops had perished; it had cost the Dominion government over four million dollars and the Indians and Métis their pride; Poundmaker and Big Bear were imprisoned (the former died within a year, the latter in 1888); nine others were executed at Battleford; and Riel was hanged on November 16, 1885 at Regina. Prairie steamboats had chalked up their best season of the 1880's, having transported 1,600 men and thousands of tons of profitable freight. But the ironic bounty of 1885 merely disguised the unavoidable truth. The golden age of the prairie steamboat giants was fading.

CHAPTER FOUR

Walterdale Steam

"When it was all over but the hangings, we were sent down the river on the boats; the biggest and best of the lot was the *Marquis* and of course most of the officers were on board." Thus scoffed one low-ranking militiaman returning from the '85 campaign; he was one who suspected his superior officers' proclaimed unselfishness and loyalty to the cause. "At the stern of this big boat on the saloon deck was a row of latrines and one of them was padlocked. I was curious and asked the guard whose station was there. He lifted me up so I could look through the space over the door . . . the place was packed to the ceiling with bales, bales of fur belonging to General Middleton." The general was later accused of pillage. Similarly, this same militiaman criticized the lavishly equipped *Marquis;* her white oak, mirrors, and carpets were beautiful, yes, but her four-foot draft was impractical for the Saskatchewan River.

Not long after the fighting, the Saskatchewan proved his point. Captain Julius Dougall, who had brilliantly piloted the *Marquis* out of Shell River ice in 1885, skippered the 202-foot sternwheeler on her first commercial mission of the 1886 season. It was nearing the end of July when she approached the crooked Thorburn Rapids, 120 miles below the forks. Captain Dougall had threaded the *Marquis* through the worst of the mile-long rapids when her hull caught a starboard rock; she pivoted, lost her forward motion, and broadsided back onto an eight-foot boulder. Sparring proved fruitless. In thirty minutes, water had filled her hold.

Recalling his navigational feat on the Grand Rapids, the Winnipeg and Western Transportation directors contacted troubleshooter Peter McArthur at his Westbourne lumber yards, and offered him a contract for twenty thousand dollars to repair the Marquis. By the end of September, McArthur and his hand-picked 35-man salvage crew reached the wreck location. Water in the river had retreated sufficiently to allow his crew to work dry-shod. Quarryman Jim Young extracted the boulder from the belly of the *Marquis,* which was then jacked up and hoisted thirty feet up the riverbank along timber slipways with horse capstans and ten sets of block and tackle. With every line under stress, McArthur reported "the foreman had an idea that the bow line was dangerously taut, so he eased it off a bit. The number two line took the added strain and snapped; in no time they all snapped. With a roar and a crash the great boat went hurtling down to the river bed, all at work fleeing before her onslaught. Six weeks labour [was] lost." McArthur repeated the jacking and winching, but winter was moving in and now more than just the hull needed repairs – the tumble down the riverbank had shattered the luxury boat's main steam pipe and severed her supporting hog chains. The following spring would bring McArthur and another crew back to relaunch the Saskatchewan's largest steamboat, but that winter the severe prairie frost quietly crept into the weakened timbers of the *Marquis* and stole away her spirit.

McArthur retraced his steps to Thorburn Rapids in 1887 and successfully refloated the crippled *Marquis,* after which the salvage crew celebrated and feasted in her dining saloon. But fluctuating water levels and the ever-deviating river channel chased the deep-draft Saskatchewan queen to her berth at Prince Albert in 1890 for the last time. There the *Marquis* died. The *Northcote* had already met a similarly inglorious end. In the same disastrous autumn of 1886 that saw the *Marquis* grounded at Thorburn Rapids, Captain Jerry Webber, home from Wolseley's relief expedition up the Nile, assumed command of the battle-worn hero of Batoche. He struggled vainly with a Saskatchewan so low at the "cut-off" that he was forced to beach his steamboat on the shores of Cumberland Lake. The *Northcote* never sailed again.

The harmony that a westward-pushing CPR had shared with the Hudson's Bay Company-backed steamboat line along the frontier crumbled during 1885. Politicians, unable to find pennies to move pebbles from the Saskatchewan, jumped to finance a thousand miles of prairie track because of Louis Riel. Steel rails were far outrunning steamboat paddles. The tentacles of the CPR had penetrated the domain of the Winnipeg and Western Transportation Company fleet – her own Saskatchewan River – at Prince Albert in 1890 and at Edmonton in 1891. An uncooperative river had first claimed the *Lily* and the *Manitoba;* then dry seasons had grounded the *Baroness, Alberta, Northcote,* and *Marquis.* Rivermen insisted that the low water was temporary, but that problem had become academic; the fatal stroke (like the one that had made derelicts of the *Cheyenne, Dakota, Selkirk, Alpha,* and *Marquette)* came to the Saskatchewan fleet with these CPR spur lines. Now the Saskatchewan steamboats were not only high and dry on the South Saskatchewan, but they were also miles from the new rail-steamboat terminals on the north branch of the river as well. Overnight the ravenous CPR broke down the delicate symbiotic transportation network of the Northwest. The age of gussy steamboats was fading. The Northwest would build no more Mississippi-style dinosaur paddlewheelers; the survival of prairie steamboating depended upon smaller utilitarian steamers, working locally on shorter runs, closely tied to a blossoming industrial economy.

Steamboats had thrived on a frontier that had gratefully accepted anything that passed by its doorstep. Now the Northwest had grown fickle; if locomotives were more fashionable than paddlewheelers, the railway got more public attention. The Saskatchewan steamer had survived, because half a century's river experience was at its helm. The American riverman was the best. He nurtured steamboating on Canada's prairie, but, for the same reasons, he abandoned it. To a riverman, home was the gingerbreaded view from the pilothouse, evenings dining in the saloon, the rumble of each steam engine stroke under foot, the splash of a strong paddlewheel at his back, and a crown of woodsmoke overhead. Fussing with cargo ashore just interfered with the skipper's love affair with the river; he lived aboard for half the year. And because he was American, this riverman rarely stayed in the Northwest. When steamboat trade declined he moved to the next frontier, if there was one; when he grew too old, he retired to the United States. He rarely took root along the river that employed him, to sell his ability locally. So, as the golden age of the great steamboats on the Saskatchewan began to falter, the American riverman migrated to new boats on the Athabasca, Mackenzie, or Yukon; or he returned south to die. Thus prairie steamboating was adopted by the prairie farmer, the native small businessman or the tradesman and settler, whose home was not just the river, but the riverbank too.

By the 1890's Captains John Davis, Aaron Russell, Frank Aymond, and Jerry Webber had withdrawn to their United States; Captain James Sheets and Captain John Griggs were dead; and soon skippers John H. Smith and Julius Dougall would join John Segers steamboating on the perimeter of the far Northwest, from one hundred miles north of Edmonton to the Arctic and the Klondike. But the Lamoureux brothers had just arrived.

Two of the sons of Marguerite Therien-Lamoureux and François Lamoureux – François and Joseph – had left their Eastern Townships birthplace about the time of the great Overlander migrations to the gold fields of the Northwest Territories and British Columbia. Taking separate paths – François through Illinois and Joseph up the Oregon trail – the brothers met at the Pacific years later. Cariboo gold strikes evaded them, but not the glowing tales of the North Saskatchewan riverbanks that were ideal for settlement. Through the 1870's and 1880's François and Joseph established themselves, their families, a Catholic community, and a healthy business on the North Saskatchewan across from the North West Mounted Police barracks site at Fort Saskatchewan twenty miles below Edmonton.

There they built a cable ferry that netted 50 cents a head every crossing; their Sturgeon River Milling Company ground 100 bushels of grain per day; and in one load their timber rights yielded 160,000 feet of lumber, 115,000 shingles, 20,000 feet of lath and 10,000 feet of dressed lumber for their Edmonton market. In August of 1887 the Lamoureux brothers turned to the river. "They purchased the tug *Minnow* from the Galt Company ...[to] leave Medicine Hat for Edmonton on the 29th," reported the Edmonton *Bulletin*. "The steamer will carry thirty tons of freight. She is pronounced entirely satisfactory by her owners, who will run her for all she is worth." Run her they did. For eleven years the *'Minou',* as François and Joseph called her, peddled Lamoureux lumber, limestone, coal, and flour on the North Saskatchewan between Edmonton and Battleford.

Optimists filed to the Northwest. Some prospected for gold; others homesteaded land. The young Lachambre family, out from Quebec, had worked temporarily in one of the small store businesses that clung to the North Saskatchewan at Battleford. A booming Edmonton suggested greater opportunity, but a 1,300-mile railway trip via Saskatoon, Regina, and Calgary wasn't inviting. "Somebody told us to take the steamboat instead. The *Minnow* was coming to Battleford with a cargo of flour," the eldest Lachambre daughter recollected. Young Annette thrilled with the excitement of loading family and belongings aboard a Saskatchewan freight steamer bound for a new home in Edmonton.

On the first of August in 1895, Captain François Lamoureux welcomed the Lachambre and Mercer families aboard the *Minnow* and piloted his miniature sternwheeler into the North Saskatchewan current on a seventeen-day cruise to Edmonton. "It was quite a sight. Half the town was there to see us off," bubbled Annette. "We stopped every night; the crew took wood that was piled on the riverbank as the supply for the next day. One morning, after two days travelling, as they started the fire for the engines, a spark jumped to the freight and our furniture caught fire. We didn't notice it right away. Finally we smelled the smoke and got busy putting out this fire with the very little equipment that they had. We lost quite a bit of our furniture.... Around the outside of the boat, there was only a plank about two feet wide and a rope for a railing. One day my aunt's two little boys were playing and one pushed the other into the river.... He was all blue and panicked ... he was going toward the paddle. But Mr. Mercer ... immediately ran to him and pulled him out just as he was going under the paddle.. . . .

"But it was a beautiful time of year and a beautiful trip. And fun. Mr. Mercer was a hunter and that season there were a lot of ducks and geese – a hunter's paradise; so when we stopped, he usually did some hunting. My mother and Mrs. Mercer were both good cooks and so they took over in the kitchen. . . . The cook didn't object. It was a picnic all the way; singsongs at night and the half-breeds played the fiddle or banjo . . . while the coyotes howled at night. We were kind of crowded. The boys slept on mattresses outside at the stern. . . . It was no Queen Mary!"

"They broke themselves with the boat," scorned one Lamoureux descendant. Joseph and François, likely overpowered by a Galt Company executive, had pooled one thousand dollars to buy the *Minnow* and then "poured their profits into the boat. If they had used horses they would have been all right." The runt steamboat struggled more often through heavy sand barriers than against the water currents of the North Saskatchewan, and lost more in repairs than she made. Late in the summer of 1895, the Edmonton fire brigade got an emergency call to the riverside; the fire engine raced through the Jasper Avenue dust to the flats by the river to find the *Minnow* enveloped in . . . sand and water, sinking. Edmonton's fire department recorded its first steamboat rescue as the fire engine's water pump drew the river water from the hold of the foundering boat. By this time the Lamoureux brothers were prepared to accept whatever they could get for the unprofitable *Minnow*. When a British remittance man, Percy B. Cunliffe, offered the sum of two hundred dollars in 1898, they quickly accepted. The Cunliffe and Bell flour mill burned soon after, Percy Cunliffe died, and with him died a tramp riverboat.

A die-hard holdout of the Saskatchewan fleet, the *North West* survived the invasion of railway terminals on the North Saskatchewan by slashing river rates; the once-celebrated "Greyhound" too had become a tramp steamer. The CPR, with millions of dollars to recover from expensive construction, was compelled to charge relatively high rates for shipping merchandise; the Winnipeg and Western Transportation directors seized an opportunity and established rates that averaged a third less than the railway. And while the CPR locomotives consumed precious coal, the *North West* thrived on the abundant wood the riverbanks still offered.

These measures, coupled with a general austerity program, enabled the steamer to survive. Seventeen-year-old L. R. Goodridge, hired as steward, was one crew member not trimmed in the austerity drive. "There were about twenty-five men left in the crew. Most came from Prince Albert. In charge of the boat was the first mate, a half-breed named [Joseph] Smith (there was no real captain), who, with his son [Alec], did the navigation. There were two engineers [Billy McBeth and Jack Shannon] and a clerk, and about twenty half-breeds for crew. . . . Wages were perhaps fifteen dollars a month and board for the crew. I got fifty cents a day and board." Goodridge supplemented his income by selling cigars from his father's hotel to the crew for ten cents each. Life was easy; "half the time we were sleeping. We had a snap as far as work went on the boat."

Fifty head of cattle here, several hundred tons of coal there, the *North West* scrounged freight up and down the Saskatchewan between Prince Albert and Edmonton. Excursionists were welcomed for outings such as "the water trip to Battleford under the auspices of the Prince Albert Masonic Lodge," that an 1890's issue of the Saskatchewan *Times* described. "The Hudson's Bay Company steamer *North West* had been chartered and departed amid a lively scene of bustle and confusion. All the town and its wife turned out to give the excursionists a sendoff . . . the company numbering in all nearly 100. . . . The evening was pleasantly passed in dancing, singing and storytelling. Mr. Lucier's story of how three knights errant hailing from River Street, Prince Albert, emulated the achievements of the immortal Don Quixote, in boldly attacking and slaying a fierce and truculent sturgeon that he (M. Lucier) had tethered in the river to keep fresh, brought down the house."

Even late in her career, however, the *North West* still played a minor role as a passenger carrier. "There was no easy way to travel. To reach one's destination was the first consideration, and comfort, an unnecessary luxury. River traffic had had its trial and was being abandoned. This would be one of the last trips for the old boat," an 1896 prairie doctor journalized. Between the births of her nine children, and during treks across the Northwest with her husband, Reverend John R. Matheson, Elizabeth Scott-Matheson had studied medicine at the University of Manitoba. Her studies completed, she was journeying overland from Winnipeg to Prince Albert with her three small children. Reverend Matheson was to join his family there and travel with them by land the remaining two hundred miles to his mission near Fort Pitt. But instead of her husband, a letter of instructions to board the *North West* greeted Dr. Matheson at Prince Albert. The additional tedious river miles and the absence of her husband seemed an impossible strain for her to bear.

"When darkness came on the second night," she wrote, "the *North West* was still some miles below Fort Pitt. The captain decided to anchor beside an island that divided the river into two deep channels. John Matheson, meanwhile, had been waiting at Fort Pitt and decided to go out in an old rowboat, thinking at every bend to see the steamer or to hear the whistle. All night long he drifted with the current. When dawn came he was thoroughly chilled. . . . Where the stream divided, tall trees hid the steamboat from him. He chose the outer channel. Suddenly, he heard the whistle, saw the steamer through the rising mist as it began to move upstream from the inner channel. He swung his own awkward craft around, shouting in the morning stillness. The pilot heard, was sure that he recognized Jack Matheson and stopped the boat." Thus a reunited Matheson family travelled the last miles to Fort Pitt aboard the *North West*, then heaving her way upstream at the end of her fifteen-year career.

The front page of the Friday, April 22, 1898, Saskatchewan *Herald* carried this advertisement: "The Hudson's Bay Company are offering their Saskatchewan steamers, the *North West*, the *Northcote* and the *Marquis* for sale by tender." The *Northcote* had been beached at Cumberland for twelve years; the *Marquis* at Prince Albert for eight seasons, and the *North West* had been recently hauled from the North Saskatchewan at Edmonton's Ross Flats in 1896. Not surprisingly, there were no takers.

But the *North West* had one final voyage to make. During heavy rains in mid-August 1899, as the North Saskatchewan rose twenty-six feet above her normal level, Ross Flats were swamped. "The historic steamer *North West* was torn from her moorings this afternoon and carried down the river. Half the people in town were on the hill to see the last of the boat go by," the August 17th Edmonton *Bulletin* reported. A teacher who rushed to the heights on the south side of the river recalled, "There was a buggy-full of us. We got there just in time to see the steamboat hit the pier [of the Low Level Bridge, whose construction was just under the flood waters]. . . . There was a wrenching and crushing sound and the boat passed on over the pier seemingly undamaged. Only the upper deck and pilot house of the steamer were then out of the water." The heart of the *North West's* engine works plunged through her severed hull planks into the arms of the steamboat's arch rival – the Saskatchewan. The *North West* had come home to the river, forever.

The Saskatchewan fleet dissolved. Within two years, the Winnipeg and Western Transportation Company liquidated assets to pay off its financier, the Hudson's Bay Company. But the Honourable Company was far from despondent; a new windfall was stirring the Territories. Exactly three years before the steamer *North West* went down, two hardened prospectors – George Carmack and Robert Henderson – had discovered gold nuggets on Bonanza Creek, a tributary of the Klondike River in Yukon Territory. Like the phenomenon that had lured thousands to Burbank & Company wharfs at Georgetown for river passage down the Red en route to Cariboo gold, a "yellow money" fever raced world-wide and established Edmonton as a major threshold to the Klondike gold fields. A new generation of Overlanders detrained at the end-of-steel on the North Saskatchewan, and Edmonton swelled with their numbers and their business.

Off the train, newcomers to Edmonton made their first exchange of money and their first acquaintance with one of the first Edmontonians. Stout, broad-shouldered, and radiating warmth from behind every whisker of his fully bearded face, John Walter was owner-operator of the ferry that crossed the North Saskatchewan from Strathcona on the south side to Edmonton on the north. The quiet, fair-haired Orkney ferryman named "Wapitigan", or "Whitehead" by the Indians, was openly friendly to everyone.

All his grandchildren knew John Walter's story well. He had been born on August 12, 1849, in the Orkney Islands, traditionally a birthplace of some of Britain's hardiest seagoing men. Skilled as a sailor, carpenter, and wheelwright, he had been an obvious choice for the Hudson's Bay Company officers who had come recruiting men for service in Canada. Walter left Stromness in 1870 for York Factory, where he joined the Honourable Company. Travelling through Norway House by York boat and along the frozen Saskatchewan River by dog team, the young immigrant reached his post in the Northwest in time to eat Christmas dinner at Fort Edmonton. For five years – three for his apprenticeship, plus two to finance an independent stake for himself – Walter applied his skills to building York boats for the Company at Edmonton and Athabasca Landing, one hundred miles to the north on the Athabasca River. He earned fifty dollars a year with meat supplied free.

Skipper Frank Aymond, aboard the *Northcote* in July of 1875, paddled into a Fort Edmonton settlement that had spread to the south bank of the Saskatchewan. While the Hudson's Bay fort and a majority of its pioneer neighbours had established on the heights of the north bank, ex-Company man John Walter, clad in fur cap, suspendered work pants, and heavy boots, had hewn logs and built his homestead cabin on the river's southside flats, which thus became known as Walterdale.

John's first "epic feat," wrote a fellow Edmontonian, "was a trip to Winnipeg in the summer and fall of 1881 to haul back cable for the Edmonton ferry. The gear weighed more than half a ton, hardly an easy load to carry [by ox and cart] over 1,000 miles of prairies and bushland trail. . . . In 1882 he set up the first cable ferry . . . serving the twin communities of Edmonton and Strathcona for 20 years. . . . Walter's original ferry scow, called the *Belle of Edmonton*, was the first cable-operated outfit between Winnipeg and the Rockies." Propelled by the eastward flow of the North Saskatchewan, the Belle was the prototype for cable ferries at major crossings throughout the Northwest. "All were built by Walter at his Edmonton works. It was his boat and scow-building business that literally forced John Walter to open his first sawmill [in 1893.] His earliest craft were built from hand-sawn lumber, but as orders mounted, the need for a mill became imperative." In its first year, Walter's Mill cut three hundred thousand feet of lumber from his timber rights at Big Island, eighteen miles upriver. Hammers at both his Edmonton and Athabasca Landing boatbuilding plants never stopped banging together river craft for the Hudson's Bay Company, the Dominion government, and, later, for outfits chasing gold.

Not to be out-flanked by either the Saskatchewan River or Klondike River gold strikes, Walter promised to "make boats of all descriptions and deliver them to Athabasca. The Walter yard will tackle anything. It is just completing a $38,000 gold dredge, 86 feet long by 26 feet wide, to work [for B. J. Little of Chicago] on the river here." The Edmonton ferry-man's efficiency and honest dealings had won for Walterdale a respected reputation, from those barging on the North Saskatchewan to the hungry gold-digging enterprises moving north from the United States. And when ice claimed the ferry system at Battleford in the spring thaw of 1896, the Territorial government arranged a subsidy for a steam ferry replacement to be brought down from Edmonton – provided that John Walter built it. "The steam ferry was essentially two scows, built on the catamaran prin-ciple; boiler in the front and the cabin and paddlewheel at the stern. The carrying capacity was six teams ... they loaded from the side into the centre of the ferry," noted its sandy-haired engineer Edward Howell. Howell and his young son Arthur, carried into Strathcona by the momen-tum of the Klondike rush in the late 1890's, had taken work aboard one of the gold dredges scraping the Saskatchewan's river bed. When the rig abruptly shut down, a quick and characteristically humane John Walter hired Howell the next day to direct the construction of the Battleford ferry's engines.

Dry-dock activity concluded six months later in September when J. H. Ross and J. S. Dennis, Commissioner and Deputy Commissioner of Pub-lic Works from the Territorial government at Regina, came to Edmonton. As Arthur Howell recounted, "They thought they were going to have a nice trip floating down the river to Battleford. ... Old Solomon Poitras, who came up to Edmonton on horseback from Delmas, was the pilot. ... They loaded up the ferry with hay, coal, flour and groceries for the Indian Department at Onion Lake." The river was falling rapidly when the steam ferry *Battleford* slipped away from the Walterdale boatbuilding yard downstream into the Saskatchewan. Five miles above Fort Pitt the *Battleford* grounded in shallows for three days; pilot Poitras, engineer

Howell, and the government men got her into the Onion Lake Agency, but then the boat and crew disappeared. "It was these two birds from the Regina Territorial Government that started to boss the operation without taking notice of the pilot. Solomon Poitras was no young man; he must've been fifty, but he could smell the depth of that old Saskatchewan better than most. . . . Instead of being three days coming down the river [to Battleford] they were thirteen, because the government representatives never took any notice of the pilot, so they'd take the wrong streams and get stuck on sandbars. Near Bresaylor, they ran out of grub. Poitras and [Howell] went down the river in a boat after dark; Poitras figured he could find Dave Taylor's place just by the outline of the hill." But it was almost dawn when the nearly starved rivermen found Taylor, who immediately prepared a meal, baked some bread, killed some of his sheep for provisions, and returned to dislodge the stranded ferry with his team and wagon. The ferry did get to Battleford before the freeze-up of 1900, but it was a close call.

From May to October the Saskatchewan was alive with bobbing timber, an army of lumberjacks, and, for young Norah MacDougall and her brother, the thrill of a passing steamboat. "I can remember running home from school," remarked Norah, recalling springtime on their family farm near Goose Island, sixty miles upriver from Edmonton.

"We heard the whistle and so we ran as hard as we could to get down to the river, to see the steamboat coming. It made a lot of noise and of course they blew the whistle when they came close to where they knew anyone lived. We heard it from the school; the school teacher had more of a hand in wanting to see the men than I did, so class finished and away we'd go. . . . That steamboat was a monstrous thing; I remember one time it came up the snye by the farm and I thought it was a terrible, big giant of a thing. It was exciting when the steamboat came, exciting when the river rose, exciting when the timber began rumbling downstream with the current to the mills at Edmonton – Fraser's Mill and Walter's."

Whining green timber, ripped and squared by John Walter's sawmill, had scarcely a moment to cool before it was shaped into an array of scows, ferries, dredges and a growing number of steamboat superstructures. Boilers came overland from Athabasca Landing for the first steamer built at Walterdale, the *Lillian Bee,* which had been designed for plying the small lakes north of the Saskatchewan. The new century spelled prosperity for the boatbuilding yards and sawmill works of John Walter. Yet he more than most prairie entrepreneurs shared the wealth with his employees. Lumbermen, river rats, mechanics and jacks of all trades gravitated to the flats for work, and John Walter always had it to offer. An English dredgeman, countless migratory loggers, the maverick son of a Winnipeg businessman, any fellow-Orkney Islander, moonlighting farmers, bargemen, and a gnomelike riverman named John Collins Mathias (whom everyone knew as Muchias), all found John Walter eager to salary their talents.

Abe Pearce, Great Lakes seaman and boat designer, had come to Edmonton in the early days of the Yukon gold rush; he built boats for eager Klondikers, including a bicycle-pedaled paddlewheeler. In 1903 Captain Pearce joined steamboat builder John Walter. "We designed the *Strathcona*," Pearce wrote, "put temporary machinery in that year, and managed to make a number of trips to upriver points besides making two trips with a large scow of freight to Fort Pitt for the Barr Colony settlers at Lloydminster. We had some trouble . . . but generally had a jolly bunch of passengers on board who appeared to enjoy the rough as well as the smooth. In 1904 we installed steam wheel engines and the boat did good work in connection with lumbering operations for several years, besides being a great convenience to upriver settlers."

"Captain Pearce was tops, a regular gentleman; the old steamboat was only a well built tug, but Cap Pearce was a pretty strict fellow. . . . He was a white-haired old Scot, who'd perhaps been at sea since he was a boy," pictured the *Strathcona's* young fireman. Not related to the skipper, Bert Pearce was fifteen when John Walter offered him a job hauling coal to the steamer for ten cents an hour. At the time Bert was also apprenticing with the CPR crews at Strathcona.

Nearly one hundred feet long, the sidewheeler *Strathcona* had a patch-work appearance. Below on the boiler deck, her crew worked virtually in the open with only a canvas wind-wall protecting them and the firebox, and slept next to engines purring with steam at night; atop the steamer, a solitary pilothouse and a collapsible twenty-foot smokestack towered on the hurricane deck. Nudging heavy scows in the spring, the *Strathcona* moved hundreds of trappers, traders, and timber river-drivers with their supplies to lumber camps and depots upriver, and assisted in the stringing of new cable ferries across the extremely swift Saskatchewan current.

"In the early days, Walter had a sawmill way upriver just beyond Drayton Valley," one logger explained. "The *Strathcona* was pushing a barge when she came to the Rocky Rapids [eighty miles upstream from Edmonton], which could only be climbed at high water in the spring. Captain Pearce was at the wheel under full steam . . . and John Walter himself used to sit on the safety valve and hold it down so that they could get enough pressure to walk that thing up the rapids. . . . My dad watched the boat one day. In the morning he could see the front end of the boat startin' around that bend. And in the evening, he could see the paddlewheel disappearing around the far end."

Some things never changed. While politicians, historians, pioneers, and rivermen of the Northwest heralded the expiry of the nineteenth century and the birth of Canada's century, the river maintained its inimical personality. The North Saskatchewan had not co-operated for very many of the twenty-five years that steamboatmen had known it; what made another century any different? And the river's repertoire of tricks was almost unending. "Some rivermen went ashore one time with Captain Pearce to survey fresh timber," narrated one Edmontonian. "Suddenly, they heard a scraping noise. The pile of drift logs that the *Strathcona* was tied to was pulled away by the river. First thing they knew, their boat was adrift in the middle of the river. . . . The whole works of them ran down the riverbank, up and down coulees and through timber, trying to catch the boat. The boat came to a sharp turn, a cut-bank, and brushed against the roots of a tree; the top of the tree shot out like a spear and ran through the front end of the steamer, through the engine room and shot out the rear wall, tearing boards all the way. Finally, they caught the boat by wading out after it."

"The *Strathcona* always made a hell of a racket," continued young fireman Bert Pearce. "And it got hot below. The firebox was just about level with the bottom deck, but the ash pit and such were down below. That great big old boiler could eat it up fast. It wasn't bad as long as we had good coal . . . but the wood burned just like matches. . . . Firing with coal you'd put a fire on about every five minutes, but with wood you'd just keep pushing it in – four-foot sticks and it'd lick it up. . . . We worked four hours on and four hours off going upstream. There were two of us firing; I worked with a Scottish sailor, a rugged fellow. . . . I used to laugh at him. . . . There we were up along the river with all those mosquitoes, and he stayed stripped to the waist. . . . We'd start out with the bunkers loaded with coal from Edmonton and try to get up around the rapids. When you're going through the rapids, to go a mile you'd maybe take five hours . . . that took lots of coal. But comin' down we just sat on our fannies. . . . John [Walter] always liked to sit near the front of the boat, with that old pipe in his mouth, and as happy as could be. . . . Back then too, typhoid was quite rampant. Old John Walter wouldn't let any of us boys drink water from the river or any stream; he bought tomato juice in big cans. Imagine this, back in 1906 . . . a prince, he was."

Few were the barns or fences within a radius of two hundred miles of Walterdale that did not owe their substance to John Walter's sawmill. Production reached sixteen million board feet annually. The lumber operation stretched up the North Saskatchewan's banks toward the

Rockies, employing the best cutters, log-drivers, and planers of the district. The residence for the mill's workers at Strathcona always bulged at the seams with Walter's hospitality, for while he employed a hundred mill workers, the dining tables at the boarding house usually fed many more than a hundred each day. No-one in need was ever turned away from Walterdale, not even the young Strawberry Creek couple who arrived on John Walter's doorstep on a rainy afternoon in September, 1907. Newly wed Arthur Huggett and his bride faced a forty-mile return journey overland through mire to their homestead north of Telfordville on the river. "But their method of reaching the farm wasn't to be by horse and wagon over the almost bottomless trail west of Leduc," wrote contemporary journalist C. H. Stout, who often lauded the deeds of his friend "Jock" Walter. "The couple went down to John Walter's office at Walterdale and booked passage on Walter's freight steamer *Strathcona*, which was going up the Saskatchewan with a cargo for the lumber camps. The trip was slow but scenic and, compared with the trails, quite cozy and comfortable." It was the *Strathcona's* first and only honeymoon cruise.

"We sailed from Glasgow and [came] by train to the south side of the Saskatchewan, the spring they relaunched the *Strathcona*," disclosed Walter Leslie, John Walter's nephew from the Orkneys. At fourteen, Walter Leslie had gone to sea aboard herring schooners, as had many of his countrymen; but the boy had returned severely seasick and inflicted with rheumatism. Crippled, Leslie would never be allowed to master a passenger steamboat alone; however, with his knowledge of boats and with assistance from Captain Abe Pearce, he was able to obtain master's papers for the Saskatchewan freight steamer. The *Strathcona*, reborn the *Scona*, was now a sternwheeler, lengthened and heightened with staterooms of sorts – places to hang a hat – that ringed a cramped galley on her new second deck. With her refurbished decks and new pilothouse occupant, the *Scona* resumed the hauls up the Saskatchewan for the lumber camps at Poplar Creek, and resumed the struggles over shifting sand and gravel bars. They seemed to reach out and latch on to the *Scona*; they were Walter Leslie's education. "One time, some reporters were in another boat and saw me with the *Scona* go on [a gravel reef] and by Jove, they came down to Edmonton and wrote that the *Scona* had grounded and would be there quite a long while. . . . We went over the side and dug the gravel away by hand and let the water run underneath her all night to wash the gravel down. . . . Next morning," emphasized Leslie, "I had her off and into town!"

"If you heard a steamboat comin' up, you trotted over to the riverbank to have a look at it." The warm summer days of August, 1909, resounded

Before he left the Orkney Islands for Rupert's Land in 1870, John Walter was asked what he would do there. "I have two good hands," he said, "and they will do anything but steal." *(Edmonton Archives)*

to the splash of a new sternwheeler on the North Saskatchewan. The echoes of John Walter's sparkling new freight and passenger steamer the *City of Edmonton* rose from the river bluffs and spread to the streets of Edmonton and the south Strathcona riverbank, where there were still numerous tepees and open acres of farmland. Like every imaginative youngster on the prairie, the fourteen-year-old at the Omand farm responded immediately to the new sounds from the river valley. "Practically every kid along the river ran to see the steamboat," exclaimed Teddy Omand. "I used to have a coach horn, and used to play it on the top of the bank when the steamboat went by.... I'd just make a lot of noise.... Once in a while, the engineer would give a toot on the whistle; not too often though – they didn't want to waste any more steam than they had to, because the fireman had to make that up."

Two hundred members of the British Association for the Advancement of Science brought their venerable assemblage to Edmonton the first summer that the *City of Edmonton* plied the North Saskatchewan. Their tour of western Canada included one September afternoon a cruise aboard the new Walterdale steamboat. Typically mellifluous, the English conventioneers "expressed intense interest" at this novelty. No doubt they were unaware that the *City,* unlike Brittannia's Imperial ships of the line which for centuries had been designed by the skilled draftsmen of Plymouth, was merely an enlarged replica of a small model. Her 136-foot by 34-foot hull fashioned by A. Chisholm, and her boiler and engines teamed overland from Athabasca Landing the previous winter "eclipse anything in the line of river boats that has ever been seen on the Saskatchewan," boasted the Edmonton *Bulletin.* "There are seven watertight compartments in the boat, each outfitted with two syphons, which renders it almost impossible for the boat to sink in case of accident."

The lanky Abe Pearce, who had installed the boiler and engines in the *City,* was still a few papers short of his passenger-boat master's certificate; and consequently had to sail under Captain Grant, a deaf sea navigator who was also examiner of masters and mates for the Department of Marine and Fisheries. "I naturally considered myself in an awkward position," commented Pearce. "However, Captain Grant proved to be an honourable and gentle man," and in the 1910 season successfully piloted the *City of Edmonton* (with Pearce as his hearing-ear mate) 250 miles down the Saskatchewan on a freighting run to Onion Lake. Fifteen years the Saskatchewan had risen and fallen since the old *North West's* paddlewheel cut the current between Edmonton and the lower river. At Fort Saskatchewan, Skiro Ferry, Succer Rapids, Victoria, Shandro Crossing, Paradis Crossing, Crooked Rapids, Brosseau, Hopkins Crossing, Wolf Rapids, Moose telegraph station, Frog Creek Rapids, and Vermilion Crossing, there was a generation that had never seen a steamboat on the Saskatchewan. The *City* carried but one passenger, a far cry from the days when hundreds of eager pioneers jammed the vast decks of frontier-bound steamers of the Saskatchewan fleet.

The happy clamour of crowds' voices returned to the Saskatchewan the following summer. The commotion began in May of 1911, when John Walter placed ads in the *Bulletin* announcing the first of the season's evening excursions aboard the *City of Edmonton,* departing from the riverbank near the Low Level Bridge; fares for gentlemen were fifty cents, for ladies and children, twenty-five cents. Edmonton Streetcar Number 13, loaded with Sunday-best excursionists, clanged its trolley bell steadily and rattled down the 97th Avenue hill to the riverside those evenings. The *City,* that winter stripped of her few cabins to make way for a second-deck dance floor, and dressed in her fresh coat of white paint, hissed steam at the shore.

It was just after 7:00 P.M. when the last fares would be collected and the *City's* moorings cast off. The Lyon family joined the excitement along the deck railings on one of those first evenings; for their daughter Eva, it was a dream come true. "We steamed downriver as far as Fort Saskatchewan," she reminisced. "Of course we had such long evenings in the summer ... moonlight excursions.... It was another excuse for young men and women to get to meet each other.... The girls fancied themselves up; but it wasn't your Dawson Creek dance hall.... There was just one very large room with seats all around. You could go out onto the deck to sit and watch the trees, or the odd animal on the shore, or whoever you were with.... If there was romance to be found, it was on the boat.... But all I was interested in was to be wherever there was music, dancing, and motion.... They had an orchestra, playing favourites.... Dancing With Tears In My Eyes, In Sympathy, Darktime Strutters Ball, and When You Beat Your Feet In the Mississippi Mud.... I danced every minute.... Next to sea-going liners, the dear *City of Edmonton* was like a little doll's house, but I thought it was absolutely beautiful then."

John Walter soon realized the exuberance that had attracted him to the river flats thirty years before could be shared among many fellow-Edmontonians. And while the *City of Edmonton* freighted up to lumber camps and downriver to budding settlements, she could easily devote some of her time and steam to excursions along the summer Saskatchewan. Eighteen miles upriver, the Saskatchewan splintered into several channels, creating Midnight Island, Fraser's Island (named after another pioneer lumberman in Edmonton, D. R. Fraser), and finally, a fifteen-acre stretch of rich river silt and towering poplar groves named Big Island. In July of 1911, John Walter purchased this lush reef from the

Dominion government, built a debarking pier, planned a resort pavilion, and began holiday excursions to Big Island on the *City of Edmonton*. The golden age of picnicking debuted on the Saskatchewan.

Oddfellows' picnics, high school picnics, Knights of Columbus picnics, church picnics, police picnics, union picnics, and YMCA picnics all booked the *City of Edmonton* for a holiday dash to Big Island. At 10:30 in the morning of a Victoria Day, a Dominion Day or any Saturday, the *City* left her dock at all six knots of upriver speed. "Nearly six hundred persons attended the annual picnic of the Edmonton United Commercial Travellers . . . held at Big Island," read a typical 1911 Edmonton *Journal* column. "Among the events: a pumpkin pie eating contest; fat man's race; egg and spoon race; smoking race; needle and thread race; forfeit potato race. On the outward trip, a volunteer band played for an impromptu dance, which later developed into a baby-judging contest. Throughout the day, the commercial travellers vied with each other in selling novelty items to one another. On the return trip, a kangaroo court was established; W. S. Hurst was judge, and offences, judgements and penalties were in the spirit of the gay outing."

While the *City of Edmonton* picnicked her way up and down the Saskatchewan, Walter Leslie and his *Scona* tried to steer clear of the levity and stick to their work schedule. It didn't always happen that way, Captain Leslie found. It was 1912 when a group of English surveyors booked the *Scona* for a trip upriver to inspect Rocky Rapids as a potential power-dam site. "The fellow that had chartered the boat had a lot of liquor on board," recalled Leslie. "I told him that the *Scona* wasn't like a ship at sea [that honoured the sanctity of cargo] with these thirsty rivermen around. 'If they see that liquor,' I says, 'I can't keep them under control. Take that liquor into your cabin.' The fellow said, 'I'm chartering this boat and this is part of the cargo.' So I said, 'Alright, but remember I warned you.' Next morning I heard this fellow out on deck just jumpin' and hollerin'; the deck was littered with empty whiskey bottles; those river-hogs had raided the whiskey and the entire crew was drunk. The crew was so sick with hangovers, we had to tie up for a day while they recovered."

Rum candy was the wildest refreshment aboard the *City of Edmonton* for adults and children like Walter Leslie's teen-age sister, Mary, who had travelled from the Orkney Islands to live with her uncle John Walter in 1910. Her uncle always playfully teased young Mary as she joined the bustle of Edmonton and the thrill of evening excursions aboard the *City*. "No liquor on the boat," Mary explained, "but you didn't need anything but sandwiches, cakes, and cookies. . . . They made their own ice cream on the boat; us kids flocked to the ice cream because it was such a treat for five or ten cents . . . and it always tasted best on the boat. . . . Everyone put on their best; I had a nice cream-coloured dress especially for picnics. . . . The boat sailed at 8:00 from the north side of the Low Level Bridge, never on Sundays; but there was a big crowd Saturday nights. . . . People would be talking and meeting friends they hadn't seen for a while. . . . There were hardwood floors for dancing . . . and Lynch's family orchestra – Charlie played violin, Carman played piano and Ducky played drums – the best band in the city. . . . The Methodists on board the boat at first didn't believe in dancing, but eventually they did. . . . It was a beautiful boat, with treats, the dance hall, waltzes, one-steps, two-steps, the best city band, and all for fifty cents."

For one Edmonton boy, it was a pleasant break from ballgames and picnics to meet the city's young ladies aboard the steamer; another recalled the boat as a "merry-go-round affair," the only place in town he could learn how to waltz or two-step; the worst punishment in the world to one Edmonton teen-ager was to be grounded for a week, unable to take the Saturday night excursion; to a riverman aboard the excursions, the greatest entertainment came from Captain Pearce's successor, Pete Christenson, who "could get the best rag out of a fiddle" he had ever heard; for a girl who was too young to take the excursion alone, the evening was pined away on the river heights as she watched the *City,* all lit up with lamps and music, disappear around the last bend on another excursion to Clover Bar Bridge. For Teddy Omand, the bugle enthusiast, the joy of boat excursions was captured in one moment. "Coming back from Laurier Park on the boat one night, Tyne Richards from the Strathcona band gave a cornet solo, and I think with the echoes back and forth across the river, that's the sweetest music I ever heard in my life."

One coal teamster encountered prairie steamboats only once. Hired to haul coal from the Standard Coal Mine to the riverside power house in five-ton loads, he received a distress call one afternoon from Walterdale; the *City of Edmonton* was stranded four miles below her wharf; her coal bins were empty, and the steam was gone. Andy Livingstone hitched his team, loaded a "jag" of coal (roughly two tons) and raced the two miles to the riverbank where the *City* had lost power. "It was quite a job getting the wagon and horses, up to their bellies, in water, toward the boat," he described, but a skiff then came from the steamer and the fuel was transported to the steamer a few pounds at a time. Crises like this somehow added to the fun of a Saskatchewan excursion, unless one happened to be a member of the All Saints Church Choir, half way to a Big Island picnic. A cylinder blew out on the boiler deck and the *City* stalled completely. After a moment of surprised silence on board, the 136-foot craft swung around, drifting aimlessly downstream. The crew madly poled the steamer toward shore to lasso a tree, but not until they had bumped their way to Whitemud Creek did they catch a tree solidly. There the excursion ended; everyone had to make his way the full eight miles back to Edmonton on foot through uncut brush and a recently arrived rain shower.

"Victoria Day Excursion," a May, 1914, Edmonton *Journal* announced. "The steamer *City of Edmonton* will leave Government Wharf, foot of McDougall Avenue at 9:30 A.M. for trip [to Fort Saskatchewan] returning about 7:00 P.M."

Twenty-one-year-old Floyd Baker (later the Clover Bar Social Credit MLA in the Alberta Legislature), a multi-talented tradesman transplanted from Ontario, invited Stella Sherwin to join him on the annual May 24 excursion to the Fort. Entertainment, food (provided at no extra charge), drink, and music awaited them at a Fort Saskatchewan park, and the weather was perfect – a balmy spring day. At 9:30 the *City of Edmonton's* paddlewheel splashing and whistle blowing echoed across the valley and the excursion began. "We took this excursion to the Fort each year," Baker said. "So this particular excursion of May 24, 1914, we were about three-quarters of the way downriver; the Saskatchewan wasn't too high and all of a sudden. . . . "

"I saw a rock ahead," recalled mate Walter Leslie. "We were about 15 miles above the Fort with about 350 passengers. I dashed to the wheelhouse and old [Pete] Christenson was at the helm. I said to him to keep her out from the shore. And he said, 'No, there's a bar there.' 'There's a rock dead ahead of you,' I shouted, but he was just too late and it just caught her under the bluff of the bow and put a big hole in her. . . . "

Pushing her crumpled nose into the south bank under Gillis's farm, the crew "put planks from the boat out to the shore," continued Baker. "And there we sat. . . . It was a pretty long day; nothing to do, nothing to eat, and the Fort fair went by, while we sat on the riverbank as the mosquitoes feasted on us. . . . "

Mate Leslie went ashore to get word to his uncle [John Walter] "to get the *Scona* boat ready, for we were sunk. He wasn't very happy. Cook Sewells was up there at Edmonton and when I arrived he and I took the *Scona* down. And John told me before we left, to be sure to make two trips, not to take them all at once. . . . "

"The marooned excursionists . . . whiled away the time from 11:00 A.M. to 4:30 P.M. as best they could," a Fort Saskatchewan *Conservator* reporter wrote. "The steamer is now lying in the river partly submerged. Her upper deck is quite high and dry, though, and it was here that some of the boldest of the passengers danced after they had been grounded. . . . "

"By golly, when I pulled the *Scona* in along side the big *City,* they all jumped aboard and I couldn't stop'em," recalled a panicking mate Leslie.

"But surprisingly, the little boat took'em all. . . . "

"It took all the rest of the day to get back upstream to Edmonton. Most people weren't too happy when we got home at midnight," but Floyd Baker claimed no-one demanded refunds. It was one of the hazards of the game.

Loaded every moonlit evening as the *City of Edmonton* was, and as active in the freight trade as the *Scona* became, John Walter's steamboats ran in the red throughout their years on the North Saskatchewan. Despite the high cost of maintaining the boats, the old Orkneyman, in his mid-60's, never overcharged for the river service. "The *Scona* would go up-river sometimes," a crewman remembered, "and would come across someone with a wagon stranded there on the bank. John would have the crew and boat haul the rig upriver and charge so little that it wouldn't pay for the grease on the steamer's paddlewheel. John was always helping others; and yet he often found people stealing logs out of the river, logs with the Walter Mill mark on them." And he once bailed from custody a man who, the same night, had stolen from his steamboat offices.

Despite – or perhaps because of – his generosity, Walter's success was impressive. His two prosperous sawmills ran day and night every summer, trimming millions of feet of timber and employing hundreds of Edmontonians. The two mills, the coal company, the power generator that ran Edmonton's first streetcar system, and the vast river property on which he had lived for over a quarter century made Walter worth nearly two million dollars. He supported artists and schools and supplied free lumber to church builders. All had come from the Saskatchewan, his home and provider, the river he respected and loved, even after 1915 when it struck him down.

"There was no warning," recalled his niece. "John had a water marker right beside his house on the river flats. The first thing he did in the morning when he got up, he put his shoes on to go out to see what the water level was. Every day of his life he watched the water. Oh the whole thing seemed an impossibility." A friend told of Walter's "walking up and down the bank saying that it will never come over." On the morning of June 28, 1915, John woke at 6:00 to find the North Saskatchewan rising at a rate of a foot an hour; by 10:00 the current had climbed the crest of the riverbank and was moving onto the Walterdale flats, toward the offices, workshops, the livestock barns, the sawmills, the endless acres of neatly piled lumber ready for sale, and toward the beached steamboats. Spring, delayed for weeks by stubborn ice and cold, had suddenly broken onto the prairie. The Great War had set Europe afire the previous summer and choked off all Walterdale manpower and its potential merchandise sales; the cluster of industries that Walter had built from scratch lay open and vulnerable before the flooding Saskatchewan.

Walter Leslie, by his uncle's side, saw the end come. "The flood settled everything; it ruined everything. . . . Everybody was getting off the flats because the water was so deep. But old Pete Christenson, the *City's* captain, rushed down to the river to the boat. . . . He kept up steam aboard and blew the whistle and kept blowing it, until crewmen Henry Burger and Bob McBride went down there to help. . . . They pulled her in on top of the bank behind the carpenter shop and tied her to a big tree to ride out the flood. John Walter too, had told old Christenson to get off the boat and let her go, but stubborn Christenson stayed with the old boat and he saved her. . . . But the flood broke the Old Man. Down at the mills, the yards were full of lumber. . . . When the War started in '14 there was nothing going on at all. No sales. . . . The double storey piles of lumber started to topple, and down the river they went; hundreds of thousands of dollars of lumber gone. And no insurance. It ruined him."

Several gold dredges, barns, sheds, dozens of houses, livestock, three sawmills from the flats, the power station, and tons of wreckage floated to the upriver side of the Low Level Bridge. Like a giant net, the bridge displayed the Saskatchewan's flood collection. The bottom of the bridge just skimmed the surface of the swollen river; it stayed intact only because the CPR tracks above were weighed down with a string of gravel-filled freight cars, held in place at either end of the bridge by two locomotives. Each day the salvage crews dynamited the debris jammed against the bridge, and each day less proof of John Walter's existence on the riverbank remained. Ironically, the only survivors of the 1915 flood were the steamboats, *Scona* and *City of Edmonton,* the least fruitful of his enterprises. While all the Walterdale operations – especially the mills – could have functioned and expanded with Edmonton long after 1915, the only remnants, the steamboats, rarely left their riverside berths again; their income and use dwindled to nothing. But their presence by the river as monuments to a once prosperous Walterdale even outlived their creator. John Walter died on Christmas Day, 1920, fifty years to the day after his arrival as a Hudson's Bay Company boatbuilder.

CHAPTER FIVE

Saskatchewan Tramp Steamers

Gaping holes on the boiler deck walls beneath the plaque proudly inscribed "Marquis" told the tale of the Saskatchewan's glamour steamboat. While the river itself had disposed of the golden-age sternwheeler *North West* at Edmonton, time and vandalism were erasing nineteenth-century steamboating from the riverbank near Prince Albert. The burgeoning industry of Prince Albert had plundered the once-splendid vessel, ripping out her boiler, her precision Iowa-built engines, every foot of steam piping, her gauges and polished brass, her shaft iron, and every scrap of solid steel bolted into her structure. Her pilothouse towered erect, like a crane on stilt-like upright beams; bits of unclaimed gingerbread trim hung limp from the bare struts. Scavengers had stripped her hull and decks of the Wisconsin oak, and the staterooms and the saloon, once glistening with chandeliers, mirrors, carpets, and polished woodcarving, had been ransacked. Her mammoth drive shafts jutted out astern toward non-existent hubs and the scattered hoop remains of a sternwheel that had once powered at speeds of up to sixteen miles an hour. So little of the *Marquis* was left by the turn of the century that her naked frame listed in the wind like a cripple, leaning on rough timbers wedged into the bank.

The derelict *Marquis* was not at all a representative symbol of the community where she had been left to die. Goshen – an industrial and agricultural region named in honour of a factor from the Hudson's Bay Company, and coincidentally the biblical name for the land of milk and honey, was swelling with the new century boom. Several thousand had settled there, the CPR line to Prince Albert had run for ten years, tax collection was a fact of life, and the Chamber of Commerce boasted of the town's prosperity. Each spring, hardware, pitch, tallow, oakum, and lumber materials cluttered the river's edge for the annual scow construction to transport settlers' effects and Hudson's Bay Company merchandise downriver to the Northeast. The Company owned and operated one of three flour and grist mills, while the Saskatchewan bristled with winter cuttings of the three major lumber outfits in town – the Sanderson, the Cowan, and the Telford Brothers mills. Threading her way through the spring log jams and spitting puffs of woodsmoke into the river air, the tiny sidewheeler *Josie* guided logs from collector booms at the mouth of the Little Red River to the Cowan Lumber Company saws at Goshen. At the helm of this rather diminished descendant of the Saskatchewan steaming fleet stood the first certified captain on the Saskatchewan River, Richard Deacon.

Captain Deacon was nothing if not impulsive. From the skipper's quick imaginative mind originated a host of business ventures – livestock raising, metal working, carpentering, hotel managing, running an electric light plant, or establishing industries along the river – each seemingly a passing fancy and none designed to revolutionize the Prince Albert community. One Prince Albert resident remembered that Captain Deacon "had built a boat up on Central Avenue, which was rolled on logs down the main street to the riverbank and into the water . . . Deacon was quite a character."

Out from England, Deacon briefly apprenticed in Montreal as a silversmith in the 1860's. Eager for action he volunteered to repulse Fenian raids on Montreal, then travelled to New York during the American Civil War. When the Red River Settlement uprising broke out, he quickly joined the Wolseley Expedition to the Northwest. The following year he married Mary McBeath, the daughter of two original Selkirk settlers, and accompanied her family on their overland trek to the village of Prince Albert. Settling in the Prince Albert area, Deacon soon became one of the community's most self-asserting citizens. On one occasion he stormed into a meeting being held by Louis Riel, and denounced the Métis leader to his face. Deacon survived the incident, and the fighting in 1885, to initiate construction of his own steamboat fleet.

The fleet did not consist of magnificent vessels such as the *City of Winnipeg* or the *Marquis* (as she had been in her prime); rather, Deacon's flotilla was made up of utilitarian, almost motley vessels, designed specifically to perform efficiently at their jobs. Recalling the Deacon fleet many years later, a Saskatchewan lumberjack described two of its boats: "One [built in 1890] was called the *Josie,* after Deacon's daughter and the other was the *Pathfinder* [built in 1903]. They were just little tugs, each with an upright boiler; they ran on gears, no drive shaft, just one small gear, to a larger one, to the paddlewheel. And there was just a small deck at the back and front. . . . The crew was two men. Cap. Deacon steered and always had one of his boys – Bert, Art or Alf – on the engine. All he had to do was throw in slabs, fire up the engines and keep water up in the boiler. . . . You started the thing and she run. . . .

"Those two sidewheelers used to take forty logs at a time; they'd go up-river along the shore, tie up and winch each raft of logs upriver . . . and when they got so far up the river, they'd swing the raft across the river, and dump it into the pond to go up to the [Billy Cowan] mill. . . . The old fellow Deacon was the pilot. He was a little short fellow and kind of a cranky old guy because we used to sneak rides with him. . . . Right after school we'd catch the boats as they were going across to the Little Red . . . and when they'd break rafts, we'd pile on to them logs and ride them down into the pond."

What Deacon lacked in physical stature he made up for in his outspoken and officious manner; everyone encountered his blunt, high-strung ways, from town merchant to grandchild. "He was very positive about his opinions; he knew that he was right," one of his grandsons recalled from experiences aboard the Deacon boats. "He was red-headed and had a fiery temper. . . . There were very few dull moments. . . . Bert never minded firing for Art when Art was at the wheel; Art had some sense. But the old man was all hustle and go. . . . He had two whistles; when he'd come through town, he'd blow the big one to let them know he was comin' and have hardly enough steam left to make the landing, and that meant more work for Bert. . . . It was all hand-to-mouth stuff."

Ferrying groceries employed the Deacon boats when the log drive slowed, but the Saskatchewan's Horatio Hornblower never allowed a dull trip under his command. On one occasion his sidewheeler was hauling a load of sowbelly bacon into Prince Albert's Sixth Street landing, when the cordwood and Deacon's temper let out at the same moment. The steamer stalled in the current and in the silence of the afternoon, Deacon's frantic orders could be heard echoing off the north bank: "Fire in the bacon, fire in the bacon. Keep those engines running!"

Richard Deacon was not a businessman, his grandson confirmed. "Anything he went into, he went into in a big way for the times, and the finance beat him. He never seemed to have any interest in money. But he was always interested in boats; he got the wood and little bits of machinery together, built the boats and got them running. . . . Captain Deacon had his papers in the wheelhouse . . . but it's not so much being able to command a ship of any size as being able to take a working boat or pleasure steamer through waters where you had to be able to tell by the look of the current whether you'd have water or not. His boats drew twenty-four or twenty-six inches and were aground as often as not. . . . The Saskatchewan was a tricky river to navigate; he'd come upriver and suddenly have no channel. He'd tie up, get out, wade in and prod with a pole to find out where the current had run. He'd go upstream to a suitable point and peg down a few branches with rocks and in a few hours he'd have a channel. He would divert enough current that the water would sweep it out again." Deacon's sole business was the river; he always treated it seriously. He was a temperate riverman and only when he took the odd excursion of school children or a church picnic upriver to the open riverbank at Lily Plain, did he allow anything as frivolous as music and a band aboard.

Deacon's commitment to the community extended beyond steamboating. In 1904 the town incorporated as the City of Prince Albert, with an area of nearly eight thousand acres; inside a year Deacon would be elected one of six city council aldermen. Sewer construction began beneath the city streets; the city's first post office inaugurated services; an electric light plant left the planning boards for implementation to make Prince Albert "the brightest city in the West"; new industries included cement production, lime burning, pork packing, and the manufacture of railway ties and telephone poles; and with the District of Saskatchewan's entry into Confederation as a province only a year away, the city broke into summer celebration with parades, picnics, and concerts.

The boom came to Prince Albert. The CPR line up from Regina fed a steady flow of immigrants to keep the new city alive with the clatter of construction. Among those attracted by the city's activity was a 22-year-old newcomer, Cuthbert H. Woodhouse. After a short stint homesteading and odd-jobbing in the countryside around Prince Albert, Woodhouse moved to the wooden sidewalks and muddy streets of downtown to take up his native trade – steam engineering. Passing the necessary examinations for his engineer's licence, the young Englishman was drawn to the River Street waterfront, where workmen were busily assembling the new generation of steamboats for Prince Albert's blossoming riverside industry.

"There were two built in 1904, not quite so big as the *Marquis,* but fairly good-sized steamers," stated Woodhouse. "The Saskatchewan* belonged to the Hudson's Bay Company, and the second steamer, owned by Captain [Fred W.] Coates and [Rufus] Mosher, was the *Alberta***.... Coates had come from Rat Portage [Kenora] where he had run steamers, and his partner, Mosher, was later one of the discoverers of ore for the Flin Flon mines during the First World War.... I went aboard both steamers while they were being built. The lower deck was for cargo with the boilers forward where the stack went up; space in the middle was for fuel; the engines were aft near the paddlewheel, with a shaft and two

*Not to be confused with Peter McArthur's Lake Manitoba sidewheeler of the same name built in 1893.
**Again, not to be confused with the *Alberta* sternwheeler built by the North West Coal and Navigation Company in 1883.

112

cranks, one cylinder for each crank to turn the wheel. Rangy-looking engines and not much power, but they got along alright. . . ."

"My father was a painter and he came out to Prince Albert from Nova Scotia in March of 1904," noted riverman-farmer Ted Harris from his father's diary. "One of his first jobs was a month-long job putting the first coat of paint on the new steamer *Saskatchewan*. One day another fellow came to work with him as a painter. They had a plank outside the boat for the two to work on; this new fellow was painting away, walking backwards, and first thing you know, he walked over the edge of the plank into the river. He didn't finish that first day. . . .

"The *Alberta* ran as an excursion steamer during the summertime every evening. . . . The night the rest of the [Harris] family came into Prince Albert, my father had just got off one of the *Alberta's* excursions." While owners Coates and Mosher had built the *Alberta* to handle freight, her greatest take was cash from the Saturday night excursions; she provided one of the few early outlets for the boom fever in Prince Albert. On calm summer nights the *Alberta* lit up the Saskatchewan River for miles above and below Prince Albert, with the magic of deck lamps, friendly townspeople, the sawing of two country fiddlers from Glen Mary, singing, square-dancing, and a "catch-as-catch-can" atmosphere.

"Twice a month I used to rush home to get dressed up (I had a pretty pink dress to the ankles) and hurry back past the firehall down the riverbank where the boat was lined up ready to go on the excursion. It pulled out about half past 7:00." The sights, the motion, and the music invited adults, children, and teen-aged girls in groups of three. One eighteen-year-old riverside resident absorbed each moment of an *Alberta* excursion. "There was always a big crowd, maybe fifty or one hundred. . . . We walked around the upstairs deck and watched the shoreline with poplars, pine, spruce, and soft maple. . . . There was dancing in the cargo space of the main deck, maybe fifty by twenty feet, to the city band (twenty musicians in suits) playing tunes like The Orvetta Waltz, The Merry Widow, Sweet Bunch of Daisies, and After the Ball. . . . There were lots of eligible fellows. . . . There were parents with their children feeding their faces. . . . They sold bananas, oranges, candies, and ice cream for five cents a cone. . . . Indians didn't come on the excursions – they were too poor. . . . The boat was painted white and there were hanging lights that swung with the motion of the boat. . . . The steamer made a chucking noise and the whistle blew when we turned around to come back from the far side of the island; when we got back, the lights were on along River Street."

The *Alberta* shuttled more than just excursion groups and their entertainment. On the spring flood waters of 1905, the Coates-Mosher sternwheeler escorted Prince Albert's latest and most awkward-looking immigrant upriver – a 100-foot gold dredge. With most of the city's boat-building in their hands, Fred Coates and Rufus Mosher had hired out their expertise to two British gold-diggers, Roughsedge and Ramsay, who in turn had convinced avid investors (eight thousand miles away from the truth) that their fortunes were to be found in the gumbo at the bottom of the North Saskatchewan River.

"When I first saw the gold dredge early in 1905, the hull was under construction on a low flat at the edge of the river in Goshen. . . . The dredge machinery was stored in a shed and I was asked if I could assemble it." This seemed a reasonable enough challenge for recently licenced C. H. Woodhouse, "provided a good set of blueprints could be produced . . . and if everything required was actually in the huge pile of castings." Woodhouse then learned that years before the dredge apparatus had been shipped to a Central American republic from New York, just in time to be greeted by "one of those periodical revolutions." The rejected materials had then been shuffled back to the United States and resold to "Doctor Roughsedge, who should have stayed with veterinary work, and his partner, Colonel Ramsay, a military man from the old country; his uncle had been Governor General of India once, and in fact, he was a personal friend of King Edward VII as far as that goes."

Bent on cornering the supply of Saskatchewan River gold, the two Englishmen packed their contraption off to Prince Albert – two upright boilers, one vertical single-cylinder engine, one double-cylinder engine, chains, buckets, sluices, winches, and a tailings conveyor. Anticipating a maximum dredge capacity of one thousand cubic yards per twenty-four hours, Roughsedge and Ramsay launched their steam-powered dredge and latched it to tow lines from the *Alberta*.

"When we were hauling the dredge the seventeen miles upriver to Gunn's Island, where it was to be moored, we got into a bit of a tangle during the night," Cuthbert Woodhouse reminisced. "The Indian pilot got kind of lost among the sandbars. . . . That was the trouble with the Saskatchewan: the bottom was too near the top. Shifting sandbars. . . . One month I stood on sand at the water level; the same fall there was about nineteen feet of water there. . . . But Coates was a very cool-headed, pleasant sort of chap. He'd come from Rat Portage and Lake of the Woods where there was lots of room to get around; so he anchored the steamer for the night and the next day did a straightforward job of delivering the dredge." Battling sandbars was only the beginning of the dredgemen's headaches; a marine inspector for Saskatchewan condemned the boiler because of faulty rivet holes; delays in shipment of new equipment set the gold production back a year; and finally, the Saskatchewan riverbed foiled the venture.

Woodhouse noted that "they had mining blankets over which the sand passed, leaving behind the gold, but also much black sand which soon clogged the blankets. . . . The black sand was iron ore and no progress was made in solving this problem . . . so during the winter, Dr. Roughsedge took me with him to California to learn more about the business, as there were extensive gold-dredging operations there. That was 1906, the year of the earthquake and great fire in San Francisco; the city looked like the pictures of bombed out cities in World War Two. . . . We visited several dredging sites near Table Mountain and Poker Flat. . . . We showed those experienced dredgemen the sample mixture of black sand and gold we had collected. They shook their heads and said there was lots of that stuff in rivers in Oregon, but nobody had managed to separate the gold from the heavy sand. Samples had also been sent to a firm of assayers. . . . There was gold and platinum, so their report said, but to my mind not enough to make the venture a paying proposition. . . . The difference of opinion ended my connection with gold dredging."

Messrs. Ramsay and Roughsedge continued to thrash the river bottom with dredge buckets above Prince Albert in search of that evasive gold dust; evenings the *Alberta*, collecting fifty cents per excursionist, frolicked her way in and out of the harbour; and meanwhile the third 1904 product of the Goshen flats, the sternwheeler *Saskatchewan*, steamed round the clock for her Hudson's Bay Company masters. Her bread-and-butter runs below Prince Albert began before sunrise. By three o'clock her steam and crew were up and the first leg of her routine downriver to the mouth of the Bigstone River would be underway; the next day she would moor at the powder house of the Company's depot at Cumberland House with staple supplies for redistribution to the outposts of the Company's Northern Department (the territory between Hudson Bay and the Rocky Mountains, and north as far as the Arctic Ocean).

"When we docked there at Cumberland, we anchored out from the shore and pulled the gangplank in, because the dogs would get up on the boat and eat everything on it. Those huskies were starvin'; you could throw them a big bar of that hard soap, or a leather shoe, and they'd eat it." Crewman Jimmy Soles had grown up with river steamers, the logging industry, the Prince Albert settlement, and the Saskatchwan River tradition. Just before the '85 conflict, Joseph Soles had rafted his family the six hundred river miles from Medicine Hat to Prince Albert; in 1893, when he was six, Jimmy had fearfully clutched his mother's hand as the *Marquis* whistle bellowed at the Prince Albert pier; at eight, he had lost his mother and learned to pull his weight at the family's Steep Creek homestead; and by the time the Hudson's Bay Company had launched the *Saskatchewan* from the Goshen bank, Soles had driven logs on every major prairie river. So when he joined the *Saskatchewan* crew, Soles brought with him invaluable experience. He also brought a sense of fun.

"We danced at every place we stopped downriver – The Pas, Cumberland, Chemahawin, Cedar Lake – if we were going to be there overnight, we had a dance. . . . The Indians called them fiddle dances," mused Soles, who called at all the dances "especially if I knew I didn't have to get up 'til about noon the next day. . . . Oh those square-dances. . . . The first trip I made with the *Saskatchewan*, we had a dance at Cumberland and there was an Indian fellow playin' the fiddle. He had a fiddle alright, and a willow bent with horse hair on it. And he only could play the one tune, Little Brown Jug. We danced to that all night."

Her freight deck loaded to the rafters, her gunwale boards straining with a cumbersome side-barge, nosing a fish barge, the following morning the *Saskatchwan* rejoined the channel on schedule for the seventy-mile stretch to The Pas. With no more manoeuvrability than a floating city block, the *Saskatchewan* and her cargo meandered the final one hundred miles to Mossy Portage at the south end of Cedar Lake. "There were about five teams there to haul freight for the Hudson's Bay from tugs on Lake Winnipegosis over to us; then they'd load up with our fish load. About five o'clock in the morning, those fellows had all the fish cleaned and caviar packed, ready to catch the tug down the lake." Inside a week, the *Saskatchewan* and her crew had covered half her eight-hundred-mile circuit, had injected vital supplies into the Hudson's Bay Company network, and had overcome all the river's quirks.

"When I was out front sounding the river, I watched the pilot at the wheel all the time. That pilot read the water; he could tell where the bars were. . . . Those bars move. They're here today when the water's high, and when the water's low, they're someplace else. And he had to know how to go over the rapids – back up the rapids full steam, and go down rapids bow first with the paddles full reverse. At Cole's Falls we'd go down so far on the south side and then we tacked across to the other side to get out of the big rocks and white water, to get over to black water to go through on. . . . You ain't got all day to work on it, you had to think quick and act quick. . . . The captain depended on his pilots. They were about forty years old, those Sayes brothers [Moyes and Baptiste Sayes, Métis rivermen from Fort à la Corne]. And they never put a scratch on the bottom of that boat; they never hit a rock."

A perfect composite of prairie timber, eastern enginery, Lake of the Woods design, and Hudson's Bay Company colours, the compact sternwheeler *Saskatchewan* functioned like a well tuned instrument, from her safety valves to her cabin sashes. A still finer harmony was the combination of crewmen who led the steamer through her short career on the

Saskatchewan River's bends and straights. Those two huge half-breed pilots said little, but summer after summer their flawless sixth sense of the river spoke for them. Charlie Nelson, backed by two centuries of Hudson's Bay culinary tradition, and trained in the lumber camps of the Northwest, served the best the Company offered – moose meat, bacon, pies, canned fruits, and marmalades. When mid-summer furnished the river with long hours of daylight, the *Saskatchewan* carried a double crew – two pilots, two engineers, two firemen, a couple of deckhands, a purser, and a ship's carpenter named Bathro, who farmed near Wild Rose, Saskatchewan, some of the time and repaired broken paddles and deck planks the rest of the time. Each crew worked a ten-hour shift – sounding the river, cleaning ropes, repairing flues, replenishing the *Saskatchewan's* fuel (eight cords of wood at each loading station), or cleaning the boiler of muddy water and scales once a week. A fatigued crew prayed for bad weather or the few hours of total darkness at night that would halt the steamer. "Too noisy to sleep?" Soles laughed. "We got used to that grunt-grunt-grunt of the steam exhaust surging. Hell, when you're young, you don't need to be rocked to sleep. . . . And if we didn't sleep we'd just sit around and smoke, or play cards; we used to play whist, bridge or pinochle. Oh yea, if we had a minute we were downstairs at a game of pinochle."

Fireman John Scales had an easy-going nature on board the *Saskatchewan* – so easy, in fact, that he frequently slept during the lulls between firings. And while Scales napped, engineer Jack Shannon nipped; on one occasion what started as an innocent eggnog concoction ended up mostly rum, and the usually quiet Shannon went into a rage, tossing chairs off the top deck into the river. On the opposite shift was the other extreme, the sober-faced, slight engineer. "Willard Goodfellow was an awfully quiet guy, a little fellow who hardly ever talked," Soles explained. "He could get a job anywhere; if it was available, he was at it; that was his business and there weren't too many of them then. He was a good engineer . . . inconspicuous and he saved all his money. A nickel never got away from him. . . .

"But the very best was Captain [E. B.] Haight," insisted Soles. "He was a happy-go-lucky character, a little short fellow . . . but he'd never back down from anything. . . . He always wore those thin gaiters with the elastic rubber in the sides. . . . He was smart; it didn't take him all day to get around. . . . If Haight had anything to say, he just stepped out on the deck and hollered to get on the ball. And he spoke Cree as well as English; he'd talk all day to the Indians just as fast as they'd talk. . . . His son, Gordon, was twenty-two and worked on the boat with us as a deck hand; he could talk Cree too, in fact, he'd lived with the Indians. . . . Mrs. Haight was

117

very religious and he was just the other way. He enjoyed life and was into everything. . . .

"One September we loaded the survey party that surveyed the road to Churchill at Prince Albert. The water was low so we had to build a big scow to tow beside the boat for supplies. We took them right to the north end of Moose Lake. . . . The first day out of P.A., that first afternoon, Haight had some of those guys with him up top. . . . He phoned down to Jack Shannon in the engine room, and he told Jack that he was sendin' this one fellow down to pick up some stuff to be brought back up to him. Well, Haight had put about fifty pounds of them big pipe wrenches and old iron in the bag for this guy to haul way up to the top there. . . .

"And the evening when we'd gone about sixty miles and tied up, Haight had two or three of them all worked up about catchin' rabbits that night. He got them all a bag and he took them ashore and got them up there on a rabbit track. He got the bags propped open with sticks and he told them to go and sit back in the bush while he went away to chase the rabbits in. Well, he came back down to the boat and left them all sittin' there. . . . He was quite the guy," nodded Soles.

"I remember Haight as a flash," recalled an old northern trader from Prince Albert who nevertheless didn't think too much of steamboats. "I worked in the [Hudson's Bay] Company office; Haight worked on the boat and he was in and out of the office all the time. I don't remember anything very distinguishing about any of them. I just checked the freight aboard – tea, flour, sugar, lard, jam, butter, bolts of material, and dry goods – for the Company. . . . Ah, I thought that the York-boat days were more romantic than steamers . . . built on the spot . . . all over the North . . . ten men on sweeps . . . a bowsman and a steersman. . . . The *Saskatchewan* . . . she was just a wet-ass steamer, running the odd excursion for two-bits upriver while they waited for the freight to be assembled."

Astern on the *Saskatchewan,* just ahead of the paddlewheel spray on the exterior of the rear engine-room wall, were painted the letters "H B C", after the steamer's owner; not all those in her service or aboard as passengers agreed that the inscription stood for "Hudson's Bay Company". All the seasons that the *Saskatchewan* plied the river, she chauffeured the Company's district factor, Commissioner Hall. So autocratic and possessive of the steamboat was the commissioner that some interpreted the "H B C" to signify "Hall's Boat and Crew". As was his annual custom, Commissioner Hall came down from his palatial home on the hill in Prince Albert to supervise the re-launching of "his" steamer from its Goshen winter drydock; each spring the *Saskatchewan* took him on a round trip to Edmonton. Accompanying the commissioner and "his" crew in May of 1905 was his daughter Caroline, and also an excursion group that included Willard Goodfellow's sisters Mary and Emma and his mother, all of whom were headed for Battleford.

Extraordinarily proud of the steamer and all it stood for, Commissioner Hall strolled the decks with the aura of British royalty. Under his surveillance, the trip to Battleford, normally a two-day steaming, swallowed up five days of the excursionists' time; Hall insisted on pulling in to shore each time a meal was served, as if he were in command of a cruise visiting exotic Caribbean ports-of-call. For thirteen-year-old Emma Goodfellow, the adventure of a river journey was limited to the steamer's short fifty-foot cabin deck and her bunk in one of six tiny staterooms. A coil of rope at the bow of the *Saskatchewan* provided a crow's-nest-like perch, and soon became her post to ward off boredom.

"It was nice being on the water," Emma admitted, "but it was very confining. . . . Yet the Commissioner was rather entertaining. . . . The boat set out at 3:00 every morning. And Mr. Hall used to get up to see what they were doing; he'd come out on deck in this long night shirt, his raincoat on over top, his feet shoved into old slippers, and one of those cow-breakfast hats on. . . . He'd watch and give orders while Captain Haight just got out of the way. . . . I used to get up too because of the noise . . . and Mr. Hall would come out and show me how they used to skate in the old country, with this old raincoat and nightgown flappin' around his legs. I used to laugh. . . . And Mr. Hall had a little black spaniel called Nigger, and he was bound that Nigger was to go ashore that early in the morning to have his run. Well, Captain Haight didn't see that to be held up for Nigger. . . . So to get Nigger back again, the engineer used to go down and give two big toots on the whistle, and we'd see this little bit of a dog flopping along and sliding down the bank and onto the gangplank in a second. . . . The old fellow Mr. Hall was funny. . . .

"At night the captain went to bed about ten o'clock, but a bunch of the crew would go up, knock on his door, get him up, make him dress himself and come down to dance. These fellows square-danced down below, and he'd get up and go down to whoop it up with the rest of them. One fellow played the mouth organ and those four or five men would dance there 'til after midnight. . . . Captain Haight was a jolly type and got on well with his crew."

"I was hired back on the crew of the *Saskatchewan* and made that trip to Edmonton in the spring of 1905," explained John Scales, by then promoted from fireman to second engineer. A 23-year-old Stanleyville homesteader originally from Ontario, Scales, like Cuthbert Woodhouse, Jimmy Soles, and many others, had come down to the foot of Eighth Avenue East to join the construction crews of the *Alberta*, the *Saskatchewan* and the gold dredge. Working on the *Saskatchewan's* superstructure, Scales had crowned her pilot house with fretwork salvaged from the nearby *Marquis* wreck. At Battleford on that May, 1905, excursion, Scales and the rest of the Saskatchewan crew helped Emma Goodfellow and her family to disembark; the intention was to pick them up when the steamer returned to Prince Albert a week later. "However, en route near Fort Pitt," Scales continued, "we ran onto a gravel bar, puncturing a number of holes in the hull. The water was dropping at the time and we ran the steamboat onto a hard sandbar, where we managed, with ingenuity, to repair the damage. Captain Haight went below with folded blankets, which he underlaid between the broken planks; we cut planks to size and braced them with posts to hold the repaired surface solid. Thus the boat was saved from sinking." However, the delay for repairs extended the Goodfellows' planned four-day excursion to Battleford to six weeks while they waited for the *Saskatchewan's* return. For Scales and the crew, the delay did have certain advantages because ". . . we had a shipment of beer from Whitiman's which was later refused as being condemned. A number of the crew didn't find too much wrong with it."

For wages and sport, the crews returned to the river and the steamboats year after year. Steamboats on the Saskatchewan still held a fascination for those on board and for those on shore. All along the river after 1904, the steamboats' splash in the channel and resonating whistle moan had a magnetism that few could resist. A stir all along the riverbank followed the Prince Albert paddlewheelers whenever they ran excursions upriver toward Edmonton.

Countless persons were involved with the steamers in one way or another, even if only for one passing moment, and each had his special favourite recollection. As boys, Fred and Robert Anderson rode horseback from their farm five miles inland to the Wingard ferry, where the steamers sometimes stopped for fuel; for a half-hour's work helping to load cordwood, the boys earned a steamboat ride up to Carlton. The eldest daughter of the Jubenville family emigrating from Minnesota to a farm near Meota helped her father drive cattle across the North Saskatchewan the day a steamer whistled through; to her the steamboat was "a beautiful ship, but built so high, that I thought it might tip over." When he was twelve, Ralph Parkinson saw woodsmoke spewing from the funnel and spray from the paddlewheel of a steamer fighting upriver against the current; he was "tickled" when the steamer crew tied to a nearby cut-bank overnight to refill the boiler with fresh clear water from Baljennie Creek bubbling through the Parkinson farm.

At Battleford, the shriek of the *Alberta's* whistle "would wake you up in the morning because they came with the daylight," complained veteran teamster Charlie Stodders. Steamers arriving from Prince Albert

120

Once his Prince Albert-based steamers *Josie, Pathfinder,* and *Marion* had delivered orders for his Red Rock Brick Yard, Captain Richard Deacon might allow
an orchestra-accompanied excursion or boy-scout outing aboard. *(Saskatchewan
Archives Board)*

Pilot house commands were transmitted below through the boiler room whistle.
Between "ahead slow," "reverse engines," and "danger" the firemen and engineers stoked fires, adjusted steam pressure, cleaned machinery and played
pinochle. *(Emma Goodfellow)*

required the local skill of Battleford ferryman Joe Nolin to help pilot them through the channel in low water, but because Joe was such an ungainly riverman, his daughter often feared for his life as he scrambled from the low deck of the ferry to the higher deck of the steamer in mid-stream. When the *Alberta* secured her lines at Battleford one evening on an excursion from Prince Albert, all the gentry in town donned their finery for a soirée of sedate waltzing and lemonade refreshments on the steamer's boiler deck. Upriver from Battleford, near Bresaylor, when the *Saskatchewan* sounded her whistle, farmer George Dymott and his son "would run a mile to a high point on the land at the river to see the steamboat pass." Young Arthur Howell had to haul all the homestead milk down to the riverside near Delmas one night; his father had sold every drop of it to the crew of a tramp steamer on the river. And when the *Saskatchewan* whistled again on the approach to the last cable-ferry crossing before Edmonton, at Hewitt's Landing, Frank Hewitt remembered his excitement when "I ran to the river to help drop the cable down to the bottom of the river so the steamer could pass."

Fire ripped through the Telford Brothers sawmill on Thursday, April 13th, 1905, and despite all efforts of the Prince Albert volunteer city fire brigade to douse the flames, the mill and most of its lumber was destroyed. By autumn of the same year, the Telfords had rebuilt the plant but in doing so had left themselves without sufficient working capital. One of Prince Albert's three major lumber operations sat idle, and for the community, just lately incorporated into the fabric of the Dominion as part of the new province of Saskatchewan, the future suddenly looked bleak.

From the birthplace of northwest steamboating and from the same watershed that had fostered the rivermen and machines for the Red River steamer trade a half century before – the heart of Minnesota – came a wealthy, well organized, and flourishing lumber family. Beginning in 1889 with a mill operation at Wausau, Wisconsin, within a decade David Nelson Winton and his brother Charles Joel Winton – "the Saw Dust Twins" – had extended their Winton Brothers Lumber Company to Thief River Falls. Then, in 1905, word that a refurbished but bankrupt plant in Canada might be available attracted the "W's back-to-back" trademark to Prince Albert. By Christmas of 1905, Winton Brothers had bought out Telford Brothers and had established the Prince Albert Lumber Company. Money and Americans moved to the Saskatchewan River system looking for timber, and with them came work for thousands of prairie rivermen and a boost to paddlewheels on the Saskatchewan.

"The big time came to Sixteenth Avenue East," one jack claimed, "when the Wintons moved in from Thief River Falls." The Wintons brought finances, western river-driving and lumbering experience, and a Norwegian named Peter Aberhart, whose lifetime of Mississippi River work was invaluable. When Aberhart landed at Prince Albert, the Goshen flats bounced to life again with the clatter of renewed boatbuilding; then a call went out for an experienced engineer to join the construction teams.

"Willard [Goodfellow] was always an engineer, right from the start. He had gotten the books and studied the courses at home for stationary and marine engineering. He had originally worked for the Hudson's Bay mill in East Prince Albert. Then Dad started a sash and door factory and a planing mill of his own, and Will worked there for years. And when they wanted him to go on the boats, they'd just go down and ask Dad to release him," explained Emma Goodfellow, beaming with pride at her brother's reputation. Goodfellow worked in the engine rooms of the steamers *Alberta* and *Saskatchewan* from 1904 to 1906, and then at the construction cribs of the Wintons' Prince Albert Lumber Company. In the spring of 1907 "they called Will to install the machinery on the *City of Prince Albert.*"

With her 100-foot length and 24-foot beam, her flat-bottom, single-decked superstructure and plain sternwheel, and her unglamorous log-hauling career, the *City* epitomized the tramp steamer. And yet, amid her ugly appendages and dinginess, lay a certain beauty. Just ahead of her bulky smokestack, and nearly as tall, stood Peter Aberhart's greatest riverboat invention – the grouser. An upright 14-inch by 16-inch by 26-foot fir timber with heavy angle irons on the corners and a heavy steel point, all inserted through a well in the steamer hull and joined to a hoist, the grouser was the Saskatchewan adaptation for an anchor. To stop the motion of the *City of Prince Albert,* or to position her on the river for winching log rafts against the current, crewmen dropped the grouser through its well and into the riverbed. With her grouser, the *City* could secure herself anywhere on the river.

City deckhand Tom Lewis described how the grouser worked. "A winchman on the bow ran out a length of the cable, probably a thousand feet; we'd drop the grouser right into the river bottom, and then start winchin' the rafts upriver. We couldn't just pull them by wheel; we had to winch them to the sawmill, and the steamboat was runnin' backwards all the time. . . . We ran steady six hours on and six hours off. . . . The mill ran twenty-four hours."

Logs swamped the Saskatchewan night and day during the summer. Thousands of jacks worked the riverbanks and rafts; every day the *City* manoeuvred four rafts, each with 1,400 logs, upriver from the Little Red

River; every second day, crews on the Shell River floated two rafts with 3,300 logs downstream to the mill. Daily, Winton saws chewed up as many as 100,000 feet of timber. The Prince Albert Lumber Company bought out all the smaller sawmills in Goshen and all their timber limits, which cut deep into the heart of the province's northland. Nine out of every ten logs floated to Prince Albert were destined for the Winton mill. The Saskatchewan's current never rested during the logging months – April to October. If timber didn't clog the river, the steamers churned it so thoroughly, insisted some young Prince Albertans, that all the gold-eyes stayed away from their baited fishhooks. The *City's* paddlewheel slowed only twice a day, when the boat crew landed at the mill boarding house for meals.

"I could always tell when the steamer was comin' in by the sound of her shrill whistle," recalled Ellen Bayes. "I worked in the dining room and had to look after the boat crew; they had a table by themselves. . . . It was a big boarding house and there were five hundred men to serve. . . . The boat crew had a better appetite than any of those in the sheds or the yard; there were five of them and I had to make sure they were well fed. . . . That's how I met my husband. . . ." The man she married was riverman-deckhand Dan McLeod, one of nine McLeod sons, all of whom worked along the Saskatchewan River from Prince Albert to The Pas.

Evelyn Cook worked in the boarding-house kitchens as second cook from seven o'clock in the morning until eight o'clock at night, preparing meats, eggs, bread, vegetables, and twenty-five pies a day. "My specialty was pies. . . . There was a huge table with baking materials left out all day, because it was pies everyday. The stoves could only cook twelve pies at a time – apple, raisin, and prune pies. . . . Sometimes if we were too busy," Evelyn chuckled, "we wouldn't take the stones out of the prunes either. . . . On Saturday night when the boatmen came in for their supper, they'd tell us about the steamboat leaving for uptown, and we'd all hurry to get our work done. We'd rush home and dress up in long dresses, big hats and blouses with puffed sleeves, and go down to the boat . . ."

Saturdays ended with a shriek as the *City's* whistle shouted out the commencement of the evening's festivities. Rivermen, loggers, millers, boarding-house workers, and many Goshen residents scurried to the mill to catch the *City of Prince Albert* for the mile and a half upriver ride to the foot of the city and the landing at the firehall on River Street, where they were let off. "There was the Bijou Theatre for only ten cents and it was worth it," continued Evelyn. Funny movies and cowboy shows starring William S. Hart. . . . No talkies, but Miss Winnie Parker played piano along with the movies. . . ."

"Big go Saturday nights," deck hand Jimmy Soles exclaimed. "We'd come into town and the barber shops stayed open 'til midnight and all eleven liquor outlets stayed open 'til midnight. We'd have to get into the barber shop first before anything, and get all dolled up; we weren't open for business 'til about eleven o'clock. But we were open from then 'til Monday morning. . . There was ballgames and roller skating and I was always a dance fan. I'd never miss a dance and when I got home I'd be soakin' wet from dancin' so hard." All those jacks, all that celebrating, eleven liquor depots open to midnight, and Prince Albert still had only one city policeman.

The music of the boom had carried Prince Albert ten years into the new century. Downtown business supported a half-dozen banks and the prosperity opened up a crop of new hotels. Prince Albert's population was approaching six thousand and its city limits stretched to both banks of the North Saskatchewan. By 1910, a railway-vehicle-pedestrian swing bridge joined the north and south banks of the river; two full-time workers would rotate its two centre spans whenever the whistle signals of approaching steamers were heard. A Buckland resident hauling gravel across the bridge to the city with his horse teams recalled "when the whistle blew, the two men cranked the bridge open with a huge six-foot key, like a clock key, and they'd walk round and round to turn it and open the bridge. . . . I'd have to wait half an hour for them; longer on a windy day." And about that time Sir Wilfrid Laurier whistle-stopped at Prince Albert on his 1910 prairie tour, and the whole city dropped everything to hear another of his twentieth-century-for-Canada speeches, and to shake hands with the Prime Minister.

"When business suddenly started to boom, Captain Deacon started to haul gravel," related a grandson, whose boyhood revolved around the construction and excitement of Prince Albert's frenzied expansion. "Then he found brick clay across from Goshen on the north bank. It was part of a strip of sand roughly eight miles wide, that ran from Shellbrook in the west, east to Steep Creek on the north side of the river. It was where the jackpines grew, and that's where he found clay that would make brick. . . . He called it Red Rock Brick Yard because there was a big sandstone red rock stuck out of the riverbank just upstream from it." Seated in his grade five class at the riverside Connaught School, Dave Wilson often spotted his grandfather Deacon's newest boat the *Marion* "chuggin' upstream with a load of brick. Her engines weren't marine engines; they were makeshift engines and exhausted to atmosphere, not into a condenser. She was quite wasteful on fuel and you could hear her puffin' away to beat the band. . . . She was just a little tug, with a three-foot propeller, and she pulled a scow on her side . . . it made her a wide job and hard to handle." Notwithstanding the slightly makeshift nature of his equipment,

Deacon's Red Rock Brick Yard helped build the city, and he also received orders from as far away as eastern Canada and the United States.

But the brick skipper didn't hold exclusive rights to the river. In the 1911 season, Deacon dodged not only the lumber-hauling steamers, but also a steamboat and crew that were the product of the building boom radiating well beyond Prince Albert's city limits. The Cole's Falls rapids – one of the old Saskatchewan fleet's earliest stumbling blocks, 30 miles below Prince Albert – became the site of a project to dam the North Saskatchewan and harness the current for 15,000 horsepower of hydro-electric energy. A plebiscite had authorized the pursuit of a three-million-dollar loan; cement was massed at Prince Albert for the construction; and the East Prince Albert flats gave birth to another steamboat, the *George V.* Her captain, John MacLeod, and first mate, John MacKay, had both grown up in the Hebrides; as homesteaders northwest of Prince Albert they were two of many, but as skipper and mate of the *George*, their talents were unique.

"When they were building the Cole's Falls dam, the *George* ran night and day carrying supplies," MacKay's daughter explained. "As pilot on the steamboat [MacKay] could tell where the rocks were under the river, by the sound of the water on the rocks. . . . He had been at sea as a young man and knew water very well. . . . But there was a bit of a rivalry between Captain MacLeod and Captain Deacon; now and again they'd race into Prince Albert up from the Falls; they'd throw bacon into the fireboxes to make extra steam and race to town. . . . Captain Deacon often sent reports to the city too, that Captain MacLeod was a danger to navigation. . . ."

"One night I was wakened with the flare of fire outside my window. Somebody had set the boat on fire to get the good hardwood lumber loose from the boat structure." A pioneer teacher's recollection of the final destruction of the derelict *Marquis* symbolized how completely the people of Prince Albert had forgotten a bygone era. "After that, people kept taking more and more pieces from the boat . . . 'til there was nothing much left." The prizes were pieces of brass, scraps of oakwood, or chunks of steel to melt down for some other purpose. Ashes remained on the riverbank.

Other changes were pushing Prince Albert out of the spotlight of the boom. By 1913 the city fathers were struggling with the debts that piled up on the Cole's Falls dam project; a risk-free investment in the future suddenly turned into a civic white elephant. The decision was made to scrap the project, but the taxpayers of Prince Albert would be paying off loans for half a century. Hungry Winton Brothers' saws had eaten deep into the Prince Albert Lumber Company's monopoly timber limits; the deeper the loggers cut into Saskatchewan timber, the more expensive it became to haul the logs back to the Goshen mill site. There were but a few seasons of cutting left at Prince Albert before the Wintons would have to move on. Once again, railways were penetrating territory previously dominated by the river and her steamers; the Canadian National Railway had established a rail head at The Pas, Manitoba, 125 miles downriver to the north of Prince Albert. Prince Albert's existence as the threshold to the Northland, that had begun with the arrival of the CPR twenty years before, crumbled.

Those young fishermen returned to peaceful riverbanks, and the rotating spans of the swing-bridge rusted with disuse, as fewer and fewer steamboats plied the river. A Winnipeg navigation company had dispatched their most seasoned skipper, Captain Levi Bellefeuille, to fetch its recent purchase – the 100-foot sternwheel steamer *Alberta*, which could no longer pay its way in Prince Albert. The excursion trade had dropped off rapidly for Captain Fred Coates and his partner Rufus Mosher; in fact, Mosher had joined other members of his family to go prospecting in the north for commodities more lucrative than excursion fares – gold, copper, and iron. And thus, after a farewell pleasure cruise out of Prince Albert one June day, the *Alberta* embarked on a 1,000-mile adventure back down the Saskatchewan and across Lake Winnipeg to the Red River.

"You can get gold anywhere in the Saskatchewan River; when you get down to the gumbo at the bottom of the river, below the rocks, you can get gold, but it's very fine stuff. When it's dry it'll blow away," claimed the last night watchman aboard the Roughsedge and Ramsay gold dredge. "Roughsedge was erratic, but he was inventive too; he invented the table to get the gold out of the sand. The dredge had corrugated rubber, sloped tables, a centrifugal pump, a 14-inch suction pipe and a 35-horse steam engine ... and then the Doctor took it to Miners' Creek above Gunn's Island. But the iron contamination killed it," Ted Harris concluded.

And as the gold dredge rotted on the North Saskatchewan above Prince Albert, downriver the steamer *Saskatchewan* was returning from delivering surveyors and equipment to the lower river. Working aboard that season, deckhand Jimmy Soles recalled, "when we came back from Moose Lake that trip, we went right to The Pas and we drydocked her there. They set her up on blocks and locked her up. . . . That's the last time she ever floated. She was all wrecked and broke up there." By 1913, the *Saskatchewan's* steam engines had been crated and were en route to

127

the hull of a new steamer on the Mackenzie. Her hull was converted to a barge, and the rest "people carried away, just like the *Marquis*. . . . Those days on the steamboat were the best, the very best."

"When the boom came in 1912 [Captain Deacon] had mortgaged everything to get more machinery for the yards, because he was selling bricks to the States and to Ontario. He had crews at the yard and on the boats and he could hardly ship enough bricks to answer all the orders," a granddaughter described. "But when the War broke out, the boom broke and the companies shipped the brick back because they were going into war work. He couldn't do anything with them and had no money, so he went out of business and moved away. . . . He was the type of person that could do anything that came along, but he was too old then, and this wasn't the country for him; he had come out with his wife's family. I think he would have been better off in a large city. . . ."

Slumping industry, the scare of a looming European conflict, and the setting of the sun on Prince Albert's heyday all seemed to spell disaster. And yet, as the timber zone thinned, as the Hudson's Bay Company transplanted its distribution depot northward again, as the excursion fever along the Saskatchewan vanished, and the hydro-electric scheme collapsed, one activity in and around Prince Albert continued to flourish: immigration. If all else disintegrated, the constant influx of confident faces and new-world optimism would salvage the momentum of the century's prosperous first decade. The people boom had begun.

"Nineteen-thirteen broke all records for immigration to Canada. . . . It was salesmanship in Scotland and everywhere. Somebody would go back home and he'd be paid a dollar for every immigrant he could get to come to Canada." Handsome and hoping his thin moustache would give him a more mature look than his twenty years, John McCuaig and his older sister Flora had spent forty pounds of their mother's savings to cross the Atlantic and half of Canada to make sure that their brother and his homestead were faring well. "We arrived on the seventh of August 1913, up from Winnipeg on the CN. It was raining. At that time there was an immigration hall in Prince Albert and an immigration officer met each train. . . . I remember his asking me why I left Scotland and I said that it rained too much over there. 'Well,' he says, 'by the look of P.A. you must have brought it with you.' It had been raining for three days. . . .

"We were stationed at the immigration hall . . . and the immigration officer was anxious to get us on our way, but we couldn't get out to Steep Creek and my brother's homestead by the road . . . so somebody suggested that we go down on the boat," John continued. Moored just below the firehall was the *George V*, ironically the only survivor of the Cole's Falls fiasco; in fact, the McCuaigs learned that the steamer was in the process of salvaging the steel and cement remains from the abandoned dam project very near Donald McCuaig's farm. "We boarded Sunday night with our straw bags and a couple of cane trunks. . . . There were just three aboard that night: Captain John MacLeod, his mate John MacKay, and the cook. . . . They had set out some folding beds for us; they were going to take us downriver as a favour. . . ."

Before sun-up, steam engines aboard the *George V* were barking and pushing her sternwheel into action. From the hurricane deck, her two weary passengers took in the terrain of their new home. "The captain didn't talk too much," Flora noted; "he was at the wheel and staring at the river all the time. . . . The boat moved quickly downriver through shallows and rocks, but I was busy looking over the side to see the land. . . . I had made my mind up that I wasn't going to be scared of anything anywhere. If I was goin', I was goin' to see all I could. . . . Coming down I saw a fellow on the crew eating something for breakfast instead of porridge. I asked what it was and he told me 'corn flakes.' I'd never seen anything like that before. . . .

"At about twelve o'clock on Monday noon, the boat pulled into the Falls and Donald came running down the ramp. . . . I hadn't seen Donald for seven years. . . . He brought some skinned rabbits and I had brought some eggs over from the old country for him . . . and we had a feast there on his homestead. . . ."

Immigrant arrivals like this at the homestead had become commonplace since 1905. Prairie lands beyond the developing towns and cities emerged as the next focal point of an expanding nation; and while healthy industry came and went with the economic times, the crop of new Canadians and their thirst for 160-acre farms seemed endless. And again the steamboat won a new lease on life across the prairies, as a tool of land promotion.

CHAPTER SIX

The Queer Apple

"Buy New, Rich, Cheap Land."
"Join the Last Stampede for Cheap Homes."
"Farm too small," the brochure asked?
"Come where you will have Good Neighbors."
"Come where Land Values will double in a few years," it promised.
"Buy Bigger Acreage for the Best Price," said a similar leaflet.
"Come where crops are safe from drought; where farmers enjoy fishing and shooting."

The propaganda was directed squarely at Americans, still first genera-tion immigrants to the United States. The bait was enticing and blunt. *"Canada is the Only Country for Americans to emigrate to,"* and *"Laws are Enforced in Canada!"* The piles of posters were shipped off for notice boards, church socials, magistrates files, dust-worn telegraph poles, and rural bulletins. Pamphlets showed white clouds dancing over a placid plain, an insignia of a ribbon-bound wheat sheaf, and attractive slogans proclaiming a new promised land: *Last Mountain Valley, Prairie Wheat Lands, Saskatchewan, Where Wheat Is King.* So read seasoned (and sometimes defeated) farmers near Omaha, large-familied Chicago mer-chants on losing streaks, young New Yorkers looking northwest to adventure, and countless rural Dakotans within a stone's throw of Sas-katchewan.

The Last Mountain Valley literature seemed both intimidating and sil-ver-lined. It shunned all overtones of "pioneering"; glorified the area's healthfulness; pledged the reliability of the climate; and forecast the bounty of the harvests by quoting overwhelming statistics of twenty-five to thirty-five bushels per acre and higher. Pamphlet after pamphlet rang with phrases like *"a single crop often pays for your land."* Every advanta-geous facility was claimed; every other word was *"success"*; and as the agents of a new religion (*"land is wheat is cash"*) shouted the good tid-ings, they introduced a new era for south central Saskatchewan: *"Last*

Mountain Valley Always Delivers the Goods!" But what, thought thousands, was Last Mountain Valley, and where? And who were the people proclaiming this mecca, the William Pearson Company Limited in Winnipeg, Canada, with the hundreds of thousands of beckoning acres?

By the time this neat packet of promotion was in the hands of prospective land buyers, William Pearson was a man en route to a well earned fortune – and a place in history as the architect of a unique steamboating story.

In the beginning Pearson had been just a farmer, a dairy farmer in western Manitoba when the credit was cut off. His creamery there went bankrupt, so instead of fighting the raw end of business on the prairies, he decided to sell real estate for commission to American farmers who were constantly moving into the country. Real estate made a new man of him, but it required that he pack his family off to Winnipeg, then the capital of Canada's only western province. He learned to speak often with Liberal government officials and soon he nestled among influential bankers and prominent lawyers to form an investing group to purchase CNR land grants of the Northwest Territories (in what was soon to become central Saskatchewan) for resale to an influx of Americans and nomadic eastern Canadians still looking for the ultimate farm.

Englishman, ex-farmer now real estate cruiser, a tall, moustached, broad-faced William Pearson set out in the spring of 1902 on what was his most significant venture. He had no lettered education; he wasn't a genius, but he did read widely and constantly. In doing so he acquired all the knowledge he would need, and cultivated to a fine edge the instincts and awareness of hard experience. Experience had taught him how to read the land, and how to deal with failure; he knew too that the inability of the railway builders to cross the Qu'Appelle River into the region north of the settlements, along the transcontinental CPR line, had left the country to the north neglected and little known.

Calculating carefully the opportunities open to him, Pearson left Fort Qu'Appelle piloted by an Indian guide and headed into that wilderness. West he travelled over vacant plains and to the ends of the Qu'Appelle tributaries, mounted the final rise before the Palliser Plain, and proceeded the final ten miles to the edge of Last Mountain Lake, or Long Lake, as it was also called. Here he would begin his life's enterprise, the establishment of the celebrated William Pearson Company.

Professor John Macoun's widely circulated 1879 survey for the CPR had already described the area in glowing terms. "Long or Last Mountain Lake," noted the professor, "lies in a region that has a general descent from the east extending over ten miles. The waters of the lake are sweet and pleasant to the taste and of great depth.... Before many years, steamboats will be plying upon its waters, and lovely land bordering on its shores will be dotted with farm houses. One of the richest tracts in the Qu'Appelle Valley lies adjoining Last Mountain, and when known will be speedily taken up by the farmers." A quarter century before Pearson stood next to Long Lake, his land-selling literature had already been written!

Pearson's next step was to complete his deal with the CNR, incorporate himself, establish credibility among landseekers, and organize a means by which he might transport his customers to his real estate.

Pearson took an option on ten thousand acres of Last Mountain Valley, polished his shoes, and set out for Grand Forks, North Dakota, Virden, and Brandon in western Manitoba to start selling. Months later he began appointing representative agents in centres across Ohio, Indiana, Michigan, Illinois, Iowa, Nebraska, Kansas, and even as far east as New York State.

Pearson's scheme attracted some very high-powered directors, such as the politician George Brown (later to become Lieutenant-Governor of Saskatchewan) and the financier George Perkins. Officially, the William Pearson Company amassed an impressive seven hundred thousand acres, but in fact their holdings may have been even greater – an employee later suggested that the total amounted to more like "a million acres, purchased through the generous offices of George Brown." In return, the company assumed a major role in advertising the area and in generating settlement. "Their agreement with the government was that they had to colonize both sides of the lake where this land was. They didn't have much money so they got the million acres for a dollar an acre; just raw prairie, no railways there, nothing." It was the perfect combination: Brown the political power, Pearson the promoter, and Perkins the pot of money. Through 1903, 1904, and 1905, the Pearson Company customers were pouring into the odd-numbered sections north of Regina, while homesteaders broke sod for shacks and first crops on the even-numbered sections.

But it was one thing to close a deal a minute with land-crazy Americans; it was another to live up to the slogan splashed across the William Pearson brochure, to "Always Deliver the Goods". Life on the valley land was far from ideal – smaller centres were dotting the eastern slope, but where were the convenient marketing points for farm produce? Where were the banking resources? What of grain elevator facilities? And for how many more years would farmers have to travel the long journey to the south railhead at Lumsden, or across the north end of the seventy-mile Long Lake to Davidson to purchase staples and machinery? Few had even slow-ambling oxen, and fewer had horses to cross the miles and

132

days in pursuit of provisions. The immediate need of his landseekers and the previously settled farmers, and the vision he saw of his company expanding into provisions outlets, lumber sales, and even resort hotels, called again on Pearson's ingenuity.

Why not a steamboat as a solution to the transportation problem? The idea of a steamer on Last Mountain Lake was not new. McKillop and Benjafield, two real estate men from Regina, had launched their own steam-powered barge the previous year, which paddled up and down the lake transporting grain to the south on a regular basis, unless there was a strong wind, or unless the captain himself got under the weather. And so, wedged and secured to a CPR flatcar, Pearson's solution arrived on a switchback rail line at Craven in the summer of 1904. On the Rainy River, then a flourishing boating lane, he had found the answer: a tiny, flat-bottomed paddlewheel steamer for sale.

The clatter and hum of a work crew assembling the new Pearson acquisition near Cowan's Beach just outside the village of Silton attracted continued attention that summer of 1904. To 23-year-old Tom Johnston, the hammering and rasp of saws were a familiar and friendly sound. Out from Birmingham, England, only three years before, Johnston and his two brothers had searched for paying employment, a place to build some permanent shelter, and perhaps a piece of farmland. The dominating presence of a monopolistic CPR in Regina made the cost of living and building too high, so they turned away. Last Mountain Valley required the talents of carpenters to fashion the beginnings of new town sites and there it was they headed.

"We built a school at Earl Grey, one or two churches and quite a few houses," Johnston recalled, "but then we got on with the Pearson Company. They planned to haul wheat down from around Arlington Beach [at the north end of Long Lake]. They'd brought up this boat from Fort Frances; they'd brought along a ship's carpenter with it and they'd unloaded this boat at Craven when the water was still high and we took it up to Silton. On the ways there we cut it amidships and built twenty feet into her. My brother was a more accomplished joiner than I was and he did most of the interior cabin work while I worked on building some scows for them. We worked for a couple of months on these boats around Silton."

Lengthening the Pearson steamer was only part of the reconstruction program; the boatbuilding crew stripped away her entire shell and redesigned her from the keel up. A flat-bottomed steamboat was at home on rivers in northwestern Ontario, but on narrow, storm-prone Long Lake, a prominent keel was mandatory. With these modifications underway Pearson appeared to have all the construction problems under control, especially with a ship's carpenter present to conduct the ministernwheeler's transformation to the substantial screw-propelled lake steamer *Welcome.*

The company's intentions for the boat were plain enough, even to carpenter Tom Johnston (who would later take up politics and then sit twelve years as speaker of the Saskatchewan Legislative Assembly). "Pearson planned to run personally conducted tours," described Johnston. "He hoped to bring up special trainloads of landseekers from the United States; he would entertain them on the boat, the *Welcome,* with lots of liquor and a good time; bring them up and hire democrats to chauffeur them around the countryside. Took damn good care that they never saw any other farmers, because they [the company] didn't want the homesteaders to make any deals with the landseekers." Americans were open game, for it was more than a rumour that these Pearson customers had sold their American farms for upwards of eighty dollars per acre, and could easily afford the cheaper twelve to twenty dollars per acre that Pearson expected.

As weather permitted throughout the winter, the face of the *Welcome* took shape. The south end of Long Lake was booming with activity. In the town of Lumsden, there was building everywhere; the town streets sprouted a flour mill, grain elevators, three churches of Anglican, Methodist and Presbyterian faiths, two hotels, a bank, Balfour's store, Troughton's store, Pettigrew's Implement Shed, Silverthorn's Livery Barn, and, on James Street, the main branch office of the William Pearson Company. By spring of 1905 the Pearson specials began to arrive at the railhead loaded with landseekers by the hundred. All this success and progress continued until the day the *Welcome* came down the ways at the Company's new lake harbour, Port Hyman. Cutting the lake water she quivered, answered the shore-lines to return, but never fully righted herself. And there she floated – a year's work, unbalanced and lopsided, completely useless at the very moment she was most critically required.

The *Welcome* died at that moment, but Pearson, who had invested two years, much of his savings, and all his confidence in this enterprise, did not lose heart. With the Company's water-transport plans delayed, he doubled his horse-drawn vehicle capacity to meet the onslaught of eager buyers arriving to tour the million acres for sale. Back on the ways, a redesigned steamer was soon under construction amid the very ribs and deck planks of the *Welcome,* to be christened and launched the following season as the *Lady of the Lake.* When the *Lady* hit the water in her 1906 debut, the passage of landseekers and supplies by water at long last began, but Pearson's steamboat headaches persisted. In the final week of May the Company announced that "an unfortunate breakdown of machinery on the new steamer *Lady of the Lake*" had crippled the movement of people and provisions again. The steamer hadn't even a month's experience logged. As if the boat's failure weren't depressing enough, the whole Pearson exploit took on laughingstock proportions; on the west side of the lake there was even a young boy who persisted in taking pot shots with his bird gun at the steamer's smokestacks. He scored two hits.

There were more serious problems with the boat than mere bullet holes in the smokestack, however. The *Lady* was too narrow for such a blowy lake; her keel could not accomodate the strain of barge-towing; her makeshift engines weren't powerful enough; the landseeker projections called for greater carrying capacity; the boat needed a newer, more attractive appearance; and, all in all, the Company's prestige needed a boost to overcome insults like bullet holes in the Pearson colours.

Despite its numerous setbacks with its seemingly ill-fated steamship, the Pearson Company was prospering mightily. Settlers poured in to Last Mountain Valley; the first crops were planted and then harvested. Almost immediately, tremendous quantities of building materials were needed by the new farmers, since the open prairie offered few if any of the bare essentials for building shelter. Pearson answered the demand by importing lumber from British Columbia and the American mid-west; five lumber yards joined agents' offices and shoreline settlements at Port Hyman, on the west side at Arm River and View Haven, at Arlington Beach on the east shore, and at the most northerly point of lake navigation, Watertown. The Pearson Company hired an army of teamsters to haul rough timber from boxcars at Lumsden to their head of navigation at Port Hyman. Docks were planned for the land-lumber offices along the lake; a system of grain elevators lay waiting on paper for construction at Port Hyman; supplies poured into the Company warehouse; four lake barges reached completion; and coal arrived for the hungry fires of a new steamer taking shape on Cowan's Beach.

The *Lady of the Lake* was hardly recognizable through the winter of 1906 to 1907. Her old structure lay in ruin at the hands of her new makers. New, more practical towing gear was installed, and her keel was reinforced. Extended to sixty-two feet in length, with her breadth increased to seventeen feet, and the draft to four feet, the steamer now weighed fifty-one tons and had a gross capacity of eighty-two tons. Boasting these bigger and better statistics, the new Pearson steamer slid down the ways as the newly christened *Qu'Appelle*. In the space of three years the William Pearson Company had obtained what was initially a sternwheeler's frame, and altered its structure inside and out, once to become the *Welcome* in 1905, a second time to emerge as the *Lady of the Lake* in 1906, and finally to appear as the *Qu'Appelle* in 1907. Acutely aware of the face

135

lifting it needed in public the Company ferried its prize to Port Hyman's docks to apply the polishing touches.

A year before, William Pearson's son A. M. Pearson saw Lumsden and his father's Long Lake empire for the first time. Out from Regina with a team and democrat, young Pearson had described the valley as "breathtaking"; he was equally intrigued with the refurbishing process that was transforming the *Qu'Appelle*. "I was seventeen then. I was going to school in Winnipeg at that time and came up on summer holidays; at least I had intended it to be a holiday more than anything .... The *Qu'Appelle* had been launched by the time I arrived and it was at Port Hyman tied up to the docks. The superstructure was just being built. They were putting another deck on her and placing the new wheelhouse on the top deck, instead of down on the main deck. And the captain's cabin was installed right behind the wheelhouse. New posts were built at the stern for a hitching rope to slide over for towing barges. Wasn't long before I was sitting down below in the boat, pounding away with a hammer on the inside of the hull, pounding the caulking into cracks to keep water out.... I liked working on the boat at anything I could do, really, like coaling up ... working without pay of course.

"There were about five carpenters working on the construction of the superstructure. Two of them were homesteaders just east of Port Hyman there, Bill Tanner and John Cook. Two lads, Jack Link and his brother, they came out to work on the boat too; they'd been homesteading up on the west side of the lake near Dilke."

Young Pearson watched all this activity carefully – his was a vested interest in the company his father had created. Many years later Pearson's son would return from World War I and take up a major role in the Company as a land inspector, but for now the construction of the *Qu'Appelle* was attractive enough. "First the frame came together; the big job here was setting the windows in before the wind blew you and the window away. The pilot house was large enough to take fifteen or twenty people in it. At the rear of the bridge deck there was a canopy-covered area. Below the bridge deck was a saloon or dining room with several tables and the galley; then below the main deck was the engine room and crew's quarters."

A crew came together quickly and without formality. Harold Gatenby, skilled at cultivation, simple carpentry, and the art of surviving on his own cooking, became the galley chef. The Link brothers moonlighted from their homestead; engineer Hobbs left stationary boilers to learn the quirks of the steamer's marine engine; and a ship's mate arrived from the Great Lakes. But crewmen brought more than their trades aboard. Mate Theodore Clarke brought a biting sense of humour with him from

The William Pearson Co. steamer *Qu'Appelle* on a tour of Last Mountain Lake, entertaining new American residents at View Haven, 4 July 1909. *(Saskatchewan Archives Board)*

Peace and quiet in the rear quarters of the *Qu'Appelle* for owner and friends: (left to right) author Emerson Hough, company president William Pearson, John Ridington, and Duncan Pierce of Cannington Manor. *(Saskatchewan Archives Board)*

Deseronto, Ontario. Both Jack Link and Harold Gatenby aspired for the hand of the maid employed at the Company's Port Hyman hotel; at every opportunity one would row with the lady on a moonlit night, while the other fumed; Mate Clarke knew it and always precipitated arguments between the two suitors, until he tired of the game and tossed them both in the lake "to cool off." By far the most impressive feature of the *Qu'Appelle* was tucked into the rear cabin on the main deck. Curtained windows partly obscured a kind of private executive's lounge designed to accomodate particular guests. In a room panelled with mahogany, they sat on leather armchairs around an elegant oak table; or relaxed in a sofa cushioned with red velvet, and smoked imported cigars. And it was all serviced by modern toilet facilities and the dim flicker of table lamps. Pearson ensured that if his company boat were utilitarian, it would also be luxurious. Proof of the *Qu'Appelle's* success was the pride she instilled in her crew who insisted "when she was freshly painted white and the sun shone on her, she'd knock your eye out! She was an attraction!" By July 1907 the *Qu'Appelle*, or as her friends knew her, "the Queer Apple", was up the lake hauling barges loaded with lumber, fuel, groceries, and mail. And no-one was happier than William Pearson.

The skipper of the Apple, W. C. Huggins, had come to the doorstep of the prairies as a young man twenty-five years earlier, on a sidewheeler down the Red River into Winnipeg. His family had lived on what his father earned mule-teaming between Winnipeg and Portage la Prairie; but young Huggins, more attracted by the life of the lakes and rivers, learned steamboating from the water up, on a fifty-foot sturgeon-hauling steamer on Lake of the Woods. Sturdily built, a drifter, W. C. Huggins followed the work his master's papers provided: to a sternwheeler running between Fort Frances and Rainy River, and on to the prairie steamer that would outlive them all (including Huggins himself), the *Keenora*.

Middle-aged and equipped with all the attributes of a seasoned skipper, including uniform, a cocked eye, tales of inland boating, and a full beard, Huggins continually studied his adversary, Last Mountain Lake. The lake had no tricky currents, few shoals to speak of, and only a few points spotted with reefs. Her trump card, however, was her erratic depth. In her narrowest stretch, from View Haven to Glen Harbour, Long Lake was perhaps a hundred feet deep at the best of times. Generally, however, her wider regions to the north and to the south gave her that unique prairie personality: shallow waters that passing winds blew into chaotic waves. Huggins soon knew the features of the lake well and respected them, for at her top speed of twelve miles per hour the *Qu'Appelle* couldn't easily outrun a storm.

By seven o'clock every other morning, crew and steamer were away from Port Hyman for their northward trip; across the lake, Cain's Point pier received supplies and passengers; View Haven had a lumber yard to replenish; at Glen Harbour passengers could be met readily because that east side had deep water for docking; steaming over to the west shore again the boat came to the Big Arm where Pearson Company lumber was unloaded for American buyers; by three in the afternoon three-quarters of the lake's length was behind them at Arlington Beach (home of the Company hotel and resort); and finally at five, the *Qu'Appelle* reached Watertown, with its lumber yard and land office located at the top or "fingers" end of the lake. Most of the crew took for granted that the route was a guideline and not a strict schedule. Docking late didn't matter, as long as the boat was in one piece.

"Steaming up pretty close to the Big Arm heading north and we ran into a hail storm," grimaced the captain's son. Cyril Huggins stepped in to wheel for the mate one season; he knew the tricks of sailboating, but hadn't piloted the lake on steam before. Long Lake waits for novice wheelsmen. "I couldn't see where I was going. I could only spot on the compass and take a blind bearing before we went into the storm. The life-boat on the top deck filled with two feet of ice, solid hail. . . . It came across from Davidson in a streak, flattening all the grain, pounding it into the ground. Couldn't go ashore. It was too shallow, so we ploughed through. Hail as big as walnuts was splashing up the water and smashing windows." Despite the hazards they got through afloat.

Barging a collapsible dock north to the Arlington Beach resort, young Huggins learned that the lake could strike more than once. A gale whipped away the barge, tore off the Apple's anchor, and blew the steam out of her boiler. Ordered below, Cyril joined the brigade trying to rebuild steam. "We didn't have much wood, but we did have quite a few cases of bacon; so we threw in about ten slabs of bacon, then a bit of wood, then coal and finally got steam up and made it, dock and all." Veterans got to be veterans by the tricks they learned merely to survive.

The *Qu'Appelle* usually steamed along the west side of Long Lake; she was restricted to the lake's deeper sections by narrow channels and by a cautious William Pearson, who had no wish to see ten thousand dollars' worth of double-compound engines, the velvet cushions, or his reputation washed ashore in ruin. But despite the storms that continued to roar in unannounced from the Saskatchewan plains, the Apple, though she remained top-heavy, weathered the test of her one-day-up and one-day-back routine.

The greatest storm the Apple had to withstand was the rush of company landseekers onto William Pearson's model acreages. Agents for the company had fanned out over a dozen American states looking for unhappy or adventurous farmers – not homesteaders, but farmers who had the money to purchase land. Their pitch seemed flawless: for $2.50 a day and part of the train fare a potential land buyer could travel to the main American depot at Minneapolis, then by Great Northern to Winnipeg, then by Canadian Pacific to Lumsden; he would ride in an open wagon to Port Hyman and board the *Qu'Appelle* to the landing of his choice and in two or three days see virgin territory "begging to be tilled"; he could eat, sleep, and celebrate for three days at the Company's expense and get full return of his expenses if he bought Pearson land. Fifty to two hundred American farmers and some investors joined each excursion to the great unexplored unexploited Northwest. It seemed more a holiday than an investment.

Pullman sleepers, strings of dining cars, and supply laiden boxcars rolled in behind a labouring CPR locomotive from Regina at least once a week those summers. If the Company's American agents had been persuasive, Pearson's Long Lake employees could expect over two hundred customers for the trek across saleable sections. When a train load arrived in the night, the town of Lumsden woke and began a great Canadian catering service. The three-day sprees, paid for largely by the Pearson Company, meant business for local merchants and work for every spare team and buggy within fifty miles.

Before seven in the morning the landseekers were fed and then loaded into the wagons for the exodus to Port Hyman and the departing steamer, or overland to other points for a land viewing. Upwards of a hundred head of horses hauled Americans to the east and west sides of Last Mountain Lake, while the *Qu'Appelle* accommodated as many as seventy landseekers each trip up the lake itself. Some came aboard with their customary Negro servants or cooks "who made black coffee that'd make your hair stand on end," while others mounted the gangplanks in mid-July carrying sheepskin coats and fur hats in expectation of snow on an eighty-degree Saskatchewan day.

Only the men came on these excursions. As a kind of prospector, the male head of an American family had paid out the daily fee and gone off to the Canadian West to seek a future site for his family. So as the spotless *Qu'Appelle* chugged along from one port of call to the next, the entire boat load of landseekers got down to the business of gawking at the shoreline from the boat's highest vantage point.

"These American lads had sold their land for eighty and ninety dollars an acre, so they could pick and choose the best land." Harold Gatenby, the cook, by this time had talked his younger brother Ron aboard the

Apple as a deckhand. For the sixteen-year-old Yorkshire boy, steamboating was a lot of work and very little glamour. He was low man on the totem pole; when the Americans arrived Ron's day consisted of wheeling coal, bucking lumber, mopping deck, polishing brass, and "keeping the landseekers from falling overboard." "Jim Morrison, one of the managers of the Company, he used to go up the lake with us," Ron Gatenby continued. "He had this big megaphone and he'd announce where we were going and give them a line of b.s. We'd go ashore and so many would get off at that point. The company had a barn and livery with their own horses and democrats. The manager there took them out then to the plots of land that were for sale; he'd spend two or three days leading them around by the nose."

Pearson's son and heir meanwhile had begun to pick up the land-selling end of the business, and joined the district managers and their tours out to Cupar and Govan where the prime chunks of farmland were displayed. The whole affair provided as much fun as it did head-to-head bargaining. "We'd stop on a piece of land; some would want to rest and others were eager to start something up," young Pearson explained. Even the boss's son stirred some sport. "They put on wrestling matches and races. One trip they had a runner from Nebraska; he was a champion hundred-yard-dash man. I had been doing some training by running behind the horses and wagons. So they decided we'd better have a race there on the prairies. Off we went across the fields in bare feet, me and the champion from Nebraska. . . . Well he beat me, but only by a few feet.

"We drove them until seven in the evening. At night tents were set up on the prairie. There would be a hundred and fifty people, thirty to a tent, in tents that were sixty feet long; and there were three or four tents to house the horses with mangers and feed. Most of these fellows were so tired that they were quite willing to lie down and sleep as soon as they got their meals. So they bundled up in their heavy clothes and slept. A few gambled, though; they brought out the cards and money and played their High-Low Jack in the Game." Three days later the *Qu'Appelle* on her southbound journey to Port Hyman rendezvoused with the weary landseekers on their way to Lumsden and their America-bound special trains.

The Pearson machinery was always in motion. Landseekers departed with down payments made on their future farming plots; livery barns filled again with stock preparing for the next onslaught; new train specials thundered into the Qu'Appelle Valley now humming with settlers; families who had purchased sections the previous summer arrived to break their land for the first time; settlers' effects arrived; the supplies continued to flow in; coal cars kept the stream of black fuel to the steamer constant; fliers full of propaganda and publicity photos (taken by Harold

141

Gatenby on his old British Kodak box camera) flooded south; the Apple had steam up around the clock for the hectic six-month season; and the Company counted the profits. Pearson had taken a hunch and had built it into a force felt as far away as Ottawa.

In 1907, with political power and money, and with the prairies' future inhabitants rushing in like so many head of cattle, Pearson knocked on the door of the Federal Minister of Public Works, Sir William Pugsley. As quickly as the CPR could marshal him there, Pugsley arrived at Last Mountain Lake to look over the proposed dredging of a channel through the marsh at the south end of the lake, which would enable the company boat and barges to reach the planned new head of navigation at Valeport, a mile down the lake from Port Hyman. Pearson foresaw a second bustling company town beyond Lumsden, at the newly surveyed and named townsite of Valeport. Pearson made plans for new grain elevators and barges to be constructed at Valeport, and for the offices, docks, and the steamer itself to be transferred there. Valeport would be the Pearson headquarters – but it was a boom town that would never be.

By 1910 the government dredge and the *Ruby*, a small steam tug, began cutting the lake bottom for the channel to Pearson's Valeport. The dredge needed a crew, and Arthur White, a wholesale silk merchant looking for any available work, took on a new profession: trip man for the pile-driving section of the dredge operation. For three years he worked forty feet above the water while the top-heavy dredge "bobbed like a duck." But he took it in his stride, and like so many with that pioneering instinct, he never knew when he was beaten.

In time, enough dredging was done to allow the *Qu'Appelle* to steam down from Port Hyman to Valeport, where the new company shop was established and where the crews' antics continued. Usually these centred around the *Ruby's* constantly-plotting engineer. "Old Joe Seaforth from Craven was quite a character, full of the devil," Ron Gatenby maintained. "The caps at that time weren't on the CPR bridge at the south end of the lake, and there were just the piles sticking up. Dunc MacMillan had crawled up onto one of these piles from the earthworks; he carried a sixteen-foot spear. . . . He was up about ten feet or so from the water, well, Seaforth starts to agitate MacMillan. 'By God, Dunc,' he says, 'here comes a big one.' This was a really big twenty-five to thirty pound jack, a beauty! 'Here he comes, Dunc. Don't miss it,' he yells! Well Dunc missed it and in he went. The water was running fast and he was wearing these hip-waders; of course when he went in they just filled right up. He came pretty close to drowning; the boys got him out, but old Joe just thought this was a great laugh."

When the dredging to Valeport was complete, Captain Huggins took

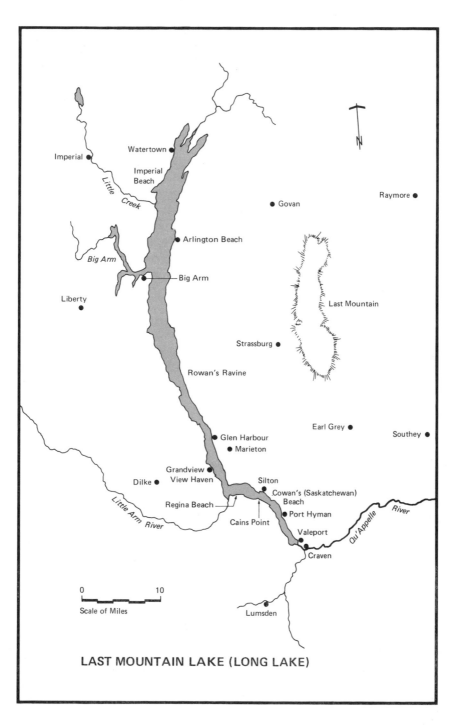

Imperial ●

Watertown ●

Imperial
Beach

Little Creek

Big Arm

Liberty ●

Arlington Beach ●

Big Arm ●———— Big Arm

Rowan's Ravine

Govan ●

Raymore ●

Last Mountain

Strassburg ●

Glen Harbour ●
Marieton ●

Grandview ●
View Haven ●

Dilke ●

Little Arm River

Regina Beach ————

Cains Point

Silton ●

Cowan's (Saskatchewan)
Beach
● Port Hyman

Valeport ●

Craven ●

Earl Grey ●

Southey ●

Qu'Appelle River

0   10

Scale of Miles

Lumsden ●

N

LAST MOUNTAIN LAKE (LONG LAKE)

the new company steel barge through on a trial run; with his son Cyril on the stern and the boat purser steering this huge ninety-by-twenty-foot barge, the captain directed the placing of markers in the channel. On one over-energetic throw, Cyril tossed anchor, chain, marker, and himself overboard, to the delight of boat and dredge crews. It was another near miss as Cyril swam fiercely to escape being run over by the barge, but afterwards it seemed humorous.

The steel barge, the only survivor today of the Pearson Company era, began a new phase of operation along the Company's lake and lands. In anticipation of high grain yields, Pearson finally began building the grain elevator of Valeport; a dancehall joined the waterfront; the lumber business boomed from its largest Valeport yard; and rail spur lines moved closer to Pearson's new land office centres. So quickly did the steel of CN and CP approach that the need for some of Pearson's initial transportation links diminished, including the one to carry landseekers over water. The railway had come to Earl Grey, Southey, Strassburg, Raymore, Craven, Davidson, and beyond, forcing the steamer Qu'Appelle into a secondary position.

In the same venturesome spirit of Pearson's original hotel and resort at Arlington Beach, new centres emerged as urbanites from Regina and Moose Jaw discovered the delights of Long Lake. Cain's Point was soon renamed Regina Beach; Cowan's Beach became Saskatchewan Beach; and the town of Imperial, ten miles from the northwest side of the lake, established a summer satellite on the shore called Imperial Beach. Last Mountain Lake took on a summer festive air. With the majority of the Pearson lands sold and the people now settled beyond the survival stage, the Company evolved from pioneer pathfinder to supplier and inter-port communications link. For the Apple there would be a new clientele: fun-seekers instead of landseekers.

When weekend excursionists arrived at docks along the lake, they met a new steamer suited to their jovial moods. The Qu'Appelle sparkled with scrubbed white planking; she was decked out in bunting and flags fluttered from every available pole and mast. The barge that had carried lumber north and wheat south on one day would be strapped to her side to provide a floating dance floor and sightseeing deck the next. Musicians would lift the excursion to singing and dancing, and the normally utilitarian steam whistle of the Apple frequently rang out her shrill blast to complement the occasion. For fifty cents the excursionist could dance, sing, or fish for several hours while the wind of the open lake dashed around him and the decks of the Qu'Appelle. Excursionists flocked to the beaches; Sunday picnics and national holidays on the first of July or the twenty-fourth of May were all an excuse for a trip on the steamboat. And William Pearson took full advantage of this opportunity to recover the operating expenses of the boat, although as everyone knew, the *Qu'Appelle* continued to operate in the red.

"Americans populated nearly all of the Big Arm and the town of Liberty. Every July we'd go up there for a special day and take them for a cruise. . . . Fourth of July 1910 we were taking an excursion of Americans over to Arlington Beach from the Big Arm. It was a beautiful, calm day; the lake was like a mirror. Capacity on the steamer was around seventy passengers, but the boat was overloaded, way overloaded. The skipper was after making some money for the Company," frowned deckhand Ron Gatenby. "That was old Captain Howett." For at least a season Captain Huggins, who loved farming and fishing as much as he did the Apple, retired temporarily to his homestead near Imperial. This July of 1910 the Company had imported Howett from Winnipeg, where (rumoured the crew) he owned a house complete with madam in the red-light district.

"Howett was a character; a gentleman, but two in one," continued Gatenby, reflecting on that innocent excursion of Americans celebrating the Fourth of July. "Coming back from Arlington Beach we ran into a thunder storm. Long Lake is one of the dirtiest lakes in the country. At that particular point it was four miles wide from Arlington to the Big Arm; there we were out in the middle of the widest part of the lake, overloaded and into this storm. It was a cross wind and a dirty wind and we were sure shipping water. The waves were short chops, not like on the ocean where the water comes in long rolls and long troughs; so the Apple listed badly and nearly stood on her beam ends. She didn't have the weight or the width for anything like that.

"The people began to panic and they nearly capsized her. They wanted to go from one side to the other on the upper deck as the boat rocked in the waves. Well, the old captain had a revolver; he saw something had to be done and he was scared for his life and his licence; he knew he'd done wrong by overloading the boat. He got up into the wheelhouse with his big megaphone that he'd used to point out sights on the lake. He bellowed through that thing like an old bull, 'I'll shoot the first man that next moves to the other side!'"

The storm roared around them for another half hour while the crew lined up the panicking passengers in the centre of the boat. Children and adults moaned and vomited with each roll the Apple took from the lake's breakers. The storm blew in from the northwest, so the captain brought the steamer around with the wind to ride it out. Gatenby never forgot his fear on that trip, watching each rising wave threaten the two-foot clearance between the lake surface and the main deck of the *Qu'Appelle*.

The fury of an occasional storm over Last Mountain Lake did not dampen the enthusiasm of either excursionists or steamboatmen. The *Qu'Appelle* could hardly meet the demand for weekly trips out of Regina Beach, the Big Arm, and Imperial Beach, let alone conduct her milk-run supply trips up the lake. She continued to cater to small storekeepers, farmers, the Pearson lumber yards, Canadians and Americans alike. In fact, her excursions back and forth between Canadian homesteaded settlements and American-settled centres helped to integrate nationalities. Sometimes, however, the meetings between the two got a little heated. One year, for the Fourth of July holiday, the *Qu'Appelle* had gathered Americans from around the lake to join in the celebrations at Watertown. As the Apple approached the Watertown dock and the predominantly American excursion moved towards the disembarkation gangplank, a tough rather bear-like blacksmith named Scotty Galt stepped forward, brandishing a double-barrel shotgun. Nothing stirred as the angered Scotsman pointed at the mast atop the Apple. Two flags were flying, but to Scotty, flying in an insulting configuration. The Stars and Stripes for the day's commemoration fluttered above the Union Jack. "Take that damn rag down," boomed the smithy's burr, "or I'll blow it to ribbons!" And before anyone had time to react Scotty pulled one trigger, then the other. Both times the hammer clicked without a shot. A light-footed crew member dashed to the controversial mast and removed the American flag. Scotty disappeared into the dock crowd and the day's celebration continued without incident.

No excursion across Long Lake to a picnic or outing on the *Qu'Appelle* and her barge was complete unless musicians came along. A tarnished cornet, tattered drum, or untuned fiddle did the trick; it didn't matter what was played or how skilled the talent – excursionists expected music. Especially after 1910, communities around the lake frequently sponsored town bands and challenged their neighbours to competitions, so it wasn't uncommon to have ready-made music on board the Apple as she made her way down the lake carrying one band to a match with another. The steamer was often transformed into a floating rehearsal hall for community bands brushing up before a musical battle; and if the Apple's passengers enjoyed the rehearsal en route, it could even mean future employment for a band.

Brass player Remington Warwick grew up on a homestead outside Imperial; the community band for a while was the centre of his world. After two years of determined practice the band travelled to Valeport to compete against the best. The Imperial band took the prize from the Strassburg and Liberty bands and went on to jobs all over the valley. "The most memorable trip," Warwick wrote, "was on the *Qu'Appelle*. We were engaged to play at a large picnic and dance at Arlington Beach, and the *Qu'Appelle* was chartered to take us and all others who wanted to go. On our return trip, the lake was calm and the moon shone brightly. There were many other passengers so we gave a little concert as we sailed along. We had just received the music for a song that was fast becoming everybody's favourite, 'Meet Me Tonight In Dreamland'. The setting was perfect and it was encored many times."

During quiet moments aboard the Apple when the excitement of a sightseeing cruise had passed, mate Theodore Clarke pulled a harmonica out of his coat pocket and buzzed a tune. When steam was down and a day's haul tucked away on shore, the half-dozen members of the permanent crew often sat in the galley and played that High-Low Jack card game that the Americans had introduced. When the perch were biting by dusk, someone would go astern and bait up a hook; Gatenby would use the fillets for breakfast. Coffee went around, and invariably some conversation about tomorrow's weather, while Clarke kept blowing melodies from the upper deck into the night air.

Even with a six-man crew plus the skipper living in such close quarters, one man knew little more than the surface of another. Most were bachelors who kept to themselves. The only difference between one and another was a year or two of experience and a few dollars pay. Skippers Howett and Huggins earned a hundred dollars a month and board; the cook, Harold Gatenby, took away sixty dollars a month and board; and his brother Ron as deckhand earned forty dollars a month and board (on the *Qu'Appelle* or at the boarding house).

"Forty dollars a month and I was just a kid. It looked pretty good when we got paid at the end of each month. I would get three ten-dollar gold pieces and two five-dollar gold pieces. No paper money, except twenty-five-cent shin plasters . . . but there wasn't any place to spend it – you got groceries and tobacco at Skone's store in Craven, but that was it."

Pay was good for the time. Any work was welcome. Often the work was bland, but each member of the Apple's crew had at least one feature that his mates remembered him by. Old Ted the chief engineer was a cranky chap. Everything in his engine room had to be just right; brass and steel stayed spotless and all five-foot-four of Ted tangled with anyone who soiled his mechanical kingdom: "you almost had to take your shoes off to go into his engine room." As far as Ron Gatenby was concerned, Old Ted was just crusty.

Ron recalled stories about some of the crew, and just images of others. "Captain Howett was clean shaven . . . Captain Huggins had a beard . . . the fireman was Iky Jones, a thick-set, stocky fellow from Ontario. We'd have little bets on the boat, especially if anybody new came on; we'd bet on Iky. He could take a ten-pound sledgehammer by the end of its thirty-inch handle and hold it straight out from his side. Nobody else could do it. . . . Mate Clarke was a pretty stuffy fellow. We were building the cradle to pull the boat out in the fall of 1911; he was hopping around rather close to the edge of the pier where there was about ten feet of water. He was an awful man to swear and I wasn't used to it; I was young and had never heard a bad word in England. But he cursed and swore 'til all he did was repeat himself – limited vocabulary. Well, he fell head first into the lake and I was all doubled up laughing when he came up. He clambered up there and got me by the back of the neck and he sure kicked my backside. Then I got out of there as quick as I could. Outside of that, he knew his business well."

Each spring for nearly five years a crew came back to Cowan's Beach to re-launch the *Qu'appelle* after the winter freeze-up. The crew might have new faces, a different mate, or fireman, or deckhand, but the procedure was always the same. They re-caulked the hull and slapped on a new coat of white paint; they refilled her twelve-by-six-foot boiler; and the engineer oiled the tired joints of her machinery. They stripped the boards protecting the pilothouse and freshened up the captain's and mate's quarters for the coming season. Then, as gently as she had come out of the lake the previous autumn, the steamer was winched back down the two twelve-by-twelve-inch ways on her custom-made cradle and brought to Valeport to begin another summer of routine runs.

Heaving planks that the Company sold, or shovelling the three to four tons of coal that the Apple consumed in one trip, made the work feel like slave labour. Docks at the ports-of-call supported mini-railways constructed of two-by-fours and flanged steel on which ran small push trucks. The pushing wasn't difficult – it was loading the trucks from the barge or vice versa that wore a crew down. Below deck, the fire-box of the steamer's boiler always roared for more fuel. And if he didn't drown in sweat in front of the open furnace, a fireman nearly suffocated from lack of air because the fire ate most of that up. Hot summer days had the Apple's crew praying for an early sunset or a storm to force them ashore to wait for calm. "At night the skipper and the mate had their bunks behind the pilot house on the top deck. Gatenby the cook and Hobbs the engineer lay on mattresses in the back cabin, while the rest of the crew just slept out on the deck. As for me," explained A. M. Pearson, on as deckhand one summer, "I slept down in a little hole in the front end of the boat, right up in the bow. It was all I could do to stretch myself out." However, if you were Captain Huggins's son, the day's work might never end. One night Cyril bunked with his father in the top bunk of the skipper's cabin. Not long after the light went out Cyril hopped out of bed. With a determined look on his face he marched down to the main deck, took a hammer, pounded a protruding deck spike back into the wood, and, still in his pajamas, climbed back to the cabin and into bed. It wasn't until the following morning when Captain Huggins told his astonished son about the night's activities that they realized Cyril had been sleep-walking.

The *Qu'Appelle* fostered crewmen from homesteads and farms that dotted all of Last Mountain Valley; most of those lake veterans felt that life aboard the Apple was the best. Work never ceased from May to November, but the company provided anything a man needed. Food on board was no exception. A roast of beef, potatoes, and gravy were not unusual; vegetables always dressed the plates, and lean bacon constituted the basis of many meals. If the boat's crew stayed at Arlington Beach to build a dock, or worked late hours to unload needed lumber at Glen Harbour, nearby residents faithfully offered fresh eggs and bread in return. Occasionally the hospitality of the feast was returned. A resident of Imperial recalls dining aboard the *Qu'Appelle* one evening. After the savory fish meal, Gatenby answered the compliments by cleaning off a tin plate and passing it around for contributions. "Fish were unbelievably plentiful. Harold could throw a little bit of a net overboard any time and get plenty of fish for a meal," claimed one-time *Qu'Appelle* fireman Bert Elderton. "And we loved fish the way Harold cooked it. I've seen the fish so thick when we docked at the Big Arm in spawning time that we could wade into the water and catch them with coal shovels and pitchforks!"

Sailing on the *Qu'Appelle* and working that life seemed the best of all possible worlds. Fresh breezes waited just outside the steamer wall in the morning and by six o'clock the smell of bacon and coffee coaxed each man out of the bunk. The skipper called down the speaking tube to bring the pressure up to a hundred and ten pounds, and the coarse scrape of a shovel scooping coal put everyone into motion. By seven the Apple's tiny whistle, perched on one side of her smokestack, blew a departure signal, and the steamer pushed northwest up the channel from Valeport to the open lake. So many mornings like this glowed with blinding sunshine. In the early days before the Regina Beach resort was built, Cain's Point would be black and white with pelicans and cormorants. Once she cleared the channel the steamer didn't require much attention, and the crew relaxed and watched the shoreline glide by. After the *Qu'Appelle* passed Billy Rowan's Ravine on the east side, the lake stretched open to the north.

"About thirty-five miles up the lake was the horizon. Beautiful day. We were going straight north. . . . And here was a steamer, up at the other end of the lake coming south!" Ron Gatenby knew that the *Qu'Appelle* was the only steamer on the lake, but "the smoke was pouring out. Then we saw the funnel, then the decks as she rose out of the horizon. . . . It was a mirage of us. She came right up into view and then disappeared altogether. I never saw anything like that before or since."

But Last Mountain Valley was changing. Hundreds of people now lived in the blocks of land once called Pearson land. Farming had developed beyond the subsistence stage, and settlement was now past history. The emphasis switched from scraping bare necessities from the ground to cashing in a profit from a year's production. The Pearson Company had been a colonizing enterprise, but with that phase now completed, Pearson had little left to offer.

The *Qu'Appelle* was showing her age too. Her continuing deficits became more onerous for the Company to carry, and her maintenance was a case of making do with whatever was available. After nearly a decade the company had moved away from primary lake transportation; the steamer, as the *Welcome,* the *Lady of the Lake* and then the *Qu'Appelle,* had evolved from a workhorse to a company frill. When she wasn't ferrying Sunday excursionists on the lake, she retrieved unsold supplies or measured changes in the lake's depth in anticipation of a prosperous new season that would never be. Each season and its activity offered less and less for the Apple to do, and her annual retirement to the Cowan's Beach ways occurred earlier each fall.

The disaster that nearly struck the steamboat and her crew on her final trip down in 1911 made the Apple's age and obsolescence all too obvious. That autumn the company had pulled the steamer off the normal run early, and relegated her to hauling leftover lumber home to Valeport to be shipped by rail instead of by water the following season. As deckhand this last trip, Ron Gatenby saw the death of an era and came within a deck board's breadth of disappearing along with it.

"The 16th of October, 1911, is a day I shall never forget. We'd gone up with the two barges and we started at Watertown emptying the yard there. We went to Arlington Beach next; then we did the same at the Big Arm and View Haven. After ten days we had the barges heavily loaded with seventy thousand feet of lumber.

"Coming down the Big Arm we had ideal weather. We'd had frost and the leaves had turned. We were out into the lake and a Nor'wester hit us. It turned cold and started to snow and the water got rough. A three-inch tow line connected the barges to the stern, and with the load we were shipping water half way up the boat. The heavy load behind wouldn't allow the stern of the boat to come up. Old Frank, a horse we had along to help haul the lumber to the boat, stood in a stall on the second barge;

we all watched as the water rose to Old Frank's belly. He'd snort and a leg would go over the edge and then he'd climb back up. And the skipper would call 'There goes Old Frank . . . Oh wait, he's okay!'

"Nearly everybody was sick. At one point I went below to the toilet in the crew's quarters. And there was the old skipper leaning over the bowl. I could see his stomach heaving. He turned 'round, looked at me in the door and said 'You son of a bitch, I'll kill you if you tell the boys.' He was really sick; you knew it was pretty bad when he was sick.

"Snowflurries kept reducing visibility. My brother Harold stood with a cleaver in his hand on the stern of the steamboat waiting instructions from the captain for him to cut that tow line. It was that close. But we didn't have to cut it; we got down the lake safely. . . . The next morning we were unloading this lumber at the dock when the old skipper came down; 'Look boys,' he says, 'I want to show you how close you came to getting it.' He stood on the dock and he lowered his foot toward the boat hull to just above the water line; he kicked the plank there just above that water line, and his foot went right through it. It was absolutely rotten. There was only a skin of several coats of paint to keep water out. And only he had known that. Nobody else did."

The Gatenby brothers never crewed the Apple again. That week the hull was patched with two-by-eight planks of oak and taken to her ways on the beach. For three days Old Frank and the crew laboured with the shore winch and a tow line that creaked "like a fiddle string" as the Apple came ashore. Once secured, the steamer was left for winter. The following spring Harold and Ron left for Alberta. And things would never be the same. A new cook came aboard the *Qu'Appelle,* but he had worked the merchant marine and he made pie crust half an inch thick and tough as leather.

Captain Huggins, twenty-year veteran of inland lakes, worked fewer runs on the *Qu'Appelle,* and spent more time fishing off Imperial Beach dock and telling stories of the good old days. When he did skipper the Pearson steamer, he came along more as an ornament. In tough spots like channel navigation and night wheeling, the younger eyes of son Cyril proved more accurate and reliable. In two years Captain W. C. Huggins would retire; not too long afterwards he was dead.

Though Regina had grown in a decade from a whistle-stop on the CPR to an incorporated city of thirty thousand, in the summer of 1912 its prosperity seemed to be slowing. William Pearson had lived up to his commitment and had filled Last Mountain Valley with citizens for the young province of Saskatchewan. The government now controlled the sale of the remaining vacant sections, and Pearson, unless he felt the urge for a pleasure trip to the Valley, remained in Winnipeg. The six-foot-six speculator who had invested all his energy and personal earnings in the future of Long Lake and her surrounding watershed, rarely appeared aboard the *Qu'Appelle*. Severe-looking and ominous as president and manager, it had nevertheless been his custom to take a drink of whisky and smoke his pipe with the rest of the crew. A great organizer, a pioneer salesman, and a self-made businessman, Pearson still read avidly and socialized with his employees. But as prosperity disappeared so did Pearson.

Valeport never did boom. The ties and steel that Pearson envisaged linking his valley enterprise with the rest of the world by-passed him. By 1912 railways paralleled both shore lines of Long Lake, making the *Qu'Appelle* obsolete. Another line built on an embankment of rocks and earth literally severed the lake, the boat channel, and the water communication line of the Pearson operation. Not only did this rail line cut off navigation on the north side of the lake from the south, but it isolated the *Qu'Appelle* from its wooden barge, the *Ruby*, and the dredge.

Economic recession settled on the prairies. Even the forces of nature seemed to conspire to deepen the gloom. On June 30 that same summer of 1912, the *Qu'Appelle* and her crew at Valeport sat moored in a kind of resigned inactivity. The wind rose in a low grey sky when the crew spotted a "huge black funnel" swirling in the southwest. Though it did not touch the lake or its valley, the cyclone ripped into Regina; it was the finishing touch that conclusively ended the boom. The Apple was a front row seat to the path of destruction that the twister made into the capital; the steamer and her lake escaped without a scratch, but their turn would come later that season.

Docked at Valeport, the *Qu'Appelle* lay waiting for a crew to winter her on the beach. Cyril Huggins, the mate, was the sole crewman living aboard, with only the galley wood stove for heat and a stray cat to share his potato rations. "Ice was about four inches thick up the lake when that storm blew in. The wind and waves broke the ice up and pushed a huge chunk of ice down the channel and punched a plank right out of the steamer's side. So she sank at the dock side." The *Qu'Appelle* underwent another patch job; her hull was pumped out, the gaping hole temporarily plugged, and straw placed all around her as she froze into the November ice. In the spring of 1913 the Apple was jacked up between a scow and the dock while her crew filled in this latest wound, but with each puncture the boat grew weaker and less able to compete against the elemental forces of Last Mountain Lake.

Throughout 1913, a sagging economy so reduced the *Qu'Appelle's* excursion business that the company all but abandoned her. In September of that dismal 1913 season, the Apple, plagued by engine breakdowns in the Big Arm, was forced to return to Valeport minus another vital organ – the Company's second pride, the ninety-by-twenty-foot steel barge, which had to be abandoned. The Apple limped home to Valeport never to return to the barge, which soon after was sunk by local farmers who wanted a permanent fishing wharf*.

If the Apple ran at all in the 1914 season, the squeak of her whistle and the puffs of coal smoke were hardly noticed. Just as the *Qu'Appelle* had come to Long Lake a decade earlier, so a new competitor arrived, on the back of a CPR flatcar from Regina. The *Maearta*, some suggest, was the product of a compromise between owner Walter Corbeau's alcoholic vice and his parish priest's demand for penance. Whatever the reason, citizens of Regina woke one morning in 1914 to discover a Catholic church half torn away and Corbeau's forty-foot launch inside. Constructed inside the church and then transported by railway to Last Mountain Lake, the *Maearta* and her gas-fueled engine terminated the *Qu'Appelle's* reign over the lake waters. A luxury boat from bow to stern, the *Maearta* displayed teakwood decks, spacious cabins, glassed-in wheelhouse, stove and toilet facilities aboard, and all the conveniences overnight cruising demanded.

The emergence of this new competitor virtually spelled the end for the *Qu'Appelle*, but if this had not been sufficient, the final blow to the Apple's career came on the fourth of August, as Canada suddenly found herself at war, and all concerns were forgotten save one.

As men enlisted, everything stopped dead, including the company and the *Qu'Appelle*. "During the War the boat had the side cut out of her," recalled A. M. Pearson, who himself went overseas in 1915. "The engine and boiler were taken out, hauled away, put on the railway for Vancouver, and sold to a Japanese outfit. The body of the steamboat sat up on the ways there at Cowan's Beach near Silton. And that's the last I saw of her . . ."

Some valley residents dashed off to join the cause; others took part at home. The Great War absorbed everyone. Women young and old knitted socks for soldiers; children learned about patriotism; the Red Cross took blood; and people supported the effort with fund-raising bees. Meanwhile teenagers and children, though they heard about catastrophic events over the ocean, continued to play and grow up around the lake. Young people still found time to be carefree. The summer still offered a baseball game or a brass band concert. The war limited many pleasures, but Long Lake remained a playground to the young. The beaches were still the best and so was the swimming. New gasoline-powered boats occasionally cruised the lake, boats like the Plaxton's *Edith*, the new

---

*Unlike most other Pearson landmarks around the lake, which faded quickly and irrevocably, the steel barge would live a second life. George P. Plaxton, hero of the 1904 Lumsden flood, used the barge to build a dance pavilion for the Roaring Twenties.

Maearta, and George Bedard's boat the *Empress.* The old run-down Apple, rotting over on Cowan's Beach, still attracted some – the ship's log lay open in the pilothouse for a boy's imagination, and what was left of the lounge and galley provided an ideal place for bathers to change. But beyond this, there was scarcely an intimation of glamour.

"Armistice night they just fired it." That year, eleven-year-old Eva Elliot had been sworn in as assistant post mistress; with the war in its fourth year, everyone had learned to take on unexpected responsibilities at Regina Beach. The eleventh night in November, Long Lake was still free of ice when news of peace came across the wire. The air was cold and brisk but the warmth of knowing that friends and relatives would soon return home stole the chill away from the night.

"It was just after supper." Eva recalled the excitement the air held that night. In the mood for celebration, a dozen or fifteen teenagers boarded the *Empress* with George Bedard at the wheel. "I went along with the party. We just got on the *Empress* and went over to Cowan's Beach to make a bonfire out of the old steamboat. The torches went to it and it burned up while we jigged around the rocks. It was a huge bonfire and really was put on for the benefit of people across the lake back at Regina Beach to see.

"Then we came back to Regina Beach and whooped around all night on the knoll in town. Then our parents joined in on the party. Somebody's underwear was taken off the line and stuffed . . . then this effigy [of the Kaiser], hung on rope between two poles, was carried around and burned on the hill. . . ."

Patriotic songs echoed down Long Lake, while the full eighty-foot hull of the *Qu'Appelle* was engulfed in flames. Her proud pilothouse and masts crumbled into the heart of the fire and her keel and rib timbers, oiled for protection and highly inflammable, burned the reflection of a fiery skeleton onto the lake. Embers of the steamer lay glowing as the last chorus of God Save the King faded away at Regina Beach, and by morning she was gone. The pride of a Company, the excursion queen of American landseekers, the Sunday amusement centre of Last Mountain Lake, and luxury steamer of William Pearson's dream-come-true, the Apple lay in her shore berth, a pile of blackened charcoal on the land and lake she had pioneered.

CHAPTER SEVEN

J. K. Cornwall and his N.T.C.

Sodbusters, tradesmen, and city streets were no longer foreign to the heart of the Canadian prairie. Miners continued to root out the seams of coal from riverbank shafts in the prairie southwest; plains fishermen harvested enormous catches from the Manitoba lakes; a bumper crop of millers ground to flour the gold from the fields of the Palliser Plains; industrialism, transplanted from the south and east, propagated itself from city to town to rural municipality all along that backbone of the prairie, the Saskatchewan River; and timber from the prairie north was cut and spiked into buildings, throughout the Dominion. And yet, even at the turn of the century, when the core of the prairies hummed with the activity of settlement and development, the far northwestern prairie fringe, equally fertile and rich, remained substantially untouched.

A hundred miles north of Edmonton, seed planting and booming industrialism were non-existent – the Klondike shone more brightly than anything the Lower Athabasca River or its surrounding Swan Hills could offer. The river was a means to an end, and the riverbanks only a stop-over on the route to Yukon gold. Typical was Athabasca Landing in the spring of 1898. Just another Hudson's Bay Company settlement, little more than a clearing in the spruce bush, the Landing consisted of a cluster of low-lying log buildings – the Company post, Company warehouses for supplies (freighted in during the winter for spring distribution on scows into the far North), the seat of the Anglican diocese, and a church school – hardly a beachhead of civilization. But that spring, like the previous two, gold fever, plus the annual flurry of Company scow and boat-building attracted an inrush of builders and carpenters and overlanders by the hundreds to the sloping sandy riverbanks at Athabasca Landing.

With urgent speed the great flotilla of barges and flat-bottomed scows took shape, in readiness for launching. With high water, the rivermen dragged the boats from their innumerable construction sheds to the river bank, loaded them with tons of staples and other supplies, and began poling them downstream, northeast on their 250-mile journey across two major rapids and into Fort McMurray. Meanwhile, York boatmen for the Company launched their craft and began tracking upriver, northwest toward depots along the Lesser Slave River, Lesser Slave Lake, and the distant areas of Peace River country, nearly three hundred miles away. Amid the barges and York boats, Klondike-bound gold seekers in packed canoes dodged the islands of floating Hudson's Bay Company provisions. Also fighting the Athabasca's current upriver were two young employees of the Alberta Railway and Coal Company in a gold-digging vessel of their own.

"My partner and I had bought a little steamer at Edmonton from butcher John Gaynor; it was a scow boat that had packed and carried groceries for the gold miners on the Saskatchewan River. We bought the *Daisy Bell* intending to run a passenger line from Athabasca Landing upriver to Lesser Slave Lake," remarked James Wallwork, who claimed that "millionaire ideas were free for everyone" during the Klondike rush. But if the passenger service idea was free, the overland transport of the 40-foot, 5,000-pound boat from Edmonton to Athabasca Landing was not; she had to be totally dismantled, carried the 100 miles to the Landing in pieces, and reassembled. For Wallwork, "the million" would be a long time coming. "The river was too low; we couldn't get up the Lesser Slave River. . . . It took us four or five days to go up four or five miles of the rapids. . . . Well, then I lost my partner . . . That trip up we were carrying a party of three; they had two canoes and they loaded their stuff finally from the steamer into the canoes. They were three men and two canoes; so they asked my partner Charlie Roberts to go along with them to the Klondike. . . . And off they went, my partner, another fellow, [W. F.] Bredin, and J. K. Cornwall. . . ."

Broader than his squared shoulders, his casual grin and the brim of his high-peaked fedora, James Kennedy Cornwall's idealism and imagination were directed inevitably to the Northwest. His trek to this frontier was just another in a string of adventures he had woven into his twenty-nine years. Born two years after Confederation, Cornwall found little attraction at his home in the East; neither his Scottish-Irish parents nor the Brantford, Ontario, farm kept him long. By age fourteen, he had run off to the United States; in Buffalo he sold newspapers on the streets, and in Boston he discovered the sea and her sailing ships. He crossed the Atlantic three times as a stowaway, toured Europe on foot, followed the route of the Trans-Siberian Railway through Russia, and then returned to North America to ship inland on the Great Lakes where he won first mate's papers. What his travels and travelling acquaintances didn't teach him, Cornwall read in books. Ohio riverboats provided him with work in the mid-West and then railroad construction marshalled him to the frontier and a new curiosity. In the winter of 1893, Cornwall came north "because," he explained, "I asked a man that year, where I could go and keep out of debt. . . . I was 24 years old when I tramped into Edmonton from Montana with a pack on my back, on my way to the North country."

The ephemeral gold of the Klondike held Cornwall momentarily, but the land, the rivers, and the wildlife of the north prairie fringe proved a stronger attraction. There was more to the north than just the glitter of Yukon gold, and at the turn of the century Jim Cornwall, with his bright bandana and broad-brimmed frontier hat – trademarks of his simple informality – was back from the gold fields piloting boat loads of gold rustlers through Grand Rapids on the lower Athabasca River at twenty-five dollars a trip.

"I got my start as a trapper killing bears north of Edmonton," recalled Cornwall. "You see, I had a rifle but no money to buy traps in starting into the North. So I took to shooting bears. I suppose I killed two hundred that winter and the hides were worth money. I lived with the Indians then and for several years. . . . they taught me their language and ways . . . . It was the basis of my success. . . . They used to entrust their furs to me to bring out of the North. I could sell them for the Indians and received a commission for my work. Then I began to carry back with me goods to trade. I became a free trader and free trapper. . . ."

Cornwall formed a partnership with his two ex-Klondike mates, W.F. Bredin and Charlie Roberts, in direct and open competition with the Hudson's Bay Company. The independent "Bredin & Cornwall Traders" introduced night travel to the trading trails, more frequent service on shorter circuits, and a more personalized approach to its customers; its practices and its success undermined the Hudson's Bay Company's two-and-one-half-century monopoly on trade in the territory. And his string of posts across the Athabasca Valley and into the Peace River country gave Jim Cornwall a reputation for honest trading and friendliness, and a faith in the land, its resources, and its people.

The more Cornwall saw of the North, the stronger became his love for the great wild land, and his determination to serve it as best he could. In 1905, as the Dominion of Canada reached out to incorporate much of the Northwest Territories as the province of Alberta, Cornwall was impressed by the political under-representation the area – the Athabasca and Peace River districts comprised two-thirds of the province, but were to send only two representatives to the 39-seat Legislature. This indicated to Cornwall where he could serve most effectively. "I saw the country's future, and knew I could do more for it down at the capital than on the trail".

157

And so Cornwall abandoned his traplines, sold his trading post to Revillon Frères of Paris, printed up campaign posters in Cree and English, and ran for the Peace River-Athabasca seat in the Alberta House. Elected, "Peace River Jim", as he became known, found himself representing a constituency nearly void of constituents. And though the formality of the Legislature was foreign to him, he saw his purpose clearly. "Every man wants to leave something of himself behind in this world," he declared. "I wanted to leave a name connected with opening up this country." And not the least among the ways this "Apostle of the North" would leave a major impression was through the leadership of his fledgling steamship line, the Northern Transportation Company.

"For the first steamboat, they rolled the boiler all the way from Edmonton to Athabasca Landing." For 16-year old Raynor Whitely, whose family had moved up to the Landing from Namao at the turn of the century, that spring of 1905 was a thrill a minute. "The boiler was supposed to be shipped in mid-winter with teams over the snow. Due to factory hold-ups, it didn't arrive in Edmonton until the snow was gone. It was eleven feet long and eleven feet six inches high, and weighed eleven tons, so they built a frame 'round it and covered it with planks, hauled it with six horses and moved it just like a big land roller. . . . Everybody thought it was impossible to get it those one hundred miles. . . . Lighter loads kept passing it on the way, so every day in Athabasca we knew where the boiler was. . . . The only hold-up was when they'd run over a large stone and break the planking; they'd stop and repair the plank and feed the horses. . . . Then they rolled it right down the main street of Athabasca to the hotel and turned toward the building site for the steamboat. And when they turned, they had to cross a little bridge. One of the horses was crowded over the edge of the bridge and fell into the mud and water, and the boiler tipped over on top of the horse. They got the ferry capstan and pulled the boiler off the horse. Well, he got up, crawled out, shook himself and didn't even have a scratch . . . a miracle. . . . When they finally got to the river bank, they jacked up the boiler, and the hull was built under it; the steamboat was put together 'round the boiler."

The *Midnight Sun* slid from the ways the following spring, almost lost in the annual shuffle of scow building at the Hudson's Bay warehouse; forty or fifty Company scows came together for every steamboat constructed. But the launching held sufficient significance to draw the entire Landing population, even if that was only twenty people. The Company's staff of four arrived in full colours; the Hislop & Nagel free-trading outfit attended; Raynor Whitely forced his family into town from their homestead at Perryvale for the occasion; Jim Wood, owner and builder of the boat, brought along the building crew of half a dozen, as well as his own christening speech. And overnight, a number of Indians from the lakes east of the Landing camped by the riverbank to pass judgement on the Landing's first fire canoe.

Almost as the *Midnight Sun* hit the waters of the Athabasca, MPP Jim Cornwall bought into the Landing's first steamboat venture and immediately became its president; if people responded to his favourable descriptions of the Athabasca-Peace River country, J. K. wanted the Landing to be ready to service their transportation needs. Cornwall envisioned an agricultural and immigration boom, launched from the Landing. Then nothing could impede the region's rapid growth.

The steamer *Midnight Sun* inaugurated the Northern Transportation Company steamship fleet; she would run passengers and freight from Mirror Landing where the Lesser Slave River joined the Athabasca, through Athabasca Landing, and downriver 150 miles to Grand Rapids. Within a year Jim Wood's crews also put the finishing touches on the *Northland Trader* for service on the Mackenzie River, and the *Northern Light* to ply the Lesser Slave River and eventually the Lesser Slave Lake. The whole plan, as one observer noted, was all part of Cornwall's "balanced imagination."

Jim Wood was a competent carpenter and had a sense of politics (he was Athabasca Landing's first mayor), but if the Northern Transportation Company were to run smoothly, it needed a general manager with river proficiency and a gambling instinct to boot. Upriver from the N.T.C. boatyard, a Bluenose skipper managed his own crew of ship carpenters in the construction of the Landing's fourth paddlewheeler, with which he intended to launch his own steamship venture. "Captain Charles Barber came out with his mother and two sisters," recalled an early Landing resident. "The captain was a pretty serious fellow and kept to himself most of the time; he lived on his steamboat . . . . But one July First a team of surveyors going north came through Athabasca. Some of the homesteaders nearby, as was the tradition, challenged the surveyors to a baseball game. The surveyors expected they could easily defeat the local people. Captain Barber thought otherwise and bet five hundred dollars on the homesteaders to win; he never left his boat to come to the game, but won himself the five hundred dollars just the same." Shortly afterwards he won the position of general manager of the N.T.C. as well; and with him Captain Barber brought his sternwheeler, the *Northland Sun*, his expertise, and his wireless telegraphy experiments. "Betting Barber" was the first to pilot a steamer across the rapids between Mirror Landing on the Athabasca River to Saulteau Landing on the Lesser Slave River; by the spring of 1907, Barber and the sidewheeler *Northern Light* had carried the Northern Transportation Company to Alberta's largest lake, the Lesser Slave. The N.T.C. had the command of the territory – all it needed was the attention of the public.

That was the next task. In 1908 Cornwall co-sponsored a promotional committee report with the Edmonton Board of Trade, that detailed modes of travel, distances in miles, passenger tariffs, freight tariffs, and time tables from Edmonton to a string of destinations across two thousand miles of territory north of Edmonton, all seemingly tamed by the N.T.C. The reports encouraged the hunter, prospector, trader, trapper, merchant, and eager settler to discover the North and its "delightful and invigorating climate, equal, if not superior to anything that India, South Africa, Australia or South America has to offer." The paddles of the N.T.C. were synonymous with Jim Cornwall, fair play, Northland hospitality, a disappearing frontier, and the reshaping of the lives of his constituents in budding communities like Sawridge, Lesser Slave Lake Settlement, and Athabasca Landing.

"They'd blow the whistle down the river about ten miles and everybody'd hear it. She'd be chuggin' away makin' about three miles an hour. Finally, she'd stick her nose around the last bend and she'd be half an hour gettin' into the Landing, plenty of time to get down to the dock," smiled Raynor Whitely. The climax of the week was the *Midnight Sun's* arrival; Whitely could confidently stride aboard because he knew the cook and Charlie Bunn knew him, and there was always fresh pie and coffee for a friend of the *Sun's* cook. "She'd tie up and they'd unload furs and start loadin' supplies for the way back. She didn't stay very long at the dock. . . . Everybody was interested in who'd be on the boat. . . . When the passengers came off there were always a few from out of the North country. . . . There'd be writers who'd taken a trip aboard to make notes on the North and to take in the posts . . . and there were always old-timers to talk to about the trips and weather along the way. . . . Lots of women missionaries went on those trips down North to the Roman Catholic and Anglican missions. . . . And there'd be surveyors. . . ."

"We were part of a federal survey party from Ottawa, laying out Indian Reserves because of the impending encroachment of agricultural settlement in 1908." In pursuit of a law career at St. John's College in Winnipeg, J. Fortescue McKay had taken summer employment as a lead chainman cutting bush, running lines, placing pins and monuments each half mile, and labelling land for future cultivation. Accompanied by his survey partners, eighteen-year-old "Forty" travelled by a wagon loaded with stoves, tents, blankets, food, and survey equipment from Edmonton toward the shack town of Athabasca Landing.

Before leaving Edmonton the survey team had learned that the *North-land Sun* departed Athabasca Landing each Saturday and Wednesday at 7:30 P.M. "We arrived on a Friday evening expecting to sail on Saturday, at Athabasca Landing," McKay related. "We soon found ourselves gazing with a certain amount of admiration at an archway where we read the following inscription: 'Of all inventions, that of printing excepted, those which contributed to the cause of transportation have done the most in the promotion of civilization. This is the Gateway to the Northern Transportation Company's shipping yards.' So we pictured ourselves travelling up the river in luxuriously appointed steamers. . . . To our consternation, sailing was postponed till the following Wednesday on account of some trouble re: hands on the boat plying on Lesser Slave Lake. . . . Twenty-five other passengers were disappointed . . . so the Company received its share of attention, inasmuch as a hearty discussion and expression of various opinions too pointed to be recounted constitutes attention. . . . Soon realizing that they were not masters of the situation . . . the passengers resignedly went in search of amusement. . . .

"Wednesday, we were aboard well before 7:30, all eager for the journey. All hands were on deck. Steam was up in anticipation of a start the moment the passenger stage from Edmonton arrived with the Captain [E. B. Haight, formerly of the Hudson's Bay Company's *Saskatchewan*] who, knowing Athabasca Landing better than we did, had gone to Edmonton the previous Saturday to enjoy the bright lights. And now he was late. When he did arrive, he announced that we would not sail till 5:00 A.M. the next morning. As ten more passengers had arrived with him, and some of these for reasons of state *had* to have staterooms, some of us smaller fry were dispossessed. And by this time the rooms we had vacated at the only hotel were occupied by other arrivals. . . . So we slept on the upper deck with nothing above us but the haze of the midnight sun and nothing beneath us but the hard deck of the *Northland Sun*.

"Shortly after midnight, the stokers began to get up steam again; cinders fell from the smokestack to our blankets. We too got up and walked the decks till dawn. . . . Wonder of wonders, the good ship *Northland Sun* weighed anchor at five o'clock and after much puffing of smoke, blowing of whistles, and ringing of bells, the gangplank was lifted. Easing her bow into the current, she began to nose her way up the river. We who of necessity were early on deck saw the sun rise above the wooded banks and the morning mists clear away. And soon a bend of the river hid the little town. Nothing remained to disturb the silence of the centuries but the echo of our engine throb and a widening swell that spread to either shore and lapped the beaches after we had gone. . . ."

Like his enterprising predecessors of the previous century – Norman

Kittson of the Red River Transportation Company and Alexander Galt with his North Western Coal and Navigation Company – Jim Cornwall realized the value of a railway system as part of his grand plan. Though his steamship line was a profitable element of an efficient transportation network into the frontier, J. K. campaigned for a rail link between Edmonton and his N.T.C. docks. He anticipated that his Athabasca Railway Company could break the Athabasca-Peace River District wide open to transport, trade, and immigration. For three years his push for support and funds fell on deaf ears and empty pockets. In 1908 he sold his rail interests to an eastern syndicate, but undaunted, he persisted in his apostolic philosophy:

> *I believe that the Northland is the richest, undeveloped extent of country in North America. . . .*
>
> *that our 3,500 miles of natural waterways mean to the Northland what the St. Lawrence and Great Lakes do to the East. . . .*
>
> *that what is known as the Peace River country contains the largest and richest area of unoccupied land in the Dominion of Canada. . . .*
>
> *that more hours of light and sunshine are experienced here than in any other grain-growing country in the British Empire. . . .*
>
> *that the climate and soil will sustain and are capable of the same development as Manitoba, Saskatchewan and southern Alberta. . . .*
>
> *that with all these advantages, unless men, money and railroads are forthcoming, they are of little value. . . .*
>
> *that it is the solemn duty of every Northland man, irrespective of creed or colour, to keep before the public the virtues and requirements of the country. . . .*
>
> *and that with faith, hope, and time, and lots of good, well directed, hard work, the Northland will come into its day and generation.*

A junket! Bring the Athabasca-Peace River District to the attention of the outside world. In the winter of 1909, Cornwall and Herbert Vanderhoof, editor of the CPR's *Canada West* magazine, launched the greatest promotional stunt the northern prairie had ever seen. J. K. sent invitations to writers and scientists across North America to join a free expedition into the Northland, which, MPP Cornwall said, was aching to be explored and tamed. Owning no land in the territory, expecting no cash return for his efforts, confident that the country would present itself well enough to earn glowing tributes in journal and newspaper reports, Peace River Jim organized, financed, and attracted a score of Canadian and American adventurers to a see-for-yourself party into the Prairies' Northland fringe.

By the spring of 1910, Cornwall had assembled an impressive entourage of tourists. The Grand Hotel, a handful of private stores, scattered residences, the white-washed walls of the Northern Transportation Company offices, and the plain-faced *Northland Sun* breathing an easy stream of wood-smoke over Athabasca Landing, greeted the eager press party that included some of the most eminent correspondents, agronomists, naturalists, and academics in North America.

The party set sail in July, 1910, and just as Cornwall and Vanderhoof had hoped, the response was ecstatic. "The *Northland Sun,* commanded by Captain Barber ... is a modern well fitted up and complete steamboat," reported Leroy Kelly, one of the journalists on board. "She is a stern-wheeler, 130 feet long by 25 feet beam, lighted by electricity, and with berths for 30 to 40 passengers. The meals served on board are well cooked and well-served, and the steamer is as modern a craft in every way as could be desired." Cornwall had calculated the necessary accommodation, transportation, and food requirements of the four-week junket precisely, and as he expected, the Athabasca-Peace River District, ripe for settlement, did the rest. "Some of the members of the party were inclined to be disgruntled, for they said that they had expected to have to rough it, and here they were getting as much comfort as though they were travelling on a steamer down the Atlantic coast. . . .

"But the sturdy engine of the *Northland Sun* chuckled to itself and whirled cheerily along, past ... mighty stretches of timber, aboriginal moose tracks and beautifully lined dugouts. Both banks of the Athabasca are very heavily timbered with spruce and poplar and birch. . . . When these heights are cleared off there will be along the Athabasca some of the richest farms in Alberta ... [and] back from the banks there are many open spaces, ready for homestead, covered with thick and strong hay, grown on the rich black soil; when there is a demand for pulp wood, the banks of the river will be cleared as if by magic, and farms will dot its shores. . . ."

J. K. Cornwall and *Everybody's Magazine* editor Robert Dunn discussed the settler's chances of ultimate triumph over the Hudson's Bay Company's Northland sovereignty. Dunn's inquisitive attitude about the tour was exactly what Cornwall had hoped for. "No. This time the Company will lose. It knows it," Cornwall stated. "Privately it acknowledges that it will lose. . . . The trapper and the gold-seeker are incidents. The farmer is permanent."

Conversations like this went to syndicated print across the United States and parts of Canada; this was the only repayment Cornwall expected from the junket. He had put his reputation and a good deal of his life savings on the line. If he could keep his guests entertained and excited by the parade of passing riverbank scenery, perhaps their published comments would attract others and open up the Northwest he loved. And entertained they were; as the steamboat drew near bear country, warlike preparations were underway on board. One passenger cleaned his large .405, another polished his small rifle, and a third sighted down the barrel of his Savage. The skipper, the engineer, the purser, J. K., and three deckhands brandished their revolvers, .30-30 carbines, .303's, and .22 rifles. "The deck looked like a pirate ship ready to spring a surprise on some unsuspecting merchantman," remarked Kelly. "In every corner stood the guns and rifles, in every attitude of readiness the hunters sat or stood, while the deck hands placed the pike-pole handy and the pilot steered with his rifle leaning against the wheel. . . ."

"In our first afternoon out from the Landing, I heard shouts and hurrying on the deck above, and soon the popping of rifles. 'What's up?' blurted out startled naturalist Benjamin Miller. 'Oh, just a bear,' the captain said. 'Lots of them all along here. Engineer killed one yesterday, just above the Landing. Got his hide down below.' He hardly turned to see the result of this particular bear chase. The bear was more than a quarter of a mile away, running up the steep broken country . . . no-one hit him. In the summer time these bears come down to the river to feed on the saskatoons and red willow berries, which are especially abundant on the large islands in the river. When approaching one of these islands, it is the custom of the steamboat men to blow the whistle, and then pot the bears as they swim out. This doesn't sound a very sporting proposition, but as actually seen it certainly is curiously interesting. . . . In the mercy of Divine Providence, our general and somewhat careless rifle fire killed no bears that day." And, fortunately for them, no travellers either.

Two thousand miles later, the weary troupe of scientists and writers returned to Edmonton under Jim Cornwall's able wing; he had shown them fields begging for cultivation, game as dense as the forest timber, the Peace River country's accessibility, a temperate climate, and a good time. And, to a man, the press party believed that Peace River Jim's country held the greatest prospect as "a granary of the empire in Canada," as "a sporting country," as "a new home of the plough, edging its way north," and as part of "a new civilization." As their composed copy came to print, the spotlight of immigration and boom swung to the Athabasca and Peace River territories.

Theodore Basarab's Austrian birthplace seemed a lifetime away as the stage coach to Athabasca Landing bounced him and his young wife toward their rendezvous with the steamer for Peace River Country and 160 acres of Alberta homestead. The New York City newspaper advertisements had pictured a Garden of Eden in the Northwest; but as Basarab saw it, the artists had forgotten to sketch in the mosquitoes, rains, and mud that plagued them en route to paradise. At twenty-four, a summer after the Cornwall publicity tour, Basarab had tired of his track-laying job in a Pennsylvania coal mine, and of the abundance of guns and disorder in America; with the ad in his hands, on an impulse, he had left his brother George, then at work in Henry Ford's new-born automobile assembly lines, for the fertile lands along Lesser Slave Lake and a farm life about which he knew nothing.

"They felt ridiculous," his daughter Nettie recalled. "Most of the other immigrants came dressed for the country, with packsacks and rugged clothing. But he did not come prepared; he was dressed in a suit, his oxfords – city clothes – and his little Panama straw hat.... And my mother, with her parasol and one of those big hats with ostrich feathers . . . completely out of place!"

The thrill of waterways and paddlewheelers had passed with Basarab's younger days in Appalachia; he had travelled aboard American steamers along inland branches of the Ohio River. But when the familiar clouds of grey woodsmoke and the hiss of steam escaping from the pressured engines welcomed him at Athabasca Landing so many miles from civilization, his love of river steamers was rekindled. Up the Athabasca from the Landing the journey went smoothly. But after the portage to Saulteau Landing and the transfer to the smaller steamer *Slave River,* things became cramped, "especially for the many European immigrants," continued Nettie Basarab. "They sat down everywhere on the boat looking for room; and there they ate the lunches they had packed with them – black bread and sausage. There were large families and it was difficult travelling so far with small children. Cabins cost extra, and there weren't enough cabins for all the people packed on the boat. It was a rough trip if you didn't have money."

Hopeful that his 3,000-mile journey had in fact delivered him to the promised land of the New York newspaper advertisement, Basarab removed his Panama and stepped off the steamer at the Lesser Slave Lake Settlement. He immediately filed on a homestead, and travelled with his wife to the land on which he hoped to plant their first season's produce. Theodore arrived at the location of his 160-acre homestead to discover it submerged in flood waters shoulder deep. "That was the sad part. He expected a lot better than what he walked into. And my mother often said that if they had had the money they'd have gone back immediately.... But they relocated on a homestead at High Prairie and struggled to make a living." And they succeeded; ultimately, the Basarab farm survived them both.

The same spring that Theodore Basarab and hundreds of other foreign immigrants responded to Peace River publicity, workers at Athabasca

Landing were building new derricks and cables for the ferry joining the Edmonton stage with the Athabasca's northeast bank where the old Klondike Gold Trail began. The construction, designed to give steamboats greater freedom around the Landing, delayed the river-crossing by Archie Goodwin and several of his twelve children who were bound for Peace River country to escape poor farmlands and sad memories. The Landing was exciting and romantic to ten-year-old Alta, who imagined that the port was a city; stage coaches and freight wagons arrived, unloaded, loaded, and departed, and "the biggest event of all was the sternwheeler *Northland Echo* [the latest steamboat in Jim Cornwall's N.T.C. fleet] rounding a bend with a hoarse blast of her whistle, and nosing in to the bank to tie up."

"We left the Landing the First of September. It took seven days to make forty-five miles." Lea Goodwin shook his head. He recollected the carcasses of horses and oxen half sunk in the mud, the mosquitoes, horseflies, deer flies, bot flies, blackflies, the hoof rot and swamp fever. When the humidity of the muskeg eased at sunset, the frost along the Klondike Trail chilled a night's sleep at places marked with crude signs: Hell's Hole, Killer Muskeg, Dead Horse Valley, and Devil's Canyon. "And that was the only road; there was no other road to the Peace River Country. After forty-five miles we stopped and built a stopping-place and put up hay down along the river. . . . In winter, everyday we served freighters; as many as fifty-three teams stopped at our place overnight . . . and in the summer the boats would run hauling freight and passengers and drop them off for the trail. . . . Those steamers were well built. If you couldn't see them, and you didn't hear the puff of the boiler, you'd hear the paddles pounding; we could hear that paddlewheel up on the road, two miles away.

"One time, my brother came down from Lesser Slave Lake to take my aunt and cousin back up; he came down on the boat and got off at our place near Tomato Creek. He told the boat crew that he'd be back when they came back upriver. But they were late coming back. It was really dark that night when we heard the steamer comin', so we built a fire down on the riverbank, and he took a burning stock out of the fire and waved to the boat. That was exciting. . . . He flagged them with the fire and I'll never forget that big coarse whistle that answered as they pulled in . . . and they didn't have a single light.

"The steamboat crews were healthy, strong fellows, but not boozers; they'd never take a boat when they were drunk. Some deck hands used to go aboard half-shot, but they only handled freight. . . . They were a good-natured, happy bunch, and worked to beat the devil when they stopped to get wood; one would throw it down over the bank, the next would grab

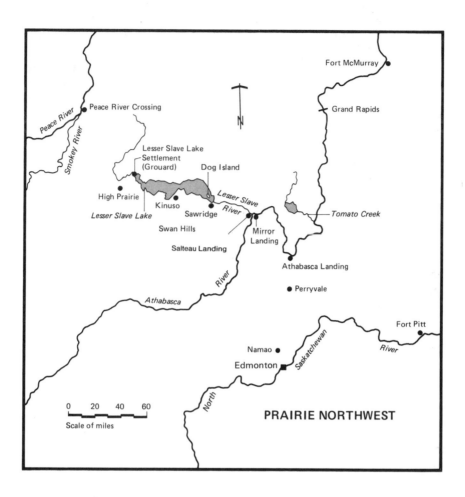

Fort McMurray

Peace River Crossing

Grand Rapids

Peace River

Smokey River

Lesser Slave Lake
Settlement
(Grouard)

Dog Island

High Prairie

Kinuso

Lesser Slave River

Lesser Slave Lake

Sawridge

Tomato Creek

Swan Hills

Mirror
Landing

Salteau Landing

River

Athabasca Landing

Athabasca

Perryvale

Fort Pitt

Namao

Saskatchewan

River

Edmonton

North

0   20   40   60

Scale of miles

PRAIRIE NORTHWEST

it and heave it onto the boat, 'til they got enough to last up to the next pile. . . . The fireman, stuffin' wood in the fire, he worked the hardest of anybody. . . . And one of the pilots was Joe," Lea's memory suddenly flashed. *Northland Echo* pilot Joseph Bird, son of Hudson's Bay Company Factor James Bird, came to Athabasca in that 1911 season; he was a huge, eagle-eyed man, part-Indian, whose skin was almost black. "Joe Bird really knew his work. His mind was always on the river for sandbars or rocks; he'd never tie the wheel down just to go and talk to somebody; his attention was always ahead. And if the water was high, he had to watch for driftwood or he'd bang into it at night, punch a hole in the boat and sink. . . ."

Another steamer on another night the following spring pounded her way through dangerous waters. On her second night out of her home of Southampton, England, on Sunday evening, April 14, 1912, the unsinkable White Star Line *Titanic* grazed an iceberg and tore open her steel hull. The largest, most luxurious steamship on the seas – 852 feet long, over 46,000 tons displacement, and carrying 2,223 persons aboard – sank, taking down 685 officers and crewmen and 832 passengers to their deaths.

"My trunk is at the bottom of the Atlantic! I was booked on the *Titanic* until a lady told my mother, 'There's a big boat goin' down. I wouldn't let Rennie go on a big boat like that. Get him cancelled from the passenger list,' she said." Rennie Hall, 19-year-old son of Joseph Hall, who had been working his way across the Canadian Prairies and north into Peace River country since 1909, finally booked on a smaller steamship out of Calais, but failed to retrieve his baggage from the *Titanic* before it set sail. Late in April Rennie Hall crossed to Canada in search of his father. His mother, two younger brothers, and his eleven-year-old sister Elizabeth booked passage on the *Empress of Ireland* to Quebec City in August 1912. And with steel then complete as far northwest as Athabasca Landing, the Halls migrated across Canada by train.

"Athabasca was all mud," described Elizabeth, who had been dressed in her best skirt, blouse, and bow-filled hat for the entire journey. The belongings they carried remained intact, but those packed in their trunks – china, furnishings, and a sewing machine – were smashed by the travel. "We stayed overnight at the hotel and when we were going from the hotel to the boat I got stuck in the mud. . . . But it was nice comin' upriver on the *Northland Echo.* . . . I watched on both sides to see the land; there were blueberries on the riverbank and bears swam in the water; they were never scared of the boat; they just waited for someone to throw bits of food. . . . I had a cabin where there were two bunks, but you couldn't sleep at night for the frogs croaking. . . .

"They had pursers on the boat and a big kitchen with a cooking stove where they cooked bacon, ham, and whitefish. . . . I was a little nervous to leave my mother, but I went into the engine room once and the fireman, Harold Haight, threatened to take my doll out of my hands and throw it in the furnace with the wood. . . . We had to get off at Mirror Landing and transfer to another steamboat at Saulteau Landing, the *Northern Light,* a double-decker that brought us upriver to the first stopping-place, Sawridge. . . . The boatmen were jolly and all got along. . . . Charlie Hutton worked on the boat with the cook and when he got drunk he saw snakes in the water and used to drop eggs overboard to feed them. . . . We arrived at Sawridge [later Slave Lake] on the seventh of September, 1912, and father and Rennie were there to meet us. . . . When I was comin' off the boat, I stepped onto the shore and fell head-over-heels over a wood pile. . . . I was the first white girl to stop and settle at Sawridge. . . ."

"People by the river and especially the natives ran to the boat when it came in," Rennie added; he and his father had already taken on a contract to cut cordwood at $1.25 per cord for the steamboats to help finance their winter provisions. "And they had the funniest mail box ever I've seen. It was a little old shack where they used to go and dump the mail on the floor, and everybody was supposed to run in and get his own mail. . . . In the summertime we used to take vegetables down to the riverbank and sell them on the boat – radishes, lettuce, cabbage, potatoes, and different things. . . ."

Sawridge became a bustling communications centre; the telegraph office buzzed with world news communiqués, Northland business transactions, N.T.C. and Hudson's Bay Company boat schedules, and countless other items of vital information. During one of his few slack periods, Sawridge's first telegraph operator, Charlie Schurter, a stout, transplanted Ontarian, rested on the steps of his station in the afternoon sun. The settler boom had come to that southeastern end of Lesser Slave Lake – boat and cart loads of immigrants – and Schurter recalled his own migration. A twenty-year-old runaway from Bruce County, Schurter had been sitting in a Regina barbershop chair one March day in 1909 when he overheard a fellow recruiting for construction of the Peace River telegraph line. Without a second thought Charlie joined the foreman on the train to Edmonton and Athabasca that afternoon, eager "for adventure, two bucks a day, and everything I found." When telegraph wires reached Sawridge en route to Peace River Crossing, Charlie had taken on the operator's job at the first telegraph office in Sawridge. For three years he had been the messenger of J. K. Cornwall's dream – the discovery, settlement, and cultivation of Peace River country – who had transmitted the news that endless lines of Europeans, Americans and Eastern Canadians were migrating en masse northwest toward Peace River Jim's country.

Among the thousands that he attracted to the Northwest was a maritime captain from Germany. Like the Indian trappers, the old Company York boatmen, carpenter Jim Wood, pilot Joseph Bird, and skipper Charles Barber, all of whom Cornwall had caught up in his enthusiasm for Peace River country, Captain Herman Nicklas was an expert in his trade. Nicklas had earned his master's papers on a windjammer running between the Prussian fatherland and its West African Cameroons colony. The survivor of a Valparaiso shipwreck, a South Seas mutiny, tropical malaria, and German autocracy, Captain Nicklas migrated to Canada and attempted homesteading with his wife near Melville, Saskatchewan.

"But to step down from captain of a ship to farmer on a homestead didn't work, and they proceeded to starve, so he moved to Edmonton in search of work," related a longtime friend, Julia L'Hirondelle. "And Captain Nicklas ran into Jim Cornwall, who explained that he needed captains at Lesser Slave Lake, people who knew navigation, captains who had papers to run the passenger steamers. So Cornwall said, 'You and I will homestead Dog Island [just off Sawridge] as partners.' And that's how Captain Nicklas became the skipper of the *Northern Light*."

Captain Nicklas stood out from the rest – his curly brown hair suggested Mediterranean ancestry, a trimmed moustache and goatee gave him the air of nobility, and his uniformed, sturdy build looked overpowering. Nicklas had his own peculiar temperament, which alternated unpredictably between hot and cold. On one occasion a *Northern Light* passenger returned aboard after a celebration at an Indian camp; he had "got so friendly with the Indians, in spite of the warning of Captain Nicklas, that he brought some of their cooties back to the boat," narrated a fellow-traveller. "One large grayback, the aristocracy of cooties, was said to have walked boldly across the Captain's belly in plain sight. The captain, being an excitable man, hopped out of bed and threw his mattress and hat overboard, to the accompaniment of all the sailor language he had learned on his trips around the world." The skipper argued frequently, including one time on a narrow gangplank with an angry deckhand, who promptly knocked the captain into the lake. Unruffled, "Captain Nicklas laid a charge against the hand. Normally, that act committed on the high seas meant a death sentence. Instead," smirked Charlie Schurter, "he was fined ten dollars." In contrast, the next minute Nicklas would bury his temper and socialize; the Nicklas homestead on Dog Island was often the scene of summer picnics and teas for the mainlanders.

Captain Nicklas shared the timber profits of Dog Island with J. K. Cornwall and helped initiate Lesser Slave Lake's fishing harvest of whitefish, goldeye, trout, pike, and pickerel. Yet the Captain was most at home at the helm of the fully loaded *Northern Light,* pivoting her from the wharfs of Saulteau Landing on her routine weekly run northwest as far as the town of Grouard (formerly Lesser Slave Lake Settlement, now newly renamed after Roman Catholic bishop Emile Grouard). After thirty miles of thrashing around hairpin river bends of the Lesser Slave River, the sidewheels of the *Light* met the eastern edge of the sixty-mile-long by fourteen-mile-wide Lesser Slave Lake, that Nicklas claimed would "often bare her teeth" in whitecaps.

"Captain Nicklas was right on the button," emphasized telegraph operator Schurter, who for three trips aboard the *Northern Light* took on the job of wiring the cabins and decks for electricity. "One trip Nicklas had a big cargo of telegraph wire and insulators, which was all dead weight. And they ran into a terrific storm about four miles past the island headin' west. He wanted to turn around and get back into the lee of the island, but they got caught in a sea trough; and being a sidewheeler, the steamer couldn't get out. . . . The deckhands and a survey crew aboard got hysterical; they figured she was going to sink and decided to take charge of the boat. They went up to the wheelhouse and claimed the Captain wasn't on to his job. The Captain, he got mad and said that it wasn't the first ship he'd sailed. He wouldn't be dictated to. . . . The only two that kept their heads were the two women aboard – the cook, Mrs. Nicklas, and a surveyor's wife. They kept a level head and didn't see any danger. . . . So the Captain had all the heavy stuff thrown off and then was able to get out of the sea trough and back to safety."

Shortly after the debarkation of immigrants and supplies at Sawridge, Nicklas piloted the *Northern Light* back out to the lake and into what was known as "the narrows", a channel five miles wide that ran the full length of Lesser Slave Lake. Only a few of the shoreline towns received doorstep service from the *Light* (and the Hudson's Bay Company steamer *Slave River*) because of unsuitable depths ashore for harbouring. Exceptions were made at Nine Mile Point, where a wooding-up spot coincidentally shared land with a stopping-place frequented by American whisky traders. Ironically, exception was made too for the alarmingly prevalent railway navvies aboard, and their steel and ties; railway depots on the south shore were creeping northwest, deeper into Peace River country, skirting steamboat shipping lanes. Thirty miles up the lake, Nicklas would reach for the *Light's* whistle cord and blast the spruce woods and south shoreline with her whistle. From a landing just north of the settlement of Kinuso, a row boat would appear, most often with J. C. Hunt, local merchant and settler, at the oars. A go-between for the district, Hunt picked up the mail and delivered butter, milk, and eggs for sale at Grouard. Occasionally, oarsman Hunt brought passengers to the *Northern Light.*

"Old Man Hunt took me down to the lake with him in a democrat to get the mail," reminisced Paul Sowan about his one and only trip on a lake steamer. It was summer, school was out, and the young Indian wished to see his friends at Grouard. By land the trip would take days; by canoe, he would have had to follow the shoreline all the way, but the steamboat went straight across. Mr. Hunt knew the captain, so he took me out in his row boat to meet the steamer quite a way from shore.... It was a big paddlewheeler.... We left at ten o'clock in the morning.... I was on the top deck and I could see all over; the lake was quiet ... and some fellow showed me how to play rummy. It was fun, even though I couldn't speak English.... The trip took only two hours...."

Folding lake water in waves ahead and thrashing it up on both sides, the *Northern Light* announced her arrival with three long whistle calls. Almost immediately the town would drop everything from prayer book to pool cue to meet the steamer. Recently established merchants anticipating supplies, farmers expecting seed, Company men from the Hudson's Bay warehouses waiting for provisions for Peace River posts, children ready to charade their pirate fantasies, and natives eager for an afternoon's wages unloading freight, all moved to the docks. A berth was readied to welcome the *Light* and her crew, as Nicklas piloted his steamer into the final port-of-call on his circuit.

Northern Transportation Company steamboats touched both ends of the Athabasca-Lesser Slave Lake system by 1912, and serviced everything in between; Jim Cornwall's exploration of the North and his casual advertisement of "North America's richest territory" had paid off. J. K. had taken his promotion to the Edmonton capital and his boats to the heart of Peace River country. Though telegraph lines and railway construction were outrunning the steamboats northwest toward Peace River Crossing, N.T.C. captains Barber, Haight, Bird, and Nicklas rarely slept nights through the summers of 1911 to 1914. In daylight and darkness, produce was freighted out and immigrants were shunted in: a Nebraska farmer who marvelled at Athabasca steamers because "all I had ever known was corn, beef, hogs, and talk of the Missouri River"; a petrified Illinois farmer's daughter, who was hypnotized by the steamboat's "ferris-wheel"; a curious traveller who spoke of a "shrouded" monster that "beat the muddy waters into froth" and woke the dead with "the raucous shriek of its siren"; and scores of Britons who compared the Slave River and Lake steamers favourably to the "tubs on the Thames." As Peace River Jim Cornwall had hoped, he left "a name connected with opening up this country," and as he had professed, agriculture had rooted on the northern prairie fringe because of the immigrant's drive to come, persistence to stay, and instinct to survive. "The farmer is permanent."

CHAPTER EIGHT

Dontianen Lives

Lawrence Mullin, for most of his sixty years, knew next to nothing about prairie steamboats. The *Northcote's* assault on Batoche in 1885 was an all-but-forgotten history lesson. Sternwheelers pounding the Saskatchewan River seemed a myth. Sand from barley fields filled Mullin's boots, not the clay of riverbanks where steamers had once come ashore. He had never experienced the feverish excitement that accompanied a steamboat docking. Lawrence Mullin, born ten years into the new century, cared little for the river or her steamboats. But his indifference would end very suddenly; the river and the boats would become part of him. A distant and almost magical steamboat would affect him and those around him like nothing else ever had. A stranger, a dream lost, and a dream found, were to involve him in the mystery of a steamboat builder's fascination with the Saskatchewan River.

If ever anyone believed in fate it is Lawrence Mullin; the way he looks back on his life, his encounter with a piece of history was inevitable. Shortly after his family moved to the Lake Valley district northwest of Moose Jaw in the late twenties, Moon, as everyone called him, heard an incredible story that would one day become an obsession with him and totally dominate his life. The curator of the community museum at Riverhurst showed him an odd-looking gear made by an eccentric Finlander named Tom Sukanen, who, unaided, was building a steamboat on his farm in the middle of the prairie, to steam down the Saskatchewan River away from the bad times that lived with everyone.

Not many knew of this strange Finn, and those who did usually regarded him as something of a joke. If Moon's own relatives didn't laugh, they certainly frowned at the man's waste of time, or else questioned the storyteller's sanity. But young men are often more receptive to fantastic stories, and years later, after World War II, when he again heard about this "madman Finn", Moon's interest was rekindled in the little-known "prairie mariner", the "lunatic shipbuilder", the "Finnish superman", the "crazy old Tom Sukanen" and his prairie steamboat that was never launched.

Shivering in the anonymous hold of a New York-bound immigrant carrier, Tomi Jaanus Alankola dreamed of a promised land, a refuge from the economic chaos of nineteenth-century Finland. Born on September 23, 1878, in Koronkyla (a tiny settlement in the province of Vassa in western Finland) Alankola had learned the only trade available to him, and now, aged twenty and on the shores of America, he hoped to earn his living through his finely tuned skills in the art of shipbuilding. However, he was arriving amid the hungry throngs of workers from innumerable lands, with whom he would have to struggle to earn a living; and so he pressed inland, into Ohio, Michigan, Minnesota, and Wisconsin, searching for work merely to survive. He tried homesteading and mining, among other pursuits. He married and fathered a son and three daughters.

Here the story takes its first twist.

In the autumn of 1911, after perhaps a decade of labouring, Tom Sukanen (the name he registered in America) suddenly picked up and left. With no money to speak of, a growing family to care for, no business instinct to send him off on a wild enterprise, and no visible reason for his impulse, Sukanen set out, on foot, in search of a brother who lived in Canada. He carried on his back the basic necessities for the trip, and nothing else. How he found his way through the wilderness of badlands, vacant plains, and parched prairie brush is undocumented and unexplained, but a Finnish sailor who could navigate the open sea was not to be daunted merely by unfamiliar terrain. What made a sea of plains any different from the Baltic?

Whether by instinct or by luck, six hundred miles after Sukanen left his Minnesota homestead he crossed the final rolling hills onto the Macrorie-Dunblane pastureland of central Saskatchewan. Near the tiny hamlet of Birsay (some seventy-five miles southwest of Saskatoon) he found people who knew his brother, Svante. Sukanen decided to stay; on October 23, 1911, he filed entry for a homestead comprising the northeast quarter of section 14, township 26, range 9, west of the third meridian, about a half-dozen miles west of Macrorie. To his neighbours, farmers like Vic Markkula, Herbert Fredeen, and W. A. Cahoon, Sukanen seemed just another immigrant farmer-settler who worked hard and made the most of each season.

His nephew, only a small boy at the time, heard Sukanen referred to as a "well-to-do" farmer. "I think he often worked out for his neighbours," suggested Elmer Sukanen, rather vague about all the facts surrounding his uncle's strange, almost completely forgotten story. "He used to go and help them stook and work on thrashing outfits. But he never visited us too much, partly because we lived ten miles apart; he was more of a loner."

Sukanen was also inventive, even creative, in the variety of gadgets he dreamed up and constructed, most of which benefitted no small number of the community's farming families. As Moon Mullin observed, "Tom made the first grain-thrashing machine, the first in the district . . . a power thrashing machine. He also made a sewing machine, so that women [of the area] could mend clothes . . . things that helped people. And then he showed a lot of people how to build homes for themselves when they first came. He was just a little different, more of a stand-out man than the average." Sukanen wasted nothing; during the mid-Depression, he knit himself a suit of clothes out of binder twine that "wore real well."

"Another time he had built a camera," continued Moon. "He went to visit a lady . . . to take her picture. The camera, I guess, burned magnesium. Tom arrived and he asked her to step in to the doorway, and of course she didn't know what was going on. . . . There was this terrible explosion . . . and Tom, he disappeared over the hill, his outfit in hand. But two weeks later he came back with this beautiful photograph to show her how that machine that he'd made worked. That was the way he was. He thought he could do these things, and he went ahead and did them."

"I can remember that bicycle, too," added Elmer Sukanen, "cause I used to fool around with it all the time. You didn't have to pedal it; you pulled it like a hand car. I was about eight or nine years old," continued Elmer. "I can remember his place, which resembled a silo built on a hillside with a staircase running through it and a mirrored periscope mounted on the top for looking around the countryside. And he had this car rigged up. He wouldn't start it because once he had the doggone thing in gear and he had a crank in front. He flipped it and it took off; damn near run him over. So next thing he went and rigged up a crank beside him so he could crank it from inside the car. That's how I remember him. And he had a violin he'd made and he played it, although I never heard him play."

By May of 1916 Tom Sukanen had received patent for his homestead, and by prairie (and wartime) standards, had succeeded in homesteading and farming – as a grain-grower, livestock raiser, and farm manager, he had amassed approximately nine thousand dollars, an enormous sum for those days. And still a wife and four children waited patiently a half thousand miles away on another homestead for Sukanen to return. In 1918, after nearly seven years with no communication to or from his family, Sukanen walked the same six hundred miles to Minnesota; he was full of a new spirit of triumph and news of the home he'd build for his family. On his return he found no-one on the homestead. His wife had died of influenza and his three daughters and one son had been scattered to the wind by local authorities into various foster homes. The boy was the only traceable member of his family; his name had been changed to John Forsythe. Sukanen gathered up his son and started home, only to be caught south of the Canada-United States border by the authorities. The boy was returned to the foster parents, but lived in expectation of another planned escape with his father. Authorities prevented John's second escape attempt and immediately threw the boy into a delinquent orphan home, and expelled his father from the United States.

The Crash of 1929 spread ruin throughout the prairies. Everywhere was chaos and collapse. With depression surrounding him, both economically and mentally, Sukanen began to draw in his mind's eye a bizarre, almost incredible plan, unlike any other in the history of prairie steamboating, that was uniquely his own. In the dust of those Dirty Thirties, he would build a steamboat on his homestead which he would drag seventeen miles to the banks of the South Saskatchewan River, and then sail down the Saskatchewan to either the Nelson or the Churchill River, through Hudson Bay, past Greenland and Iceland, and home to his native Finland. Of shipbuilding, navigation, and marine lore, Sukanen still remembered much from his youth spent among Finnish fiords; and for courage and determination he was unsurpassed. With the decision made, Sukanen considered the expedition as good as complete. "Dontianen" was born in that vision.

The first evidence of unusual activities in the northeast quarter of section 14 came in the shape of large quantities of sheet steel, cable, copper, and other such supplies brought in from Port Arthur at the Lakehead. Sukanen began sinking his entire life's savings and every ounce of energy he could spare from his farming into the construction of the steamboat. Soon his sowing and reaping would be left aside in his obsession to complete and sail the vessel. As soon as materials arrived at the Macrorie railway station from the eastern factories, Sukanen would collect them and, with the help of a neighbour, haul them to his farm.

"Dontianen" (a Finnish word meaning "small water bug") rose in three sections: a keel, a hull, and a superstructure, the latter consisting of a cabin, a wheelhouse, railings, and other trimmings. The design resembled a mid-nineteenth-century Scandinavian cargo freighter that could be converted conveniently from sail to steam power at will. First to take shape was the hull, some forty-three feet in length and thirteen feet at its greatest width, and ten feet from keel to deck. Once Sukanen had positioned the ribs of the hull which formed the main frame, he then shaped the exterior of her body with lapped planking, which he both tarred and caulked. Beyond this sealed hull covering he secured a second layer of non-lapped planking, and then applied the final protective covering of one-sixteenth-inch sheet steel, which he shaped and cut by hand with his self-designed tools at a forge he built expressly for the purpose. On each sheet of the outer steel shielding he crimped the edges in order to interlock the pieces of steel for greater strength. He intentionally left the deck wide so that the steam boilers and engine mechanisms could be lowered into the heart of *Dontianen* at a later date.

The North American steamboat's grandfathers (the Mississippi keel boat and the Northwest Territories York boat) usually had flat-bottomed shallow-draft hulls to facilitate passage across the sandbar and snag-ridden shallows of the mid-western waterways. But Sukanen knew that an ocean-going steamship would require a keel to keep her upright and stable in rough currents and gale-force winds. Ballast and freight could be taken on in the keel as well. Nine feet high and nearly thirty feet in length, the keel was double-planked, as the hull had been, then tarred, and then enclosed by sheets of galvanized iron, which Sukanen laced together with unbroken steel wire. This way the keel would be durable enough to support *Dontianen's* superstructure, and would also be flexible on the high seas. Sukanen then sealed the keel section by smearing it with horse blood, a process he calculated would protect the underside from the corroding effect of salt water. By preparing each section of the steamboat separately, he hoped to insert the hull section into the keel, double-boiler style.

To crown these lower stabilizing sections of *Dontianen*, Sukanen designed and built two eight-foot-high cabin arrangements, each with four-foot-tall railings to be trimmed with some of the softer metals he had purchased from the East. While the one cabin toward the bow was the wheelhouse (enclosing the steering mechanism), the second cabin, astern, would provide living quarters and the space to store needed supplies. The upper deck quarters would not only hold navigational instruments and a unique water-clock chronometer, but also cupboards, bunks, and living space. Heat from the wood-fired steam engine and the smokestacks would pass through or near the cabins on deck, as the heat was expelled. Sukanen also forged – by hand, from solid pieces of flat steel – pulleys, gears, funnels, a propeller with driveshaft and universal joint, a lifeboat, and numerous chains. Incredibly, this was all done while Sukanen was in his late fifties, and during the Depression, when most prairie people were concerned with bare survival.

What was Tom Sukanen like? Though few of his neighbours were in accord about his psychological stability, most agreed regarding his physical appearance: chiseled facial features; skin stretched taut over a symmetrical face; blown, unkempt coal-grey hair; wide, expansive forehead; square chin; deep-set eyes; indistinguishable neck; dominant, muscular shoulders; tall, massive frame. "He was a giant of a man . . . because men six-feet-two, when they talked to him, they looked him right in the eye. . . . And his chest was a lot larger than an ordinary human being . . . his strength, the strength of three men . . . and he often proved it."

"He was a husky guy," recalls Elmer Sukanen. "His hands were all bloody always, 'cause he was workin' with barbed wire barehanded."

The small-community nature of the West, combined with the conditions of the Depression, exaggerated Sukanen's stature and his unconventional behaviour out of all proportion. Fear is not too distant from amazement. Macrorie district town and farm people saw the man as "different", all but condemning Sukanen when they labelled him "superhuman". "No man on earth could put up them big planks and steel like he did, unless he was a superman in strength. And his chest expansion, well . . . a man told me he himself had been a big man, and yet when he put on Tom Sukanen's coat one day, he said, 'Lord,' he said, 'it hung on me like an oversized overcoat.' That same man weighed 270 pounds when he was younger. I know. I seen him and I can imagine. And at 270 pounds Tom's coat was still big on him."

Another man, named Stone, saw Sukanen perform a remarkable feat of strength. Two railway workers were lifting a set of train wheels. As Stone remembers, one of them said to Sukanen, "well, you're a big strong man, you get on the one end." And instead of getting on the end, Sukanen walked over and picked up the wheels in the middle and put them above his head. Then he just threw them out and let them fall. The railway workers figured afterwards the wheels weighed six hundred pounds. The two workers, according to Stone, were among the biggest men in the district, but even using tools the two of them couldn't lift the wheels.

For six years, day and night, summer and winter, without a single interruption for relaxation or illness, Sukanen drove himself fanatically to complete his ship. The keel and the hull neared completion at his farm, the superstructure took shape at the river's edge some distance away, and all along the route between the homestead and the river, portions of *Dontianen* were spread about. Sukanen lived in the overturned hull or in the cabins of the superstructure, depending on where he was working at the time. Still arriving from eastern factories was the sheeted steel Sukanen rolled into pistons, shafts, rivets, a smokestack, cylinders, boilers, valves, pipes, and a wide assortment of cabling and rigging. Throughout at least

"Tom Sukanen . . . was soft spoken and friendly, but his eyes never smiled. He was obsessed with building the *Dontianen*, but died in the attempt." *(Moose Jaw Prairie Pioneer Village and Museum)*

After his death, Sukanen's riverside building site became known as "the home of the mad Finn." The oddly shaped cabin was the *Dontianen* superstructure to be assembled downriver. *(Don Thurber)*

one winter he worked night and day over his forge, cutting the boiler, the pumps, the propeller, the gears, and the other steam-driven mechanisms out of shapeless steel.

The arrival of spring some six years after *Dontianen's* birth redoubled Sukanen's obsessive urgency. He was approaching sixty years of age, and inevitably his strength was flagging. His neighbours doubted his sanity. His spirit was beginning to break, in part through the recently arrived news that John, his son, the only surviving member of his family, had died. And not only did *Dontianen* have to be transported those seventeen miles overland to the Saskatchewan, but in addition nearly all her interior work – the steam engine, the boilers, the bilge pumps, and other major components – still had to be forged, assembled, and installed.

But ferocity, not of temper but of creative energy, was Sukanen's great resource against criticism, the elements, and the frustration of encroaching age. So he began the arduous task of moving the shell and soul of the *Dontianen* he had nurtured so long toward the fast-flowing waters of the Saskatchewan. He had to abandon his quarter-section homestead, the home on which he had laboured so arduously for the benefit of his supposedly waiting Minnesota family.

Planning began for the final stages of assembling the steamboat. Sukanen intended to strap together a raft at the riverside for transporting himself, a horse, and the superstructure. The raft would tow the 43-foot hull (complete with steam engine and boiler parts) and the nine-foot keel, which would float air-tight on its side, downriver to the point of assembly. Sukanen expected to shove off on the spring flood waters of the Saskatchewan and allow the high river current to carry him and *Dontianen* quickly into the complex lake and river system of northeast Saskatchewan and northern Manitoba. The farther downstream Sukanen rafted the deeper and stronger the water flow would be. Then, reaching the deep delta of the Nelson or the Churchill, on the threshold of Hudson Bay, he would flood his keel upright, assemble *Dontianen's* parts, and make his way to ocean waters.

But seventeen miles and stupendous labour lay between Sukanen's creation and its planned launching. Using a system of anchored posts and winches, and his sole remaining horse, Sukanen dragged the cumbersome hull towards the northeast. With the determination of ancient engineers, he built primitive wheels, eighteen inches wide and twenty-four inches in diameter; these wheels were mounted on the underside of the keel, which lay on its side and rode behind the hull. Interminably, twenty-foot stage after twenty-foot stage, anchors driven into the ground, pulled up, moved ahead, driven again – Sukanen winched *Dontianen* toward the River. Gullies obstructed his hauling path. Sukanen fashioned wheels made by rolling willow trunks strung together with steel bands in tandem, and crossed them. Nothing could resist his determination. But after two seasons he had still only transported *Dontianen* a distance of two miles.

"I couldn't see where he'd get any place with it." Elmer Sukanen remembered the futility of his uncle's attempts to get the steamboat moved to the River. "I'll tell the truth. I don't think he ever would have made it. . . . But I helped him move part of it. It was the top of it, the captain's part where he was going to live, that we moved first. I went over with four horses and I started movin' it, and it broke. He had taken an old wagon and made it wider, but he didn't make it strong enough, so we had to rig it up and put it on a different kind of set-up. Some of the rest of it he pushed in a wheelbarrow from there to the River."

Inevitably Sukanen's health deteriorated, physically (and according to some, mentally). Years before he had owned nine well bred horses, but with time and the Depression closing in on him, he began grinding up the last of his homestead's grain into meal for his own consumption; even the team of horses he eventually butchered and ate one by one to keep himself going. Then his last horse, the one he used to winch the barbed wire cable through pulleys that towed *Dontianen* toward the River, finally went. Of the nine thousand dollars he had accumulated for purchasing the materials for the boat, and the seven thousand dollars received for crops after construction began, every cent had been poured into the dream. In the latter years, age and malnutrition had rotted his teeth; he pulled them out with forceps he had made, and fashioned a metal mouth plate so that he could chew the tough grain meal. And still he wielded a sixteen-pound hammer all day long shaping the steel and fastening the rivets.

"He would have to swing it too, to shape that boiler up," vouched Elmer. Half-inch steel, cold rolled steel and that chain. I can remember a bit of it when he made it; he'd pound it and round off the links. Then he heated steel for the boiler and punched rivets through it . . . hot rivets. And it was a perfect job on them rivets. They was just like a factory job. Oh yes, he knew what he was doin' alright, but he started in a bad time."

"I feel sorry now," admitted a farm neighbour, "because I had the power and equipment at the time to pull his ship to the water, but I thought if I did, other neighbours would think I was crazy like him."

To some degree the problem lay with Sukanen as much as with his neighbours. No-one could help him. He was too proud to take charity. And if he did take anything, he insisted upon paying back in money, supplies, or labour. Even the West family, farming the west bank of the Saskatchewan where Sukanen forged *Dontianen's* machinery, discretely offered help. Sukanen never took something for nothing. "I was frightened when my husband consented to Tom's working at his boat on our land . . . alone out there near him," remembered Mrs. West. "We offered him fresh eggs. . . . During the cold months we had extra old clothes. . . . I lied and said we were getting new dishes so he could have some of our clean china. . . . But we could never give him anything. He refused our help because he couldn't pay us back. He refused to fish in the river, because the fish weren't his.

"He ate rotten horse meat and old wheat chaff. . . . He lived in squalor; he was so black from his stove with no chimney, that he was shiny. . . . He never drank. . . . He was soft-spoken and never laughed. He just hammered on his anvil. . . . We could hear the steady rhythm of his pounding for days on end."

Sukanen was strange, certainly, which separated him from his neighbours, but his particular sense of humour served to heighten the barrier, rather than decrease it. "I know one time his neighbours came over to my Dad," illustrated Elmer. "Tom had butchered a pig. It was a cold day and he didn't bother to skin all the hair off real good; so he left it – he hung it like that. These guys asked, 'What's the matter that you leave the hair on the pig?' 'Well,' said Tom, 'it keeps you warmer when you eat it with the hair on.' So they figured that there was something wrong and they came running to Dad right away, that they better take him away."

In the last two years Sukanen failed rapidly, and it was obvious to anyone who had known him. The man who had performed prodigies of strength, the inventor who had built the township's first thrasher, the Finn who had always given freely to anyone who asked, was rapidly approaching the point that he could not even care for himself. Health was critically important to him; at the end Sukanen had withered into a ghost of a man, barely recognizable even to his relatives who saw him "going without." The wheat he ground and ate to keep himself going was hardly edible, let alone nutritional. He sold the pieces of his now-overgrown homestead: a mower, bits of steel, utensils, for whatever food he could gather. For a time he saved what money he could spare to buy eggs from his river neighbours, the Wests, at five cents a dozen, but when his last funds ran out his diet consisted of straight wheat and nothing else. Sukanen did not own a gun, so he didn't hunt; he never fished in the Saskatchewan because he abided by the law that prohibited river fishing.

Attrition and exhaustion took their inevitable toll. The ring of Sukanen's hammer dwindled to a sporadic tapping. Both his life and his life's savings had been invested in this project; increasingly it became clear that it would not pay off. He was alone and isolated, psychologically as well as physically. "He never wanted nobody," recalled Elmer Sukanen. "If you went there he wouldn't work at all; he'd stop, 'cause he didn't want to work when anyone was watching. I used to go there once in a while with my Dad, but he'd quit working; he had to work alone . . . one thing though, he kept one day sabbath, never worked on Saturday."

The end came when Sukanen discovered that all the fruits of his years of work, the hull, the keel, and the superstructure of *Dontianen* had been stripped by vandals. This blow to his pride, this final insult, broke him. His neighbours notified the Mounties, but more to complain about his activities than to report the vandalism he had suffered. Tom Sukanen's work was halted on the technical grounds of his obstructing His Majesty's thoroughfare. Sukanen was taken to an institution hospital at North Battleford.

"Don't ever let that ship go. Don't let them tear it apart, Vic," were Tom Sukanen's last words to his last friend, Victor Markkula. Even as Sukanen spoke vandals were tearing *Dontianen* apart body and soul. Lumber was scarce on the prairies; steel was valuable; *Dontianen,* unprotected, was at the mercy of any passer-by. People with no understanding of the labour in every notch and board of the steamboat's body carried away what they needed, and smashed what they didn't want.

Tom Sukanen died on April 23, 1943, penniless and almost forgotten. The municipality offered money for his burial, and Vic Markkula, with what they say was his last forty dollars, purchased *Dontianen's* remains from the municipality; immediately he hauled the steamboat keel, hull, and assorted machine parts to his own farm a mile or two away, where he employed the structures as granaries during World War II. In the fifties, while planning the present Gardiner Dam-Diefenbaker Lake complex, Praire Farm Rehabilitation Act officials hired Tom Whitely, a local engineer, to rid the South Saskatchewan's banks of debris. Whitely, only too obliging to dispose of "the work of madman Tom Sukanen," dynamited *Dontianen's* boilers. Victor Markkula died during that era, but before his death he entreated his son Wilf, "If I die don't you let the boat be ripped up. The right man will come along to put the boat together."

Shortly before World War II, Moon Mullin acquired a farm in the Lake Valley area, and began in earnest a hobby he had enjoyed all his life: collecting junk, artifacts, fragments, old cars, early farm equipment, rusting tools, buggies, and dozens of other odds and ends that soon spread themselves over the greater part of the farm.

Surrounded by this strange array of relics from the prairie past, Moon became more and more caught up in his interest in history. One day, for no particular reason, he recalled the story told to him more than twenty years earlier of an eccentric farmer who had built a steamboat to sail to his native Finland. "It had slipped my mind until after the Second World

War," Mullin explained. "And then I got thinking about it again, about this man; I wondered how he made out. All of a sudden it just kept working on me, one thing to the other, something just driving me on; I don't know what."

Slowly Moon developed an obsessive interest in the story of Tom Sukanen. On countless occasions he travelled into the Macrorie-Dunblane territory looking for clues of the now dead and seemingly forgotten Finn. One evening Moon and a couple of companions were travelling in foul weather about a hundred miles west of Lake Valley. They barely knew the region, and by sheer chance discovered a hotel in the tiny southwestern Saskatchewan town of White Bear, where Moon and his companions sat up with the hotel keeper for conversation. The hotel keeper listened intently as Moon related all he knew about the strange story of Tom Sukanen and his steamboat dream. When Moon had finished his story, the hotelman hesitated a moment, then asked him how he regarded Sukanen – did he take him seriously, or did he see him as some sort of half-crazed madman? Finally, after Moon had assured the man of his sincere interest in Sukanen's story, the hotel keeper told him his name and of the artifact that he, Wilf Markkula, had in his possession.

Moon, who has long believed in the predetermined design of his life, was convinced that his meeting with Wilf Markkula was but further proof of the fateful role he felt himself destined to play in uncovering the mystery of Tom Sukanen. Long after Moon had gone to retrieve the steamboat from Wilf Markkula's inherited farm, he came across a letter which Tom had written to his sister sometime before he died.

"A man will follow a light," Moon recited by heart, recalling that it was a light that had drawn him to his discovering the locale of *Dontianen*. "Four times there will be men who attempt to raise this ship, and three times they will fail. And the fourth time, a man will start the raising of her. And the ship will go up. My ship will be ready, and then I shall rest. . . ."

Continued Moon, "I was the fourth man, unknowingly, to come along. Other men worked in the summertime. They had more money to move it. They could have moved it into different towns. But something always turned up to stymie them. Either the valley flooded and they couldn't take the ship out, or something happened. But with me, it just went like silk."

Moon, his obsession with *Dontianen* a dominant concern in his life, steadily worked away at making enthusiasts of everyone who would listen to him. Few could remain indifferent or sceptical in the face of his irresistible passion for Sukanen's steamboat. Among his key converts were members of the Moose Jaw Prairie Pioneer Village and Museum, originally an antique car club that blossomed into a museum when the car buffs felt some monument ought to be fashioned to commemorate the prairie pioneer spirit. And when Mullin discovered the *Dontianen* on the Markkula farm, his obsession to preserve and restore Tom Sukanen's legacy became infectious. By January, 1972, a feasibility study was complete, seven hundred dollars in donations had been collected, and the museum members had gathered a *Dontianen* retrieval crew.

"We got up there about twelve miles northwest of Birsay; we had Ray Butts, a professional mover from Moose Jaw, with his diesel rigs and his big moving outfits, two of them, to take the hull and keel out of the valley," recalled Moon. "We just slipped down there, worked on her and got the ship loaded and that night she went up the hill. I can see the big diesels a-bellowing away yet. We got the boat on top and the old Finlander standing there (Torval Skelly, who had watched over the ship for years to protect it from vandals), he said, 'She's going home, boys, she's on her way.' And I can hear that yet."

Almost forgotten, all but buried by years of scrub overgrowth and a cobweb of twitch grass, nearly lost in the snowscape of a prairie winter, and only a foggy memory to those who cared to remember, Sukanen's steamboat had returned from the dead. A plain framework barely stolen from the elements that had claimed her, the awkward fragments of *Dontianen* made their way overland to their new home.

CHAPTER NINE

Laird of the Saskatchewan

The Prairies disguised its steamboating mavericks well. Those men destined to become the barons of the prairie waterways most often came west undistinguished among the mass of faces; their fortunes and personalities suddenly blossomed when they built, purchased, or took command of prairie steam craft. Thus an American fur trader became a Manitoba steamship commodore; a British expeditionaryman created a prairie warship; an Orkney Island tradesman founded a river industry in a booming Alberta city; a silversmith's apprentice from Quebec initiated a flourishing prairie business with his North Saskatchewan steamboat fleet; a frustrated merchant launched an international real estate scheme with a Saskatchewan steamer; the wanderings of an Ontario trapper broke open the far Northwest with paddlewheel power; and a land-locked immigrant farmer from Finland dreamed of escape from the Canadian plains to the open sea aboard a self-made steamship. The southwestern prairie was typical of a West that might completely absorb the newcomer in its anonymous landscape, but then again might re-fashion him in a radically different image.

A witness to very little excitement since the coming of Canadian Pacific Railway steel and, shortly after, the invasion of Dominion troops on their 1885 campaign, Medicine Hat in the 1890's remained just another crowded canvas town. Prairie winds dumped the gardens of Lethbridge into the Medicine Hat coulee, while the summer sun bleached a sandy dinginess into every tent and shack. A town with "all Hell for a basement" (as Rudyard Kipling described massive sub-surface natural gas deposits), the Hat displayed a universal grey that was superimposed on its citizens – miners, cowboys, trappers, prospectors, farmers, and streetwalkers. Only the tiny, stubborn brush of the South Saskatchewan riverbank offered visual relief from the dust-clogged streets and the churning river brown.

The first colour to hit Medicine Hat after the '85 conflict appeared one

June evening a decade later. En route from Calgary to Winnipeg via the Bow and South Saskatchewan rivers in little more than a glorified rowboat, a stocky, ragged Scotsman tied his prairie launch to the Medicine Hat riverbank for the night. Ashore, the Scot looked like just another penniless transient, but Horatio Hamilton Ross was actually of the gentry. Born in 1869 the son of Sir Charles and Lady Ross of Rossie Castle, Scotland, he had run off to sea, sailed around Cape Horn, landed in gold-crazed San Francisco, trekked overland by wagon into the Canadian Rocky Mountains, ranged livestock on the prairies, and played polo in Calgary, all before the age of twenty-five. Until then Ross had shrugged off the nobility of his blood. But Medicine Hat struck his fancy. What began as a one-night layover turned into nights and days of partying at the ferry operator's riverside shack. Suddenly the flamboyance of his Scottish rank and youthful energy surfaced.

It was 1898, a year of madness. Medicine Hat emptied and filled daily with overlanders rushing to stake out Klondike gold. These adventurous Klondikers attracted the young worldly Scot. So to provide himself and a collection of his new-found friends with ample accommodation, Horatio Ross built a $30,000 hotel in the centre of Medicine Hat. Ross revelled in the entertaining of his guests; so much so in fact that the grand opening of his Alberta Hotel prompted two full weeks of celebration.

"That's where he made his headquarters," declared another Klondike-era resident of the Hat. "When I walked to school, I often saw him perched there on the veranda of the hotel." But with the novelty of the initial celebration gone, the mad Hatter tired quickly of life in a static cow-town. And so Innkeeper-Captain Horatio Ross launched his first sternwheeler, the seventy-foot *Assiniboia*, designed to propel the young skipper into a booming freighting career on the Saskatchewan River in 1903. But Medicine Hat had little cargo to offer, so the *Assiniboia* sat idle for much of its first seasons. Yet if the venture was not a commercial success, it was certainly a social one. Captain Ross introduced steamboat excursions out of Medicine Hat on short hops up and down the South Saskatchewan, again to amuse friends. Entertaining aboard the *Assiniboia* peaked in the autumn of 1905, when Ross and a party of Hatters decided to steam all the way to Winnipeg via the Saskatchewan River and Lake Winnipeg, just as it had been done a quarter-century before. The first thousand miles passed smoothly and gaily until the Saskatchewan river system stone-walled the excursion at Cedar Lake with sandbar-ridden shallow waters. Amid the first snow flurries of winter Ross ordered the excursion to abandon ship. He hired two nearby Cree Indians to guard the *Assiniboia* over winter, paid them with food and blankets from the galley, marshalled his party by dog team to the nearest rail line, and disappeared. That year Captain Ross booked trans-Atlantic passage and sailed off to winter in Egypt.

What the lake ice hadn't shattered of the *Assiniboia's* hull, the spring waters carried away. Yet a Sahara-brown Captain Ross returned to the scene of the abandoned excursion to find two faithful Indians safeguarding the half-buried steamer engines and boilers at Cedar Lake. Ross rewarded their loyalty and continued southwest back to Medicine Hat. Prepared to sell his Alberta Hotel, Ross found the Medicine Hat of 1906 an incorporated city. The Hat was bigger now, and alive with talk of tapping her underground natural gas. Ross's next venture was eagerly awaited by a flock of investors, including CPR station agent J. W. McLean and the city's first mayor, prosperous and prominent William Cousins, "who had money in anything that was taking a chance – a good gambler."

Barely old enough to know anything of the world beyond her First Street home, Isabel Cousins, like all curious Hatters, watched a 130-foot sternwheel steamboat rise from the South Saskatchewan riverbank during the winter of 1906-07. At Ross's docks, affectionately known as the New Edinburgh Yards, a Scottish boatbuilder named McQueen supervised six hired workers and expended over $28,000 of Ross's bankroll fashioning the Captain's latest floating enterprise. On June 4, 1907, Isabel was dressed in a bonnet and her Sunday best; the new steamer flaunted its dazzling white paint and a panoply of flags and bunting appropriate for the spring day ceremony. The mayor had proclaimed a half-day holiday to honour the marriage of the city's maiden steamboat to the South Saskatchewan, for better or worse.

"My father had invested money in the steamboat," Isabel recalled, "and it was decided that I would christen the boat at its launching. A great crowd of people came to the river. . . . There was a bottle of champagne, which I broke over the boat and I said, 'I christen you the *City of Medicine Hat* and I wish you luck.'"

"It is Sunday," wrote one *City of Medicine Hat* excursionist, "a very important day for all good people in the Hat and a day of special interest for those excursionists hurrying along the wharf, down past the Royal Hotel (whose bar is closed as the law requires). . . . They troop down to the level, covered deck of the flat-bottomed vessel, greet their friends and the orchestra members, and await the great moment when the ropes will be cast off. . . .

"The vessel floats freely upon the river, unattached to land. It is a passenger vessel, going somewhere. It has legal rights. It exercises them. The bar opens! Later there will be music and dancing as the threshing paddles drive the vessel as far as Bow Island, and then with less force bring it back in the moonlight, the passengers full of the romance of the prairie night and something to keep out the chill of the evening, always so treacherous at high altitudes. Captain Ross guides his vessel home. . . . The *City of Medicine Hat* glides along the wharf. The ropes are thrown and fastened. The bar is closed. The Home Waltz is ended."

For Medicine Hatters, the *City* steamer offered a chance to relax; for Ross, an escape from boredom, as well as bankruptcy. The launching of his steamer meant income from the transport of drilling equipment thirty miles downstream to Bow Island, and from the fares of weekend excursionists. Captain Ross resumed his favourite pastime – entertaining friends – aboard the double-decked *City*, complete with seven staterooms, a parlour, and an orchestra in tow on a barge. He took shareholders on special excursions, led hunting parties after lynx to Bow Island, threw parties on board for nurses in training, and occasionally steamed north-east for quick visits with downriver cronies.

"When Captain Ross blew the *City's* whistle rounding the last bend to the Landing, father would yell at us children, 'Run to the attic and put up the flag! Here comes Ross!' " The teenaged daughter of Frank "Chub" Goodwin knew the Saskatchewan Landing riverside well; she had been born and had grown up the eldest of eight children not a mile from the Saskatchewan's river bank. And Muriel's father (an ex-North West Mounted Policeman) had operated the cable ferry there, so she knew just about everyone who passed through by land or water, including that stocky uniformed captain from Medicine Hat. "Immediately I would run to the roof top to hoist our Union Jack. And with that Captain Ross would blow the whistle again. . . .

"Ross was quite a talker, even though he spoke softly. He was clean shaven and mostly wore a uniform with silver buttons, braids, epaulets, and a captain's cap. . . . He looked like some high official in the army and acted like it. . . . When the boat came into the Landing we ran down to the wooden walkway . . . I didn't pay much attention, but my father and Ross used to tell each other military stories about the Rebellion, while my mother fed the lot."

Intended primarily to return capital to its investors, the *City* supplied a blossoming gas-probing industry at Bow Island with equipment, and maintained a life line for the Alberta Land Company. But daily work-runs up and down the river were tedious; Ross merely went through the motions to please his shareholders. The true eccentric Cap Ross dawned with the evening and weekend excursions. Attired in his spotless white ducks, a gregarious personality with an irrepressible effervescence, the *City's* skipper assumed his most comfortable role – the river's jovial host. With each twilight excursion or the two Sunday outings, at one o'clock and seven, Ross entertained a hundred passengers with whisky, orchestral music, and fine cigars. The summer of 1907 seemed an endless celebration.

The season of 1908 was launched on a sour note, however, when the Lord's Day Alliance prohibited Ross's Sunday liquor cruises. It was a hint of things to come. Business slumped. Excursions tapered off. But setbacks never thwarted the Scottish laird of the river. Determined to prove his paddlewheeler's worth, Cap Ross initiated the first commercial steamboat venture down the South Saskatchewan from Medicine Hat since the steamers *Baroness, Alberta,* and *Minnow* had transported troops to the Batoche front in 1885. Loaded to capacity with flour for Winnipeg and freight for riverside ranchers, Cap Ross and his full company of crew set out from "Chub" Goodwin's Saskatchewan Landing ferry crossing in the first week of June.

The Saskatoon that Ross and his mates found on the first Saturday evening following their upriver departure was vastly changed from the Temperance Colony of tents, Victorian villagers, and medical corps officers that had greeted the Canadian militiamen a quarter century before. The tiny shack town that had housed few more than a hundred souls during the spring of '85, in 1908 bulged with land speculators peddling real estate and railway gangs stringing track on three separate bridges across the Saskatchewan River. Saskatoon was a hub. Saskatoon was a boom city. And with the rise of her notoriety, her temperate reputation vanished. It was more than the railway lamps and railwaymen singing on the upriver side of the Grand Trunk Pacific bridge at the southwest entrance to the city that invited Cap Ross and his *City* crew to tie to shore that Saturday night. Bars and brothels clung to the river's edge like barnacles.

When Sunday arrived, both the South Saskatchewan and the crew of the *City of Medicine Hat* were in severe states of overflow. Still hungover, Ross's boatmen had to face a river current that was in its climactic days of spring flooding. The river's rise further complicated an already tricky passage through Saskatoon's maze of bridges. Navigation past the bridgeworks of the Grand Trunk line proved relatively simple. But the Canadian Northern Railway bridge, whose clearance had been tremendously reduced by the flooding, posed a serious barrier for the 130-foot sternwheeler. Cap Ross, in apparent control of himself and the situation, ordered the *City* to anchor directly upriver from the Canadian Northern bridge, to survey the obstruction.

"The crew of the steamer began taking measurements," recalled Tom Pendlebury, a pedestrian walking across the 19th Street traffic and foot bridge, another low-lying bridge located just downriver from the Canadian Northern trestle. "They found that if they let the smokestack down slightly, they could get under the bridge. Presently they came through, clearing the underside of the Canadian Northern bridge by inches. But the CNR's telegraph wires, which were strung low along the side of the bridge, were hidden just under the surface of the flooding river. The sternwheel and rudder got entangled in the wire, and the captain lost control of the boat. And the railway bridge wasn't very far from the pedestrian bridge. . . ."

It was plain the *City* would not clear the 19th Street pedestrian bridge. With her steering mechanism snagged in the telegraph wire, the *City* didn't respond to Ross's tugs on the helm. The skipper rang for full steam astern, but the current was far too strong.

"This great excitement came down the river that morning." Russell Griffith was another attracted to the uncommon appearance of a steamer on the Saskatoon waterfront. "They couldn't steer the boat. It was drifting downstream and they were all running around hollering. . . . Then one fellow threw a rope off, swam ashore and tied it around a tree. . . . But with only the one end tied to shore, the other end swung around, drifting towards the first pier of the bridge. . . ."

"Two of my uncles, Bert and Jack Potter, were bringing out the town herd that morning," recounted Roy Potter, then just a young prairie lad. "Every three or four families owned a cow in the city, and my uncles would gather up the cows and take them across the bridge to pasture on the east bank during the daytime. . . ."

"Just then," announced Pendlebury, "these fellows came onto the south end of the foot bridge with a herd of cattle. At the same moment, the steamboat slammed sideways into the bridge and the cattle stampeded. So we stampeded too, into the upper part of the bridge, to save ourselves. . . ."

Rattled by the collision and the panicking cattle, the Potters watched in horror as the crippled steamer slid up the pier of the bridge and began to roll. The *City* splintered, whined, and listed to port at a 75-degree angle. "Everybody scrambled up onto the bridge to safety, except the engineer. He popped out of the engine room and jumped into the water. By the time he reached the river bank, he had drifted a mile downriver, the current was so strong. . . ."

The Saskatoon *Star* described the wreck of the *City of Medicine Hat* as "the greatest marine disaster in the history of Saskatoon." No lives were lost that June seventh, but a $28,000 Ross investment and tons of flour were dumped into the South Saskatchewan. A year and three days after her launching, the *City* lay impaled on the 19th Street bridge, the current tearing at her timbers and brass fittings. Saskatoon engineers claimed the *City* was undermining their bridge, so they pried her loose and tossed her back into the river. Not a stick was salvaged. Only her ribs and the boiler remained when spring flooding receded. Concluded Tom Pendlebury, "She was a total loss."

A loss of pride maybe. But Cap Ross had disappeared. Damages, he expected, would be compensated by Ottawa; so that's where he went, to collect. Ottawa proved delightful to the funseeking Ross. More influential people. More attractive parties. More of just about everything, except recompense for his sternwheeler *City of Medicine Hat.* She was a dead issue. But would Ross accept instead an appointment as Fisheries Inspector at The Pas? Absolutely. It was only September; prairie waters still ran high enough to carry Captain Horatio Ross to his new post – all that the new Fisheries Inspector needed was a new steamboat to get him there.

A crowd gathered at the Collingwood waterfront on Georgian Bay several weeks later. Five hundred miles from the national capital, the impulsive Cap Ross had reappeared with five thousand dollars in his pocket to purchase the brand new 18-ton 47-foot propeller-driven steam tug *Sam Brisbin.* Not wasting a moment, Ross hired a green crew and announced an inaugural cruise. Then, befitting the Ross reputation, the skipper promptly christened his *Brisbin* with a bottle of vintage champagne and launched a traditional floating celebration. Flags flew. Corks popped. And the engine-room bells rang "full speed" for the open waters of Lake Huron. The *Brisbin* responded beautifully until an overzealous guest pitched the anchor overboard with the tug steaming full throttle; three captains and a chief engineer took headers over the bow. But nothing could tarnish Ross's pride. The *Brisbin* was a work of art. And her appointments – a modern telephone system, polished brass fittings, strategically placed gold cuspidors, and a binnacle prestigious enough to have come from a trans-Atlantic steamship – dazzled even the wettest of Ross's guests.

So pleased was the bon vivant of the lower Saskatchewan with his first Collingwood purchase that Cap Ross returned to Georgian Bay two years later, in 1910, to shop for another tug. His fisheries-inspection operations and business prospects were expanding in the Northwest. And that season the Collingwood shipyards watched Old Man Ross christen one more of their creations, the *Le Pas,* named in honour of Ross's new navigation headquarters. A Canadian Northern branch railway line had reached The Pas the year before, establishing the town as depot and jumping-off point for lumber, fur, minerals, and religion prospectors. Chains of river scows, loaded with fish, furs, timber, or supplies for missionaries, traders, hunters, and railwaymen, carried Ross's name deep into the North. The Ross Navigation Company was born. Nevertheless, serious business rarely interfered with Cap Ross's party spirit, as evidenced by the morn-

The trademarks of Captain Horatio Hamilton Ross: blue and white ensigns, limitless capital, strict protocol, decisiveness, infinite optimism, and original steamboat designs. *(Grace Cousins)*

ing his general manager, young Harvey Weber, hesitantly informed the Old Man that both Ross Navigation steamers were contracted with outbound cargo, and would therefore be unavailable for another of Ross's impromptu cruises.

"Oh Hell!" snarled the master. "I'll just have to go buy another boat!" Almost immediately the skipper returned, on the bridge of a newly purchased steamboat from downriver. And immortalizing the significance of his remark, Ross christened his third propeller-driven tug the *O'Hell,* and launched yet another pleasure excursion.

"The *O'Hell?* I worked on her a while", stated Joe McAuley. Lanky and slight and eager to catch as much summer work as he could, Joe, an Indian from Cumberland House, had joined Ross Navigation because "I was young. I didn't care. . . . Sometimes we worked all day and all night. Sometimes we travelled all night keeping watch along the river and then loaded freight all day. . . . Towing railway ties downriver, that's what we hauled when I was a deckhand. We used to haul rafts of them down to The Pas. . . . They built big rafts of ties. One time we lost a raft of ties up the river. Well, the captain went to shore too fast, the boom busted, and there were ties all over the river. . . . The roughest spot was the rapids between Cumberland House and The Pas, getting up those Big Stone Rapids. They kidded this fireman trying to keep up steam one time. They told him to run and get some coal oil for the fire to keep up steam pressure. Well, coal oil's just as clear as water and we'd put water from Sturgeon Lake in the coal oil can. So instead of firing up the flames with coal oil, the fireman panicked when he threw this water on the fire and lost steam. Funny! Oh we laughed. . . .

"Wood was the fuel to fire the boilers. Talk about hot. And in the evenings we would stop and anchor on the riverbank, where there were millions of mosquitoes. Couldn't sleep. . . . And in the morning those big pistons began again, pounding up and down. They could hear a steamboat coming for miles. . . . And when we arrived there was lots of excitement alright. Kids were everywhere. We unloaded pretty near all night, getting everything ashore into the warehouses. Then we loaded up with wood – spruce and some poplar wood – all piled there on the banks. Then we'd have dances and a good time. They had violins and Scot tunes, all kinds of reels, square-dances, and waltzes. I enjoyed that dancing. . . . Lots of music."

Playing first cornet in the Citizens' Band of Prince Albert filled the gaps between jobs and between seasons for steam engineer Willard Goodfellow. At thirty-five, Goodfellow had plane milled in East Prince Albert for the Hudson's Bay Company, fired aboard the Coates-Mosher excursion steamer *Alberta,* manned the engines of Commissioner Hall's

Saskatchewan, and directed the installation of machinery into the hull of the sternwheel *City of Prince Albert.* In the spring of 1913 he signed up with Ross Navigation, packed away his cornet, and moved northeast to The Pas for work. He arrived to find a Ross crew polishing the fourth of the Ross Navigation tugs – the *Minasin* – and a second all-Indian crew ready to move north to build a fifth Ross steamer under his (Goodfellow's) direction. For an entire season Goodfellow spoke not one word of English, and worried to the point of insomnia about his first assignment. Despite the quiet engineer's concern, however, the *Notin,* another sleek prop-driven tug, slid down her ways into the Saskatchewan on schedule and on a perfect keel.

So it could be said of The Pas. Its future looked sound despite economic lags elsewhere in Canada. The northern prairies finally experienced a boom. The Pas had been incorporated as a town. O. Herman Finger, since 1910 the sponsor of the huge Finger Lumber sawmills, was elected the town's first mayor. Though a flash fire had razed the east side of Fischer Avenue, frame houses were outrunning town planners. In the face of opposition from eastern politicians to completing the railway north through The Pas to Hudson Bay, piers rose from the Saskatchewan riverbed for the steel railway bridge called "The Gateway To The North". And even Laurier's federal defeat on the Reciprocity issue hadn't stunted the town's economic growth. New industry and business flourished. The Canadian Bank of Commerce opened the town's first branch; the first school was completed; churches abounded; and general stores, a furrier, a drug store, and several real estate operations joined the boom. And the town even installed its first sewer and waterworks. Not the least prosperous was the Ross Navigation fleet. Cap Ross's assets from river traffic climbed steadily, even as Europe exploded with World War I in 1914. And, as if plotted as another of Ross's string of successes, mineral prospectors announced the largest strike in prairie history. The boundless deposits of copper, gold, and iron ores at Fred C. Jackson's Mandy Mine played right into Captain Ross's pocket book.

The Mandy mine was a thousand miles from the nearest refinery (at Trail, British Columbia), a hundred miles north of The Pas, and accessible only by waterway. Firmly established as the major water transporter out of The Pas, Ross Navigation therefore held exclusive monopoly over the movement of ore, men, and supplies. Ross portaged his steamers *Notin* and *Minasin* north of the Sturgeon Weir to carry Mandy ore from its source, known as "The Glory Hole", along the first leg of its journey across Schist and Athapapuskow lakes. And from Sturgeon Landing, on the south side of the weir (or portage), Ross Navigation would barge the ore via Sturgeon Lake, Cumberland Lake, and the Saskatchewan River to The Pas. Rail transport would then complete the haul, eight hundred miles to Trail.

Riverbanks at The Pas came alive again. Steamboats had reclaimed the lower Saskatchewan. Boatmen converged on Captain Ross's doorstep to earn Ross Navigation pay. And again Horatio Ross vanished. While his fleet commanded all movement on the Saskatchewan, and his enterprise, under able assistants, continued to profit, Ross had answered another whimsical call. An advertisement in a Saskatoon office window had caught his eye late in 1914. On the spot, Ross had booked passage to the Atlantic by rail and steamship to the British Isles. He missed both the first train east and the ocean liner, but negotiated his Atlantic crossing with the master of a tramp steamer, and arrived in England too late to enjoy English Yule. The Great War dominated everyone's thoughts, and quickly absorbed the impulsive Scotsman; Ross soon found himself assigned to special duties for the British government. These carried him to the Far East, to investigate the possibilities of deploying a fleet of sternwheelers up the Yangtse River. Yet as quickly as he shipped out, Ross lost interest; his thoughts wandered back to the Saskatchewan, and before the War was over he had rejoined his busy prairie steamboat fleet.

"In 1917 I was at Mud Lake cutting cordwood with the boys when I saw this nice steamship," reminisced William "Steamboat Bill" McKenzie. McKenzie, a half-breed, had grown up at Cumberland House, the long-time pivot point of steam navigation on the prairies. To him, the steamers entering the east bay of Cumberland Lake were as common as mosquitoes in summer. McKenzie's great uncle was the first to scout the white water upstream from Cumberland through some of the Saskatchewan's most treacherous bends and snags. Bill's mother had travelled aboard the massive *Northcote,* and his father, a Scot, had earned mate's papers aboard the Hudson's Bay Company's steamer *Saskatchewan.* But of all the riverboats Bill had seen or heard about, this ninety-foot sternwheeler, with her decks telescoping up out of the water and a brigade of ore-laden barges strung out behind, was the most magnificent.

"She was the *Nipawin* of the Ross Navigation Company. And I had enough guts to go up to ask Captain Ross if I could work aboard her," bragged Steamboat Bill. "Well, he was up there at the bridge deck. And he says, 'Come next week.' I started as fireman. Holy smokes, I could hardly lift the cordwood I was so young. But that's how I started. . . . Worked next to those big boilers of hers, always going at high speed. . . . You thought she was going to tear the river in two!"

As Ross Navigation skippers and crew familiarized themselves with the routine on the river route northward, boatyard gangs began grinding out ore scows and supply barges. A handful of engineers constantly pored over blueprints, while carpenters hustled thirty and forty-man crews all across the waterfront. A workman standing still soon found himself jobless. At Ross Navigation warehouses and offices, clerks juggled the industrial future of the north country on paper; all money, men, and machines in the North seemed to lead to Ross Navigation ledgers. Cap Ross found success as easy as uncorking wine.

And nothing was quite so attractive to businessmen hardpressed by the War as the prospect of successful investment, wherever it might be found. Not surprisingly, Ross's success attracted other entrepreneurs to The Pas. One such enterprising prairie group, led by Captain F. E. Simonds, purchased Prince Albert's city sternwheeler *George V* (left unemployed by the abandoned Cole's Falls dam project), enhanced her appearance with a fully-equipped second deck addition, and relaunched the steamer for The Pas.

"This syndicate of businessmen figured they could make money in the Saskatchewan River trade. There were prospectors and Lord knows what going up into that Mandy country. There was quite a rush on," emphasized one early Canadian Northern railwayman. "This syndicate expected to cash in on the big rush for gold around Flin Flon. . . .

"On the trip down to The Pas, Captain Coates [from the *Alberta*] skippered the *George V*. Art Deacon was the mate, Bert Deacon was wheelsman [sons of Prince Albert skipper Richard Deacon] and Hudson's Bay man Moyes Sayes piloted. . . . Downriver from Prince Albert Captain Coates took a notion to check the water depth below him by pulling up to a Dominion government water gauge. . . . Well, they had a deck hand aboard . . . a character who always seemed to fall over his feet. And as they nosed in, Bert jumped ashore to receive a line. A rope was coiled in the forward hold and this deck hand swung it round and round his head. He let it go and it wrapped around his neck and took him over the side. . . . The fireman saw the deck hand go, but he was driftin' away down stream. Art was trying to keep the boat up in the stream, and to keep from running over the deck hand; Bert was trottin' down the bank watching this performance; and the fireman got the rope, pulled him in and up over the side, then reached for him, but back out he went again. Did this twice before somebody got it in the fireman's head to hang onto the rope as he helped the man aboard. . . ."

At the Pas the *George V* found a new home. Innocently tied ashore, her plain tramp-steamer exterior gave away no secrets. Yet under her skin the sternwheel newcomer was outfitted with luxuries unfamiliar to this rugged territory. Elaborately furnished cabins crowned the port and starboard sides of the second deck, while the *George's* lower level housed a dining room and entertainment features that came alive, in the Horatio

Ross tradition, when the steamer cast off for open water. Prohibition had closed down Saskatchewan liquor bars in 1915, but although more than four hundred hotel bars in the province had dried up with the legislation, liquor salesmen merely changed signs and locations. Booze began to flow to the Saskatchewan faithful through general stores, drug stores, and mail order houses in Manitoba and Alberta. And to the syndicate owners of the *George V* now established at The Pas with their paddlewheeling liquor store, quick runs across the border into Saskatchewan brought a lucrative income for "missions of mercy". So while Ross Navigation steamers worked for their daily bread from dawn to dusk, the *George V* quenched thirsts in northeastern Saskatchewan by night.

"She was beautiful," one boatman confirmed. "You could see those rooms on both sides of the steamer. And there was dancing in three sets of squares when they wanted to. A piano was close to the dining room and a girl played the piano while the crew played the violin. . . . Just for the rich ones . . . with the gold . . . *George V* might push off toward Edmonton when there was lots of water; but then she'd be back, tied up behind the swinging span of the CNR bridge. They'd open the bridge for her and tie her up at one of the piers. . . . She was just for the bigshots. . . ."

Deckhand Joe McAuley agreed that the *George V* worked strange hours and in odd locations. "They had her anchored out on Cumberland Lake. You knew she was anchored out there. . . . You could see the lights. . . . They didn't land at all . . . and you had to use canoes to reach her. . . . They sold whisky aboard her. Canoes went back and forth all night long. It's a wonder nobody drowned. . . . But there was a girl who disappeared. She fell overboard and they never knew. . . . And then a young guy – he was from Edmonton, a half-breed fellow – he was missing off that boat too. Never found either. . . . That was the *King George V.*"

"She was just for rich people," frowned another Métis riverman. "Don't know who they were . . . but they took out gold. . . . I think those people had all the money they wanted. . . . They just didn't care much at all."

"After the Prince Albert [Lumber Company] mill closed down [during World War I] their steamer sat moored down by the firehall for several seasons." Young Bill Lovel and his schoolmates, who had often acted out buccaneer fantasies on the riverbank and collected empty whisky bottles worth ten cents each, had witnessed the passing of all their riverside playgrounds. Fire had gutted the proud *Marquis*. A rejuvenated *George V* had left for greener pastures. And all three steamers of Captain Richard Deacon's fleet had rotted into the Saskatchewan. Then, in the spring of 1920, the renewed vitality of The Pas waterfront industry drew the last of the idle steamers at the Goshen riverside away from Prince Albert. "One June Sunday afternoon there was something special going on. I went down to the *City of Prince Albert* boat. . . . The captain up in the wheel-house was talking to a deck hand below, and the fellow on deck was tell-ing him that the water had come up a few inches in the last twenty four hours. Cordwood was piled on the deck and steam was up. . . . They all watched the level of the river, hoping it would rise so that they could take the steamer down to The Pas." At The Pas, she would join her new owners, the Mandy Mining Company, who were now extracting eight thousand tons of copper and gold ore annually from "The Glory Hole".

Not far behind the tired steamer *Prince Albert* on the river road to The Pas came the hungry Winton Brothers. From an 1880's Wisconsin lumber mill, David N. and Charles J. Winton had branched onto the Canadian prairies, beginning at Prince Albert in 1905. Their "W's back-to-back" trademark had attracted and employed hundreds of prairie woodsmen and boatmen. But by 1918 dwindling central Saskatchewan timber had chased the Wintons downriver in search of new resources. Their bank accounts carried much weight and by the end of the War the Wintons had purchased the controlling interests of Herman Finger's lumber works. Thus by 1920 The Pas business community recognized a powerful new industrial concern, The Pas Lumber Company, backed by Winton Broth-ers dollars. Purchase of the Finger Lumber setup included rights to tim-ber inside the vast "Saskatchewan triangle", a million and a half acres of virgin woodland upriver from The Pas, enclosed by one hundred miles of the Saskatchewan River on the north, seventy-five miles of the Carrot River on the south, and fifty-five miles of the Sipanok Channel on the west.

Hundreds of eager lumberjacks and miles of fresh timber were waiting. The white spruce that had attracted the Winton saws to the northern prai-ries grew 3,000 to 5,000 feet to the acre. The Wintons put 1,400 men, 400 horses, and several Phoenix half-track steam log haulers through a mil-lion and a half work-hours – cruising, cutting, trimming, skidding, and piling their spruce. And when water ran in the spring, the Saskatchewan, the Carrot, the Sipanok, and The Pas channels came alive with logs en route to The Pas Lumber Company mills. But despite this abundance, The Pas Lumber Company was immobile – they had no timber steam-boat. With their purchase of the Finger Lumber setup they had acquired two steamers, the twin-screw *Emma E.* and the sidewheeling *C.R. Smith,* but both were useless on the Saskatchewan because of the excess weight of their machinery and their deep draught.

Then came a break for the Wintons, if not for some of the other resi-dents of the area – Prohibition overtook the whisky-wielding *George V.*

Just three seasons after Captain Simonds and his prairie syndicate had purchased and remodelled the luxury steamer and transferred her to the thirsty ports-of-call north of The Pas, the *George V* had run afoul of the authorities at Sturgeon Landing and Cumberland House. Detained at The Pas, she was moored, against warnings, to the downriver side of the Gateway railway bridge. Over the winter, her hull planks and keel froze to the riverbed, and in the spring, when the ice broke up, so did the notorious sternwheeler. Waiting in the wings, the Wintons purchased the remains and hired cornet player cum engineer Will Goodfellow to salvage the steamer's boilers, engines, and sternwheel from the icy river current.

But greater carrying capacity still was needed, and so the Wintons brought in Peter Aberhart, a Norwegian boatbuilder who had built Mississippi riverboats, flat-bottomed sternwheelers with shallow draught ideally suited to river conditions; he had also built the Winton's first steamer, the *City of Prince Albert.* Throughout much of 1920, Aberhart supervised the construction of the 120-foot *David Nelson Winton,* in readiness for launching the following spring.

The Saskatchewan's spring thaw rose so quickly that year that the river lifted the still-unfinished *D.N. Winton* right off her nine-foot-high construction blocks; fortunately, no damage was done by this unscheduled launching – the Winton owners merely arrived early to celebrate the birth of their latest enterprise. Typically, they shared the cheer. "After she was all built and painted up . . . the Wintons gave me a bottle to christen her," recalled Tom Paquette. At thirty-six, Paquette had served aboard everything from fish barges to lake steamers; like many other transient rivermen, he had for a time been taken under the protective wing of Horatio Ross. Now he was hired aboard the newest, most powerful sternwheeler on the Saskatchewan. "Well, I was supposed to break this bottle on the iron on the front of the boat. . . . So they gave me a bottle to tie on a string to christen her. But the string broke and the bottle went into my overalls. So I christened the *D. N.* at home. . . . The Wintons were a good outfit to work for. . . ."

"We had no steel bunks or mattresses or springs in the lumber camps up 'til that time," noted lumberjack Alan Kennedy, recalling his earliest days along the Saskatchewan. "When the company moved into The Pas, though, they started everything new. So they decided to purchase enough double deckers, springs, and mattresses to accommodate a thousand men . . . . As I remember, the *David N. Winton* was on her maiden voyage that spring . . . there was good water up the Carrot River . . . and the manager [Al Mattes], the president [David Winton] and vice-president [Charles Winton] were aboard. . . . Both the bottom deck and the roof top were

200

loaded with all those steel beds and mattresses. . . . What a sight. All those officials and beds!"

A floating powerhouse, the *D.N.* never let up steam throughout her summer season. Downriver she guided log booms; upriver she hauled tons of gasoline, kerosene, powdered milk, canned vegetables, flour, sugar, coffee, tea, lard, dried fruits, oats, clothing, and parts and tools to the Company's westernmost supply depot – the Saskatchewan Warehouse – which fed nine different Winton lumber camps. Each of the *D. N.'s* twelve 36-inch by 16-foot paddles thrashed through the river fifteen times a minute, powering the steamer up to ten miles per hour toward her next pick-up or drop-off.

"The old *D. N.* could push or haul four eighty-foot barges . . . even in the toughest rapids. You'd have to hold a stick up and look at a tree in the bend of the river to see if you were moving sometimes. Slow. Took hours. But you'd get up alright. We never rushed things. We just took it slow," rambled one smiley and solid deckhand.

Shortly after the launching of the *D. N. Winton,* boatbuilder Aberhard began constructing a smaller steamer of the same design, to freight barges to the lumber camps up the Sipanok as far as Red Earth and up the Saskatchewan nearly as far as Nipawin. She was to be called the *Alice Mattes,* after the daughter of The Pas Lumber Company manager.

"Well, Aberhart was short-tempered," remarked Alan Kennedy, at that time an employee of The Pas Lumber Company. "He began building the *Alice Mattes* smaller and with lighter machinery than the *D. N. Winton* . . . . At the same time, the Ross Navigation Company was building the *Tobin* to carry freight and passengers to Cumberland and Sturgeon Landing. . . . The *Tobin's* builder maintained that Aberhart didn't know how to build a boat . . . that he had her machinery too far forward, that her sternwheel wouldn't even catch the water. . . . Unfortunately, the Winton managers questioned Aberhart too. . . . 'Alright,' said Aberhart, 'Let him build the boat. I'm leaving in the morning. . . .' Aberhart's managers tried to bribe him with a bottle or two of Scotch . . . until he consented to stay and complete the *Alice Mattes.* But with this liquor in him, Aberhart wasn't so steady on his feet . . . and tripped coming downstairs. He had to supervise the finishing of the *Alice* with a broken leg." But when the ninety-six-foot sister steamer to the *Winton* hit the Saskatchewan in 1921, her grace dispelled any doubts about Aberhart's design.

Good design was important to Aberhart and the Winton owners, but to the uninitiated the mere sight of a riverboat was a striking experience. The first boat Jack Doyle saw as a kid on the Saskatchewan was "something out of this world." He could hardly believe they existed, much less that he would one day work aboard one. Born in England in 1902, easy-going Doyle had emigrated and grown up in time to join The Pas Lumber Company in Manitoba in the early 1920's. Young Doyle started in a lumber kitchen, but from scraping pots he quickly moved to scraping rip-saws across raw spruce, and then on to river driving in the summers. "And that's where I got involved with the boats. . . . I think I really started to work on the steamboats from my rafting work . . . about 1923. See, the *D. N.* used to pull logs from the mouth of the Carrot down to The Pas. And crew men did everything. . . . Getting aboard the *D. N.* was a promotion, we thought, but the money was no different. . . . I started on the water at $2.50 a day. Long hours . . . daylight 'til dark. But you got three square meals a day and that was the big payoff. . . .

"Bolt for bolt the *D. N.* was just like the oldtimers. . . . Beautiful she was. . . . No storm she couldn't handle. Mind you, it used to get miserable and you'd have to do a lot of wheeling around to keep things straight, especially if you was steaming with a string of boom. . . . It might drift you over and your boom might shake logs loose and break a boom chain . . . . Then the air got blue with profanity. . . . Well, you'd go into shore, swing around and chase your boom downriver." As one of four deck hands on the *D. N. Winton,* Jack Doyle sweated through numerous twenty-four-hour workdays. Some seemed like forty-eight hours. *D. N.* deckhands fired for engineer Tom Paquette, measured depths for skippers Pete Allison, Vern Walker, and Mackie McLeod, heaved lines for winching up rapids, bucked cargo for the lumber camp foremen, played a little penny-ante poker, and occasionally stole a nap behind a vegetable crate when the pace slowed, "but you slept with one ear open. When there was work to do, you didn't fool around. You did it. . . ."

"Wintons sawed fifty million logs a season . . . and as a rule, the *D. N.* went upriver and towed boom logs down and turned them loose in the pocket three times a day to keep that mill going," continued a second nimble *D. N.* deckhand, Charlie Otterbein. As a tall and boney youngster, Otterbein had joined the Great Lakes merchant marine and had shovelled coal into the furnaces of lake steamers the thousand miles from Duluth, Minnesota to Buffalo, New York. Each summer after 1910 Charlie returned to the Lakes and laboured his holidays away in the bellies of ore and lumber carriers. Until a huge passenger ferry at the Cleveland docks rolled over with 1,200 excursionists aboard. He quit to join the Canadian army. After the First War Charlie moved north to the Canadian prairies to trap and homestead, and there The Pas Lumber Company attracted him, in 1922. Soon after, Otterbein worked his way to the *D. N. Winton,* her endless days, occasional poker games, and the bacon and eggs of cook Ernie Mortimer, nicknamed "King of the North".*

*Jack Doyle told the story how Ernie Mortimer received his title. "We were goin' out in the

Life aboard the *D. N. Winton* could be described as hard work punctuated by a great deal of good-natured fun. Teasing was never unkind; everyone was a prankster's victim sometime. But a sense of humour was vital. It was a sixth sense to ward off loneliness during heavy winter cutting, to ease the breakneck pace of the spring river drive, or to suppress panic in a tough spot out on the river.

"We had no river maps . . . The pilot would more or less mark his own map. . . . A bend . . . or a sandbar. . . . There was nothing scientific about it. Never ran by compass . . . just common sense," Jack Doyle emphasized. Doyle and his *D. N.* crew mates always kept their heads when a gale blew waves violently enough to shatter their paddlewheel, when spring ice tossed rocks and hazardous tree roots into the centre of river channels, or when flood waters re-directed the rivers and left no channel at all. "That's what that damn flat country is about . . . and that's how it used to get us. . . . Going down a new channel near Cumberland . . . you could take umpteen bloody channels before there was one you could get through. . . . One time we'd headed out across Cumberland Lake. Away we went, all set to make record time from The Pas to Saskatchewan Warehouse. . . . We comes up one channel and she's a blind channel. . . . Up another and we end up hittin' sandbars. . . . We didn't know where to turn. Instead of making a record we were two days late."

Canoe hunting parties, fish tugs, passenger steamers, and ore scows all crossed the paths of Winton steamers *Alice Mattes* and *D. N. Winton*. In the early 1920's the Saskatchewan River and her family of lakes and tributaries became a frenetic highway. Ross Navigation and The Pas Lumber Company entered a decade of prosperity. Ports along the lumber, fish, and ore routes soon recognized familiar faces among the visiting boat crews. And whenever friends found themselves ashore overnight, minor celebrations ensued. The captains liked their illegal liquor strong; it was almost expected that one boatman would play fiddle or a hand saw for square-dancing, and another crewman had to call. From the streets and boat decks townspeople and crews gathered 'round, the happy and the troubled alike. "One night there was a dance at Cumberland," remembered Joe McAuley, an Indian loading ore for Ross Navigation. "We all went ashore. The passenger steamer *Nipawin* was anchored right beside us; she'd been going to Sturgeon Landing, but got windbound that

spring . . . after the winter camps. . . . Everybody'd be drunk the day before . . . and we had all gone down to see a bunch of the winter jacks off. One drink led to another, until one jack, Bill Cook, starts talking to Ernie. . . . Ernie was no hell of a cook, you know . . . but Bill Cook pats Ernie on the shoulder, telling him what a wonderful cook he was, and all this sort of baloney. . . . Four or five gathered around Ernie and Cook pulls this bloody pie out . . . and bringing the pie right down on Ernie's head, Cook says, 'I hearby crown you King of the North!' " Mortimer laughed as heartily as the rest.

night. . . . The Pas Lumber boat was there and a dredge alongside. . . . It was a great dance . . . but next morning . . . at breakfast this one guy never showed up. So one of the boys went to wake him up. . . . Came back and told us something had happened. . . . He was lying up in the front of the boat all covered in blood. . . . Sent guys out for the police. I ran back there and I just seen his throat with his Adam's apple going up and down, like he was about to die. He only spoke a word to the captain. Told him he'd shot himself. . . . I was there when he died. . . . Blowed his guts right out. . . . We couldn't do anything 'til the Mountie got there, so we built a box . . . smashed up some ice to put inside the box . . . and that night the *David Winton* shipped the body to The Pas. . . . Nobody ever found out why he did it. . . . Helluva nice guy. . . . Kind of friendly too." Bill Carson. Irish. Thirty-eight years old. Married. His wife at The Pas couldn't see going so far upriver to stay with him. While shouts of his dancing mates and the hiss of escaping engine steam filled the night, Carson had turned a shotgun on himself in the loneliness of the tugboat's forward compartment.

"All kinds of people . . . anybody travelled as passengers aboard the *Nipawin*. . . . Bigshots, bishops, government people, mayors. . . . Indians goin' from Cumberland to Grand Rapids . . . businessmen, RCMP . . . merchants, traders . . . lots of Russians goin' to the mines at Hudson Bay, Norwegian trappers going way up to Reindeer Lake for fox, mink, and lynx furs." Boatman William McKenzie had seen them all. An apprenticeship with Ross Navigation had carried "Steamboat Bill" from washing decks to ship's mate by the early 1920's. As pilot, McKenzie guided the $50,000 passenger steamer *Nipawin* through hundreds of miles of Saskatchewan River bends, fog, snags, deadheads, rapids, blind channels, and three hundred cords of wood per summer, six days a week, day and night. "The *Nipawin* of Kenora, she was a good old boat. The dollars I earned aboard her. . . . Best outfit I ever worked for."

"A luxury steamboat, that's what the *Nipawin* was," affirmed Cumberland trapper-guide Pierre Carrier, a northern prairie name long associated with river activity. From the earliest canoe transporting days of the Hudson's Bay Company, through the heyday of the York boat brigades and into the steamboat era, the Carrier family had guided river traffic. But even the stories heard on his father's knee of the *Northcote's* elegance didn't match the *Nipawin*. "You travelled in style. Cabins. Running water in the basins. The rooms weren't very big, but comfortable, with nice beds. . . . I travelled on her in the twenties. . . . I really enjoyed shooting down the rapids. The Big Stone Rapids. . . . When they shot down those rapids, they'd reverse the sternwheel . . . to slow her speed. . . . What a commotion. . . . I watched in the boiler room. . . . They were really busy trying to keep enough power. . . . You could hear the pistons and rods working, going back and forth. . . . But the most exciting thing about it was that you were going so fast and yet those [crew] men knew exactly where to shoot so they wouldn't hit boulders!"

"Shh shh went that old steam engine. . . . And the low-pitched whistle of the *Nipawin* scared me as a kid." The Settee family of Prince Albert had no other way to reach relatives at Cumberland House than to take the train to The Pas and the *Nipawin* upriver to Cumberland. And though he had grown up beside the Saskatchewan where his stepfather worked aboard a steam dredge, young Tom Settee always jumped at the chance each summer to ride that "beautiful steamboat. . . . The *Nipawin* was a double-decker with a sternwheel. . . . She could go twenty-five or thirty miles per hour. . . . And there were cabins on the boat, space enough for say thirty people . . . and then down below there was space where the poorer people – the Indians – would be. Most white people stayed on the top boat class . . . for fifteen or twenty dollars. . . . Meals were brought to you. . . . But what impressed me was that big sternwheel. I used to go down to the back to watch the shafts turning this huge wheel. And the water would be churning and gushing. We'd really be movin' along. Never forget that. . . . And the captain impressed me too with his blue uniform and brass buttons. . . ."

"All those captains, with gold medals in their caps and brass buttons. Well, they're skippers sure. They know how to launch or land the ship. But when it came to the rapids, somebody had to be there to tell him where to steer," scoffed Steamboat Bill. "I was born and raised beside this river channel . . . and I knew the channel from the moment we left The Pas 'til the time we got to Sturgeon Landing, night or day. . . . If I didn't know the channel, she'd have sunk to the bottom. . . . I was runnin' a $50,000 ship. . . . I didn't need no map, I just used these," McKenzie announced, pointing proudly to his eyes. "If I started to look at a piece of paper, I'd hit a rock. Never used maps. We had a compass, if it was foggy in October, or going across a lake at night. . . . But you don't need to ask me anything about maps or rocks, because I know the channel. That's why I was pilot. . . . I had guts and I knew what I was doing. . . . But captains with all their brass buttons, they'd never make it!"

Behind the polished buttons, brimmed caps, creased jackets and curtly delivered orders of Captains McLeod, Deacon, McKinnon, Weber, Haight, Coates, Simonds, Bridges, and others were men – men who knew protocol, routine, and seniority. The river was their work. Even among these remarkable individuals, however, there was one skipper who was unmistakably unique – Captain Horatio Hamilton Ross. Behind the smart uniform and the formal manners, Ross was a *personality*. The Saskatchewan was his life. "Cap Ross was a man of medium height, blocky build . . . and all business." Harold Kemp, one of Ross's innumerable acquaintances, felt intimidated at his first meeting with this "typical Royal Navy officer type." Ross was "an educated Scotsman, complete with Oxford accent, all that "Ol' Chap" business, a typical old salt . . . the kind you'd imagine as the captain of the *Queen Mary.* . . . As a skipper he was a martinet alright. The crew really stepped around when the old captain barked at 'em. . . ."

Hard-nosed Ross showed his true colours to Kemp, however, when the latter journeyed upriver from The Pas one season to break in the new post operator for Reveillon Freres at Cumberland House. "I came upriver on one of Ross's boats this one time with a fellow named Rothwell and his wife. I just happened to be standing on the bow of the boat, watching as we came into Cumberland. The rear of the boat ran into a barge and I went overboard. . . .

"I came up without a stitch on me. I clambered up and they pulled me back onto the doggone boat. And Old Ross says, 'My Gawd! You're such a mess! Who's got some clothes?' Well, nobody had extra clothes but him. 'They're in my cabin. Hike down there and get them,' Ross says. . . .

"There I was in the wheelhouse with everything peeled off. So I headed for his cabin at the stern of the boat. I'm down the steps and through the saloon. . . . Must have been the first official streaker. . . . And who's sittin' right there but Mrs. Rothwell. Oh, did I go through there in a hurry . . . with Captain Ross roaring with laughter all the while. . . ."

Cap Ross's laughter disappeared from the Saskatchewan suddenly in 1925. On a February night, in his fifty-sixth year, the crusty skipper who was "always afraid of guns" cleaned a rifle at his office on the bank of the Pasquia River in The Pas. Alone as usual, Captain Ross was killed when the loaded gun discharged a bullet into his stomach. It happened as quickly as his notorious impulses.

Friends mourned long after. The white population at The Pas fashioned a salute to the Captain at the old Christ Church (the only piece of The Pas older than steamboats on the Saskatchewan). Beneath a sunlit stained-glass window, a font, and a chalice, they inscribed: "To the memory of Captain Horatio Hamilton Ross of Rossie Castle, Scotland. Died in The Pas February 11, 1925. A tribute from his many friends."

Forever capturing the opportunity, Captain Ross had always been first to act, regardless of the risk; and had always managed to reap enough from each venture to employ his comrades and to finance his next enterprise. Ross dreamed and realized dreams; he worked himself hard and worked his associates harder, but never without reward. Ross Navigation thrived as a result. Boat mates and total strangers were always welcomed; the Captain had even adopted young Harvey Weber, his first Ross Navigation engineer. Cap Ross refused no-one work. Perhaps those who most grieved the master's passing were his Indian companions.

"Heavy drinker . . . but he shied away from any fighting," remarked one Indian deckhand, who owed his job to the Old Man. . . . "Big spender, but he helped a lot of poor people too. . . . He spent quite a bit of money on poor Indian people. . . . Made money. Didn't care how he spent it."

Copper ore loader Joe McAuley at first didn't know too many whites on the Saskatchewan, but "I knew Captain Ross. . . . He was a nice old guy. Kindhearted. . . . Indians liked him very much. He was sort of a jolly guy, this Captain Ross. . . . He always liked to joke."

Mathew McGillvary landed his first job with Captain Ross in 1919 aboard the *Nipawin*. It was after the War and work was scarce, but "he took me in and I stayed with him in his shack for the first while . . . and that first spring I went on board for the trip to Cumberland House. . . . Worked hard, but Captain Ross never made me work in a place tougher than I could handle." Following five hot summers of firing, the broad Indian McGillvary was promoted from his forty-dollar-per-month deckhand position to pilot aboard the Company's last sternwheeler, the *Tobin;* but in the beginning "when I was broke," Mathew nodded, "and needed some money, 'Sure. How much do you need?' Ross would say. And he'd never ask me for it back. . . .

"I don't know how Captain Ross missed unloading that shotgun. . . . He never liked guns. . . . Whenever a gun was around he saw to it that it was unloaded . . . but it went off and he shot himself. . . Lived just across from the office, alone in his own shack there, just off the Saskatchewan River. . . ."

In their Indian cemetery, a huge gathering of Crees and whites witnessed the burial of the old Saskatchewan skipper. Ross Navigation rivermen crowded into the pine shade on the west bank hill called the Big Eddy, overlooking the Saskatchewan. Medicine Hat would remember his excursions; Saskatoon, his wrecking the *City of Medicine Hat*. Collingwood wouldn't forget the colour of his money; nor The Pas his floating parties. Ross Navigation honoured his name for the remaining few years of its success in northern Manitoba, while other Saskatchewan River captains faded in memory. Yet all remembered Ross's personality, a personality unique to prairie steamboating.

A simple headstone was raised that spring, "to the dear memory of Captain Horatio Hamilton Ross, 1869-1925. He was greatly loved."

CHAPTER TEN

In Defiance of *la Bête Noire*

Although railway steel had first spread through the prairies in Manitoba territory, and then stretched north and west to the resource heartlands, from the first appearance of the railway in 1883 until well into the twentieth century much of Manitoba remained a steamboat sanctuary. Dashing for the Pacific, the CPR had struck due west from Winnipeg; and, out of convenience, the Hudson's Bay Company had launched its steamboat traffic straight north across Lake Winnipeg to the mouth of the Saskatchewan and points far into the Northwest. Both major routes – the steamboat and the railway – circumvented the province's two other principal inland lakes, Lake Manitoba and Lake Winnipegosis. Here, in isolation, inland steamboating flourished.

First to supply a young Winnipeg with lumber in the 1870's; first to build an exclusively Manitoban steamer, the *Prince Rupert,* in 1872; first to bring harvested grain back from settlement up the Assiniboine River in 1877; first to run a steamer fleet, the *Prince Rupert, Marquette,* and *North West,* up the Assiniboine to the Qu'Appelle River in 1881; and, in 1882, the first to successfully navigate three Hudson's Bay Company steamers, the *Marquis, Manitoba,* and *North West,* up the four-and-one-half-mile Grand Rapids cataract to the Saskatchewan River, Peter McArthur had become one of prairie steamboating's first refugees.

Relieved of his HBC Inland Navigator's post in 1882 when he refused to ship whisky up the Saskatchewan, and muscled out of his North West Navigation Company directorship by William Robinson, Captain McArthur had retreated to a quarter-section farm outside the hamlet of Westbourne near the southwestern shore of Lake Manitoba. Discharged but not dispirited, the wiry Scot looked north to nearly four thousand square miles of untouched inland waterway and heavily timbered shoreline. Lakes Manitoba and Winnipegosis, virtually detached from the traditional paths of transport, lay on McArthur's doorstep. With the help of Indian guides, he set out to survey both lakes; he rode horseback, paddled canoes, and drove dogsleds through the best timberland the two lakes had to offer. Adjacent to the Westbourne settlement, McArthur built a family cottage; at the nearby landing, he constructed and outfitted a mill to plane timber that he would ship from his newly established sawmill at Fairford, 120 miles up Lake Manitoba; and to haul that timber, skipper McArthur designed his fourth steamboat.

Fashioned just below the Manitoba and North Western Railway trestle that spanned the Whitemud River at Westbourne, the *Saskatchewan's* 110-foot hull housed a six-foot-deep holding space, two steam engines, and a ten-foot boiler. Her sidewheels would power a full company of crew, passengers, and freight, as well as timber barges across one hundred miles of perhaps the shallowest major lake on the continent. Built at a cost of thirty thousand dollars, McArthur's *Saskatchewan* was launched in 1883, to the delight of the six McArthur children.

"The Saskatchewan was licensed to carry passengers," wrote McArthur's daughter Agnes. "I remember Charles Mair, the Canadian nature poet, on his way up the lake for a trip. . . . Father was very good about letting us children go up the lake when he went for a load of timber. . . . I liked to see father giving orders to the crew from the top deck when we were casting off. I'll tell you, those men hopped to it! We would back down the river a little way into Perch Creek to turn around; then down the nine miles of the beautiful Whitemud with its overhanging elms, past Totogan to the broad and marshy mouth of the river to Lake Manitoba.

"Mother would take along her sewing machine and on board there was a little square-shaped rosewood piano, which had come from England by way of York Factory and had been carried over the portage on men's shoulders. . . . We children raced up and down the long tarred and sanded upper deck behind the huge smokestacks. And we never wearied of leaning on the railing behind the paddle wheels watching the rainbows in the spray."

The *Saskatchewan* paddled the McArthur family through some of its happiest moments. Up on the bridge Peter McArthur piloted the millions of feet of spruce timber per year across the lake, while at the rosewood piano on the cabin deck, Pauline McArthur accompanied daughters Eva, Agnes, and Isabelle in singsongs. The summer and the lake-scape offered new vistas each minute. At The Narrows, Lake Manitoba's shallow strait where Cree Indians claim they hear the voice of their god Manitou in the water's turbulence, the Sifton family would row out to the steamer to collect their mail and to treat all on board to wild strawberries and cream, welcome relief from the English cook's cornstarch pies. Loading timber at Fairford, to fill Peter McArthur's contracts for railway ties, the *Saskatchewan* would sail the McArthur mariners home, but not without a final adventure. There was always trouble plying back up the Whitemud River; at every bend the steamer's nose would stick fast in the soft riverbank; the last few miles were a struggle. But by sunset, an exhausted family and crew would moor again at McArthur's Landing.

Success had barely touched McArthur's enterprise when fire gutted the planing mill in the 1893 season. And that same summer, settlers along The Narrows witnessed a second blaze when an entire barge of lumber and planks burst into flames in the channel. The *Saskatchewan* was bound down the lake on her final trip of the season, with a hired British skipper in charge. In addition to her usual timber freight, the steamer carried bags of sawdust on deck.

"The whole barge caught fire and burned in The Narrows," wrote one witness. "The cargo spilled into the lake, where it drifted in the wind . . . and the *Saskatchewan,* hauling the flaming barge also caught fire." The crew went wild with fright, and could do nothing to extinguish the fire. The crew abandoned ship in the only rowboat, and watched as the *Saskatchewan* burned to the waterline and sank at the south end of Horse Island in fourteen feet of Lake Manitoba water.

"Not one of the Lake Manitoba steamboats operated at a profit at any time," McArthur's eldest son Duncan commented somewhat acidly. "The reasons are numerous and varied. It seemed to be a tradition. The steamer *Lady Blanche* was the first, built by Reginald and Walter Pratt in 1879 with Oakville, Manitoba, oak planking and powered by a Montreal harbour tug's machinery; it towed cribs of logs down from Dog-hung-Creek but could never keep Pratt's Totogan sawmill running. Father's steamer *Saskatchewan* carried too small a cargo and had the grace to burn to the bottom with little insurance. . . . Finally, the *Petrel* was built in 1898 by hardware merchant C. W. Maloan, who planned to ship limestone from The Narrows of Lake Manitoba. . . . The steamer was constructed by a Nova Scotia deep-sea builder; it was a ghastly failure and half broke the hardware man, who sold the *Petrel* to the Manitoba Gypsum Company, which teetered on the brink of ruin itself until Rod MacKenzie built the 100-mile Gypsumville railway branch to haul out the ore, and the boats were scrapped. . . . Nothing but woe unrelieved."

But destruction never meant the end. For McArthur, these fiery losses were only setbacks. Later that disastrous season of 1893, Captain McArthur purchased Reginald Pratt's weary steamer *Lady Blanche;* refurbished, retrimmed, and redressed, she became the boatman's fifth steamboat creation, the *Isabelle,* a screw-propeller steamer with an eighty-foot hull and limitless tow capacity. Four years later the indefatigable skipper entered the fish business as Lake Manitoba's agent for the Booth Fish Company of Chicago. McArthur circulated the lake purchas-

210

ing every pound of whitefish taken, for a cent a pound, then barged the catch aboard his steam tug *Victoria* (an 1885 troop carrier refitted to haul fish), and froze and stored the fillets in his newly erected ice-house.

It was inevitable that Captain McArthur – an incurable optimist despite his seemingly interminable series of setbacks – would soon look beyond the seventeen-mile horizon of Lake Manitoba. At Winnipegosis, the tiny fishing village named after the lake "little muddy water", 120 miles north of McArthur's Landing, the nomadic Scot planted new roots. By 1898 he had borrowed $25,000 from his American in-laws to finance a new sawmill at Winnipegosis; his Standard Lumber Company, which would specialize in spruce flooring and siding, was the first lumber operation on Lake Winnipegosis. Moving himself and his family to the new village site was a simple overland trip, but transferring his vital tow steamer *Isabelle* from Manitoba to Winnipegosis proved more complicated a task.

"The Winnipegosis country is . . . one of the most inaccessible regions of the North-West," a Toronto traveller had noted two decades before. "The Water Hen River is the only floating entrance into Winnipegosis; it adds 30 miles to the water stretch, and is the worst part of the route . . . It will always be the *bête noire* of lake navigation . . ."

"In 1898 father built the mills at Winnipegosis, taking the *Isabelle* up by water," recalled McArthur's daughter Agnes. "But on reaching the mouth of the Water Hen River, the water was so low, and the boat having a deep draft, the captain despaired of getting her through. But father had two small empty barges in tow, and these he lashed, one to each side of the tug, to give her more buoyancy. And empty barrels they were carrying were sunk to help raise the tug over sand bars until finally they got the Isabelle through to Lake Winnipegosis."

McArthur's successful climbing of the Water Hen seemed to signal a general migration of lumberjacks, boatmen, trappers, and fishermen to the salty waters of Lake Winnipegosis. Hugh Armstrong of Portage la Prairie and his Armstrong Trading Company, a Booth Fish subsidiary, promptly threaded their steamers *Lady Ellen* and *Osprey* through the Water Hen from Lake Manitoba; Booth's outside manager, Charles White, followed with the financing. McArthur repeated his feat with a Lake Manitoba tug, *Ida,* soon after; and in 1899 his Standard Lumber Company imported another steamer, *Iona,* by rail from Collingwood. That same season the new North West Fish Company arrived, with manager Captain Coffey piloting the steam tug *Lottie S.* from Lake of the Woods and his own steamer *Mockingbird* by water all the way from Port Arthur. And with such thick competition for Winnipegosis fillets, lake fishermen brought in fleets of Collingwood-built yawls and sloops. During those early years fifty Booth and North West sailing boats rivalled each other for the pickerel, whitefish, jackfish, and perch that were freighted by steamboat to Winnipegosis, where freezer cars of a recently arrived Canadian Northern Railway spur line waited to carry the catch off to Winnipeg and Chicago.

But Captain McArthur was no longer interested in fish – he had given up his Booth Fish agency to pursue the prime timberlands around Lake Winnipegosis, stands of spruce he knew could yield twenty-four dollars per thousand feet of two-by-fours and twenty-seven dollars per thousand feet of first class siding and flooring. First the skipper pressed the *Iona* and *Isabelle* into day-and-night navigation, towing giant log booms from a series of Standard Lumber camps along the north shore and islands south to town.

"We towed logs from across the lake," recalled *Isabelle* fireman Mike Harrison, who at fifteen had come with his father from the Ukraine to Canada in search of 160 free acres in 1899. After working for the CPR digging clay for two cents and a loaf of bread a day, Harrison had joined McArthur's boat brigade and there remained for thirty-five years of loyal service. "We had to supply that big sawmill in Winnipegosis, a hundred men putting through one hundred thousand feet of timber in an eleven-hour day . . . I fired aboard the *Isabelle* night and day for fifteen dollars a month. . . . We built booms up the lake; it was alright in calm weather, but when it got rough we'd lose half the lumber. . . . But that steamboat was reliable. We knew we'd get there. . . . The *Isabelle's* engine was an old-timer, a big upright engine, bolted and braced to the floor to keep her from tipping in a storm. . . . That old steam engine, she must've worn out three or four different boats. . . . "

"Just a chuck-chuck-chuck sound was all you'd hear of that engine, and up in the pilothouse I'd never hear it at all, she was so quiet," added mate Harry Brown, who wheeled for McArthur aboard the *Isabelle* after the steamer had undergone her third face-life in 1902. "My first couple of trips, Captain McArthur stayed in the wheelhouse to teach me the lake; he knew it well. . . . You got to know the lake and its reefs by hitting them. . . . Peter McArthur was tall and slim. He didn't smoke or drink; he just used to carry baking soda water in his pocket and take a sip of it once in a while for his ulcer. . . . Aboard the *Isabelle,* we used to take the hot lids from the wood stove, wrap them in newspaper and put them on his stomach to relieve his ulcer. One time the lid was too hot and the paper caught fire – well, he wasn't long throwin' the lid overboard . . . but he wasn't one for fun. Peter McArthur was all business. . . ."

Each of Standard Lumber's half-dozen camps up Lake Winnipegosis employed twenty-five to thirty jacks and fifteen mill workers, while each of McArthur's tugs was crewed by a captain, a mate, two engineers, two firemen, two or three deckhands, and a cook. Winter trappers took summer work with McArthur; freighters who hauled Hudson's Bay Company goods north by horse teams moonlighted for him; European tradesmen looking to support their homestead claims with part-time labour came to the town mill; and fishermen like Billy Johnson, who knew every quirk on Lake Winnipegosis, came for hire to Standard Lumber. Born in North Dakota and packed off to the wilderness with his family at the turn of the century, Johnson had fished and sailed in most of the lake's bays and narrows; twice he had survived a capsized sailboat and several times he had saved companions from exposure to the lake's stormy elements. Johnson began working for McArthur as a teenager at fifty cents a day, unloading lumber plank-for-plank with grown men.

"McArthur was kind of odd, but not a bad soul," recalled Johnson. "He was awfully strict keeping his crews moving, but he was good to me. . . . Some years later his captain aboard the *Isabelle* jumped the job and he had one more raft to tow down from Grave's Point, 145 miles up the lake; so he asked me to bring her down. She was a good-sized steamer; she trembled with power. This trip he was pulling out the mill; he'd loaded the mill's steam engine, all the camp horses, the crews, their families and their tents, everything, aboard the raft.

"First we struck some rough weather. Then the boiler blew a stay-bolt in the front end. There was steam everywhere and my feet were cooking in the pilothouse from the heat down below. We cooled her down and repaired that. . . . Then we got to the seven-mile crooked channel at Maggie's Island. It was dark. A stiff breeze from the west. And the Old Man was in his kimono about to go to bed and advised me to anchor. . . . But I decided to chance it because I knew the channel well. McArthur agreed to it, came back all dressed and paced up and down the deck all night, 'til I got through at the break of day. . . . Once through, the old fellow went below and made me a cup of tea. And when we got to town he handed me ten dollars extra, a lot of money in those days!"

"Boatmen didn't have money enough to spit on," Hawley Burrell laughed. "I worked two years on the *Isabelle* as mate; my cousin was skipper then, Joe Burrell, and he used to argue with old man McArthur. . . . The two of them argued about the weather and where to put up in case of a storm. But one time we got caught. We were going from Pemmican Island; we got out about three or four miles, and it really started to blow. One said to continue, the other said to put in. Well, half the lumber worked its way out of the rafts and went ashore. Lot of the farmers along there got stable and barn wood out of that. . . . Being the mate, I was caught in the middle of every argument between the skipper and McArthur. But whatever McArthur said went, or else."

If McArthur appeared consistent to one man, to another he was unpredictable, a mosaic of contradictions. He was always setting an example through his determination and leadership, as on one occasion when he led his crew through a five-day blizzard on Lake Winnipegosis – but he could be terrified by ancient Scottish superstitions. In the bush he used rocks for pillows, but he would drink nothing stronger than weak tea. He fired a lumberjack for calling him "Pete", but never refused a man in need of work. Above all, McArthur's priorities were determined by his sense of enterprise. The *Mockingbird* incident is a case in point. By 1901 the *Mockingbird,* Captain Coffey's luxury sixty-foot steam yacht, had freighted and towed North West Fish Company barges regularly for two seasons. That July her five-man crew steered the *Mockingbird* away from the High Portage wharf at the lake's north shore. Astern on the steamer sat a heavy load of cordwood, which forced her bow up out of the water and reduced her manoeuvrability. Half-way down Winnipegosis, before the crew could stow the firewood below, the steamer encountered a gale. Three large breakers poured over her already depressed stern.

"Just opposite Big Island, the steamer swamped and sank fast," reported a Standard Lumber employee. "McArthur operated a sawmill at Big Island. And one fella from the steamer swam the two miles in big seas to shore. He ran right to the mill. Peter McArthur had steam on the *Isabelle,* but he was going to use it for some other work. So he told his men to steam the other tug up, the *Iona,* to go out and rescue the rest of the survivors. . . . Took two hours to steam up the *Iona* . . . I guess he had no feelings, old McArthur."

Ironically, the remainder of the foundering steamer's crew scrambled onto the floating cordwood that had sunk the *Mockingbird* in the first place, and drifted safely ashore.

Fish versus Lumber. Already Lake Winnipegosis had grown crowded with its two major industries. From a small mill in the urchin-like Winnipegosis settlement at the mouth of the Mossey River, McArthur's Standard Lumber monopoly had boomed up both sides of the lake and onto most of the lake's major islands. The Booth Fish Company had gained control of the richest fishing grounds, had established a host of fish camps across the north end of the lake, and had acquired countless acres of grazing land, on which they pastured cattle for winter beef and their thirty teams of horses for winter fish-freighting to Winnipegosis. Rivalry on land and water sparked incidents that engendered grudges on both sides. Fishermen complained that the sawmills' cuttings spilling into the lake harmed their fish. Lumbermen found spikes in their cut timber and swore that resulting saw breakdowns were the work of crazed fishermen. Stan-

"A strict Presbyterian, Peter McArthur was a traditionalist, who spoke like an Oxford professor, never socialized, rarely did physical work, but possessed acute business sense." *(Edna Medd)*

Between 1893 and 1904, McArthur's *Isabelle* had a dozen skippers, freighted everything from jam to jackfish, and weathered every storm on Lakes Manitoba and Winnipegosis. *(Provincial Archives of Manitoba)*

dard blamed the fishermen for broken boom chains; and Booth blamed the loggers for torn nets. And sabotage was suspected when Standard boatmen found the *Iona* submerged to her decks while moored at their planing mill. Competition up and down Winnipegosis, however, was productive. By 1900 Peter McArthur had invited James Parker from New Brunswick to convert Standard Lumber's inefficient boom-towing operation to a more sophisticated raft system, whereby lumber sawed up the lake would be constructed into temporary floating barges for the haul to Winnipegosis. Rafts were more stable, transported a greater volume of semi-prepared lumber, and doubled as scows for carrying men, supplies, machinery, and livestock.

That year Booth Fish manager Charles White supervised construction of the largest freighting steamer yet seen on Lake Winnipegosis. "A full 105 feet long . . . the *Manitou* could carry 40,000 pounds of crated fish." Ed Redonets, experienced with steam shovels, dredges, and CPR steamers, worked in the boiler room aboard the *Manitou* as three times a week she hauled 700 to 800 boxes of frozen fish 100 miles down the lake from the company's fish camp at Whisky Jack Island to Winnipegosis. Forward, the *Manitou* consisted of hold space; amidships above decks, was the cabin deck and galley; above that rose the captain's and mate's quarters; and aft were the crew's eight bunks, the ten-foot-long boiler, and the two steam engines that powered her twin-screw propellers. This machinery hold was Ed Redonets's home at sea.

"Smooth as velvet those engines. . . . From the boiler, steam goes through the small forward high-pressure cylinder, then into the larger aft low-pressure cylinder, so your steam is used up twice. Then the steam is pumped through a condenser, and, as water, is pumped back into the boiler. Never waste any steam. Never lose any water. . . . Silent engines. Made in Goderich, Ontario. I slept next to the engine room, too – my head was right beside the engine. . . . Just a constant whoosh-swhoosh sound. Once I got used to it, it was like somebody playing piano . . . and with the rocking of the boat, it was just like a cradle."

"I can still hear the whistle of the old *Manitou*. I loved to hear that whistle blow. It was a long, mournful . . . very deep, melodious moan. It was the nicest of all the steamship whistles I thought . . . the old *Manitou*," Ruth Patterson called to mind.

Born in Winnipeg, Ruth came to Winnipegosis as a young girl and grew up with the town and its infant industries. No longer the helter-skelter collection of fishermen's shacks of the 1890's, Winnipegosis had prospered, particularly with the fish harvest and the related steamboat traffic. Previously nursed by a Hudson's Bay Company trading post, Winnipegosis after 1900 sported T. R. Whale's general store and accompanying warehouses (equipped with private telephone lines); the Canadian Northern Railway station; John Seiffert's hotel and the Ross brothers' Lakeview Hotel; a public school; a Methodist Church, a Roman Catholic church, a Presbyterian church, and later an Anglican and a Greek Catholic church; a skating rink and four sheets of curling ice; and two town doctors. As wood-burning was the chief source of energy for this developing town, firewood lined the streets of Winnipegosis. Piled as high as the houses and several rows wide, poplar and tamarack cordwood stretched nearly a half mile from the railway station down to the fishermen's docks and warehouses. And here, at the lake's edge, was the focal point of Winnipegosis, that Ruth Patterson remembered so vividly.

"Fish were caught fresh and put in boxes with chipped ice all around them at the northern fish camps. And then they were brought down by steamboat. As the *Manitou* would enter the channel at Winnipegosis, she would whistle. That was the signal for men at the warehouses to be ready. It was really a scene of activity; half the townspeople and all the children would flock to the docks to see the big steamboat come in loaded with fish. Talk about a beehive. Real excitement. Men would be running with wheelbarrows and ice boxes to the docks; the fish were unloaded and re-iced and packed into the warehouses and then later transported by train out of Winnipegosis. Wages were low, sixteen cents an hour, but the men considered themselves lucky to have work.

"The first time I went aboard the *Manitou* I was thrilled to death. I thought it was the most beautiful and the most huge thing I'd ever seen in my life. . . . They used to call the *Manitou* 'the old tub', because of the way she was built, she wasn't very stable in a storm and would roll badly. I recall this one particular fall, me and two of my girl chums were going right to the far north end of Winnipegosis as passengers on this trip. The *Manitou* was heavily loaded. We were taking winter supplies north on the *Manitou* to Whisky Jack and all the fishermen's cabins. We were taking lumber, empty fish boxes, nets, winter grocery supplies, a fisherman's pony, and dogs – all the supplies necessary to live the six months during winter ice fishing.

"Well, we got caught in a terrible storm. And that old *Manitou* would roll right over and I'd swear she would never come back up again. Finally, they had to throw the pony overboard and a lot of the lumber, because we almost capsized. I was frightened . . . I went down to the galley at meal time. But the galley was one place to stay out of when it was rough. . . . Even though things were fastened down, dishes were sliding all over the table and pots falling on the floor. But some managed to eat. The worst of it was that the cook had made roast pork, really rich roast pork. Well, I took one look at the food and my stomach rolled. I dashed for our cabin. One of my chums was already lying on the bed and green around the gills. 'Move over,' I said, and I rolled in beside her. Oh, were we seasick. In fact, many of the crew were very sick. . . . "

"I remember rough water aboard the *Manitou*. That steamer carried ten or fifteen passengers every trip. None in the family was particularly fond of travelling, but we used to go north on this boat in the summer when I was small. This one trip, with my mother and two sisters, I was a small boy and I remember the storm and sliding from one end of the stateroom to the other. But those excursions were fun," recalled Delroy Grenon.

Grenon's family had pioneered commercial fishing on Lake Winnipegosis. Before the Armstrong Trading Company, before North West Fish and before Booth Fish, had been the Grenons. An early student of fish propagation, a former hatcheries superintendent for the United States Government in Michigan, and a proficient sailboat builder on Lake Manitoba, Joseph O. Grenon, Delroy's grandfather, had introduced the first large-scale fishing enterprise to Lake Winnipegosis in 1896. During his first seasons, Joe Grenon had taken immense fish catches, three to four tons of whitefish a day. Competition with North West Fish and other independents drove Grenon to sell his business to the Armstrong Trading Company of Portage la Prairie, itself a subsidiary of the Booth Company of Chicago. Joe's son, Joseph P. Grenon, was appointed manager of Booth's Armstrong Trading Company interests on Lake Winnipegosis. Yet Joe Sr. refused to give up his life's occupation completely; even as the *Manitou* hauled out bountiful catches for Booth, he continued fishing privately with his other sons, Walter and Harry. And in 1912, Joe Sr. was appointed Superintendent of the Winnipegosis fish hatcheries at Snake Island. Then, in 1918, after Booth Fish and Armstrong Trading had parted company, Joseph Grenon Sr. returned to active fish marketing when he allied with Hugh Armstrong and two other businessmen, to form the Armstrong-Gimli Fisheries. With two seasoned operations, Booth Fish and Armstrong-Gimli, the competition for Winnipegosis whitefish and pickerel intensified, especially when the Grenons launched a steamboat to rival the *Manitou*.

"They brought the frame of the steamboat from Collingwood, Ontario," Delroy Grenon explained. "All the forms and materials came up in pieces. And our steamer *Armenon* was then put together."

"My father and my brother Joe made the planking that went into her," added a jolly Lloyd Burrell. "For twenty-one cents an hour we drove spikes into her, putting her together. And I did a lot of painting when the hull was finished." Growing up during the reign of the Manitou over the lake, Burrell had gained his initial steamboat training aboard Peter McArthur's *Isabelle*. Then when his family took up work with Arm-

218

strong-Gimli, the youngest Burrell joined the building crew.

"After the hull was completed and launched into the Mossey River, she was moored and machinery was installed. It took several days of work with screw-jacks and timber to get the machinery ready, and then a day to fasten it all in. . . . For about two months, Captain Jack Denby and my brother supervised construction. . . . Keeping tradition, we put money under the stem post at the *Armenon's* bow for good luck. I didn't have much, but I put in my nickel. My uncle, Hall Burrell, he put his watch under the stem post that day and said, 'She'll always be on time.' "

Nearly ninety feet long and powered by the fore and aft compound steam engine and boiler extracted from McArthur's old *Iona*, the *Armenon* was slim and sturdy and perfectly suited for her Armstrong-Gimli towing duties. With her screw propeller set low into the water astern of the tow post, the *Armenon* could tow 300 feet of hauser line and a barge loaded with 1,300 boxes of frozen fish from the company's Channel Island fish camps 130 miles down the lake to Winnipegosis. At full throttle and without a load, the *Armenon* could steam a full fourteen miles per hour. By comparison, the Booth Fish Company's *Manitou*, with a wider and longer hull for hold and deck freighting, was capable of twelve miles per hour unloaded. Despite her greater age, however, and a structural defect which caused her to list to port, the *Manitou*, with her twin screws, was still a fair match for the Armstrong-Gimli newcomer. Each steamer had supply runs north and fish runs south several times a week across the same seas – ample opportunity for each crew to test the other's efficiency and speed.

Elaborated Lloyd Burrell, "I was eighteen when I started work as a fireman aboard the new *Armenon*. . . . I had to fire up the boiler about every twenty-five minutes; I'd go down the hole, swing the door open and start piling cordwood in. . . . On the lake we travelled night and day. I might be on two of the four watches, say from midnight to six in the morning and from noon to six in the evening, six hours on, six hours off. . . . The *Armenon* and *Manitou* used to freight down the lake the same time and we used to race. . . . We'd see the *Manitou* coming a few hundred yards away and when we got abreast of one another, away we'd go. Engineer Jim Bickel kept me busy. We'd be throwing oil into the furnace to keep steam up, and the engine would be wide open. . . . Couldn't race too long. It would drive the fireman crazy, but we did it happily. . . . "

"Jack Denby was captain aboard the *Armenon* for years," reminisced his nephew, Jim Denby. "Jack was a good captain. Excellent navigator . . . knew the lake A to Z . . . and was a good drinker too. . . . When she towed a barge, the *Armenon* couldn't beat the *Manitou*. Well, one night they came up alongside the *Manitou*. They were feelin' pretty good. So Jack cut the tow line, let the barge go, then circled the *Manitou* waving a burning broom out the back end of the *Armenon*, just to show 'em how much faster he was than the *Manitou*."

"Jack sure wouldn't let anybody beat him," confirmed his daughter. "He'd break his neck first!"

Steamboat rivalry on Winnipegosis was constant in all camps. But it was amiable. In the seasons that the *Armenon* and *Manitou* vied along the full length of the lake in nautical one-upmanship, there was never the likelihood that either Booth Fish or Armstrong-Gimli would emerge supreme because of a faster steamboat run. There would always be plenty of fish to catch, freight, and sell. But skippers on Winnipegosis treated their roles soberly, for the most part, imbuing the boats, their crews, and the lake itself with importance. Whereas the transient steamboat captains of the golden paddlewheel era on the prairies had come almost exclusively from British seafaring families or the American Mississippi tradition, the masters of Winnipegosis steamers had grown up locally with their trade. The lake shoreline was their home year round. And when they piloted lake steamers, they exhibited a colour and a humour all their own.

One of the first to steamboat on Lake Winnipegosis, with his *Mockingbird* yacht and the *Lottie S.* steamer, Captain Coffey was a stout man. The ferocity with which he smoked cigars and his gruff manner perpetuated his tyrannical mystique; but beneath the cranky exterior, Coffey was a lamb. And the *Manitou*, first lady of the lake, attracted her fair share of characters. During the *Manitou's* earliest trips, her crews operated under the tightest of disciplinarians, an officious skipper named Fisher. Much warmer, but equally meticulous about the *Manitou's* sanitary state, Captain Bill MacDonald was a stickler for spotless decks and immaculate machinery. Skipper-manager Charles White, ever-efficient on land and at sea, not only packed the Booth Fish warehouses with record fish catches, but on one occasion herded over ninety fishermen's dogs onto the *Manitou* for one trip north to the winter camp sites. The antics and achievements of Captain Alex Vance spread his reputation well beyond the shores of Lake Winnipegosis. First to transport loads of fresh-water sturgeon from Grand Rapids in 1897, the inventor of snow plowing and caboose fish-freighting over frozen lakes, and an innovator of more efficient methods of log towing, Sandy Vance was at home on and in the lake. One spring, with ice still thawing on the lake, Vance stripped all but his cap and swam amid the ice floes. Another time, forced ashore in a storm, he discovered an odd-coloured rock; when he later found that it contained gold, he began an annual ritual – searching the lakeshores in vain for that auric location. Captain Vance also was renowned for his carefree attitudes towards navigation. Alone on his watch, he would go below for coffee and leave the wheel unattended, complaining, "The damn boat goes wherever it wants to anyway!"

"The *Manitou* had the reputation of being a hard steamer to steer," agreed young deckhand Howard Medd. "The first trip that Vance made as captain of the *Manitou*, the year I was aboard, a dredge was marking the shallow channel at Sister Islands, halfway up the lake. They were putting buoys at each end of the channel. . . . When we reached the islands and the path that the dredge was clearing, we saw the dredge in the narrow cut and a barge right beside it. There was just room for the *Manitou* to go by along side the barge. Custom was, when you went through a place as treacherous as that, to slow down. But old Vance didn't bother to slow down a bit. He raced through at top speed. I was at the side of the *Manitou* and I could have stepped onto that barge, we were so close. Well, next trip we found that a bolt was broken and that the *Manitou's* tiller was about to come loose!"

The *Manitou* survived many near misses, some of which brought her within inches of disaster. Somehow she survived nearly two decades of navigation on Winnipegosis. Her frame had become grossly twisted out of shape – when her forward decks were level, the engine room astern had a decided slope to it – but the crew could usually improvise by loading her cargo and cordwood fuel so as to keep the boiler and machinery level. The steamer's two upper decks and pilothouse made her top heavy as well. And with her forward above decks always loaded, the *Manitou* laboured at the helm; her wheelsmen used to joke that the *Manitou* was never on course except when she crossed it. Yet all these shortcomings of age never bothered old-timer Bill Mapes. A rakish steamboatman, Mapes was a renowned storyteller, but the dashing Captain Mapes of his yarns bore little resemblance to the impulsive, inexperienced Mapes on the actual steamboat bridge.

"One September, the *Manitou* was making her run north with fishermen and their families to the winter camps: Long Point, Dawson Bay, Hunter's Point, Shoal River; and she was carrying lumber, fish boxes, horses, and dozens of people aboard," recalled one fisherman. "This was 1926.. . ."

"After the first half-day's run we dropped anchor at the north end of Birch Island," wrote second engineer John McArthur, Captain Peter McArthur's son. "The sky looked threatening in the north. In spite of this warning, Captain Mapes pulled up the hook and continued the trip north. About two o'clock that afternoon, when we were well away from shelter, a terrific northwest wind sprang up into a whole gale. Heavy seas crashed against the bows, washing an anchor from its place. . . . Water filled her forward deck level . . . and flowed through the companion ways. She sprang a leak in her bow where there was no syphon and water poured into her fore hold until she was badly down by the nose. . . ."

"Mapes was white as a sheet," claimed one of the two crewmen who had clung to the *Manitou's* wheel in an attempt to bring the steamer into the lee of an island. In the galley the cook and a bargeman braced themselves against timberheads and tried to keep the wood stove from toppling when the boat rolled. "Beet juice went flying in the middle of the storm and the interior of the galley looked like a slaughterhouse," pictured one passenger.

Related a fisherman's wife: "Everything was tossed around, from dishes to people to food. Shelves were falling. People were sick. The floors were coated in a pukey slime. No-one could stand up. And the crew had to crawl across the decks. . . . A skiff containing a dog team turned over and the dogs were drowned. And most of our food was lost or soaked."

"Fish boxes were tumbling all over the *Manitou*," described one Newfoundlander on her way north to cook for the fishermen through the winter. "I stayed in the cabin in bed. I was too scared to be sick!"

Recorded young John McArthur, "Steam was kept at full head and all syphons were kept at full capacity. But the water level kept rising and now the vessel was listing badly to starboard, so much so that she would not answer the rudder. . . . As it appeared to Captain Mapes, there was only one recourse. He gave the order for everyone to get to the lifeboats. . . . Then it came to our captain like a bolt from the blue – the deck load of lumber and fishing crates could be jettisoned. Forthwith it was, the result being that the *Manitou* righted herself, answered the rudder and we were able to make it to shelter."

Above all, Winnipegosis produced Captain Jack Denby. A mimic, a faithful churchgoer, the town chanty-singer, a wit, and author of some of the town's most colourful language, Jack Denby was the affectionate "uncle" for many of the town's youngsters. When the Winnipegosis dramatic society called for community participation, Denby was always eager; and if his characterization was not exactly according to the script, his ad-libs usually brought down the house anyway. Captain Denby's companions were many, very often the drinking variety, and all were frequently treated to an impromptu mouth-organ recital or a leftover soliloquy. Wheelsman Billy Johnson recalled nights of companionship on the lake:

"I'd come on the second watch at midnight to take her through 'til six in the morning. But Jack never left me. He'd sit there in the pilothouse and sing hour after hour, to shorten the time for me. He'd sing comical songs and together we'd sing church hymns."

"I mind the time I was first given charge of the *Iona,*" began Jack Denby about his employment with the Standard Lumber Company. "Captain McArthur was on board himself that trip and on the way down, I hit nearly every rock on the lake. It was getting dark when the boat ran aground about two miles north of Winnipegosis. McArthur went to bed, while I stayed up, got the boat off the reef, and pulled into town. I figured I'd be fired, so I beat the boss to the draw by quitting. . . . McArthur pats me on the back and says, 'Jack, my boy, any fool can run a boat aground, but it takes a good man to get one off.' "

Beginning in 1889 Jack Denby challenged Winnipegosis territory with total enthusiasm. Competitive, strong-willed, and fluent in Icelandic, French, and Saulteau, Denby grappled with the lake's treacherous channels, its cross winds and shallows, its steamers and boatmen. First with McArthur, then with Booth Fish, and finally with the Grenons aboard the Armstrong-Gimli *Armenon,* Captain Denby learned rafting, fish-freighting, and navigation by instinct – he never sailed on Friday, but, like the watch built into the *Armenon's* keel, he was always on time. Denby was tough on his crews; the air around him often turned blue with the passion of his orders, but his was a "friendly kind of cussing." In the Winnipegosis tradition, he liked his liquor, he often kept to himself, and he had bad nerves. But in a crisis his reflexes were sharp and his intuition accurate. Some said he had a sixth sense for the lake and would wake from deep sleep to avert an impending collision or grounding.

"Tension made them hard drinkers. If you didn't toe the line you were out, and you'd lose a good job. Good job? Hell, as master of the *Armenon* Jack didn't command any more than eighty dollars a month. . . . These fellas were all hard drinkers, had to have a good stiff jolt in the morning to get going," remarked Lorne Lawson, Denby's son-in-law. Lawson had come to Winnipegosis in the spring of 1929, eager to enter the fish trade; he entered, carrying cordwood to steamboat furnaces, and worked his way up from there to *Armenon* wheelsman and then *Armenon* second engineer.

"There's one trip I'll never forget. We had been making special runs. We hadn't had time to fix some leaking flues in the *Armenon's* big boiler, but we were still able to keep enough water and enough steam to make good time on these runs. We came with a full load of fish from Whisky Jack as far as Hill Island, about half way, and couldn't keep the fire up anymore; water was coming through and washing out the fire. . . . So we pulled the fire right quick, and pitched it overboard as the steam pressure in the boiler crept down.

"I didn't know what had to be done. . . . We just knew that we had frozen fish aboard and that if we didn't get them to town, money would be lost. But Jack knew what to do. . . . It was his plan to get some green birch. He got us to cut the wood down into plugs. I kept wondering what good this would do. I was all agog. . . .

"Well, he wanted a young fella; he didn't want a whisky-soak to go into that hot boiler where there was still eighty pounds of steam on. So they asked me to go to the back of the boiler to the return flue, about ten feet a way back in the boiler to plug the holes. You had to stoop over and not touch the sides because they'd burn you. So I put on lots of overalls and sweaters. . . . They laid planks down because me feet'd burn otherwise, and I walked with these plugs and a hammer. . . .

"I got to the back and I could see right away that there were three flues with scalding water shooting out of them with this eighty pounds pressure. He'd briefed me on what to do – get the plugs started in the holes and then hammer them good, to expand the metal out. I remember thinking all the time that I had to hurry or else I would faint. It seemed like hours, but it was finished. I came out and collapsed . . . and I remember thinking that those plugs would burn up, but they didn't leak a drop. And they ran three more trips before they had to cut the old flues out. Right there I learned a lot . . . and it was all Jack's idea . . . he knew exactly what to do."

Still, steamboat skippers were not the only heroes of Winnipegosis. After 1920, neither the *Manitou* nor the *Armenon* left port for open water without homing pigeons aboard. Booth manager Charlie White had seen motion pictures of these birds covering vast distances at great speeds and, at the end of World War One, decided to experiment with them on Lake Winnipegosis. To prepare the town's fish warehouse crews for an approaching steamboat load, White planned to introduce pigeons as the communications link; a pigeon would be released with details about the size of a catch just as a steamboat embarked on its homeward sailing. The first pigeon pair was taken to Spruce Island, about fifty miles up the lake. Within a few summers the pigeons had multiplied and were carrying information south from Whisky Jack, Fox Bay, Channel Island, and most steamer pick-up points along the lake's north shore. A proud Charlie White soon reported that his home pigeons were flying south to town at a mile-a-minute pace.

"There were no radios in those steam days," recounted Cecil Patterson, captain of his own steam launch on Winnipegosis. "When the fish companies caught their fish one hundred miles up the lake, they would want their men in town to know how much ice to prepare and how many railway cars to order for shipping the fish out. . . . These pigeons had a great homing instinct; once released, they went straight up 'til they found their

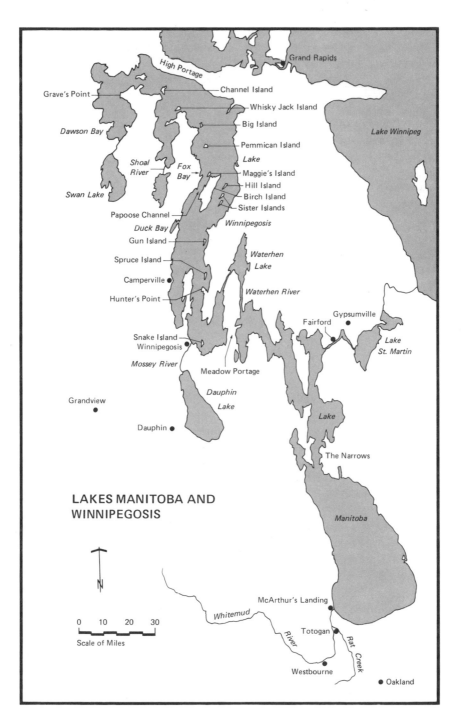

Grand Rapids

High Portage

Grave's Point ————— Channel Island

Dawson Bay

Whisky Jack Island

Big Island

Lake Winnipeg

Pemmican Island

*Shoal
River*

*Fox
Bay*

Lake

Maggie's Island

Hill Island

Birch Island

Sister Islands

Swan Lake

Papoose Channel

Duck Bay

Winnipegosis

Gun Island

Spruce Island

*Waterhen
Lake*

Camperville ●

Hunter's Point

Waterhen River

Gypsumville

Fairford ●

Snake Island
Winnipegosis

*Lake
St. Martin*

Mossey River

Meadow Portage

Dauphin

Grandview
●

Lake

Lake

Dauphin ●

The Narrows

LAKES MANITOBA AND
WINNIPEGOSIS

Manitoba

N

McArthur's Landing ●

0   10   20   30

Whitemud

Totogan ●

River

*Rat
Creek*

Scale of Miles

Westbourne ●

● Oakland

bearings and then straight home. . . . The fellow who raised the homing pigeons was a bachelor who lived alone in a small house down by the lakeshore . . . name was John Butler."

"At one time John Butler cooked on one of the steamboats, but then he was given the job of raising and training homing pigeons for the steamboats." Young Ed Kristjanson worked after school and during the summer holidays cleaning the cages and helping pigeon-keeper Butler, for six dollars a month. "He trained them by placing salt at his window for them to home to. I crated the trained pigeons and when the boats came into Winnipegosis, I put them aboard. . . . The boats then went north to meet the fish boats; they tagged the pigeon with a two-inch-square piece of onion skin paper in a small vial attached to a leg. And in a few hours the homing pigeons arrived in Winnipegosis with information about the size of the fish load, or if a boat was in trouble. . . ."

"Trouble always happened near Hill Island," frowned *Armenon* second engineer Lorne Lawson. "We broke a three-and-one-half-inch crank shaft coming through there one time. She weighed over 1,800 pounds, long and an awful thing to get out of the machinery and complicated parts. The stern bearing had gone out of line and the boat hadn't been pulled out for a few years. . . . It got further out of line and just like working a nail back and forth, it broke off. . . . When she broke, the engine ran free; we knew it'd finally happened. There wasn't a thing we could do. We were helpless. . . .

"Sent a pigeon. . . . Never went out without pigeons. They were the only way we could communicate. Imagine what 1,200 or 1,300 boxes of fish would be worth. If they'd stayed out there and deteriorated, what could you do. They wanted them in New York right now, and fresh too. The companies wouldn't stand for any losses, no matter what it cost to get that fish there in time. . . . Right away, they came out to tow us into port."

The *Armenon* captain and crew paid for the breakdown with their pride – no steamboatman relished entering the home port in tow. Reputations were won and lost from week to week. Competition was stiff, but not destructive. For as well as a sense of humour, Winnipegosis had a sense of community. There was a cohesiveness among the town's swelling population that overshadowed the severity of the Depression in the late 1920's and early 30's. One might not have a steady job, but he always had friends closeby and the lake to supply nourishment. Year round, Winnipegosis townspeople found gaiety in what their lake provided. As a town school teacher remarked, "Each spring the return of the fishermen and their families was the most exciting thing. There would be mile-long trains of horse-drawn sleighs loaded with fish, and people on cabooses strung out across the lake ice. Everybody in town could hardly wait to get down to meet this whole business. All the young men would be back in town. And there would be dances. Everybody had money again and lively times returned. . . ."

"Most fun was in the fall," smiled fisherman Jim Denby, "gettin' ready to go north for the winter. I remember they loaded horses in a sling on a crane into the steamboat holds. Some would get loose and kick everything to pieces. One time they took one horse down the eight feet into the hold, took the sling off, pulled it out, and the horse jumped right back out on the dock. Two guys on horseback had to chase it and had a helluva time catching it."

"Hall Burrell ran a little steam launch with a five horsepower engine in it, called the *Evelyn B.*," began Cec Patterson, who later owned that converted York boat and renamed it the *Rambler*. "We had a couple of pigs and some cattle on late that fall. He dumped them overboard near the shore. And one of these crazy pigs turned around and swam out toward the open lake. Well, Hall was half tight and he took after the pig in the steamboat. I told Hall to let it go . . . but Hall ran that engine flat out yelling, 'Pigs are worth too much money!' He caught up to it and turned it around."

Life at Winnipegosis was never dull. If Jack Denby wasn't serenading the town with his hymns late in the evenings, Bill Mapes might be out spinning yarns with his accomplice, Wags, a wire-haired terrier. On occasion, a towering Negro merchant named Bob Jones would steam into town aboard his launch *Irene.* Jones was noted for his tremendous strength and for his love for children. When he had arrived at Duck Bay in 1915, he ran a trading post, established a school for the settlement children, and professed to be "the first white man in Duck Bay." For the children, the summer days by the lake were an endless adventure. One game of hide 'n' seek led the group to the hold of the docked *Manitou;* when the chase concluded, her seacocks had been pulled and the *Manitou* had sunk above her bulwarks. Not surprisingly, many of the youngsters' capers originated from the shack down by the docks, where steamboat cook Bill Foley lived. There, in winter and summer, bachelor Foley told tall tales, cooked up stolen garden vegetables, and amused the boys with gadgets like his two gramophones, played simultaneously at peak volume to penetrate the peace uptown.

"Foley for a time was cook aboard the dredge," narrated Ruth Patterson, "and he used to bake pies for the crew the night before. He had a shelf where he used to line the pies up to cool. And every night after Foley had gone to bed, the crew would sneak down and snitch some of these pies in a midnight feast. . . .

"Well, Foley got fed up with this, because he'd be short of pies for the next day's meals. So he started collecting flies. He collected and collected until he had gathered a half a quart. He then made a batch of raisin pies, and he put flies in some of the pies; but the good pies weren't put up on the shelf that night. . . . So the boys came down at midnight, stole them and feasted themselves on almost all of the shelf pies.

"Next morning, Foley came down and asked, 'Well boys, did you enjoy the pies?' 'What pies?' they said, acting innocent. So he said, 'Just to make this interesting, I'll show you what you've been eating.' So he took these half-eaten pies from the shelf, and opened them up, and there were flies and raisins mixed together. Some of the fellas hit for the deck and threw up. One lost his false teeth over the railing. . . .

"Not to be outdone, one of the dredge crew offered Foley a remedy for his dandruff problem. He didn't tell Foley it was peroxide. He told Foley to rub it into his hair faithfully every night for so many nights to cure his dandruff. Well, Foley ended up with green hair. . . ."

Diesel fuel. Internal combustion engines. Steel-hulled lake boats. These marked the sudden decline of Winnipegosis steam. By the mid-1930's, old Joseph Grenon Sr. had retired, the Armstrong-Gimli Fisheries had amalgamated with Booth Fish, and the government had purchased the Grenon's proud *Armenon* for tugging barges loaded with dredge diggings. It became cheaper to operate a diesel boat. A diesel engine occupied very little hull space compared with a boiler, a large steam engine, and all the cordwood fuel that went with them. Diesels could carry more fish, or load significantly more freight. But when the first of its kind, the diesel-powered *Myrtle M.,* slid down the ways at Winnipegosis, there was naturally great animosity among steamboatmen. Booth's *Myrtle M.* had few well-wishers.

"I never made a trip on a diesel. I never liked the *Myrtle M.* I saw it, but I never made a trip on it. Diesel. . . . Ah, but I liked steam," eulogized engineer Lorne Lawson. "I learned to smoke my first GBD pipe aboard a steamboat. . . ."

"And I miss the whistle of the steamers. My old *Rambler* had a high shrill whistle," Cecil Patterson agreed. "The diesel engines didn't have the thrill. They weren't romantic like a steam engine. The smell of steam cylinder oil to me was always sweet. . . ."

For fireman Lloyd Burrell, aboard the *Armenon,* "The smell of wood burning in the furnace was wonderful. To an engineer or a fireman, there is no perfume in the world that can beat it . . . and steam was darn reliable!"

Economy won over reliability. Diesel won over steam. And years won over the old-timers. During the 1930's, Standard Lumber Company sawmills closed down and Peter McArthur sold out his timber interests and equipment to the Pine Falls Pulp and Paper Company. His steam tugs *Iona* and *Isabelle* were worn out and had been drawn ashore. Captain McArthur was in his nineties. A devout Christian, a pioneer, an acquisitive monopolist, a frontier aristocrat, an aggressive, frugal, unaffectionate, punctual individualist, Peter McArthur had probed the West, had investigated it, had invested in it, and had grown with it. It was still young, but McArthur was not.

"I remember the Old Gent after the mill had closed," pictured one steamboatman, "when he was on an angel food diet for his bad stomach. Coming down to the lake with his cane, he'd walk over the sawdust and wood slabs. And I remember his posture so well – his hands behind his back, stooped over – and his white beard. . . . Peter was kind of a Scrooge character."

"His business was the business of shipping," concluded a grandson. "Peter McArthur was a businessman, not a captain."

When he and his era died in 1936, Captain Peter McArthur's estate was worth two hundred thousand dollars. Not a monumental sum, considering the extent of his life's investment. McArthur had fathered half a dozen enterprises, most from personal savings; he had risked his business investment on such early unknowns as the CPR, Canada Cement, and International Nickel; he had survived a veritable series of adversaries, including Louis Riel; virtually alone he had pioneered four major prairie water systems; he had successfully piloted three paddlewheelers up Grand Rapids, never conquered by steam before or since. An acute sense of power and money had elevated him to the directorships of two key prairie transportation syndicates; and he had designed and outlived five graceful ladies driven by steam – *Prince Rupert* (1872-81), *Marquette* (1879-97), *North West* (1881-99), *Saskatchewan* (1883-93), and *Isabelle* (1893-1920's).

CHAPTER ELEVEN

On the Sixth Great Lake

The Plains Cree had scattered at the sight and screech of the first fire canoe along the Red River in June of 1859 as the steamer *Anson Northup* hooted its way intrusively toward Fort Garry. A quarter century later, the prairie void, once home of wandering Cree hunting parties, had been strung together with telegraph wires, caged by crisscrossing section fences, and tamed by town streets. Eastern European dialects and the whine of lumber mill saws nearly drowned out the traditional sound of Cree and Métis French. Fishermen were more prevalent than Indian hunters. Town residences displaced teepees. And steamboats outnumbered buffalo. The Red River tumbled constantly as boats threaded the channel to and from the Crees' great sea, Lake Winnipeg. And a nondescript meeting place had become a full-fledged town at the mouth of the river, housing a settlement heaving with activity, and harbouring fiery steamers. Selkirk.

Its history plagued by disappointments, Selkirk, and its riverside inhabitants of the late nineteenth century, had seen boom and bust too often. The worst blow had begun in 1873, when the Pacific Scandal had toppled John A. Macdonald's Conservative Government and with it the all-Canada transcontinental railway route through Winnipeg. The Liberal plan of elected Prime Minister Alexander Mackenzie had called for a patchwork of water and land transport links westward from central Canada, through Selkirk. Among the residents hopeful of a resulting real estate boom at Selkirk had been steamboat captain William Robinson, who had liquidated all his assets and borrowed as well to purchase land at the rumoured railway crossing location. The land investment fizzled with Macdonald's re-election in 1879. And though another boom in the form of immigration would revive Selkirk by 1880, for Selkirk businessman Robinson, the downturn had continued. His failure to transfer the Hudson's Bay Company's paddlewheeler *City of Winnipeg* across Lake Winnipeg to the Grand Rapids in 1881; his subsequent replacement as

HBC Inland Navigator by his North West Navigation Company partner Peter McArthur; and the recession of 1882, when he deliberately wrecked his steam tug *William Robinson* to collect insurance, had nearly ruined the Selkirk captain. However, in 1884, Lake Winnipeg's struggling skipper recovered. That year, at age thirty-six, Captain Robinson joined the British expedition to quash the rebellious Moslems in Egypt. By piloting specially built Yarrow gunboats up the Nile during the campaign, Robinson won battle citation and international recognition.

Back home on the Red River the next year, Robinson took stock. As the sole remaining active director of the North West Navigation Company, he still owned a Selkirk boatyard, with two surviving steamers: the veteran sternwheeler *Marquette*, and the largest Lake Winnipeg steamer afloat, the *Princess*. Measuring 154 feet from bow flag pole to stern post, and with comfortable accommodation for six hundred passengers, Robinson's *Princess* won the distinction of ferrying homebound Canadian militiamen from Grand Rapids at Lake Winnipeg's north end into the heart of a victory celebration in Winnipeg in late 1885. In January of 1886, the captain married and moved with his bride aboard the drydocked *Marquette*. There at Selkirk he planned a new enterprise and his financial recovery on the 9,000-square-mile lake he had reconnoitered a decade before. Lake Winnipeg was his future.

"Robinson had a lot of great ideas, that's for sure," stressed George Simpson. One of an American immigrant family, Simpson found employment at the age of fourteen as an office boy for the William Robinson Lumber Company. This latest Robinson venture began at Selkirk in the late 1880's; from small beginnings it carried Robinson to outright ownership of major sawmills, timber rights, fishing rights, cold storage plants, and, by the mid-1890's, to the directorship of the largest passenger-freighter fleet on the prairies. But young George Simpson never felt like the neglected cog in the larger machine: "He was kind to me . . . a friend. . . . He was a big man, about six feet or more. Light weight. He wore a bushy moustache and after the Nile expedition, he was deeply tanned. . . . He was a modest man. . . . Robinson wasn't a drinker and he built up a strong lumber and boating business."

The registry of vessels for the Province of Manitoba during the 1880's and 1890's reflected the increasing influence of William Robinson and his Selkirk-based operations. Covering entries of all water craft – sail and steam-driven – between Lake Superior and the Rockies, the Winnipeg shipping ledgers indicated a ten-year average of nearly eight steamers constructed per year. Robinson steamer entries dominated more each season. In 1881 Captain Robinson had christened the *Princess*. In 1883 the steamer *Red River* was launched. The tug *Ogema* in 1885. The *Sul-*

tana and the *Myles* in 1889. By the late 1880's, the Commodore had acquired three previously built lake tugs: the *Lady Ellen*, the *Glendevon*, and ironically, the old Hudson's Bay Company *Colvile*, from which he had first surveyed the shallow waters of Lake Winnipeg in 1875. Then, in a banner 1893 season for William Robinson Lumber, his Selkirk yards bore three new steamers: the 67-foot *Fisherman*, the 70-foot *Idell*, and a sister ship for the *Princess*, the 110-foot *City of Selkirk*.

Strung out along 240 miles of shoreline, fishing stations drew net after net of Lake Winnipeg whitefish, goldeye, and sturgeon. Methodically, William Robinson worked his way up both lakeshores buying out the independent fish interests and establishing a steamboat freighter system to relay fresh fish to new freezing plants at Selkirk. Similarly, the Robinson Lumber Company bought out weaker timber businesses adjacent to Lake Winnipeg, and initiated a lucrative market steamboating lumber south to railway contractors hungry for building planks, pilings, and ties. While Winnipeg left the Red River bank behind and looked inward, shaping its streets and crude buildings into a city, Selkirk flourished because it remained at the riverside, dependent on its incoming resources and its outgoing steamboat traffic. By the early 1890's the Robinson monopoly had revived an abandoned water highway and its almost forgotten steamers.

Not unlike Peter McArthur at Lake Manitoba, however, William Robinson suffered heavy setbacks. On a breezy night in August, 1891, fishermen at the Dauphin River station on Lake Winnipeg watched flames completely gut Robinson's tug *Glendevon*, taking one crewman with her to the bottom. Captain Thomas E. Pollock, working for the Commodore, reported the same scene three years later from Grand Rapids. The *Colvile's* crew woke on a July morning to face flames in their steamer's hold. With nothing aboard to combat the fire, the boatmen were forced to abandon ship as the blaze consumed the weary old-timer. Fire also swept through an $18,000 freezer plant at Robinson's Selkirk yards that year and destroyed an entire season's catch. Again, the insurance that might have recompensed a portion of the damages had not been purchased, and for a moment the Robinson empire tottered.

Just as American capital provided the needed adrenalin to fishing and freighting on Lake Winnipegosis, so that same money source arrived on Robinson's waterfront at this crucial point. As at Winnipegosis, the Booth Fish Company of Chicago had dispatched agents to Lake Winnipeg to ferret out potential fish suppliers for the tables of New York, Boston, and Chicago. Northwest Canadian whitefish and Winnipeg goldeye were Robinson's trump cards. Booth Fish decided to establish a branch in Selkirk, and formed the Dominion Fish Company, with William

Robinson as its manager and with his North West Navigation Company supporting the export of fish in a continuous shuttle of fish-freighting steamboats up and down Lake Winnipeg. Renewed steamboat activity lifted spirits all round, from fishermen who supplied Dominion freezers, up to Robinson and his key assistants, like Johnny Jones.

"There were three or four steamboats continually engaged in our fishing business. And those were the days for fish! Those boats'd go out in the forenoon to the fishing stations and come back in the afternoon loaded to the gunwales and with fish piled high on the decks. There was never trouble selling Lake Winnipeg fish. They were stored in the freezers at Selkirk and then transferred to refrigerator cars bound for the States."

The Booth-Robinson arrangement rejuvenated the North West Navigation boatyard as well, as new ships were continually being built to keep pace with a catch that exceeded three million pounds per year. Hired shipbuilder William Dewar commenced hull lengthening and superstructure renovations aboard the *City of Selkirk* in 1894. In 1896 North West Navigation's new silver-banded funnel emblem crowned yet another steamer, the 126-foot *Premier*. Next was the 105-foot *Lady of the Lake*, with cabin space for twenty-five passengers and freezer capacity for 250 boxes of fresh fish. The *Lady* was christened in 1897, the year of the flood.

The threat of prairie fire, drought, frost, insect infestation, and crop rust plagued farmers of the southern Manitoba plains mercilessly during the sod-busting years. But no other natural disaster could match the devastation of a sudden river flood. Perennial friend, the lower Red River had turned unpredictable foe in 1826 and in 1852, forcing Indians and settlers to take speedy refuge in the Pembina Mountains in North Dakota or on the ridge ten miles east of Emerson on the international border. Repeated in 1861, flooding on the Red sent Winnipeggers retreating to Stoney Mountain on the west and to Bird's Hill on the east side of the river. And the river's rise in 1882 had warranted the emergency use of Red River sidewheeler *Cheyenne* for assistance. But the flood of 1897 was unlike anything ever before experienced.

On April 9 of that year residents of Grand Forks, North Dakota, one hundred miles upriver from Winnipeg, fought jamming ice and rising river levels well into the night. These signs alone were evidence that the breakup on the Red in lower Manitoba would not be an ordinary one.

April 13 marked the beginning of abnormal water turbulence at Emerson, seventy-five miles up the Red River south from Winnipeg.

Storms lashed the river into four-foot waves and cloudy foam on April 17 as the 1882 high-water level was approached.

By April 21, freezing rain had fallen, swelling the river's volume and spilling its current over the banks and onto the farmlands and prairie town streets as far north of the border as Morris, Manitoba. Warehouses, old landmarks, and traffic bridges were smashed, with some loss of life and much discomfort. Livestock were removed from pastures and barns and brought into farmhouses to keep them from drowning, while families moved themselves to second floors. Trains and mail stood still. The Great Northern Railway turntable at St. Vincent was washed away, taking several buildings with it. And as hotels and shops grew crowded with refugees from the south Manitoba countryside, Emerson town officials worried about dwindling supplies. North Dakota Senator Judson La Moure of Pembina, sent an urgent telegram:

"Washington. April 19. The storm of yesterday in connection with the flood has left over 200 people destitute along the Red River in this country. Aid is needed at once. The local committee is unable to render sufficient aid."

"It came down like a thief in the night," a horrified Morris farmer reported. "We saw what appeared to be a cloud on the southern horizon. Then rivulets flowed across the fields, and, to our astonishment, before ten hours had passed, we were in the midst of a lake, and farm machinery was damaged, if not carried off!"

The North Dakota state government pressed the two-year-old excursion sternwheeler *City of Grand Forks* into mercy mission service down the Red River to Pembina on the American side of the border. The *Grand Forks'* crew and company found the territory in chaos. Any reluctance to believe the reports of destruction vanished when they encountered an entire Minneapolis and Northern Company warehouse carried miles across the prairie from its Drayton, North Dakota, site. The *Grand Forks* skipper noted "The low-lying district from the Snake River to Pembina is appalling. It is one vast sea of desolation, wreck, and ruin. In some cases the steamer was as much as two miles from the river channel. Barbed wire fences interfered materially with navigation across the Prairies, but some thirty familes were supplied with provisions. . . ."

North of the border, a woman had drowned at Morris. And a fair-sized Grand Forks house, having drifted 150 miles upside down, grounded finally at St. Mary's cemetery in east Winnipeg. Responding to Emerson's predicament, on April 22 the Manitoba government commissioned Captain E. Connell's 92-foot sternwheeler *Assiniboine* to relieve the town. Aboard with Connell's crew were Ernie Blow of the Manitoba *Free Press* and government representatives E. M. Wood and George Black, who dispensed emergency goods. An avid diarist, Black chronicled the voyage up the "Raging Ruby" River channel:

"April 22 – Started from the mouth of the Assiniboine. . . .

"April 24 – As we ascended the river, signs of the devastating effects of the high water became more and more apparent, houses surrounded by water, at various stages of submersion. Some had water up to their eaves, some with only a small portion of the roof visible; chickens, pigs and cattle seeking safety on the tops of partially submerged dung heaps and haystacks. . . . In many cases the houses were abandoned, and in others the occupants were moving out. . . . We reached Morris at four o'clock, and, looking west, south and north, water could be seen as far as the eye could reach; in fact, Morris wore the appearance of a modern Venice. . . .

"April 26 – As we approached Emerson . . . we were met by Mayor Wright and three or four citizens about three miles from the town. They came on board and accompanied us to the town. Instead of seeking moorings at the river bank, which, of course, was invisible, we steamed right up the principal street and tied up in front of the Alexandria block, the floating sidewalk in front of the building doing duty as a wharf. . . . The townspeople accorded us a hearty welcome, and we had hardly come to a standstill when the boat was crowded by citizens, all of whom were in high spirits and appeared to be enjoying the situation. The majority of people were moving from place to place in boats. . . ."

Stanchions atop the steamer wheelhouse ripped away the CPR telegraph wires, and parties on board the *Assiniboine* shook hands with amazed occupants at the second story windows of the Alexandria block buildings. Citizens and dogs flocked to the street on anything that would float. Excitement and levity ran high for six hours; a small boy fell from the moored steamboat and was pulled out in a comical rescue. Emerson's floating sidewalks were soon over-crowded with onlookers who struggled to keep their makeshift galleries stable; most often the sidewalks tipped and sank, to the merriment of all, including the victims. Captain Connell then steamed the *Assiniboine* down Main and across Church Street to the residence of Dr. D. H. McFadden to load horses. The town photographer, Roy Abbott, did a booming business capturing the historic docking, and selling flat-bottomed boats on the side. As Edward Gilbert recalled, "We'd had heavy snowfall all winter . . . and when the thaw came, everybody had started building boats. . . . Salem Ruth, the undertaker had the most stylish boat. And Welshman Davy Williams had his large family aboard a wide and deep boat. . . . In its own way, it was a picnic. . . ."

At seven cents a pound, Lake Winnipeg fish prices were inviting seamen from all sides of the prairies. American fishermen, already affiliated with Booth, joined the migration north to Manitoba. Salt-water boatmen had arrived at the Selkirk docks to search out shipbuilding labour. And fresh-water veterans, crowded by Great Lakes congestion, packed up their marine trades and their families for opportunities on Canada's sixth Great Lake. Despite the arrival of all these newcomers, however, Lake Winnipeg remained dominated by William Robinson and his Booth subsidiary, Dominion Fish. The Commodore directed the widest fish-marketing operation, with control of the prime fishing grounds, dozens of net-hauling sailboats, and an expanding steamboat fleet. Independents found next to no room. Robinson had previously absorbed the Manitoba Fish Company; then as Dominion Fish manager, incorporated Dan Reid's fish business, and challenged the Ewing and Fryer sturgeon enterprise. Another newcomer who attempted to succeed alone was former Lake Michigan fisherman J. W. Simpson, who worked for a time with Dominion Fish. In 1899 Simpson christened an independent fish tug, whose construction style few had seen before. The *Rocket* dropped away from a sheer bow, through a 76-foot-long by 15-foot-wide hull, to a long low open afterdeck. Forward, her main compartments were entirely enclosed, with the pilothouse and cabin above – in all, an 1880's Great Lakes design. But Captain Simpson and his *Rocket* could not compete, and the young steamer soon found her way to Robinson's North West Navigation Company.

Regardless of the seeming impossibility of competing against Commodore Robinson, it was inevitable that sooner or later the prosperity on Lake Winnipeg would attract more skillful competitors for the rich harvest of sturgeon, whitefish, and goldeye. Caught up in gold fever, William Purvis, a cousin of J. W. Simpson, had set out from his home on Manitoulin Island in the mid-1890's for the Yukon. En route to the Northwest, Purvis stopped over along the Red River and Lake Winnipeg; he liked what he saw. When Klondike prospecting was out of his system, Purvis returned East and transplanted his family from Ontario to Selkirk. His son Roy Purvis retraced his father's migration:

"My father came out to Selkirk to build boats on the lake. He brought out some men from his home at Gore Bay. There, at Manitoulin Island, my father had fished, but he got burned out twice.... On Lake Winnipeg, he ran a fish station near the Duck Islands...."

"About 1900," George Simpson continued, "my father [J. W. Simpson]; Jack Seaman, a steamboat engineer; Captain Tom Pollock, skipper on the lake; W. J. Guest, a fish salesman who owned the Merchant Hotel in Winnipeg; and Bill Purvis – the five of them formed the Northern Fish Company. And they made quite a success of it."

Shipbuilding began immediately in the Northern Fish camp. Full-bearded and tempered by eighteen years service with the Hudson's Bay Company, Stornaway Scot Roderick Smith assembled – unaided – the

236

Captain Joseph Connell and the flood-rescue steamer *Assiniboine* at work in Emerson, April 26, 1897. *(Provincial Archives of Manitoba)*

The Saskatchewan River drops 85 feet over the 4½-mile-long Grand Rapids cataract. On June 6, 1908, the steamer *Alberta* shot the rapids in 30 minutes and promptly sank. *(Emma Goodfellow)*

propeller-driven *Highlander*. Smith hand-hewed the steamer's tamarack keel and ribs before bolting them to hand-planed planks. The *Highlander* first freighted for the Imperial Fish Company, which helped bring together Imperial Fish and another firm, the W. J. Guest Fish Company of Winnipeg, under the Northern banner. The following spring the *Chieftain,* fashioned of beechwood and rock elm and powered by the swiftest marine engine on the lake, gave Northern a fleet of two. By 1903 Roderick Smith had christened the gem of his designing career, the 126-foot passenger-freighter *Wolverine.* Sister ship to the *Chieftain,* the *Tempest* joined the fleet in 1904. Bill Purvis contributed his first effort to the Northern group in 1905, the 120-foot *Mikado.* And that same season, Northern launched their tug, the *Alert.* Inside five years, Northern Fish had balanced the weight and capacity of William Robinson's steamer strength.

Booth's Dominion Fish Company suddenly faced a serious competitor for Lake Winnipeg fillets. Moreover, news from the north end of the lake had shaken the Commodore. Two days out from Warren Landing on a return trip, the North West Navigation steam freighter *Red River,* burdened with lumber and a capacity cargo, had foundered and sunk; no lives were lost, but overnight Dominion Fish had a gap in its fish-freighting operation. This loss, combined with Northern's organized threat, sparked Dominion into year-round production at the North West Navigation yards. William Dewar, Robinson's master shipbuilder, completed the lengthening and structural alterations aboard Dominion freighter *City of Selkirk.* In 1904, to complement the silver-funnelled fleet of Commodore Robinson, the North West Navigation Company launched a 64-foot tug, *Frederick.* And two seasons later Dewar completed a major face-lift on the North West flagship, the *Princess.* Converting the once-graceful "queen of the lake", Dewar ripped away her gingerbread staterooms for bulk cargo space. Forward of her boilers, he slashed through her hull, extending her total length to 160 feet. Romantic though they were, her sidewheel assemblies were torn loose and replaced with a steeple compound engine which drove a single four-flanged propeller. Astern, Dewar eliminated her promenade deck for a tow-line apparatus, leaving but six cabins, a kitchen, a dining room, and only a shadow of her original Victorian elegance.

"As a school boy on holidays, I scrambled over her decks playing at pirates as she lay abandoned in the slough at Selkirk. Even then, I was impressed with her lovely lines," Ed Nelson wrote. Boyhood fantasies aboard the beached *Princess* in the 1890's were long past, but now, in the winter of 1905-06, looking for work, Nelson signed aboard the reconstructed *Princess* freighter.

"The *Princess* made trips to Spider Islands, almost at the extreme north end of the lake, for loads of fish. On her second trip, I had been promoted to wheelsman on the second watch. At the fueling dock at Bull Head, I was ordered to help with the fueling in spite of my protests that I was off watch. I was at the wheel as we later steamed down the channel, and I warned the mate that I was feeling very sleepy. . . . The mate sat beside me, telling me stories to keep me awake. But eventually, he fell asleep and I dozed off too. I woke up as I was falling off the seat. We were passing Gull Light, at about 5:00 A.M. . . . The *Princess* hit the beach at full speed. . . .

"The *Princess* was released from the shore and repaired, and we left again for Spider Islands. I was paid off, as I expected, and that seeming misfortune may have saved my life."

The *Princess,* on a late summer morning of that same 1906 season, cast off from Warren Landing, the most northerly port on Lake Winnipeg. Now several years since Dewar had stripped away all her majestic features, the *Princess* appeared gray and humble. Bow enclosed. Stark pilothouse above and set well back. Austere cabins behind. Aft hurricane deck crowded with funnel, vents, tanks, and boats on davits. And a long vacant stern, cut-away and vulnerable. With the market booming, the demand for fresh fillets pushed each freighting crew to the limit. The thrust of competition between the Northern and the Dominion fish companies warranted continuous export quotas. And the pressure of strict freighting schedules caused the normal precautions of good seamanship to be tossed to the wind.

A figure in the pilothouse scanned the horizon from the pink eastern sunlight of a young day to the north and west, where breezes from unmarked skies sighed across the starboard bow. Master of this steamer, the figure rigidly guided his wheelsman toward open lake through the mouth currents of the Nelson River, up which the skipper had first come to the lake seven years before. In his early sixties, Captain John Hawes was stocky, but of dignified stature, with pointed Edwardian beard and moustache. Behind his seven years with Commodore Robinson lay a life of salt-water sailing in the service of the Hudson's Bay Company, running steamships between Liverpool and Fort Churchill. Married a second time in 1890, Hawes had moved inland to Selkirk in search of employment that would allow him more frequent visits with his family. Devout, soft-spoken, secluded, self-demanding, Captain Hawes boasted a career of superb seamanship. Yet, in the half-dozen seasons Hawes had navigated Lake Winnipeg, the veteran was only just acquainted with the lake's sudden gales, amorphous shallows, boiling reefs, and, most disturbing to an Atlantic salt, the omnipresent meandering shoreline.

So it was, with 1,200 boxes of frozen fish, hardly enough to stiffen her hull against the lake's often tempestuous conditions, that the *Princess* nosed out from Warren Landing on Saturday, August 25th, homebound the 240 miles to Selkirk. Aboard, her normal crew of thirteen included a mate, a chief engineer (her second engineer was not aboard, as he had been transferred to the *City of Selkirk* to replace a sick man), a woman cook, a stewardess, two pilots, two firemen, four deckhands, and the captain. At Warren Landing the *Princess* had embarked eight passengers – five men, a woman, and her two children – and five hours later a ninth passenger came aboard at Poplar Point, the steamer's last scheduled stop before Selkirk.

"We left Poplar Point at 4:30 on Saturday afternoon," mate Alex Joyce began. On his first watch Joyce, wheeling for skipper Hawes, set his course for George's Island, steering well clear of the Poplar Point reefs. The lake was ominously calm.

By six o'clock, wind gusts began blowing in, now from the northwest. Seas were breaking. For Joyce, the struggle was only beginning.

"The *Princess* sprang a leak about 6:30 P.M. We had then run along for two hours and were passing George's Island. Continued on our course for Swampy Island until about 10:30 P.M. At that time the water was getting worse in the fire room, so we turned around to try to get back to George's Island, and continued on that course until about 12:30 A.M. The wind was hard to the northwest."

Winds reached gale force. The *Princess* crashed headlong into paralyzing wind and 25-foot seas. Joyce maintained his course in vain. All other crewmen, up to their necks in water, were below at the pumps, as Joyce struggled at the helm.

"The water got above the damper of the boilers and shut off the fire. The engines then stopped. This was about two o'clock in the morning. From then on we were at the mercy of the wind. All the time the water got deeper in the hold. . . . The whole crew and others on board bailed with buckets, everything. But we were unable to do anything. We wanted to keep her afloat until daylight. It was the worst sea I ever saw. And we would've had no chance in the darkness."

Mate Joyce and pilots Jack Bird and Joe Star gave up the struggle to hold the *Princess* to any course. In the storm the vessel swung about, drifting broadside to the south. Hope now rested on the chance that the steamer might pile onto a sand beach at Swampy Island ten miles away.

"About four o'clock we notified the passengers to take to the boats. The girls laughed and thought that there was no danger. They thought that she would hold out. They would not, after repeated warnings, put the lifebelts on. There were plenty of them on the boat.... Poole, the engineer, was the only one who put one on....

"We had been sounding all along, as we expected to find a shallow place on the island. I made the last sounding about ten minutes before she went to pieces. As near as I could tell in the rough seas, it was eight fathoms," surmised Alex Joyce.

"About 4:15 A.M.," a passenger recalled, "the steamer gave a great lurch...."

"The captain seemed to act strangely. He had nothing to say," Joyce continued. "When Arthur Poole came up from the engine room, he remarked, 'Well Captain, we're on the island.' He just said, 'Yes.' I was in the pilot house at the time and didn't feel the blow that broke her...."

A reef below punched a hole in her hull. Disintegration followed rapidly. Bailing stopped. Rain and waves cascaded every direction. And again the *Princess* lurched. "The upper part of her split right away from the hull," another of the survivors recalled. "The sea split the whole superstructure from the hull.... The smokestack went down through the bottom.... A deck hand, making for the boats, went down through the hole and disappeared....

"[We] struggled desperately to reach the lifeboats. Mrs. James Sinclair had two small children. She threw one into the yawl boat which was afloat on the deck. When the deck rose out of the sea, Mr. Sinclair hurried across, although the waves were mountains high. With an axe he chopped loose the falls which held the yawl. The tremendous strain of the sea broke the ship at the boiler and she settled aft, going down at the stern....

"Alex Joyce, the mate, was at the stern end, endeavouring to get near the yawl boat to get it free from the davits. One large rush of water sent him headlong to the yawl. Catching hold, he managed to draw himself half-way into it. At this moment, he caught sight of Mrs. Sinclair in the water, holding her baby.... Joyce caught her by the shoulder and pulled her into the yawl.... Everyone else was swept overboard...."

"Knowing Swampy Island was somewhere in the roaring darkness ahead, and fringed with boulder-strewn beaches," recounted another passenger, who steered his load of survivors ashore with an oar, "my hope was that we would hit a stretch of sand beach.... Land appeared directly ahead.... but the expected sand beach was not there. The boat was driven among boulders completely out of control...."

It was 6:30, Sunday morning. North reef. Swampy Island. Survivors shivered in the dawn's cold. Waves rolled in gently. Eleven reached shore in lifeboats. Four rode wreckage to the beach. One floated free of the shattered *Princess* in his lifebelt. Untouched lifebelts littered the sand. Fish crates, an ice chest, storing beef, and pickles tumbled ashore. Miraculously, dry matches were found. Two days later the steamer *City of Selkirk* rescued the sixteen survivors. Nowhere to be found were passengers Joe Einarson and Loftus Gudmanson, nor Indian deckhand Charles Greyeyes, nor cook Yoba Johnson, nor stewardess Flora McDonald, nor Captain John Hawes. All six lives were lost.

"She sank out on the biggest part of the lake," Roy Purvis sighed. As a Northern Fish wheelsman, Purvis knew Lake Winnipeg's checker-board nature well – squally here, dead calm there. "We were coming down the lake that night on the *Wolverine*. Storm never bothered us at all. . . . But the *Princess* got ripped apart. She'd laid on the bank too long at Selkirk before they made her into a screw-driven boat. . . . She wasn't fit for the lake. She was rotten. . . . And the captain drowned; when they found him, he was on his hands and knees under the wheelhouse, dead."

The dead were buried. Only fragments were found of the *Princess,* a prairie steamer remembered along the Red for her historic 1881 launching and tragic 1906 foundering. Other memories persisted, scarlike, among the survivors. For years afterward, whenever surviving engineer Arthur Poole passed Swampy Island, he would climb to the bridge until the steamer he was engineering passed safely by, and only then return to his engine room.

Storms did not avoid Lake Winnipeg after 1906. That "Old Devil Lake" had not claimed the last of her trespassers. The *Myles*, the *Garry*, the *Chieftain*, and many fish sailboats would follow. Riverton Fish Company's steamer *Goldfield* one night narrowly made shelter from seventy-mile-per-hour winds and electrical flashes so intense the wheelsman was forced to wear dark glasses. Dominion's *Lady of the Lake* heaved so violently in an early spring storm that tumbling cordwood punctured her hull and nearly crushed her engine-room crew. One season's gale drove Northern's *Wolverine* ashore on Spider Island, ripping out a twenty-foot keel section; only Captain Tom Pollock's ingenuity and several mattresses stuffed quickly into the hole managed to save her. Still the steamboats and crews endured the risks. And still the routine continued. Fish was king. Gill-nets a thousand yards long were cast, their diamond-shaped meshes strung between buoys. Healthy catches were cleared with each lift. Fillets were dressed. Packers crated the millions of pounds annually into ice-houses. Freighters rendezvoused twice weekly and steamed back down the lake for Selkirk. Night and day, six days a week, June to August, then September through October, fishermen harvested and steamboatmen hauled. Just days after the catch, baked Selkirk white-fish spiced Chicago soirées; Lake Winnipeg pickerel, saugers, and tullibees sizzled in thousands of American kitchen skillets; and prized Winnipeg goldeye brought premium prices at New York restaurants. Ninety percent of Lake Winnipeg fillets were exported to the United States.

Yet there were steamboat dollars other than American to be made, particularly along the Red. After years of river hauling with his sternwheeler *Alice Sprague*, Winnipeg lumber merchant Daniel Sprague suddenly discovered an after-hours occupation on the river as excursion operator. Similarly, the sidewheeling *Antelope* began slipping into weekend bunting to attract evening outings. Overnight, a Winnipeg business consortium formed the Pioneer Navigation Company, placing their recent sternwheeler acquisitions *Alexandra* and *Gertie H.* on the Saturdays-and-holidays circuit. With a little paint, coloured streamers, ice cream to sell, band music, and the right *Free Press* publicity, no-one would notice the slightly questionable background of the pleasure steamer, nor even the unattractive murk of the current. Instantly the Red was romantic. On a clear night, the price of a fare, some imagination, and the magic of a Red River excursion could recreate a Parisian canal cruise for young lovers, or a Blue Danube waltz in the old country for old-timers, or a Mark Twain adventure for a young boy.

"As boys, we never missed the *Alexandra* or the old *Gertie H.*," wrote one young adventurer. "One skipper was a most breathtaking sight in his gold crusted cap and long blue coat with its double row of gold buttons. Maybe it wasn't real gold, but we thought it was. It was magnificent. We stood, mouths agape, as he welcomed passengers aboard. No commodore of the Cunard Line could have excited more admiration than Captain Bellefeuille. . . ."

Levie Bellefeuille represented the vanguard of a new breed of prairie captain. From relative obscurity during the dying days of Queen Victoria's era, the forty-year-old Bellefeuille climbed directly into the limelight after 1900. Pioneer Navigation's *Alexandra* was his creation, and he skippered it rigidly; he embarked and docked with punctuality and was so opposed to passengers spooning openly that he publicly lectured one couple. Recognizing his talents, a Manitoba channel-clearing firm commissioned him to build perfection and efficiency into their Red River steam dredge. Bellefeuille's expertise also attracted Winnipeg entrepreneur John L. Hyland, who proposed that Bellefeuille design a fleet of pleasure steamers to compete with Pioneer for excursion business. The compelling square-faced ship's master decided to pursue a more colourful prospect for his career, however. The Winnipeg Navigation Company, another promoting concern eager to exploit the excursion rebirth, had purchased the sternwheeler *Alberta*, a neglected but fit candidate for its excursion trade, and a captain was needed to sail her into the Red River shipping lanes. The problem was that the Alberta sat idle at the Goshen flats of Prince Albert, Saskatchewan, nearly a thousand miles by water from its new Winnipeg owners. It was a challenge – and just the right-sized feather for the captain's cap of Levie Bellefeuille.

A fast-water design built in 1904, the *Alberta* was a staunch craft, comprised of twelve watertight hull compartments, a lower or main deck, cabins on her second or boiler deck, and a hurricane deck with captain's quarters and pilothouse on the top level. An eighteen-foot-long boiler powered her engines through a four-foot horizontal stroke, which rotated her sternwheel at a top speed of fifteen miles per hour. But with five hundred miles of perverse Saskatchewan River to navigate, and an equal distance along the shoreline of a deceiving Lake Winnipeg, Captain Bellefeuille required more than an adequate steamboat design – the *Alberta* needed a crew with *savoir faire,* who could read the river and lake water best, and who knew the normal pulse of a Saskatchewan paddlewheeler. Bellefeuille hired Alfred McGillivray, a Cree from The Pas, and Louis Jourdain, a forty-year veteran of the Cumberland Lake country, to pilot, with Joe and Henry McKay as interpreters. Below, he engaged George Neil as chief engineer, with boatbuilder-engineer Willard Goodfellow as his second; the firemen were George Neil Jr. and B. Bartley; William Busby was cook; Bob Angus and Charles Hudson were taken on as deckhands.

Widespread interest prevailed among Winnipeggers in the *Alberta's* journey, which was one of the longest and most perilous voyages in prairie navigation history. Manitoba *Free Press* correspondent J. S. Evans travelled overland with the captain to Prince Albert to document the trip.

"Sharp at two o'clock on the afternoon of May 30th ... the *Alberta* swung into the stream with two barges alongside, blew a series of whistle blasts as a parting salute, and we were launched on our way to a novel experience and a journey of unsurpassable beauty and pleasure. . . .

"Twenty miles below Prince Albert, at Cole's Falls, our adventure began. . . . Rounding a bend in the river, a ferry cable stretched from two towers on either bank, was discovered. The engines were reversed and the whistle blew raucously for the ferryman to lower his cable, but there was no answer to our signals. After considerable delay, with wrath steadily mounting, a party of us went ashore and laid violent hands on this arrangement, which is regarded by every river navigator as an invention of the devil, second only in malignancy to a bridge. . . ."

Steep banks, jutting straight up from the river and crested with dense greenery, isolated the *Alberta* from the surrounding prairie. The boatmen met not a soul along the many river miles past the old site of Fort à la

Corne, past the English River, down the Nipawin Rapids, and into marshlands overpopulous with pelican and duck flocks. Each sunup and sundown splashed crimson over different terrain. At Birch Island, where the fourteenth base line met the Saskatchewan, the steamer crossed the same latitude as the main street of Edmonton. Mammoth boulders greeted them at the Tobin Rapids, while snags and sandbars slowed their passage through the Big Stone Rapids to Cumberland House, where they moored next to the rotted remains of the Hudson's Bay Company's queen steamer *Northcote*. Near The Pas, the pilots dodged treacherous whirl-pools at the Big Eddy; en route to Chemahawin, a rugged riverbank claimed one of their two loaded barges; and at Cedar Lake, gusting crosswinds halted progress. Despite the obstacles, however, by late after-noon of June 4, the fifth day of the voyage, the *Alberta* reached the upper end of the Missi-paw-wis-te-guk, the white water of the Grand Rapids cataract.

"Our skipper and Joe McKay went down the rapids in a canoe with the dean of the Grand Rapids pilots, Old Sikimish, and made soundings with a pole, finding nowhere less than nine feet of water, which was sufficient for our purposes. In a canoe, Sikimish has no superior, but his eyesight is failing, and we were strongly recommended to engage Jimmy Atkinson, another younger pilot to take us over the Grand Rapids. On the morning of Saturday, June 6, Atkinson came aboard. . . .

"There was a slight wind with mild rain when we cast off at the head of the rapids at 7:35 A.M. There was a little manoeuvring in order to strike the channel fairly and at 7:41 we were into the first chute in about as hel-lish an outburst as one could imagine. The steamer shot her nose through the first ledge with a bound and the bow rising the stern fell and struck heavily. I could feel the jar and hear the grinding of wood; the superstruc-ture jerked backwards as if it would wrench itself off, and, to use the vocabulary of a member of the crew, 'She ran like a scairt dog!'

"The chief engineer came forward and megaphoned through his hands to the pilot house. 'She's got a hole in her, skipper, and the water's com-ing in fast.' No sooner were the words spoken than there was another fearful jar and then came a succession of bumps as if the steamer were going down a staircase. McGillivray, who stood beside me, was badly scared. . . .

"A procession of hungry, jagged rocks, everyone of which had horns, tusks and a complete set of double-teeth, upper and lower, passed by the side of the boat with horrid rapidity. So close were they, that I thought every one of them would tear the boat to pieces. Fascinated by the mov-ing picture of the riverbed, I was oblivious to the passage of time and the scenery en route and when Prisoner's Island, at the foot of the rapids was sighted, the present chronicler is bound to confess that his prospects for dying comfortably in bed at a ripe old age and after a long life of unremitting industry, were vastly improved. . . .

"The experience was but of half an hour's duration, but it will last all who underwent it for the balance of their lives. The awesome roar of the rapids and the weird, piping note underlying it were enough to terrify one, but added to this was the appalling fury of the gale and rain together with the frightful speed at which the steamer ran for most of the distance. . . . . The *Alberta* had come the whole way down with a puncture in the bottom of her hull, six inches by eighteen in size. . . . After beaching opposite the H. B. Co's post, the *Alberta* settled rapidly to the bottom."

Hudson's Bay men quickly constructed a bulkhead around the large break in the *Alberta's* hull; then filled the gap with blankets, clay, and sods. Syphoning followed. But the longest delay was for the weather to clear. Nine days after shooting the rapids, Captain Bellefeuille brought aboard a new mate, John Simpson, to guide the *Alberta* south across Lake Winnipeg. Hugging the lakeshores and hiding in bays from the wind, the *Alberta* slipped unnoticed around Long Point, past Reindeer, Swampy, and Commissioner islands, across Humbug Bay, through Gull Harbour and Balsam Bay, and into the thickly fogged mouth of the Red River. Relief overcame the *Alberta* crew and *Free Press* correspondent Evans.

"On Friday, June 19, we arrived in Winnipeg early in the afternoon. . . . Whistled salutes and congratulations from locomotives, dredges, and even factories apprised us that we were at home and that the instructions to 'come through' had been fulfilled."

Surveying the damage to his prize, owner A. McKenzie welcomed the *Alberta* to her new Winnipeg Navigation Company home. McKenzie commenced immediate repairs to the steamer's structure, battered by forty-eight sets of rapids and nearly a thousand nautical miles. Within a year, the *Alberta* was commanding a healthy hauling business and even healthier weekend cruising patronage. The dimension of the *Alberta's* achievements were noted far beyond the Red River banks. Among those impressed was the Dominion Minister of Public Works, William Pugsley, who went so far as to predict "a waterway system from the Red River and Lake Winnipeg to the mouth of the Saskatchewan River and thence across the prairies to the foothills of the Rockies, 100 miles west of Edmonton. . . a direct system of navigation for 1,500 miles to Winnipeg!"

The arrival of the *Alberta* had stirred activity on the Red reminiscent of the early days of the Kittson Line and Merchants Line. Selkirk sported twenty-seven steamboats in 1910, and Winnipeg harboured seven. An American sternwheeler, the *Grand Forks,* joined its Canadian sister ship *Assiniboine* in cross-the-border excursions, the first such exchanges since the 1880's. And the Hyland Navigation Company had joined the excursion boom full steam, with festive launching ceremonies. Wrote one young steamboat enthusiast of the day:

"The majestic *Alberta* arrived with Captain Bellefeuille on the bridge. To five small boys in a leaky rowboat, he looked enormous. Since the *Alberta* was a sternwheeler, they bent a hawser around her forebitts and snubbed the other end to the Hyland sidewheeler *Winnitoba*. Captain Bellefeuille shouted orders; bells jangled; and the big paddlewheel began churning the water. . . . The hawser whipped out of the water, tightened, then parted with a report like a cannon. . . . It took a lot of rope and a lot of jerks before the *Winnitoba* finally made it into the water. Then, as the flagship of the Hyland Navigation Company, she took her part in the excursion trade. . . ."

"I knew Hyland's son," another young excursionist remarked. "So we spend our summer holidays on the *Winnitoba;* she was quite a decent-sized sidewheeler. . . . I loved the boats. I just wanted to get out of school and onto the water. We used to take the hearts off the Macdonald's chewing tobacco cans, bend them, and stick them in the slot machine for the player piano. . . . Big passenger trade. The boats were absolutely loaded those days. Later, Hyland built another boat, the *Bonnatoba,* a sternwheeler, and they both ran excursions down the river to Hyland Park."

In July of 1910, Prime Minister Wilfrid Laurier's formal inauguration of the St. Andrews Locks, which bypassed the rapids between Winnipeg and Selkirk, gave the excursion trade a substantial boost. In the seasons that followed, excursion fever spread from the Pioneer, Hyland, and Winnipeg Navigation docks downriver to the industrial steamboat harbour of Selkirk. Hyland's 1,500-passenger steamer *Mount Cashel,* the third in his fleet, began weekend service down the Red River to Victoria Beach on Lake Winnipeg. And Bellefeuille's *Alberta* ran regular trips to the lake's Traverse Bay.

Pleasure cruises were invading the realm of the lake steamers, freighters, and part-time passenger craft of Dominion Fish and Northern Fish shipping. Not to be caught flatfooted, William Robinson made room aboard his fleet vessels for greater passenger capacity; his *Lady of the Lake* and *City of Selkirk* took up some of the slack, but the loss of his *Premier* to fire left the old Commodore at a disadvantage. Northern Fish, on the other hand, with a younger fleet and a stronger sense of the times – a somewhat depleted fish and cargo trade, and a rapidly blossoming tourist trade – jumped to the forefront.

From the outset it was apparent aboard lake steamers like Northern's *Wolverine* that passengers were an afterthought. Steamboat crews knew a casual existence aboard their summer homes. But for passengers – ranging from Hudson's Bay Company officials to surveyors, geologists, and prospectors, from perennial travellers to inquisitive, if not naive, summer holidayers – accommodations on the lake boats were definitely rustic. What berths there were on board the *Wolverine* offered a cramped night's sleep, provided one could sleep at all. Lying on the decks or propped up in the companionways, natives of the lake scraped fiddles, moaned through mouth organs, and jigged and crooned the night and their liquor away. Meals, strictly frontier styled, smelled of fish, whether fish was included in the recipe or not. And each day on deck offered a new challenge to a passenger's sense of balance, as the *Wolverine* rolled her way through a 500-mile week-long round trip up Lake Winnipeg and back. For a traveller, this was adventure; for a crewman, like Ed Nelson, cruises aboard "the Wolf" were routine.

"It looked like the start of a beautiful, restful voyage when the *Wolverine* gave the customary short blast on her whistle and cast off from Selkirk that afternoon in August of 1914. A full complement of passengers and freight aboard . . . including a disposition of 120 barrels of building lime, protested by the mate. . . .

"A typical mid-summer trip. There was the usual bustle as the purser allotted berths and cabins to passengers. Luggage was checked. Passengers relaxed on deck. . . . The Wolf made her first stop at Hecla on Big Island, where the Icelandic people gave the ship and her passengers a rousing welcome as the freight consigned to them was unloaded. . . . Half an hour's running time later, the *Wolverine* docked at Gull Harbour . . . site of the federal fisheries department hatchery for the celebrated Lake Winnipeg whitefish, and popular resort where many Winnipeggers had summer cottages. Always at this stop, some passenger would complain that part of his luggage was missing – a parcel of groceries, a tennis racquet, an article of clothing – and the purser would worriedly hunt around while the captain on the bridge would fume at the delay. . . .

"At Berens River there was an Indian Reserve, with a Hudson's Bay post, and an Inn for the summer vacationists. While unloading, someone noticed smoke up the forward hatches. The lime was smoldering through spontaneous combustion. . . . The hatches were battened down, and all night long water was poured into the forward holds and pumped out again by the engine room. It seemed that the ship was floating in skimmed milk.

"Also in the cargo were forty-eight cases of scotch whisky, covered with heavy tarpaulin. During the excitement, someone cut through the tarpaulin and removed four of the cases. Shortly after dark, most of the male population of the reserve were out in the woods singing and whooping it up.

248

"Next morning the Wolf's hatches were uncovered. What a mess! Cases of canned goods were crushed flat by the pressure which had built up . . . Luckily, among the deck passengers were twenty labourers, going to the Hudson Bay Railway line; all day and night, they worked in shifts shoveling the lime out . . . Captain Vance gave permission to the Indian women and children, and the few men who had not been in on the previous night's binge, to salvage whatever was of value to them, candy, tools and lime. . . . Never within memory have the Indian cabins been so neatly whitewashed as they were that fall."

The First World War deflated whatever leisure steamboat business the major Red River and Lake Winnipeg navigation companies had nurtured for so long. Many of Selkirk's and Winnipeg's veteran boatmen enlisted in the Royal Canadian Navy, never to see prairie water again. But the southern Manitoba steam era had one fling left. Two halves of a steamboat, formerly a passenger-freighter plying Lake of the Woods, arrived by rail at the foot of Winnipeg's Notre Dame Street in 1918. A syndicate of three Winnipeg lawyers had purchased the twenty-year-old steamer *Keenora,* with high hopes of collecting receipts from a rejuvenated excursion trade on the Red. Lengthened to nearly 160 feet and dressed with two levels of staterooms and a promenade floor, the *Keenora* heralded the War's end with cruises and moonlight dances. But the hoped-for return of the earlier days of the *Alberta, Winnitoba,* and *Bonnatoba* excursions never materialized, and the *Keenora* changed hands once again. In 1923 the Northern Fish Company spent forty thousand dollars clearing her debts, repairing her steel hull, and renovating her interior to accommodate both freight and passengers. One *Keenora* ticket holder remembered her beginnings as a Northern Fish steamer:
"The dock at Selkirk on the first Monday morning in August, 1923, was a busy place. The *Keenora* was berthed closest to the old ferry; a little behind her was the *Wolverine.* . . . Smaller boats crowded in everywhere. The dock itself teemed with loaded horse-drawn drays and men with push-carts. A tall, silent, sombre individual, I was told, was Captain Tom Pollock. As he stood by a warehouse door, a stouter and more active man rushed about stirring others to greater activity by his forthright language – I learned he was Captain Simpson.
"I had been lured into the trip around the lake by the eloquence of W. J. Guest, a partner with these others, in the company owning the *Keenora,* who assured me that he had just come back from making it himself, that the water was lovely, just like a millpond. . . .
"Next day, we were heading out through the Narrows . . . and then hauled into Snake Island, where Captain Sandy Vance held us for twenty-four hours as adverse weather was approaching. We pulled out

the next morning, but the wind freshened, and we rolled more heavily. I got bumped by someone on the foredeck and rolled into the scuppers to prevent myself taking a header into the water, which seemed the only other place to go. . . ."

"Came out of the [Warren] Landing one night," narrated one *Keenora* mate. "It was blowin' so hard, we couldn't get back into the harbour. I was at the wheel, and it threw me right across the wheelhouse, and before I could get up I'd hit the other side of the wheelhouse. And I went below, down the halls; all the passengers were sittin' on the floor, slidin' back and forth. And I was laughin' as I was jumpin' over them . . . . Next morning, a woman came up to me and said, 'If it hadn't been for you laughin' last night in the storm, when you came down, we'd have been all scared to death.' "

Keenora passengers were always curious. Most were tourists, for whom everything on the lake was a discovery, even the gales. At the height of an electrical storm one summer night, the *Keenora* met a convoy of lake steamers heading the opposite direction; crew and guests bet on the number of steamboats approaching; then as the four steamers passed, the *Keenora* passengers crowded the railings and photographed the convoy each time the lightning flashed. Each of the six days out on the lake provided a new fascination for the summer excursionists. The *Keenora* was the north country residents' only link with the south; when she arrived at Warren Landing, Norway House, or Grand Rapids first thing each spring, whole communities poured onto the docks. Fresh fruit, mail, cloth, and delicacies absent for the winter had returned to their lake settlements. And this was rare excitement, shared by northern Manitobans and *Keenora* passengers alike.

"The passengers were from all over, particularly the United States – Minneapolis, Kansas City, New York – year after year," recalled a *Keenora* skipper. "Good people. Anyone coming north on a vacation was in a good mood too. Lots of teachers. . . . Nice people. We had mock marriages, mock courtroom trials. If they danced, they danced up on the top decks or sometimes when we stopped, they'd dance with the locals. . . ."

"Once in a while, passengers would get under your skin. I'd get aggravated. You see, I had come off a fish hauler to the *Keenora*. And many's the night I wished to God there were dead fish in the hold, not passengers!" complained a sardonic Stan Sigurdson, first mate aboard the *Keenora*. And yet, Sigurdson took special pride in acquainting those interested passengers in the Icelandic heritage of Lake Winnipeg.

"We had good times, but we worked like fools. . . . Anything to keep a job. We had to. Some ways I'm sorry I stayed with the lake, 'cause it was nothing but a garden-hose job. You started out in the spring; then, when

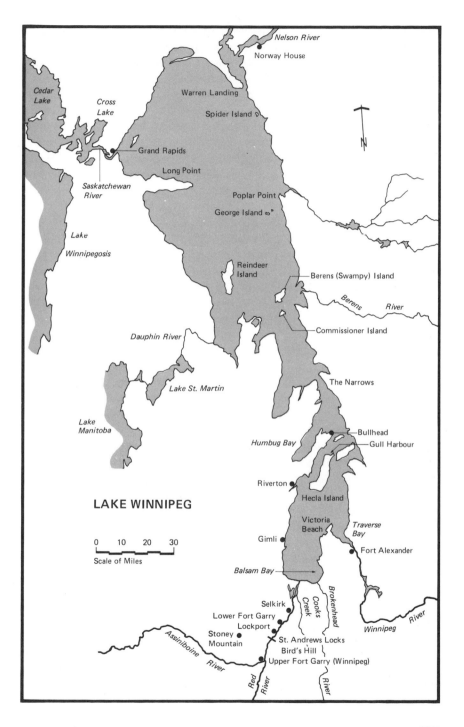

Nelson River
Norway House

Cedar Lake

Cross Lake

Warren Landing

Spider Island

Grand Rapids

Long Point

Saskatchewan River

Poplar Point

George Island

Lake Winnipegosis

Reindeer Island

Berens (Swampy) Island

Berens River

Commissioner Island

Dauphin River

Lake St. Martin

The Narrows

Lake Manitoba

Bullhead

Gull Harbour

Humbug Bay

Riverton

Hecla Island

LAKE WINNIPEG

Victoria Beach

Traverse Bay

Gimli

Fort Alexander

0   10   20   30
Scale of Miles

Balsam Bay

Brokenhead River

Cooks Creek

Selkirk

Lower Fort Garry
Lockport

Stoney Mountain

Winnipeg River

St. Andrews Locks
Bird's Hill
Upper Fort Garry (Winnipeg)

Assiniboine River

Red River

River

the snows blew and the ice formed, you were out of a job. . . . "

Then, when the snows blew and the ice formed, you were out of a job. Such was the seasonal tradition of prairie steamboating. Since the day Captain Anson Northup had steamed his unglamourous "pine basket" sternwheeler toward an unsuspecting Fort Garry, for seven decades the survival of steamboats had depended directly upon seasonal conditions. Dry seasons prohibited navigation; high-water flooding prompted a boat boom. When freight was plentiful, steamboatmen had money to spend; but when contracts were few, gloom shadowed the prairie fleets. If steamer excursions looked attractive, there was laughter along the lakes and rivers; if tourist passengers stayed away, the steamers sailed half empty. One excursionist accurately summed up this fickle breed of traveller: "The boats'd go like Billy-O for the first few years and then people wouldn't want to go to the same place."

Steamboat owners and skippers persisted, however. With blind confidence, crews arrived back at the Winnipeg and Selkirk docks each spring as a reflex of their tradition. The return of the steamboats to the Red and to the lake, they believed, was as natural as the ice thawing. After all, fish had to be hauled, lumber barged, freight run north, and tourists entertained. The lake's posts and ports would always wake to the three whistle blasts of an approaching steamer, wouldn't they? Boatmen did not fear what they did not see.

The Depression crashed onto the prairies and into the already meager salaries of Manitoba steamboatmen. Fishing returned to its beginnings – a local, non-commercial trade. Industry on either side of the lake lost momentum and faltered for a decade. The tourist trade slumped. The pleasure steamers disappeared from the Winnipeg waterfront. And the economy of diesel fuel had dated the power of steam engineering. The *Keenora,* last lady of a great prairie steam dynasty, still plied the inland waters of Lake Winnipeg. Plunging headlong into the 1930's, the Northern Fish Company operated their flagship, always expecting the next season at least to equal the last. Yet, unlike other steamer owners, Northern Fish had made changes – changes that perhaps prolonged the *Keenora's* life beyond her steam-driven sister ships. Re-established at Selkirk as the Selkirk Navigation Company, the *Keenora's* owners renovated her once again. Surgery in 1930 eliminated her main deck cabins, expanded her freight hold, and shrunk her passenger capacity to twenty-seven. Youngest and most versatile of the Selkirk fleet, the *Keenora* continued, if colourlessly, as a vital cargo lifeline for the north and an occasional tourist carrier. The *Keenora* had adapted, and while neglect and the Selkirk sloughs claimed the majority of the remaining steamers, she alone survived another thirty years of sporadic service on Lake Winnipeg.

Otherwise, the times took their toll. During the 1930's, widespread steamboating was abandoned. And the masters of abandoned steam died with their era. Excursion king Captain Levie Bellefeuille was dead. Old Captain J. W. Simpson too had died. Boatbuilder William Purvis was gone. Captain Sandy Vance had retired. And old age had overtaken the Commodore of Lake Winnipeg himself.

"A Caesar of ceaseless enterprise" and a shrewd exploiter of every opportunity, William Robinson had made the Red River and Lake Winnipeg his empire. And he had accomplished this swiftly and boldly. His stylish sidewheeler *Princess* had climaxed the first boom of the Red River steamboat packets in 1881; his flamboyance and ambition had elevated him to a stormy stint with the Hudson's Bay Company; and his business sense had thrust deep into the richest resources of central Manitoba. For a quarter century, Robinson had milked Lake Winnipeg of its fish, its lumber, its freight transport, and its cheap labour. He had muscled out the minor lumber operations around the lake; he commanded the majority of the lake's boatmen; he managed Booth Fish interests as his own; and he had wrested control of North West Navigation from his partner, Peter McArthur. Robinson had jostled and schemed for a monopoly on Manitoba waterways, and won. His sour victory over McArthur in the pair's final encounter is recorded by McArthur's son:

"A day came in the early 1900's when Captain Robinson and Captain McArthur stood together on the Selkirk river bank. Robinson pointed out the empire he had won. There were the planing mills, the great department store, the gigantic ice-house, freezer and packing plant, and the fleet of lake boats. 'All mine,' he said. The very words. Mr. McArthur was shocked. And the pawky, canny Robinson got away with it. . . ."

In 1936, the same year as Peter McArthur, Commodore William Robinson died.

EPILOGUE

Every autumn, the cloudy waters of the Red River lapped unfeelingly against the gaunt remains of more abandoned steamers. With each wave rot seeped deeper into decaying wood, protective engine oils were washed away, and corrosion and rust consumed discarded steam enginery. From as early as 1862, when the river level suddenly dropped and fatally wrecked the *Pioneer*, the former *Anson Northup*, the first steamer up the Red, to the 1936 dismantling-ten-dollar-sale-for-salvage-burning of the Northern Fish steamer *Wolverine*, the Selkirk sloughs became as much a steamboat graveyard as a steamboat birthplace.

Victims of neglect, outstripped by the railway trade, surpassed by diesel power, unequal to the demands of fluctuating seasons, and defeated by the natural elements they had long overcome, prairie steamers filed one by one to the sloughs, riverbanks, and drydocks of the west. Boneyards like the Selkirk sloughs appeared all across the three prairie provinces – at Winnipeg, up the Assiniboine, at Winnipegosis and The Pas, on Cumberland Lake and near Prince Albert, between Lethbridge and Medicine Hat, on Long Lake, and as far northwest as Edmonton. Except in the tales told by old-timers, the pirate play of children, or the re-creation by historians, the marooned steam craft never sailed again.

And yet the steamboat cemeteries did not entomb all the last remains. While fire, vandalism, rot, or flood destroyed without trace many clues to that steamer period, some memories of its folklore lived long enough to be recorded in these preceding chapters. And though no vessels from that era steam through prairie waters today, many survived to the present as re-used parts, fragments treasured as artifacts, or as scraps stored and forgotten. Where those tangible pieces of the prairie steamboats fell, and where their boatmen retired, migrated, or died, provides an epitaph as varied and colourful as the era itself.

Efforts to raise the *Pioneer* after she had sunk at Cooks Creek that spring of 1862 proved futile, and only her machinery was salvaged for a sawmill at Grand Forks, North Dakota.

Described as "an old landmark of the Northwest," Commodore Norman W. Kittson, the millionaire controller of the Red River Transportation Company monopoly of the 1870's, died early in 1888 at St. Paul, Minnesota. None of his steamboats on the Red River between Georgetown and Winnipeg outlived him. The powerful *Selkirk*, built in 1871, was wrecked at Grand Forks, North Dakota, in the 1884 season. Only her bell remains. Nine years after her construction at Breckenridge, Minnesota, the *Dakota* burned near the international border in 1881. Kittson's sternwheeler *Minnesota*, an acquisition from defeated rivals, the Merchants International Steamboat Line, was rebuilt and relaunched in 1881 as the *City of Winnipeg*. The same season, en route to the Saskatchewan River, she was wrecked on Lake Winnipeg. In 1884 Kittson's sidewheeler *Cheyenne* was grounded and wrecked at Ste. Agathe, Manitoba. The attempt to free the sternwheeler *Manitoba* from Shell River ice at Prince Albert in April of 1885, in order to aid Canadian militiamen at the Battle of Batoche, proved fruitless, and her hull and superstructure were totally destroyed in the spring breakup. The steamer's boiler was saved for the Sanderson sawmill in 1885, removed by the Prince Albert Lumber Company in 1908, incorporated into the Paddockwood mill, and finally dynamited for scrap in the 1940's. One chair from aboard the *Manitoba* resides at a Prince Albert museum.

The actual fate of Kittson's last steamer up the Assiniboine River, the unglamourous but sturdy *Alpha*, remained a mystery for eighty-five years after the fact. In the spring of 1885, on what was to be her final voyage, the *Alpha* steamed upriver from Winnipeg toward Brandon. Attempting to reduce the travelling time and distance, the *Alpha's* skipper piloted across several flooded bends in the river. On April 27, in the heart of the Spruce Woods district, the steamer ran aground outside the main river channel, and remained there, high and dry, when the flood waters receded. Temporarily abandoned while the crew sought assistance, the *Alpha's* cargo of oat seed and lumber, and even her machinery, were plundered. The Assiniboine claimed the rest; succeeding years of flooding dumped silt into the *Alpha's* hull, while cottonwood seedlings grew to trees that concealed the grave. For a half a century the river hid the site; then it cut a new channel parallel to the buried steamer, revealing the 105-foot hull like a fossil. Together with clues found in Spruce Woods communities – lamps, pieces of furniture, and trinkets made from the *Alpha's* Wisconsin oak – Brandon historian Roy Brown linked the stories and artifacts to the unearthed hulk, and verified the final resting place of Kittson's *Alpha*.

Built in 1872, the Hudson's Bay Company's first prairie lake steamer the *Chief Commissioner* survived in renovated forms for nearly a quarter of a century. Though replaced in 1875 by the *Colvile*, the *Chief Commissioner* contributed her engines, which powered the *Colvile* admirably until the *Colvile* was burned at Grand Rapids in 1894. Meanwhile, the *Commissioner's* hull served as a floating warehouse at the Company's riverside wharfs at Lower Fort Garry.

The first of the Saskatchewan fleet to perish, the *Lily* had arrived from Alfred Yarrow's British shipbuilding yards in "knocked down" prefabricated pieces in 1877. Six years later, on a navigability survey up the South Saskatchewan for the Winnipeg and Western Transportation Company, the steel-hulled *Lily* scraped bottom and sank at Drowning Ford. Her bacon cargo, all lives, and twenty thousand dollars of insurance were salvaged, but her remains have disappeared and reappeared like a phantom for years. In the 1920's, en route from Medicine Hat to Prince Albert, a canoeist stumbled across a fragment of rusted steel and a brass boiler plate, but he was never able to re-locate the site of the wrecked *Lily*.

In 1886, a year following her dubiously successful diversionary assault on the river forces of the Métis at Batoche, the Saskatchewan River giant *Northcote* lay deserted on the beaches of Cumberland Lake. Her staterooms still marred by military bulwarks and her hull laden with gunshot, the *Northcote* was just a plaything for children.

"She was supposed to be fixed the next year," claimed Cumberland House boatman Bill McKenzie. "But she was just ended by religion. . . . My mother said that old Mr. Belanger at the Catholic Church and the Hudson's Bay manager were pretty good friends. And when they found that girls and boys was flirting in the cabins of the old *Northcote*, well, they gave an old Indian, Jimmy Greenleaf, a barrel of coal oil to go and burn her down. He was told to. It must have been terrible to see."

Among the few surviving Saskatchewan rivermen, Bill McKenzie, once a wheelsman for Ross Navigation at The Pas, spends many hours combing all that remains of a golden age sternwheeler. One hundred years after their construction, the huge Cincinnati-built boilers and the scattered engine parts of the *Northcote* were mounted as a tourist attraction at Cumberland House, but the attempt at grace-saving failed. Scarred by chalk scratchings and broken glass, and scavenged by local farmers in search of scrap metal, the *Northcote's* precision innards lie corroding, ignored and knee-deep in weeds.

Inscribed: "L. M. Rumsey & Co., St. Louis, Missouri", the *Northcote's* bell now beckons a congregation to the Duck Lake Anglican Church each Sunday; while a hundred miles away the Gardiner Presbyterian Church – now Fred Light's tiny museum in the old town of Battleford – houses the *Northcote's* three-tone steam whistle. And three feet of *Northcote* deck plank functions as a refinished cribbage board in one Prince Albert living room.

Sister ship to the *Northcote*, the *Marquis*, the largest sternwheeler to sail the Saskatchewan, was beached at Prince Albert in 1890. Within a decade the *Marquis* had been picked clean of her valuables – ginger-breaded exterior, carved banisters, stained-glass lamps, brass ornaments – until all that remained was another playground for youngsters. Some fished from her decks; others dove to the North Saskatchewan from her railings; and still others assembled rafts from her hull boards.

"I was about eight or nine years old when we moved to Second Street in East Prince Albert. At that time, the *Marquis* was up on the south bank of the Saskatchewan, high and dry, and intact . . . . We started playing, as kids do, pirates and cops 'n' robbers. And when we really got going, we had a fire on the deck, from time to time. That, of course, didn't do the *Marquis* any good. And the poor old *Marquis* gradually disintegrated. After three or four fires there was practically nothing left. And I was partly to blame . . . . I don't confess to actually lighting the fires, but I guess I was an accessory after the fact," admitted Judge Walter Nelson.

Nelson eventually recovered two oaken planks from the wreck and had two gavels carved, one of which is still used today at the Prince Albert City Hall. Nat B. Webster owns a chair from the *Marquis*. The Peters Motor Company of Prince Albert pounds out steel on a *Marquis* drive shaft, while another shaft rests behind a Prince Albert museum. A sternwheel hub from the *Marquis* lies among the artifacts at Fort Battle-ford National Historic Park, and the *Marquis* steam whistle announced the morning shift at the Burns meat plant in Calgary for many years until vibration finally shattered it.

Perhaps the prairies' first case of planned obsolescence, the steamboat fleet of the North Western Coal and Navigation Company faded as quickly as it appeared. Inside the two seasons of 1883 and 1884, the com-pany's major shareholders – Sir Alexander T. Galt and his son Elliott T. Galt – had launched three steamers to haul their "black diamonds" from shafts at Lethbridge to CPR locomotives at Medicine Hat. Almost simul-taneously, the Galts constructed a narrow-gauge railway to replace the river run of the three sternwheelers. Then, despite a brief commission steaming supplies and munitions to militiamen fighting Riel's Métis, the three steamers retired to their berths back up the South Saskatchewan.

A powerful tow steamer, the *Alberta* was hauled from the river at Med-icine Hat, her boilers extracted, and her engines converted to hoist Galt coal from the low-lying banks of the Oldman River at Lethbridge to the narrow-gauge rail cars on the prairie above. Most of her cabin doors and windows went to embellish the homes of miners and ranchers along the river, and the ship's bell was employed by the town as a fire-alarm and as a curfew bell, until it was later suspended in an arbour at the Galt Gar-dens. And the shell of the *Alberta* vanished in a dozen different directions. Recalled Tom Brown of Medicine Hat, "My father, L. Charles Brown, came out from England in 1887, and was one of the few Englishmen to stay in the district. . . . Well, in 1892, he built a ranch house for the family in the Cypress Hills near Elkwater. . . . He took lumber from the steamboat hulk at Medicine Hat – foot-wide three-inch-thick fir planks – and hauled them thirty miles. It supplied wood for two ends of the house. . . . And I remember, early in the 1930's, taking those same planks to make a road culvert. Some pieces are there yet. . . ."

The *Baroness* came to a similar end. While her namesake, the celebrated philanthropist Baroness Angela Burdett-Coutts, received regal burial at London's Westminster Abbey, the South Saskatchewan's steamer *Baroness* was drawn ashore at Lethbridge and unceremoniously dismantled. Her huge boiler became the town's first public bath, supplied by hot water from the Lethbridge mines. But her mammoth hull and superstructure went the way of most prairie paddlewheel queens – torn apart by souvenir hunters, burned by youngsters, and finally swallowed up by river silt.

The tiny member of the coal fleet, the *Minnow* sat idle at Medicine Hat for two years. By 1887, she had returned to active service on the North Saskatchewan for the Lamoureux brothers' lumber and freighting enterprise. The *Minnow's* fling as a tramp steamer running between Edmonton and Battleford was brief, however. In 1895 she was struck by fire. In 1898 she changed hands to a less prosperous mill operation. And by the turn of the century, the *Minnow's* engines had been torn loose and implanted in a stationary mill at Sunnyside Crossing.

When Captain Peter McArthur moved into Lake Winnipegosis territory about 1900, he was midway through his colourful steamboat career. But in 1900 he had little to show for it. McArthur's *Prince Rupert*, the first steamer built exclusively within Manitoba, had been condemned and broken up in 1881. The Hudson's Bay Company had dismissed him as Inland Navigator because he had refused to ship whisky up the Saskatchewan. Fire consumed his third steamboat masterpiece, the Lake Manitoba sidewheeler *Saskatchewan*, in 1893. Commodore William Robinson had muscled him out of the North West Navigation Company directorship. By 1897, his second steamboat creation, the sternwheeler *Marquette*, had been disassembled and sunk in the sloughs of Selkirk. The *Manitoba* and *Marquis*, steamers he had navigated up the Grand Rapids, had been beached for good. In 1899, North Saskatchewan flood waters smashed his finest piece of steamboat design, the *North West*, against a bridge pier at Edmonton, and demolished her completely.

From all his years as a steamboat pioneer, Peter McArthur managed to salvage only one memento. "Father got the whistle from the *North West* when she was dismantled," wrote his daughter, "and put it on his sawmill at Winnipegosis. Men hearing it in the spring over at Water Hen and Crane River, thirty-five and forty miles away, would come to work in response to its blasts."

Very little remains to recognize Peter McArthur's second thirty years as a prairie steamboatman. The *Iona* is gone. Barge skeletons sometimes protrude from the Lake Winnipegosis shallows in the driest days of the summer. The huge Winnipegosis mills that trimmed millions of feet of timber have disappeared.

"The old *Isabelle* was driven up on the bank. She was condemned. They took the engines out of her and there she rotted away," one of her crewmen stated. Another confirmed, "all the machinery that Peter McArthur had, they blew up with dynamite, loaded it, and sold it for scrap!"

Few traces of the McArthur steam tugs exist. Even fewer are the tales of their trips up and down Lake Winnipegosis for the Standard Lumber Company. And scarcer still are their living crew members. One, Mike Harrison, takes pride in his survival, and in his dearest possession, the solid brass engineer's steam signal whistle from the tug *Iona*. At ninety, Harrison fully intends to construct a replica of the steam unit he worked over for decades in the hull of a McArthur steamer.

A soft-spoken sense of humour has sustained Bill Johnson, McArthur's ever-dependable *Isabelle* wheelsman, and sole survivor of the lake's early gas boat fire disaster.

McArthur employee Hall Burrell survived his engineering days aboard the *Isabelle* too, and outlived Peter McArthur himself; but the days of steam power stayed in his blood. Long after Burrell had retired and moved from Winnipegosis to Toronto, he often found himself wandering down along the waterfront piers next to the Lake Ontario steamships.

Jack Denby, the comical *Isabelle* skipper and favourite son of the town, never left the lake. Remembered a steamboat mate, "Jack had Bright's disease; he was given to fainting spells . . . . Jack was working as skipper that night. And that boat had low bulwarks, barely to your knee, and no way to catch a hold . . . . Jack left the wheel with Tommy Campbell; he was goin' back to the kitchen at the stern of the boat. And Tommy wondered why Jack didn't come back, and went back to look. The engineer had seen Jack go by toward the kitchen . . . but they couldn't find him. Well, they turned back. Dark night. Blowin' hard. But they found nothing. . . . Found his body the next spring. . . . Irony of it was that he died off that *Myrtle M.,* a diesel boat, not a steamboat. . . ."

As temperamental as the prairie lake he navigated, the squally Captain

Herman Nicklas found himself unemployed when "Peace River" Jim Cornwall's ambitions outgrew his Northern Transportation Company steamboats on the Athabasca River and Lesser Slave Lake. By the early 1920's the long-awaited railway from Edmonton finally penetrated the Peace River country, eliminating the need for Captain Nicklas's command aboard the Lesser Slave steamer *Northern Light.* In semi-retirement, Nicklas saw his steamboat stripped and torched at the Sawridge waterfront. So he and his wife migrated, as they had numerous times before. First they moved to San Francisco, where she worked in a department store and he landscaped gardens; then the two returned to their native Germany, where the captain later died in a freak accident. Strange, that Captain Nicklas could survive a Valparaiso shipwreck, a south seas mutiny, a bout with tropical malaria, the First Great War, lake storms aboard the *Northern Light,* and World War II, only to be killed when a horse threw him to the cobblestone street of Stralsund, Germany.

At Christmas in 1920, the spirit behind the thriving Walterdale flats at Edmonton died. During a half century in residence there, John Walter had made his riverbank the focal point of lumber, power, and boat production. Two sternwheelers – the excursion steamer *City of Edmonton* and the freighter *Scona* – became symbols of John Walter's benevolent monopoly on the upper North Saskatchewan. And though the 1915 flood catastrophe demolished Walter's entire riverside empire, the two steamers miraculously survived. But the reprieve was short. A 1934 Edmonton *Journal* column documented their passing:

"For a good many years now, there have been lying on the bank of the river ... two sorry-looking remnants of what once were gallant ships of the north. One was the hull of the steamer, *City of Edmonton,* which disappeared entirely by process of decay, only a year ago; and the other was the boiler of the *Scona,* which, being made of sterner stuff, has endured longer and has still a converted life before it. . . .

"[This] last remaining relic of steamboat navigation on the North Saskatchewan River is being turned into barnyard paraphernalia. . . . An enterprising blacksmith has taken the old marine in hand, with the intention of cutting it in two, lengthwise, and making water troughs of it. . . . It seems like a rather good idea from the standpoint of agriculture; but in terms of navigation it is surely a heavy fall from the glory that used to be. . . ."

Prince Albert firebrand Richard Deacon never recovered from the depression that accompanied World War I. For several decades Captain Deacon had livened the North Saskatchewan with his businesses, his antics, and his steamboats. A series of Deacon exploits from cement freighting to excursion running reached their zenith after 1900 with the establishment of his Red Rock Brick Yard. But when brick orders were returned from the United States because war had broken out, the Deacon businesses crumbled. In his half century on the prairies, Richard Deacon had witnessed the repercussions of the American Civil War, the march of Wolseley's 1870 expedition to the Red River Settlement, and a personal confrontation with Métis leader Louis Riel. Deacon had been elected to Prince Albert public office and had skippered three of his own steamboats, the *Josie, Pathfinder* and *Marion.* And when he died in 1934, Deacon left six children, two of whom became steamboat captains in their own right – Bert out of Prince Albert and Art down the Mackenzie River and in the employ of the Ross Navigation Company.

"Yes," admitted Captain Harvey Weber, general manager of the Ross Navigation Company after old Cap Ross died of a gunshot wound in 1925, "shipping is at rock bottom on the northern rivers now. I don't like to make pessimistic utterances for publication, but that fact remains."

From humble beginnings at Medicine Hat to a flamboyant reign on the lower Saskatchewan from The Pas, Horatio Hamilton Ross had never sailed a dull voyage. The skipper grounded his first steamer, *Assiniboia,* at Cedar Lake in 1905. He awakened Saskatoon on a spring Sunday in 1908 when he smashed his sternwheeler *City of Medicine Hat* into their Nineteenth Street traffic bridge. (The wreck supplied riverside residents with lumber for years. The sunken boiler was raised the following winter, and towed away. Across the frozen river and down Saskatoon's iced-over First Avenue went the boiler behind a string of horse teams, until a news-hungry photographer leaped in front and halted the entire procession for a shot. Momentum was lost, and the boiler got stuck; the city's creamery took delivery of its new heating source a little later than expected). And then Ross's whirlwind steamboat shopping spree over the next decade amassed a steamer fleet of six and launched the Ross Navigation transportation monopoly in northern Manitoba. But by the late 1920's, with Ross gone, the junction of the Saskatchewan and Pasquia Rivers was looking like a steamboat morgue. They were scrapping the *City of Prince Albert;* the *Minasin* was rotting; the tug *Sam Brisbin* had sunk; and *Le Pas, O'Hell,* and *Notin* had all gone.

Down on the docks at The Pas in 1930, on a rambling, one-story warehouse, the blue and white ensign of the Ross Navigation Company flapped in the breeze. The blackboard, labelled "Steamer Arrivals And Departures", was blank. And Harvey Weber, Captain Ross's first protegé on the lower Saskatchewan, summed up:

"Now we operate only the steamers *Tobin* and *Nipawin,* for local traffic between The Pas and Sturgeon Landing . . . [But] history has a way of repeating itself . . . and in years to come I am confident that the North-west will become a network of canals which will be used to carry the products of the country to the distributing centres. It may be fifty or a hundred years hence." Within the company's lifetime at least this was not to happen; the *Tobin* and the *Nipawin* disintegrated like all the rest.

"W's Back to Back", the emblem of Winton Brothers lumber holdings, remained on the Saskatchewan long after Ross Navigation and Hudson's Bay Company steamers had faded. Timber sustained the Wintons' The Pas Lumber Company and their two timber steamers along the northern rim of the prairies through and beyond the Depression. But by the 1950's the Manitoba log harvest had waned. Tom Paquette, who saw forty years with the Wintons – four seasons on the sternwheeler *Alice Mattes,* and the rest as steam engineering stalwart aboard the larger sternwheeler *David N. Winton* – stayed on to the end.

"They ran out of timber. The Saskatchewan Government wouldn't allow them to take out any more timber. So, they shut down. . . . The Wintons went back to Minneapolis. And I missed the sound of the *D.N.'s* paddlewheel on the river. . . . I found it kind of lonesome after they shut down. I stayed on the boat until the ice came downriver in 1954 and shoved the *D.N.* ashore and took the side out of her. Then they gave it to this fellow for the lumber, but he set fire to it instead. . . ."

The *Alice* lingered even after the last of the *D.N.* had washed away. Narrated Pas Lumber man Charlie Otterbein, "After they dismantled the *Mattes* to make a barge out of her, they left her pilothouse just sittin' there. I thought, the first chance I got, I'd take it to The Pas and make a playhouse for the kids. . . . In the fall, we put two skids on her and took her as far as Three Rivers. . . . There, I used it as a bunk house. Put dou-ble-decker steel bunks into it. Boarded it up except for two windows and used it as a bunk house in the summertime. Then I went back, and it was gone. Don't know where it went. . . ."

In 1967, the *Alice's* wheelhouse was discovered just below the newly constructed Squaw Rapids Hydro Station and Dam; it was immediately claimed by the Town of Nipawin and transported to a town storage yard. Years later, when nostalgia moved the town to preserve steam era relics, it was found that the pilothouse had again disappeared. A city engineer confirmed, however, that it had simply rotted away. Time had stolen the last vestige of the last Winton steamship.

On Armistice night, 1918, celebrants from Regina Beach partied their way across Saskatchewan's choppy, still unfrozen Long Lake. At Cowan's Beach they torched the shell of the *Qu'Appelle,* the abandoned steamer of the disbanded William Pearson Company. The thousands of American landseekers she had toured along Pearson's real estate had long been settled. William Pearson had returned with his earnings to Winnipeg. And with the immigration boom over, the *Qu'Appelle* was beached, her side cut away, and her steam engine exported to Japan. The armistice fire removed the "Queer Apple" from Long Lake forever.

"The last trip the *Qu'Appelle* made was in September, 1913," Regina Beach boatman Leonard Plaxton recalled. "They were having boiler trouble. They didn't know whether they were going to get back down the lake or not, so they left Pearson's big steel barge in the Big Arm, just off Liberty. Local farmers sank it there, so nobody would take it away; they wanted a cheap fishing pier. . . . About 1920, we bought and raised the barge, brought it back to Regina Beach and built on it. Twenty-by-eighty feet, we sank the barge with 130 tons of rock at the beach, and then we built the two-story building on it that was known as the Ark. We had a restaurant and an office on the main deck. And on the upper deck we had a dance hall. . . . The Ark was known all over. . . . We had some of the finest dance bands in the country. Tommy French. The Ding Dong Bells. Mart Kenny. The Ords. Merry Melody Men. . . . Dances ran seven days a week. Every night. Twenty-five cents admission. We were just crowded out all the time. Maybe five hundred people a night. . . .

"And I believe it was the spring of 1935 when we had high water, and quite a stormy session. . . . The Ark was buoyant, even though it had all this rock in its base. So when the water came up and raised her off the shore, it shook the Ark to pieces."

Crowds peaked in the lower Red River excursion trade during the summer of 1913. On Dominion Day, all Pioneer, Winnipeg, and Hyland company steamers paddled capacity cruises to holiday celebrations. Late in the afternoon that July First, the sidewheeler *Winnitoba* pulled into Hyland Park to assist the overcrowded steamer *J. M. Smith* ferry excursionists home. A *Winnitoba* passenger described the scene:

"The picnickers got excited and swarmed onto the dock and tried to board the *Winnitoba.* To force the people back, the skipper turned the hose on the crowd and ordered the boat to leave. Those left behind were quite angry. . . . Two nights later, the *Winnitoba* was burned to the water's edge in revenge for the dowsing. . . ."

Pleasure steamboating ended abruptly.

The *J. M. Smith* was soon beached. The *Winnitoba's* sister vessel, the *Bonnatoba,* found herself wedged in ice when the 1913 season concluded at the Hyland Park docks; she was wrecked and written off as a total loss. Fire caught up with John Hyland's lake steamer *Mount Cashel,* in 1914, and ice carried away her remains in 1919.

"About the *Alberta,*" finished one Winnipegger. "I remember during the flood of 1916, I was on the riverbank to see if the river had gone down when I saw the *Alberta* being swept to her doom at Lockport. About six men with ropes and grappling irons were chasing after her along the riverbank, some on foot and some on bicycles. . . . All in vain. . . . I collected enough firewood to last me two winters. . . ."

Beyond the collapse of the Red River and Lake Winnipeg excursion trade, through the introduction of diesel power, despite the financial drought of the Depression, and in the face of the stringent fire and safety regulations of the 1940's and 1950's, the steamer *Keenora* survived. Converted to diesel in 1960, she lasted another five years and then retired to the Selkirk sloughs, apparently to die. But conservation and nostalgia saved the *Keenora* from the way of all her steam-driven predecessors. In August of 1972, the young Marine Museum of Manitoba purchased the abandoned lady, and in 1974 unveiled a permanent artifact and period photograph museum aboard a restored *Keenora,* sole survivor of the prairie steamboat era.

Eight miles south of Moose Jaw, on the grounds of a local museum, has risen the dream of two men – of Tom Sukanen, the "mad Finn" who created the steam vessel *Dontianen* but who died before he could sail her from the heart of the Canadian prairies across the Atlantic home to Finland; and Lawrence "Moon" Mullin, who discovered and experienced Sukanen's obsession, and who in 1975 succeeded in completing *Dontianen's* reconstruction. But not without the help of other believers.

Vic Markkula to his death preserved the nine-foot-tall keel which now supports the hull and the thirty-foot superstructure. Installed are some of the hand-forged engine works, the smokestack, and the drive shaft, all saved by Markkula's son. Inside the vessel, artifacts display Sukanen's ingenuity: his hewn pulleys, found by a North Dakota hunter; his camera, discovered in British Columbia; his crafted chronometer, donated by Moose Jaw's art museum; the forceps he used to lace the sheets of galvanized steel together, offered by Riverhurst gunsmith Al Peterson; one of Sukanen's homemade tricycle wheels; his violin, which Moon Mullin spotted at a Saskatoon auction sale; the lifeboat, superstructure railings, and the sixteen-pound hammer, treasured by old friend Cluny McPherson; and photographs that relatives and neighbours hid for so many years as part of a life story best forgotten.

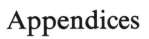

Appendices

NOTES

Prologue

page line
13	1	For Swampy Cree legend, see Clay, pp. 7-24.
13	15	For details concerning Glacial Lake Agassiz, see Upham.
15	3	For details of early prairie explorers, see Warkentin (ed.), pp. 23, 47, 72, 78-82, 99, 123, 144-91, 191-231.
17	6	Hind, p. 77.
17	24	Medd, "My Father's Steamboats", *Manitoba Pageant*, Autumn, 1971.
17	28	See Anderson (ed.).

One: First Down the Red

19	26	Bishop Alexandre Taché; quoted in "Sketch of the North-West of America", *in The New Nation*, August 6, 1870.
20	6	*Ibid.*
20	20	Bell, p. 97.
20	30	Charles T. Cavalier; quoted in "Trade Moved by Paddle-Wheels", *Winnipeg Free Press*, June 6, 1959.
21	36	The term used by Captain C.P.V. Lull; quoted in Herriot, p. 249.
22	24	Hargrave, pp. 56, 61.
23	18	J.C. Burbank; quoted in *Nor'Wester*, June 14, 1860.
23	33	Eggleston, p. 271.
24	4	R.H. Alexander; quoted in Roy Johnson, "Steamer Anson Northup Perishes Near Fort Garry", *Fargo Forum*, August, 1955.
24	26	*Nor'Wester*, May 14, 1862.
28	1	Sven Heskin; quoted in *North Dakota Historical Collections*, Vol VII, p. 278.
28	31	Pyle, p. 107.
29	9	*Manitoba Free Press*, June 13, 1876.
30	3	Quoted in "The Paddlewheeler that Stretched Fifty Miles", *Winnipeg Free Press*, April 21, 1952.
30	17	Hamilton, p. 19.
30	37	*Manitoban*, May 17, 1873.
32	3	Gordon J. Keeney, "Shackled Prisoner Leaps from Steamboat to Save Child", *Fargo Forum*, June 4, 1950.
32	40	*Free Press*, August 9, 1875.
33	28	Cabin boy; quoted in "Murder Mystery of the Red River Steamboat", by G.C. Porter, *Winnipeg Tribune*, February 14, 1942.
35	7	*Free Press*, May, 1875.
35	32	Dispatches quoted from *Red River Star* and *Free Press*, June, 1875.
36	7	W.B. Nickles; quoted in "Record Setting Steamer Manitoba Sunk in Red by Collision", *Fargo Forum*, June 4, 1950.
37	1	Passenger's letter; quoted in *Free Press*, September 26, 1878.
37	21	Dufferin, Marchioness of Dufferin and Ava, pp. 316-18.
38	3	*Ibid.*, pp. 366-67.
38	9	*Manitoba Free Press*, October 7, 1877.

Two: The Scot, The Wolf, and the Honourable Company.

43   11   Northcote, p. 6.
43   33   Peter McArthur, p. 3.
44   5   *Ibid.,* p. 11.
44   10   *Ibid.,* p. 9.
44   12   *Ibid.,* p. 7.
44   37   *Free Press,* June, 1874.
46   21   Reverend Henry Budd.
46   35   St. Paul Press; quoted in *Manitoban,* October 3, 1874.
48   13   Hill, p. 393.
49   12   Dufferin, Marchioness of Dufferin and Ava, p. 355.
50   1   *Saskatchewan Herald,* August 25, 1879.
50   31   Thomas R. Smith.
50   40   Molly McFadden, "Boats on the Red River of the North", p. 17.
52   2   D.C. McArthur; Molly McFadden Papers, letter from McArthur to McFadden, December 27, 1957.
54   6   A.D. Robinson, Journal, included among Molly McFadden Papers.
54   41   Peter McArthur; Molly McFadden Papers; quoted in letter from D.C. McArthur to McFadden, November 3, 1952.
55   19   O-ge-mas-es (Little Clerk), pp. 61-64.
56   28   Phil. B. Reader; Interview, May 19, 1974, The Pas, Manitoba.
57   9   *Ibid.*
57   19   *Ibid.*
57   39   Molly McFadden, "Steamboats on the Assiniboine", p. 8.
59   28   *Brandon Daily Sun,* May 24, 1881.
59   33   *Winnipeg Daily Times,* April 29, 1881.
60   2   *Brandon Daily Sun,* May 24, 1881.
60   9   D.C. McArthur; Molly McFadden Papers, letter from McArthur to McFadden, December 10, 1952.
60   19   *Brandon Daily Sun,* May 24, 1881.
60   26   *Ibid.*
61   7   Captain James Sheets; quoted in *Winnipeg Daily Times,* September 28, October 11, 1881.
62   39   D.C. McArthur; Molly McFadden Papers, letter from McArthur to McFadden, December 13, 1956.
63   29   *Ibid.*

Three: Paddles of Peace and War

65   13   Jessica Tyerman; Interview, July 9, 1974, Calgary, Alberta.
67   31   *Saskatchewan Herald,* July 7, 1883.
67   38   *Saskatchewan Herald,* September 15, 1883.
70   6   Obituary, *Manitoba Free Press,* April 27, 1909.
70   26   *Saskatchewan Herald,* September 15, 1883.
71   13   Clarence H. Geldert, "Tells of Terrible Trip on River After Little Boat Wrecked", *Star-Phoenix,* June 30, 1927.
71   42   *Edmonton Bulletin,* August 3, 1896.
72   27   Horace Greely; quoted in Shepherd, p. 62.
72   33   *Ibid.*
74   6   Mrs. H.E. Kelley, "Recalls First White Marriage in Southern Alberta", *Lethbridge Daily Herald,* March 29, 1924.

74 22 "When Lethbridge was a Port of Call for Steamers", *Lethbridge Daily Herald*, March 5, 1927.
75 10 D.J. Whitney Jr.; quoted in Johnston, p. 23.
76   2 Alexander Galt; quoted in Den Otter, p. 4.
76 30 William Robinson; quoted in Thomas.
76 35 *Ibid.*
77 15 *Ibid.*
78 31 Alexander Galt, telegram to A.P. Caron, March 31, 1885.
78 40 *Ibid.*
79   5 Alexander Galt, telegram to Caron, May 14, 1885.
79 14 Alexander Galt, telegram to Caron, July 27, 1885.
79 34 A.P. Caron, telegram to Major-General Middleton at Qu'Appelle, March, 1885.
80 16 Ballantine, pp. 99-100.
80 33 *Ibid.*, pp. 100-01.
81 41 George M. Douglas; quoted in Needler, p. 41.
84   1 E.S. Andrews in "Narratives of Saskatoon 1882-1912", p. 47.
84   5 Arthur Kelly, Interview, August 18, 1974, Spy Hill, Saskatchewan.
84 35 George H. Ham, *Toronto Globe*, May 13, 1885.
85 17 Louis Riel; Diary, quoted in Dawes, p. 52.
85 22 Ham, *Op. Cit.*
85 33 Ham, *Op. Cit.*
86 33 Tom Pendlebury, Interview, September 18, 1973, Moose Jaw, Saskatchewan.
87 24 George H. Ham, *Toronto Globe*, July 12, 1885.

Four: Walterdale Steam

88   1 Sergeant Davis; Molly McFadden Papers, quoted in letter from D.C. McArthur to Agnes Medd, August 14, 1949.
89   3 Peter McArthur, p. 5.
91 10 *Edmonton Bulletin*, August 13, 1887.
91 23 Annette Barry (née Lachambre); Interview, courtesy Provincial Archives of Alberta.
92 10 Hormisdas Lamoureaux; quoted in Wickenden.
92 38 L.R. Goodridge; quoted in *Ibid.*
93 11 *Saskatchewan Times*, June 16, 1893.
93 23 Elizabeth Scott-Matheson, Diary, 1896.
94 11 *Saskatchewan Herald*, April 22, 1898.
94 19 *Edmonton Bulletin*, August 17, 1899.
94 23 Mrs. D.C. McEachern; Interview, courtesy Provincial Archives of Alberta. Also, *Edmonton Bulletin*, August 17, 1899.
95 34 *Edmonton Bulletin*, December 31, 1887.
96   1 Ellen Andrews and Jack Walter; Interview, June 21, 1974, Ellerslie, Alberta.
96 12 *Edmonton Bulletin*, summer 1898.
96 22 Arthur G. Howell; Interview, June 15, 1974, Lloydminster, Saskatchewan.
97 19 Norah MacDougall; Interview, June 25, 1974, Edmonton, Alberta.
98 10 Abe Pearce, unpublished autobiography.
98 19 Bert Pearce; Interview, July 3, 1974, Edmonton, Alberta.

98   35   Marvin Combs; Interview, June 24, 1974, Edmonton, Alberta.
99   9   *Ibid.*
99   20   Bert Pearce interview.
100   10   C.H. Stout, "Honeymoon on Steam Boat".
100   18   Walter Leslie; Interview conducted by Marvin Combs, December 1, 1967, Edmonton, Alberta.
100   33   *Ibid.*
100   40   F.C. Omand; Interview, July 2, 1974, Edmonton, Alberta.
102   19   *Edmonton Journal*, September, 1909.
102   24   *Edmonton Bulletin*, August 19, 1909.
102   33   Bert Pearce interview.
103   19   Eva Johnson (née Lyon); Interview, June 25, 1974, Edmonton, Alberta.
104   8   *Edmonton Journal*, July, 1911.
104   24   Walter Leslie interview.
104   40   Mary Muckleston; Interview, June 22, 1974, Edmonton, Alberta
105   12   The Edmonton boy was Arthur J. Skitch; Interview, June 25, 1974, Edmonton, Alberta.
105   14   The waltzer was Jack L. Shep; Interview, June 25, 1974, Edmonton, Alberta.
105   19   The fiddle-lover was Don Morrison; Interview, June 21, 1974, Edmonton, Alberta.
105   20   And the girl "who was too young" was Mrs. Charles Learmonth; Interview, July 2, 1974, Edmonton, Alberta.
105   24   F.C. Omand interview.
105   34   Andrew Livingstone; Interview, June 23, 1974, Edmonton, Alberta.
106   5   *Edmonton Journal*, May, 1914.
106   16   Floyd Baker; Interview, June 22, 1974, Edmonton, Alberta.
106   20   Walter Leslie interview.
106   27   Floyd Baker interview.
106   31   Walter Leslie interview.
106   36   *The Conservator*, May 27, 1914.
106   41   Walter Leslie interview.
107   2   Floyd Baker interview.
107   10   Marvin Combs interview.
107   28   Mary Mucklestone interview.
107   32   George Honey; quoted in Byron, p. 21.
108   2   Walter Leslie interview.

Five: Saskatchewan Tramp Steamers

110   15   Jean Marvin (née Miller); Interview, September 27, 1973, Prince Albert, Saskatchewan.
110   35   Jim A. Soles; Interview, June 5, 1974, Buckland, Saskatchewan.
111   12   Dave Wilson; Interview, August 6, 1974, Saskatoon, Saskatchewan.
111   27   Jean Marvin interview.
111   30   Dave Wilson interview.
112   13   Prince Albert Citizens' Committee, unpaginated.
112   29   Cuthbert H. Woodhouse; Interview, May 7, 1974, Winnipeg, Manitoba.
113   3   Ted Harris; Interview, June 9, 1974, Briarlea, Saskatchewan.
113   21   Mary Woodhouse; Interview, May 7, 1974, Winnipeg, Manitoba.

114   7   Cuthbert H. Woodhouse interview.
114   15   Cuthbert H. Woodhouse, "The Gold Dredge Adventure of Rough-
             sedge and Ramsay".
114   28   Cuthbert H. Woodhouse interview.
115   1   *Ibid.*
115   30   Jim A. Soles interview.
116   3   *Ibid.*
117   16   *Ibid.*
117   28   *Ibid.*
117   34   *Ibid.*
118   19   Harold Kemp; Interview, June 8, 1974, Emma Lake, Saskatchewan.
119   13   Emma Goodfellow; Interview, August 8, 1974, Prince Albert,
             Saskatchewan.
119   36   John H. Scales; written reminiscence, courtesy of Emma Goodfellow.
120   5   *Ibid.*
120   34   Alma Eano (née Jubenville); Interview, June 14, 1974, North Battle-
             ford, Saskatchewan.
120   37   Ralph Parkinson; Interview, June 12, 1974, Battleford, Saskatchewan.
120   40   Charlie Stodders; Interview, June 12, 1974, Battleford, Saskatchewan.
122   10   John Currie; Interview, June 14, 1974, Bresaylor, Saskatchewan.
122   16   Frank Hewitt; Interview, June 14, 1974, Hewitt's Landing, Sas-
             katchewan.
122   41   Jim A. Soles interview.
123   8   Emma Goodfellow interview.
123   33   Tom Lewis; Interview, September 27, 1973, Prince Albert, Sas-
             katchewan.
124   13   Ellen McLeod (née Bayes); Interview, June 8, 1974, Prince Albert,
             Saskatchewan.
124   24   Sarah Evelyn Cook; Interview, June 7, 1974, Prince Albert, Sas-
             katchewan.
124   38   *Ibid.*
124   42   Jim A. Soles interview.
125   18   John A. McLeod; Interview, June 7, 1974, Buckland, Saskatchewan.
125   26   Dave Wilson interview.
126   18   Dolly Cummins (née MacKay); Interview, June 7, 1974, Spruce Home,
             Saskatchewan.
126   28   Jean Marvin interview.
127   25   Ted Harris interview.
127   38   Jim A. Soles interview.
128   4   Janet Riddle; Interview, June 7, 1974, Prince Albert, Saskatchewan.
128   24   John McCuaig; Interview, June 9, 1974, Prince Albert, Saskatchewan.
128   37   *Ibid.*
129   9   Flora Phelps (née McCuaig); Interview, June 8, 1974, Steep Creek,
             Saskatchewan.

Six: The Queer Apple

130   1   Prairie acreage slogans are excerpts from William Pearson Company
             publicity pamphlet "Last Mountain Valley", *c.* 1913.
130   27   *Ibid.*
131   39   John Macoun; quoted in Kleiner, pp. 1-2.

132 21 Ron Gatenby; Interview, July 22, 1974, Regina, Saskatchewan.
133 26 Tom Johnston; Interview by C. Higginbotham, July 27, 1963, courtesy Saskatchewan Archives Board.
134   7 *Ibid.*
134 42 *The Leader*, May 31, 1905.
135   5 The Long Lake marksman was Ernie Swanson; Interview by Leith Knight, September, 1973, courtesy Moose Jaw Public Library.
136 20 A.M. Pearson; Interviews, October 1, 1973, July 26, 1974, Lumsden, Saskatchewan.
136 29 *Ibid.*
138 15 Ron Gatenby interview.
139 14 Cyril Huggins; Interview, July 23, 1974, Regina, Saskatchewan.
139 29 *Ibid.*
140 29 A.M. Pearson interviews.
140 39 Ron Gatenby interview.
142 23 Henry White; Interview, July 30, 1974, Silton, Saskatchewan.
142 29 Ron Gatenby interview.
145   4 *Ibid.*
145 17 *Ibid.*
146 18 Scotty Galt; quoted in "Tales of Grandfather", by Remington Warwick, *Advertiser Post*, *c.* 1971, courtesy Bill Warwick, North Battleford, Saskatchewan.
146 42 *Ibid.*
147 26 Ron Gatenby interview.
147 40 *Ibid.*
148 35 A.M. Pearson interviews.
149 20 Lillian Kelly; quoted in "Last Mountain's Steamboat Era was Short Duration", *Leader Post*, August 15, 1955.
149 23 Elderton, p. 108.
149 41 Ron Gatenby interview.
150 31 *Ibid.*
152 20 Cyril Huggins interview.
152 29 *Ibid.*
153 23 A.M. Pearson interviews.
154   6 Eva Plaxton (née Elliot); Interview, July 31, Regina Beach, Saskatchewan.

Seven: J.K. Cornwall and his N.T.C.

156 11 James Wallwork; Interview, 1957, courtesy Provincial Archives of Alberta.
157   3 J.K. Cornwall; quoted in Porter.
157 15 *Ibid.*
157 41 J.K.Cornwall; quoted in Dunn.
158   7 *Ibid.*
158 12 Raynor Whitely; Interview, June 26, 1974, Athabasca, Alberta.
159 20 Dunn, *Op. Cit.*
159 28 Jettie Willey; Interview, June 27, 1974, Athabasca, Alberta.
160 11 Cornwall and Evans.
160 18 Raynor Whitely interview.

160 34 J. Fortesque McKay; Interview, June 29, 1974, Regina, Saskatchewan.
162 12 J.K. Cornwall; quoted in Briggs.
163   7 Kelly, p. 6.
163 33 J.K. Cornwall; quoted in Dunn.
164   6 Kelly, p. 43.
164 11 Miller.
165   8 Nettie Gramiak (née Basarab); Interview, June 27, 1974, Slave Lake, Alberta.
166   9 Fredrickson and East, p. 26.
166 13 Lea Goodwin; Interview, June 26, 1974, Athabasca, Alberta.
168   6 *Ibid.*
168 20 Rennie Hall; Interview, June 27, 1974, Slave Lake, Alberta.
168 32 Elizabeth Hall; Interview, June 27, 1974, Slave Lake, Alberta.
169 15 Rennie Hall interview.
169 36 Charlie Schurter; Interview, June 28, 1974, Slave Lake, Alberta.
170 12 Julia Nash (née L'Hirondelle); Interview, June 28, 1974, Slave Lake, Alberta.
170 26 Shore.
170 34 Charlie Schurter interview.
171   7 Julia Nash interview.
171   9 Paul Sowan; Interview, June 28, 1974, Kinuso, Alberta.
172 32 Hugo Carlson; Interview, June 27, 1974, Athabasca, Alberta.
172 35 Catherine Hobb; Interview, June 27, 1974, Athabasca, Alberta.
172 36 Godsell.
172 38 Rennie Hall interview.
172 39 J.K. Cornwall; quoted in Dunn.

Eight: *Dontianen* Lives

Written sources for the recounting of Tom Sukanen's story consisted of:
1) articles published in — The *Western Producer* Magazine, April 20, 1961, Saskatoon, Saskatchewan.
— *The Outlook,* January 27, 1972, Outlook, Saskatchewan.
— *The Moose Jaw Times-Herald,* January 1, 1972; March 1, 1972; March 8, 1972; June 19, 1972; Moose Jaw, Saskatchewan.
— *The Leader Post,* Regina, Saskatchewan.
— *The Riverhurst Courier,* Riverhurst, Saskatchewan.
2) unpublished notes courtesy Leith Knight of the Moose Jaw Public Library.
3) unpublished notes courtesy Saskatchewan Archives Board.

Interviews consisted of sessions with:
1) Lawrence "Moon" Mullin; September 18, 1973, October 2, 1973, July 25, 1974, Lake Valley, Saskatchewan.
2) Helen and Elmer Sukanen; October 2, 1973, Lucky Lake, Saskatchewan.
3) Erald Jones; September 18, 1973, Moose Jaw, Saskatchewan.
4) Leith Knight; September, 1973, Moose Jaw, Saskatchewan.
5) Mr. and Mrs. Frank West; July 25, 1974, Moose Jaw, Saskatchewan.

Nine: Laird of the Saskatchewan

page line
187 22 Ola Barnes; Interview, July 18, 1974, Medicine Hat, Alberta.
188 13 Grace Cousins; Interview, July 18, 1974, Medicine Hat, Alberta.
188 27   Isabel Cousins; Interview, July 18, 1974, Medicine Hat, Alberta.
188 32 *The Albertan,* September 19, 1954.
189 16 Muriel Whitehead (née Goodwin); Interview, July 20, 1974, Saskatchewan Landing, Saskatchewan.
190 39 Tom Pendlebury; Interview, September 18, 1973, Moose Jaw, Saskatchewan.
191 12 Russell Griffith; quoted by Roy Potter; Interview, August 5, 1974, Saskatoon, Saskatchewan.
191 37 *Saskatoon Star,* June, 1908.
192   3 Tom Pendlebury interview.
194   5 Captain H. H. Ross; quoted in A. J. Dalrymple, "Cap Ross of the Saskatchewan", in *The Beaver,* June, 1944.
194 10 Joe McAuley; Interview; September 23, 1973, Cumberland House, Saskatchewan.
196 20 William McKenzie; Interview, September 22, 23, 24, 1973, Cumberland House, Saskatchewan.
197 15 Dave Wilson; Interview, August 6, 1974, Saskatoon, Saskatchewan.
198 12 Pierre Carrier; Interview, September 23, 1973, Cumberland House, Saskatchewan.
198 21 Joe McAuley interview.
198 30 William McKenzie interview.
198 33 Bill Lovel; Interview, June 4, 1974, Prince Albert, Saskatchewan.
200 23   Tom Paquette; Interview, May 17, 1974, The Pas, Manitoba.
200 34 Alan Kennedy; Interview by Ernie Morris, courtesy Saskatchewan Archives Board, 1965.
201 12 Jack Doyle; Interview, September 25, 1973, May 20, 1974, Nipawin, Saskatchewan.
201 40 *Ibid.*
202 27 Charlie Otterbein; Interview, September 26, 1973, Prince Albert, Saskatchewan.
203   7 Jack Doyle interview.
203 33 Joe McAuley interview.
204 17 William McKenzie interview.
204 30 Pierre Carrier interview.
205   7 Tom Settee; Interview, June 6, 1974, Prince Albert, Saskatchewan.
205 24 William McKenzie interview.
206   3 Harold Kemp; Interview, June 8, 1974, Emma Lake, Saskatchewan.
206 29 Mathew McGillvary; Interview, May 19, 1974, The Pas, Manitoba.
207   6 *Ibid.*
207 11 Joe McAuley interview.
207 15 Mathew McGillvary interview.

Ten: In Defiance of *la Bête Noire*

209 15 Agnes Medd, "My Father's Steamboats", *Manitoba Pageant,* Autumn, 1971.

210	12	Eye witness quoted in Lucy Lindell, "Memory Opens the Door", courtesy Pauline Rowan.
210	19	D.C. McArthur; Molly McFadden Papers, letter from McArthur to McFadden, July 12, 1953.
211	7	Ferguson.
211	15	W.F. Munro; in "Winnipegosis", from Rose-Belford's *Canadian Monthly and National Review*, pp. 473, 475.
212	13	Mike Harrison; Interview, May 15, 1974, Winnipegosis, Manitoba.
212	27	Harry Brown; Interview, May 15, 1974, Winnipegosis, Manitoba.
213	13	Bill Johnson, Interview, May 16, 17, 1974, Swan River, Manitoba.
213	32	Hawley Burrell; Interview, May 9, 1974, Winnipeg, Manitoba.
214	18	Harry Brown interview.
216	13	Ed Redonets; Interview, May 15, 1974, Winnipegosis, Manitoba.
216	33	Ruth Patterson; Interview, May 10, 1974, Winnipeg, Manitoba.
217	12	*Ibid.*
218	4	Delroy Grenon; Interview, May 15, 16, 1974, Winnipegosis, Manitoba.
218	34	*Ibid.*
218	37	Lloyd Burrell; Interview, May 15, 1974, Winnipegosis, Manitoba.
219	26	*Ibid.*
219	38	Jim Denby; Interview, May 16, 1974, Winnipegosis, Manitoba.
220	4	Lenore Lawson; Interview, May 25, 1974, Saskatoon, Saskatchewan.
221	2	Sandy Vance; quoted by Howard Medd; Interview, May 5, 1974, Timmins, Ontario.
221	4	Howard Medd interview.
221	31	Jim Denby interview.
221	36	John E. McArthur, "Inland Cruising".
222	3	Quoted by Lorne Lawson; Interview, May 25, 1974, Saskatoon, Saskatchewan.
222	7	Lenore Lawson interview.
222	10	Freda Johnson; Interview, May 16, 1974, Winnipegosis, Manitoba.
222	16	Annie Bradbury; Interview, May 16, 1974, Winnipegosis, Manitoba.
222	19	John E. McArthur, *Op. Cit.*
222	39	Bill Johnson interview.
223	2	Jack Denby; quoted in Howard Medd, "Steamboat Days", p. 2.
223	20	Lloyd Burrell interview.
223	25	Lorne Lawson interview.
224	37	Cecil Patterson; Interview, May 10, 1974, Winnipeg, Manitoba.
226	4	Ed Kristjanson; Interview May 6, 1974, Geraldton, Ontario.
226	15	Lorne Lawson interview.
226	39	Ruth Patterson interview.
227	4	Jim Denby interview.
227	11	Cecil Patterson interview.
227	27	Palmer.
227	37	Ruth Patterson interview.
228	28	Lorne Lawson interview.
228	32	Cecil Patterson interview.
228	36	Lloyd Burrell interview.
229	9	Lorne Lawson interview.
229	15	Howard Medd interview.

Eleven: On the Sixth Great Lake

231 22 George Simpson; Interview, August 27, 1974, Selkirk, Manitoba.

233   6 Johnny Jones; quoted in Will E. Ingersol, "Lake Winnipeg's Commodore", *Winnipeg Free Press,* 1937.

234 13 Senator Judson LaMoure; telegram, quoted in Molly McFadden, "Two Steamships Came Sailing", *Morris-Emerson Journal,* April 6, 1966.

234 17 Mathew Lawrie; quoted in *Ibid.*

234 29 Captain J. Elton; quoted in Molly McFadden, "Steamboats to the Rescue", in *Manitoba Pageant,* April 7, 1961.

235   1 George Black, Diary; quoted in Will E. Ingersol, "The Red River Flood of '97", *Winnipeg Free Press,* May 4, 1940.

235 34 Edward Gilbert; quoted in "Shopping in Boats Style in '97 Flood", *Winnipeg Tribune,* April 21, 1948.

236 31 Roy Purvis; Interview, August 27, 1974, Selkirk, Manitoba.

236 35 George Simpson interview.

238 37 Ed Nelson "One Wrong Order, and the Freighter Broke in Two", *Winnipeg Free Press,* July 8, 1961.

240 12 Alex Joyce; quoted in *Selkirk Reporter,* August 31, 1906, courtesy Clifford Stevens, Gimli, Manitoba.

241   6 Anna Tillenius; quoted in *Winnipeg Free Press,* August 1906.

241   8 Alex Joyce; quoted in *Selkirk Reporter, Op. Cit.*

241 14 Anna Tillenius; quoted in *Winnipeg Free Press, Op. Cit.*

241 32 Donald Everett; quoted in Ed Nelson, "One Wrong Order and the Freighter Broke in Two", *Op. Cit.*

242   8 Roy Purvis interview.

243 21 Edward R. Green, "Remember Those Red River Excursions?", *Winnipeg Free Press,* June 24, 1961.

244 28 J.S. Evans, "Steamer Alberta's Thrilling Descent of Grand Rapids", *Manitoba Free Press,* July 4, 1908.

245 16 *Ibid.*

246 22 *Ibid.*

246 34 William Pugsley; quoted in "Water Route proposed by Dominion in Northwest", *Winnipeg Telegram,* May 27, 1910.

247   4 Edward R. Green, "Remember Those Red River Excursions?", *Op. Cit.*

247 14 Captain Julian Mills; Interview, June 18, 1974, Edmonton, Alberta.

248 15 Ed Nelson, "Hectic Voyage of the Wolverine", *Winnipeg Free Press,* August 13, 1960.

249 29 T.C.B. Boon, "Memories of the Keenora", *Winnipeg Fress Press,* May 23, 1966.

250   5 Roy Purvis interview.

250 28 Captain John C. Hokanson; Interview, May 11, 1974, Selkirk, Manitoba.

250 34 Stanley Sigardson; Interview, May 13, 1974, Selkirk, Manitoba.

252 13 Excursionist quoted in Beth Paterson, "The Paddlewheeler that Stretched 50 Miles", *Winnipeg Free Press,* April 21, 1952.

253   7 Will E. Ingersol, "Lake Winnipeg's Commodore", *Op. Cit.*

253 22 D.C. McArthur; Molly McFadden Papers, letter from McArthur to McFadden, December 13, 1956.

Epilogue

254   32   Obituary, *Manitoba Free Press,* May 11, 1888.

256   18   William McKenzie; Interview, September 22, 23, 24, 1973, Cumberland House, Saskatchewan.

257   6   Judge Walter Nelson; Interview, June 7, 1974, Prince Albert, Saskatchewan.

258   1   Tom Brown; Interview, July 18, 1974, Medicine Hat, Alberta.

259   1   Agnes Medd, "My Father's Steamboats".

259   11   Hawley Burrell; Interview, May 9, 1974, Winnipeg, Manitoba.

259   13   Ernie Whale; Interview, May 10, 1974, Winnipeg, Manitoba.

259   31   Bill Johnson; Interview, May 16, 1974, Swan River, Manitoba.

260   25   *Edmonton Journal,* June 19, 1934.

261   14   Harvey Weber; quoted in A.J. Dalrymple, "Ships That Pass in the North".

262   1   *Ibid.*

262   17   Tom Paquette; Interview, May 17, 1974, The Pas, Manitoba.

262   25   Charlie Otterbein; Interview, September 26, 1973, Prince Albert, Saskatchewan.

263   9   Leonard Plaxton; Interview, October 1, 1973, Regina Beach, Saskatchewan.

263   34   E. Hotchin; quoted in Beth Paterson, "Flame Leaped from Stricken Winnitoba", *Winnipeg Free Press.*

264   4   *Ibid.*

BIBLIOGRAPHY

PUBLISHED SOURCES

Anon.

"The Anson Northup", *The Beaver,* 1928.

Canadian Pictorial and Illustrated War News, Toronto, August 29, 1885.

"Last Mountain Valley", the William Pearson Company Ltd., Winnipeg, 1913.

"Narratives of Saskatoon 1882-1912", Historical Association of Saskatoon, Saskatoon, 1927.

North Dakota Historical Collections, Vol. 7.

"Prince Albert, 100 Years, 1866-1966", Prince Albert Citizens' Centennial Committee, Prince Albert, Saskatchewan, 1966.

"S.S. Keenora; Its Life and Times", Marine Museum of Manitoba, Spring, 1974.

Shipping Register of the Port of Winnipeg, 1875-1897, Provincial Archives of Manitoba, Winnipeg.

"The Pas . . . A History", The Pas Chamber of Commerce, The Pas, Manitoba, 1970.

Waterways Journal, St. Louis, Missouri, May 8, 1948, and June 19, 1948.

Anderson, Anne (ed.) *Plains Cree Dictionary,* Edmonton, 1971.

Ballantine, Archie "Recollections and Reminiscences, Steamboating on the Saskatchewan", *Saskatchewan History,* Saskatoon, Autumn, 1965.

Barnes, H.H. *Journal of a Trip to Manitoba and Back, June and July 1878,* Halifax, 1879.

Barrie, J.J. "Captain Horatio Hamilton Ross and the Riverboat City of Medicine Hat", *The Rattler,* July 2, 1975.

Begg, Alexander *History of the North-West,* Toronto, 1894.

————— and Walter R. Nursey *Ten Years in Winnipeg,* Winnipeg, 1879.

Bell, Captain Edwin "Early Steamboating on the Minnesota and Red Rivers", *Minnesota Historical Collection,* Number 10, Part 1.

Berton, Pierre *Klondike, The Life and Death of the Last Great Gold Rush,* Toronto, 1958.

————— *The National Dream, The Great Railway 1871-1881,* Toronto, 1970.

————— *The Last Spike, The Great Railway 1881-1885,*

	Toronto, 1971.
Bill, Fred A.	*Life on the Red River of the North,* Baltimore, Maryland, 1947.
Bowman, R.F.P.	"Railways in Southern Alberta", Lethbridge, 1973.
Briggs, Austin A.	"Czar of the North", *Collier's Magazine,* 1913.
Brown, Roy	"The Mystery Ship of Spruce Woods Forest", Tourism Unlimited, Brandon, Manitoba, 1971.
Butler, Effie	"Fishing in Lake Winnipeg," *The Beaver,* June, 1946.
Byron, E.	*John Walter,* Edmonton, 1967.
Campbell, Marjorie	*The Saskatchewan,* New York, 1950.
Cashman, A. W.	*The Edmonton Story,* Edmonton, 1956.
Chafe, J.W.	*Extraordinary Tales From Manitoba History,* Toronto, 1973.
Clay, Charles	*Swampy Cree Legends,* Toronto, 1938.
Cornwall, J.K., and H.M.E. Evans	"Report of a Committee of the Edmonton Board of Trade on the Transportation Facilities in existence at the present time to the Peace, Finlay, and Mackenzie River Basins from Edmonton", Edmonton, June 29, 1908.
Cotter, Chief Trader H.M.S.	"The Steamer Northcote", *The Beaver,* September, 1931.
Dalrymple, A. J.	"Ships That Pass in the North", *Maclean's Magazine,* April 15, 1931.
————	"Cap Ross of the Saskatchewan", *The Beaver,* June 1944.
Dawes, Denise (translator)	"Riel Diary, Lost 1885, Found 1970", *The Nor'Wester,* Vol. 100, No. 1
Den Otter, Andy A.	"Steamboats on the Belly. Why?", *Alberta Historical Review,* Winter, 1972.
Devore, Roy	*The History of Walterdale,* Edmonton, 1956.
Dufferin, Marchioness of Dufferin and Ava	*My Canadian Journal, 1872-1878,* London, 1891.
Dunn, Robert	"The Settler's Fight for the Fur Lands", *Everybody's Magazine",* 1914.
Eggleston, Edward	"The Kit Carson of the Northwest", *Minnesota History,* Vol. 33, Autumn, 1953.
Elderton, Bert	"Steamboating on Last Mountain Lake", *Saskatchewan History,* Autumn, 1960.
Evans, George	"Evergreen Cutline", Centennial Committee of White Fox, White Fox, Saskatchewan, 1971.
Fredrickson, Olive A., and Ben East	*The Silence of the North,* New York, 1973.

Gill, C. B., and Allyson Taylor	"Lake Winnipeg, Route of the Adventurers", Peguis Publishers, Winnipeg, 1971.
Glover, R.	"York Boats", *The Beaver,* March, 1949.
Gluek, Alvin C.	"The Minnesota Route", *The Beaver,* Spring, 1956.
————	"The Fading Glory", *The Beaver*, Winter, 1957.
Godsell, Philip H.	"The Old Peace River Trail", *Canadian Cattlemen,* December, 1958.
Goschen, Rt. Hon. George J.	*Report of the Governor of the Hudson's Bay Company to the Shareholders,* London, 1874.
Gray, James. H.	*Red Lights on the Prairies,* Toronto, 1971.
————	*Booze,* Toronto, 1972
Grenalds, William O.	"Peace River Jim, Empire Builder of the Arctic", *The American Magazine,* June, 1932.
Ham, George H.	*Reminiscences of a Raconteur,* Toronto, 1921.
Hamilton, J.C.	*The Prairie Province, Sketches of Travel from Lake Ontario to Lake Winnipeg,* Toronto, 1876.
Hargrave, Joseph James	*Red River,* Montreal, 1871.
Hawkes, John	*The Story of Saskatchewan and its People,* Chicago, 1924.
Herriot, Marion H.	"Steamboating on the Red River", *Minnesota History,* Vol. 21, 1940.
Higinbotham, John David	*When The West Was Young,* Toronto, 1933.
Hill, Robert B.	*Manitoba: History of its Early Settlement, Development and Resources,* Toronto, 1890.
Hind, Henry Youle	*A Preliminary and General Report on the Assiniboine and Saskatchewan Exploring Expedition,* Toronto, 1859.
Howard, Joseph Kinsey	*Strange Empire, A Narrative of the Northwest,* New York, 1952.
Johnston, Alexander (ed.)	"Boats and Barges on the Belly", published by Historical Society of Alberta, Lethbridge, October, 1966.
Kavanaugh, Martin	*The Assiniboine Basin,* Winnipeg, 1946.
Kelly, L.V.	*North with Peace River Jim,* Calgary, 1972.
Lass, W. E.	*History of Steamboating on the Upper Missouri River,* Lincoln, Nebraska, 1962.
Lindell, Lucy	"Memory Opens the Door", Eriksdale, Manitoba.
Macdonald, Coleman	"The Face of Yesterday", Brandon Junior Chamber of Commerce, Brandon, Manitoba, 1957.
MacGregor, James G.	*Edmonton Trader,* Toronto, 1963.

Macoun, John | *Manitoba and the Great North-West*, Guelph, Ontario, 1882.

Marcile | "The Grand Rapids Tramway", *The Beaver*, June, 1933.

McCourt, Edward A. | *Remember Butler*, Toronto, 1967.

McFadden (Basken) Molly | "Steamboats on the Red", Part One, *The Beaver*, June, 1950.

——— | "Steamboats on the Red", Part Two, *The Beaver*, September, 1950.

——— | "First of Many", *Manitoba Pageant*, April 14, 1959.

——— | "Steamboat Holiday", *Manitoba Pageant*, April 21, 1959.

——— | "Steamboats to the Rescue", *Manitoba Pageant*, April 7, 1961.

——— | "Keenora", *Steamboat Bill of Facts*, Summer, 1966.

McInnis, Edgar | *Canada, A Political and Social History*, Toronto, 1947.

Medd, Agnes | "Adventures of the Marquis", *The Beaver*, June 1952.

——— | "My Father's Steamboats", *Manitoba Pageant*, Autumn, 1971.

Miller, Benjamin K. | "Along the Peace River", *Recreation Magazine*, September, 1911.

Morton, Desmond, and Reginald H. Roy (ed.) | *Telegrams of the North-West Campaign 1885*, Toronto, 1972.

Mulvaney, Charles Pelham | *History of the North-West Rebellion of 1885*, Toronto, 1971.

Munro, W. F. | "Winnipegosis", *Rose-Belford's Canadian Monthly and National Review*, July-December, 1879.

Needler, G. H. | "The Lone Canoeist of 1885", *The Beaver*, June, 1950.

Northcote, Sir Stafford, Henry | "Report of the Governor of the Hudson's Bay Company to the Shareholders", London, 1873.

Palmer, Gwen | "Camperville and Duck Bay", *Manitoba Pageant*, Spring, 1973.

Patterson, Clara Burdett | *Baroness: Angela Burdett-Coutts and the Victorians*, London, 1953.

Pearson, A.M. | "Hills of Home", Lumsden Homecoming '71 Book Comittee, Lumsden, Saskatchewan, 1971.

Peel, Bruce | *Steamboats on the Saskatchewan*, Saskatoon, 1972.

Porter, G.C. | "Peace River Jim; Hunter, Trapper, and Trader", *Toronto Star Weekly*, July 9, 1927.

Pyle, Joseph Gilpin	*The Life of James J. Hill,* Toronto, 1916.
Ream, Peter T.	*The Fort on the Saskatchewan,* Second Ed., Fort Saskatchewan, Alberta, 1974.
Robinson, Marguerite E.	"The Wounded of the 1885 Rebellion", *Western Producer Magazine,* July 18, 1974.
Shepherd, George	"River Steamboats, Once Classic Mode of Transportation", *Scarlet and Gold,* 19th Ed., 1938.
Shore, Edna I.	"Athabasca Landing Trail", *Alberta Historical Review,* Spring, 1971.
Skelton, Oscar Douglas	*Life and Times of Sir Alexander Tilloch Galt,* Toronto, 1920.
Smith, T.R.	"The Steamboat Lily", *Saskatchewan History,* Spring, 1964.
Stout, C.H.	*Frontier Days in Leduc and District,* Calgary, 1974.
Thomas, A.V.	"Red River Man on the Nile", *Winnipeg Tribune Magazine,* December 21, 1935.
Trew, Dora E.	"Alberta's Prairie Steamer", *Canadian Cattlemen,* August, 1964.
Upham, Warren	"Report of Exploration of the Glacial Lake Agassiz in Manitoba", published by authority of Parliament, Montreal, 1890.
Warkentin, John (ed.)	*The Western Interior of Canada,* Toronto, 1964.
Watson, Robert	*A Boy of the Great North-West,* Ottawa, 1930.
Wickenden, Nick	"North-West and Minnow, Two Saskatchewan Steamers", *Alberta Historical Review,* Winter, 1957.
Wilson, Loudon	"Steamboats on the Red River of the North", *Steamboat Bill of Facts,* August, 1942.
———	"Navigation North and West", *Steamboat Bill of Facts,* eighteen articles published in September, December 1952: March, June, September, December 1953; March, June, December 1954; March, June, December 1955; June, September 1956; March, June, December 1957; June 1958.
Winton, David J.	*"W's Back to Back",* Minneapolis, Minnesota, *c.* 1970.
Wood, William Charles Henry	*All Afloat: A Chronicle of Craft and Waterways,* Toronto, 1964.

PUBLISHED NEWSPAPER SOURCES

Advertiser Post, North Battleford, Saskatchewan, 1971.
Albertan, Calgary, Alberta, 1954.
Brandon Daily Sun, Brandon, Manitoba, 1881.
Conservator, Fort Saskatchewan, Alberta, 1914.
Edmonton Bulletin, Edmonton, Alberta, 1887, 1896, 1898, 1899, 1909, 1910.

Edmonton Journal, Edmonton, Alberta, 1909, 1911, 1914, 1934, 1953, 1957.
Fargo Forum, Fargo, North Dakota, 1950, 1955.
Grand Forks Herald, Grand Forks, North Dakota, 1955, 1957.
Grand Rapids Star, Grand Rapids, Manitoba, 1961.
Leader, Regina, Saskatchewan, 1905.
Leader-Post, Regina, Saskatchewan 1937, 1955.
Lethbridge Daily Herald, Lethbridge, Alberta, 1924, 1927, 1952.
Manitoba Free Press, Winnipeg, Manitoba, 1887, 1888, 1908, 1909.
Morris-Emerson Journal, Morris, Manitoba, 1966.
New Nation, Winnipeg, Manitoba, 1870.
Northern Manitoba Weekly, The Pas, Manitoba, 1962.
Nor'Wester, Red River Settlement, District of Assiniboia, 1861, 1862.
Ottawa Daily Free Press, Ottawa, Ontario, 1884.
Port Arthur News Chronicle, Port Arthur, Ontario, 1958.
Prince Albert Daily Herald, Prince Albert, Saskatchewan, 1966.
Prince Albert Times, Prince Albert, North West Territories, 1883.
Red River Star, Moorhead, North Dakota, 1875.
St. Paul Press, St. Paul, Minnesota.
Saskatchewan Herald, Battleford, North West Territories, 1879, 1883, 1898.
Saskatchewan Times, Prince Albert, North West Territories, 1893.
Selkirk Reporter, Selkirk, Manitoba, 1906.
Phoenix, Saskatoon, Saskatchewan, 1908, 1927.
Western Producer, Saskatoon, Saskatchewan, 1974.
Winnipeg Daily Times, Winnipeg, Manitoba, 1881.
Winnipeg Free Press, Winnipeg, Manitoba, 1910, 1914, 1937, 1940, 1949, 1952, 1956, 1958, 1959, 1960, 1961, 1962, 1965, 1966, 1969, 1972.
Winnipeg Telegram, Winnipeg, Manitoba, 1910.
Winnipeg Tribune, Winnipeg, Manitoba, 1935, 1948, 1959.
Winnipeg Weekly Telegraph, Winnipeg, Manitoba, 1906.

UNPUBLISHED SOURCES

Anon, "John Walter: A Resume", courtesy Edmonton Parks and Recreation Department, Historical Division, Edmonton.
Budd, Henry, "Journal", Church Missionary Society Records, Public Archives of Canada.
Cashman, A. W., "Gainer's Edmonton Story" (series of programs aired on CJCA Radio, Edmonton), courtesy Provincial Museum and Archives of Alberta, Edmonton.
Ferguson, Eva M., "Winnipegosis – Little Muddy Water", courtesy Pauline Rowan, Miniota, Manitoba.
Kennedy, Alan, Interview conducted by Ernie Morris in 1965, courtesy Saskatchewan Archives Board, Saskatoon.
Kleiner, John, "Last Mountain Lake", courtesy Provincial Archives of Saskatchewan, Regina.
McArthur, Douglas C., "Tales of Fort Garry as told to me by my father, Peter McArthur", courtesy Pauline Rowan, Miniota, Manitoba.
McArthur, John E., "Inland Cruising", courtesy Pauline Rowan, Miniota, Manitoba.
McArthur, Peter, "Unpublished Memoirs of Peter McArthur", dictated to D. C. McArthur, Winnipegosis, Manitoba, 1934-1935.

McFadden (Basken), Molly, "Boats on the Red River of the North", "Steamboats on the Assiniboine", "S.S. City of Grand Forks and S.S. Assiniboine", and other Papers 1950's, courtesy Provincial Archives of Manitoba, Winnipeg.

Medd, Agnes, "Local History – Westbourne and The Landing, Manitoba", courtesy Provincial Archives of Manitoba, Winnipeg.

Medd, E. Howard, "Steamboat Days at Winnipegosis, 1937", courtesy Pauline Rowan, Miniota, Manitoba.

O-ge-mas-es (Little Clerk), "Steamboating on the Saskatchewan River", from Reginald Beatty Papers, courtesy University of Saskatchewan Archives, Saskatoon.

Parker, John E., Papers, 1940's, courtesy Provincial Archives of Manitoba, Winnipeg.

Pearce, Abe, "Unpublished Autobiography", courtesy Provincial Museum and Archives of Alberta, Edmonton.

Preston, Lieut. J. A. V., "North West Campaign 1885, with the Midland Battalion", Diary, courtesy Saskatchewan Archives Board, Saskatoon.

Scales, John H., "Unpublished Memoirs", courtesy Emma Goodfellow, Prince Albert, Saskatchewan.

Scott-Matheson, Elizabeth, Diary, 1896, courtesy Ruth Matheson-Buck, Regina.

Shere, L., "Transportation in Western Canada 1785-1885", M. A. Thesis for University of Manitoba, 1922, courtesy Glenbow-Alberta Institute, Calgary.

Smith, John N., "Reminiscences of Old-Timers on the Founding of Prince Albert", March 24, 1947, courtesy Arnold Agnew, Prince Albert, Saskatchewan.

Walter, Elizabeth, "Unpublished Memoirs of Mr. and Mrs. John Walter", January 17, 1939, courtesy Northern Alberta Pioneers and Old-Timers Association, Edmonton.

Wickenden, Nick, "Steam Navigation on Western Canadian Plains 1859-1956", courtesy Glenbow-Alberta Institute, Calgary.

Woodhouse, Cuthbert H., "The Gold Dredge Adventure of Roughsedge and Ramsay", c. 1960's, courtesy C. H. Woodhouse, Winnipeg.

Wright, H. A., "Fish Creek, Batoche and Events of '85 Rebellion Recalled, Personal Reminiscences by a Winnipegger of the Days Spent in Northwest with the Field Hospital Corps", Diary, courtesy David H. Wright, Saskatoon.

CHRONOLOGY

STEAMBOAT	BUILT	OWNER	DEMISE
Anson Northup (formerly *North Star*, formerly *Governor Ramsey*)	1858	Captain Anson Northup	Reconstructed as *Pioneer*, 1859
Pioneer (formerly *Anson Northup*)	1859	Captain Anson Northup	Crushed by ice at Cook's Creek off Red River, 1862
International (formerly *Freighter*)	1862	J. C. & H. C. Burbank; transferred *c*.1872 to Red River Transportation Co. (Kittson Line)	
Swallow	1868	Minnesota shippers; 1875 to Captain James Flannigan	Caught in Red River ice, 1879
Selkirk	1871	Hill, Griggs & Co.; *c*.1872 to Red River Transportation Co.	Wrecked at Grand Forks, North Dakota, 1884
Dakota	1872	Red River Transportation Co.	Burned near international border, 1881
Prince Rupert	1872	Peter McArthur, then part of North West Navigation Co.	Dismantled at Winnipeg, Manitoba, 1881
Alpha	1873	J. W. McLean; *c*.1874 to Red River Transportation Co.	Grounded at Spruce Woods, Manitoba, 1885
Cheyenne	1873	Red River Transportation Co.	Wrecked near Ste. Agathe, Manitoba, 1884
Chief Commissioner	1873	Hudson's Bay Co.	Hull converted to barge, 1875
Maggie	1873	James Bell; to F. T. Rollin	Converted to barge at Winnipeg, Manitoba, 1878

Name	Year	Owner	Fate
Northcote	1874	Hudson's Bay Co.; 1883 to Winnipeg & Western Transportation Co.	Beached at Cumberland House, N.W.T. 1886; burned c.1903
Colvile (formerly *Chief Commissioner*)	1875	Hudson's Bay Co.	Burned at Grand Rapids, N.W.T., 1894
Manitoba	1875	Merchants International Steamboat Line; 1875 to Red River Transportation Co.; c.1881 to Winnipeg & Western Transportation Co.	Crushed by ice at Shell River, N.W.T., 1885
Minnesota	1875	Merchants International Steamboat Line; 1875 to Red River Transportation Co.	Refurbished as *City of Winnipeg*, 1881
Keewatin	1876	F. T. Rollin	Wrecked in storm on Lake Winnipeg, 1884
Lady Ellen	1877	E. McMicken, N. Blacklin & J. Colclough; 1880 to Brown & Rutherford; 1885 to D. Clark; 1887 to D. Fraser; 1887 to North West Navigation Co.	Laid up at Selkirk, Manitoba, 1915
Lily	1877	Hudson's Bay Co.; 1883 to Winnipeg & Western Transportation Co.	Sunk at Drowning Ford, N.W.T., 1883
J. L. Grandin	1878	J. L. Grandin (of Bonanza Farms)	Sunk in Halstad, Minnesota flood, 1897
Victoria	1878		
Lady Blanche	1879	Reginald Pratt	Reconstructed as *Isabelle*, 1893
Marquette	1879	North West Navigation Co.	Wrecked on Red River, 1888
William Robinson	c.1880	William Robinson	Grounded on Lake Winnipeg, 1882
Pluck (formerly *White Swan*)	c.1880	Bonanza Farms; 1882 to Red River Transportation Co.	Dismantled at Grand Forks, North Dakota, 1886
City of Winnipeg (formerly *Minnesota*)	1881	Winnipeg & Western Transportation Co.	Wrecked in storm off Long Point on Lake Winnipeg, 1881

Name	Year	Owner	Fate
North West	1881	North West Navigation Co.; 1884 to Winnipeg & Western Transportation Co.	Wrecked in flood at Edmonton, N.W.T., 1899
Princess	1881	William Robinson; then part of North West Navigation Co.	Sunk in storm off Swampy Island on Lake Winnipeg, 1906
W. H. Alsop	1881	W. H. Alsop (of Bonanza Farms); 1882 to Red River Transportation Co.	Dismantled, c.1890
Glendevon	1882	Charles Gauthier	Burned at mouth of Little Saskatchewan River, 1891
Marquis	1882	Winnipeg & Western Transportation Co.	Beached at Prince Albert, N.W.T. 1890; burned c.1909
Baroness	1883	North Western Coal & Navigation Co.	Abandoned at Lethbridge, N.W.T., 1885
Red River	1883	North West Navigation Co.	Sunk in storm on Lake Winnipeg, 1899
Saskatchewan	1883	Peter McArthur	Burned at The Narrows, Lake Manitoba, 1893
Alberta	1884	North Western Coal & Navigation Co.	Abandoned at Medicine Hat, N.W.T., 1885
Minnow	1884	North Western Coal & Navigation Co.; 1887 to Lamoureux Brothers; 1898 to Percy B. Cunliffe	Abandoned on North Saskatchewan River, c.1900
May Queen	1884	E. S. Andrews	Scrapped at Saskatoon, N.W.T., 1885
Ogema	1885	Reid & Tait Fish Co.; to North West Navigation Co.	
Alice Sprague	1886	Sprague Lumber Co.	
Antelope	1887	Sprague Lumber Co.	
Myles	1889	North West Navigation Co.	Lost on Lake Winnipeg, c.1900

Name	Year	Owner	Fate
Sultana	1889	North West Navigation Co.	Abandoned at Fort Alexander Mills, 1911
Josie	1890	Richard Deacon	Abandoned on North Saskatchewan River, 1914
Fisherman	1892	North West Navigation Co.	Laid up at Selkirk, Manitoba, 1914
Idell	1892	North West Navigation Co.	Broken up at Selkirk, Manitoba, 1941
City of Selkirk	1893	Ewing & Fryer; to Dominion Fish Co.	Crushed by ice on Red River, 1914
Isabelle (formerly Lady Blanche)	1893	Peter McArthur; then to McArthur's Standard Lumber Co.	Abandoned near Winnipegosis, Manitoba, 1904
Assiniboine	1890's		Dismantled at Winnipeg, Manitoba, 1900
Ida	1890's	Peter McArthur; then to McArthur's Standard Lumber Co.	
Osprey	1890's	Booth Fish Co.	
City of Grand Forks	1895	W. J. Godfrey; to East Grand Forks Transportation Co.	Sunk at Grand Forks, North Dakota, 1912
Battleford (ferry)	1896	John Walter; 1896 to Village of Battleford	Abandoned at Battleford, Saskatchewan, c.1907
Premier	1896	Reid & Tait Fish Co.; to Dominion Fish Co.	Burned at Warren's Landing on Lake Winnipeg, 1908
Lady Ellen	1897	Booth Fish	
Lady of the Lake	1897	Stephen Sigurdson; 1898 to William Robinson; 1899 to Dominion Fish Co.; 1901 to Northern Fish Co.	Condemned at Selkirk, Manitoba, 1934
B. J. Little (gold dredge)	1898	B.J. Little	
Daisy Bell	1898	James Wallwark	Abandoned at Dawson, N.W.T., 1899
Keenora	1898	Rainy River Navigation Co.; 1918 to three Winnipeg lawyers; 1923 to Northern Fish	Beached as the Marine Museum of Manitoba at Selkirk, Manitoba

Name	Year	Owner	Fate
Petrel	1898	Co.; 1931 to Selkirk Navigation Co.; 1964 to Marine Transport Navigation Co.; 1972 to Marine Museum of Manitoba Ltd.	Dismantled, 1910
Iona	1899	C. W. Maloan	
	1899	Standard Lumber Co.	
Mockingbird	1899	North West Fish Co.	Swamped on Lake Winnipegosis, 1901
Rocket	1899	J. W. Simpson; 1906 to North West Navigation Co.	Broken up at Selkirk, Manitoba, 1933
Gertie H.	1900	J. S. Hall; to Pioneer Navigation Co.	Abandoned, c. 1914
Highlander	1900	Imperial Fish Co.; to Northern Fish Co.; to Hudson's Bay Co.	Dismantled at Norway House, Manitoba, 1916
Lottie S.	1900	North West Fish Co.	
Manitou	1900	Booth Fish Co.	Beached on Lake Winnipegosis
Chieftain	1901	Dominion Fish Co.; 1909 to Winnipeg Fish Co.; 1910 to Northern Fish Co.	Grounded on Red River sandbar, 1916
Alexandra	1903	Levi Bellefeuille; to Pioneer Navigation Co.	Wrecked in electrical storm on Red River, 1907
Assiniboia	1903	H. H. Ross	Crushed by ice on Cedar Lake, Manitoba, 1906
McKillop-Benjafield (sternwheel barge)	1903	McKillop & Benjafield	Abandoned on Last Mountain Lake
Pathfinder	1903	Richard Deacon	Abandoned on North Saskatchewan River, 1914
Saskatchewan	1903	Hudson's Bay Co.	Dismantled at The Pas, Manitoba, 1913
Wolverine	1903	Imperial Fish Co.; 1904 to Northern Fish Co.	Dismantled, 1936

289

Name	Year	Owner	Fate
Alberta	1904	Rufus Mosher & Fred W. Coates; 1908 to Winnipeg Navigation Co.	Caught in flood at Lockport, Manitoba, 1916
Frederick	1904	North West Navigation Co.	Lost on Lake of the Woods, 1912
Strathcona	1904	John Walter	Rebuilt as *Scona*, 1907
Tempest	1904	Northern Fish Co.	Broken up at Selkirk, Manitoba, 1927
Alert	1905	Northern Fish Co.	
Midnight Sun	1905	Northern Transportation Co.	
Mikado	1905	William Purvis; to Northern Fish Co.	Rebuilt as *Grand Rapids*, 1913
Roughsedge-Ramsay (gold dredge)	1905	Roughsedge & Ramsay	Shut down on North Saskatchewan River, 1909
Welcome	1905	William Pearson Co.	Rebuilt as *Lady of the Lake*, 1906
City of Medicine Hat	1906	H. H. Ross	Wrecked on Saskatoon bridge, 1908
Lady of the Lake (formerly *Welcome*)	1906	William Pearson Co.	Rebuilt as *Qu'Appelle*, 1907
Northern Light	1906	Northern Transportation Co.	
Northland Trader	1906	Northern Transportation Co.	
City of Prince Albert	1907	Prince Albert Lumber Co.; 1918 to Mandy Mines	
J. M. Smith	1907	William Hall	
Marion	1907	Richard Deacon	Abandoned on North Saskatchewan River, 1914
Northland Sun	1907	Charles Barber; to Northern Transportation Co.	
Qu'Appelle (formerly *Lady of the Lake*)	1907	William Pearson Co.	Torched at Cowan's Beach on Last Mountain Lake, 1918

Name	Year	Owner	Fate
Scona (formerly Strathcona)	1907	John Walter	Abandoned at Edmonton, Alberta, c.1918
Emma E.	1908	Finger Lumber Co.	Beached at The Pas, Manitoba
Sam Brisbin	1908	H. H. Ross; then to Ross Navigation Co.	Sunk at The Pas, Manitoba, 1920's
Algoma	1909	Levi Bellefeuille; to Manitoba Sand & Dredging Co.	
City of Edmonton	1909	John Walter	Abandoned at Edmonton, Alberta, c.1918
Winnitoba	1909	Hyland Navigation Co.	Burned at Winnipeg, Manitoba, 1913
Bonnatoba	1910	Hyland Navigation Co.	Crushed by ice near Winnipeg, Manitoba, 1913
Le Pas	1910	H. H. Ross, then to Ross Navigation Co.	Beached at The Pas, Manitoba, 1920's
Mount Cashel	1910	Hyland Navigation Co.	Burned near Winnipeg, Manitoba, 1914
Northland Echo	1910	Northern Transportation Co.	
O'Hell	1910	Ross Navigation Co.	Beached at The Pas, Manitoba, 1920's
Ruby	1910	Federal Department of Public Works	
George V	1911	City of Prince Albert; 1915 to F. E. Simmonds syndicate	Wrecked in ice at The Pas, Manitoba 1918
C. R. Smith	1912	Finger Lumber Co.	Beached at The Pas, Manitoba
Slave River	1912	Hudsons' Bay Co.	
Grand Rapids (formerly Mikado)	1913	North West Navigation Co.	Broken up at Selkirk, Manitoba, 1930's

Minasin	1913	Ross Navigation Co.	Abandoned at The Pas, Manitoba, 1920's
Goldfield (formerly *Minerva*, formerly *Frank Burton*)	c.1914	Reid & Tait Fish Co.; c.1910 to Goldfield Mines; 1919 to Riverton Fish Co.; 1921 to Gimli Fish Co.; 1936 to Armstrong Gimli Fish Co.; 1969 to Sigardson Fish Co.	
Notin	1914	Ross Navigation Co.	Beached at The Pas, Manitoba, 1920's
Bradbury	1915	Federal Government	
Odinak	1916	Armstrong Gimli Fish Co.	Beached at Winnipegosis, Manitoba
Nipawin	1917	Ross Navigation Co.	Beached at The Pas, Manitoba,1930's
W. J. Guest	1917	Northern Fish Co.	
Armenon	1918	Armstrong Gimli Fish Co.	Beached at Winnipegosis, Manitoba
D. N. Winton	1920	The Pas Lumber Co.	Beached at The Pas, Manitoba, 1954; wrecked by ice, c.1950
Alice Mattes	1921	The Pas Lumber Co.	Beached at The Pas, Manitoba, c.1950
Tobin	1921	Ross Navigation Co.	Beached at The Pas, Manitoba, 1930's
Evelyn B.	1922	H. Burrell	
Sparkle	1922	Booth Fish Co.	Refurbished as *Rambler, c.*1925
Rambler (formerly *Evelyn B.*)	c.1925	C. Patterson	Beached in storm at Coffey's Point on Lake Winnipegosis, 1930
Dontianen	c.1930	Tom Sukanen; 1942 to Victor Markkula; 1972 to Lawrence Mullin and the Moose Jaw Prairie Pioneer Village and Museum	Reconstructed at Moose Jaw Prairie Pioneer Village and Museum

INDEX

293